GRE® FOR DUMMIES®

7TH EDITION

by Ron Woldoff, MBA, MIS
Instructor and Owner, National Test Prep
with Joe Kraynak

John Wiley & Sons, Inc.

GRE® For Dummies®, 7th Edition

Published by
John Wiley & Sons, Inc.
111 River St.
Hoboken, NJ 07030-5774
www.wiley.com

Published by John Wiley & Sons, Inc., Hoboken, NJ

Published simultaneously in Canada

For general information on our other products and services, please contact our Customer Care Department within the U.S. at 877-762-2974, outside the U.S. at 317-572-3993, or fax 317-572-4002.

For technical support, please visit www.wiley.com/techsupport.

Wiley also publishes its books in a variety of electronic formats and by print-on-demand. Not all content that is available in standard print versions of this book may appear or be packaged in all book formats. If you have purchased a version of this book that did not include media that is referenced by or accompanies a standard print version, you may request this media by visiting http://booksupport.wiley.com. For more information about Wiley products, visit us at www.wiley.com.

Library of Congress Control Number: 2011932090

ISBN: 978-0-470-88921-3 (pbk); ISBN 978-1-118-10398-2 (ebk); ISBN 978-1-118-10399-9 (ebk); ISBN 978-1-118-10400-2 (ebk)

Manufactured in the United States of America

10 9 8 7 6 5 4 3 2 1

About the Authors

Ron Woldoff completed his dual master's degrees at Arizona State University and San Diego State University, where he studied the culmination of business and technology. After several years as a corporate consultant, Ron opened his own company, National Test Prep, where he helps students achieve their goals on the GMAT, GRE, and SAT. He created the programs and curricula for these tests from scratch, using his own observations of the tests and feedback from students. Ron also teaches his own GMAT and GRE programs as an adjunct instructor at both Northern Arizona University and the internationally acclaimed Thunderbird School of Global Management. Ron lives in Phoenix, Arizona, with his lovely wife, Leisah, and their three amazing boys, Zachary, Jadon, and Adam. You can find Ron on the web at www.testprepaz.com.

Joe Kraynak is a freelancer who specializes in team writing with professionals in various fields. He holds a BA in creative writing and philosophy and an MA in English literature from Purdue University and has co-authored numerous *For Dummies* titles, including *Bipolar Disorder For Dummies* with Candida Fink, MD; *Food Allergies For Dummies* with Robert A. Wood, MD; and *Flipping Houses For Dummies* with real-estate mogul Ralph R. Roberts. Joe lives in Crawfordsville, Indiana, with his wonderful wife, Cecie, their two children, Nick and Ali, three cats, and numerous forest critters. You can find Joe on the web at www.joekraynak.com.

Dedication

Ron Woldoff: This book is humbly dedicated to the hundreds of students who have passed through my test-prep programs on their way to achieving their goals. You have taught me as much as I have taught you.

Authors' Acknowledgments

Ron Woldoff: I would like to thank my friend Elleyne Kase, who first connected me with the *For Dummies* folks and made this book happen. I would also like to thank my friends Ken Krueger, Lionel Hummel, Jaime Abromovitz, and Gary Steiner, who helped me get things off the ground when I had this wild notion of helping people prepare for standardized college-admissions tests. And more than anyone else, I would like to thank my wife, Leisah, for her continuing support and for always being there for me.

Both authors would like to thank agent Bill Gladstone of Waterside Productions in Cardiff, California, for giving us the opportunity to revise this book. Special thanks to the technical editors, Frederick Sexton, MPH, and Marti Maguire, MA, of PrepSuccess, for meticulously checking the manuscript, ferreting out errors, and generously offering their own GRE expertise and insight. Also, much thanks to Chad Sievers for his patience and persistence in shepherding all the manuscript, figures, and equations through editing and production. And thanks to copy editors Jennette ElNaggar and Danielle Voirol, who carefully edited the manuscript to ensure clarity and root out errors. Finally, a shout out to Lindsay Lefevere, our acquisitions editor, who was ultimately responsible for choosing us to revise this edition and for dealing with all the minor details to get it going and keep it on track.

Publisher's Acknowledgments

We're proud of this book; please send us your comments at http://dummies.custhelp.com. For other comments, please contact our Customer Care Department within the U.S. at 877-762-2974, outside the U.S. at 317-572-3993, or fax 317-572-4002.

Some of the people who helped bring this book to market include the following:

Acquisitions, Editorial, and Media Development

Senior Project Editor: Chad R. Sievers

Executive Editor: Lindsay Sandman Lefevere

Copy Editors: Jennette ElNaggar, Danielle Voirol

Assistant Editor: David Lutton

Technical Editor: Frederick Sexton, MPH, and Marti Maguire, MA, of PrepSuccess

Editorial Manager: Michelle Hacker

Editorial Assistant: Rachelle S. Amick

Art Coordinator: Alicia B. South

Cover Photos: © iStockphoto.com/MarttiSalmeh

Cartoons: Rich Tennant (www.the5thwave.com)

Composition Services

Project Coordinator: Bill Ramsey

Layout and Graphics: Carl Byers, Carrie A. Cesavice, Christin Swinford

Proofreaders: Melissa Cossell, Shannon Ramsey

Indexer: BIM Indexing & Proofreading Services

Publishing and Editorial for Consumer Dummies

Diane Graves Steele, Vice President and Publisher, Consumer Dummies

Kristin Ferguson-Wagstaffe, Product Development Director, Consumer Dummies

Ensley Eikenburg, Associate Publisher, Travel

Kelly Regan, Editorial Director, Travel

Publishing for Technology Dummies

Andy Cummings, Vice President and Publisher, Dummies Technology/General User

Composition Services

Debbie Stailey, Director of Composition Services

Contents at a Glance

Table of Contents

Introduction

Welcome to *GRE For Dummies,* 7th Edition. Don't take the *dummies* thing personally — you're obviously no dummy. You made it through high school with high enough grades and test scores to get into college. You then graduated to join the elite group of approximately 25 percent of U.S. citizens 25 years or older who hold bachelor's degrees. And now you're standing at the entrance of graduate school.

Between you and your goal is the GRE: A test designed solely to challenge your ability to remember everything you've forgotten since high school — material you haven't touched in years. To clear this hurdle, all you really need right now is a refresher course. Well, here it is: *GRE For Dummies,* 7th Edition, is your refresher course plus. This book goes beyond simply rehashing what you've learned and forgotten and provides valuable strategies and tips for answering questions more efficiently and improving your odds of answering correctly. In this book, you also find plenty of examples, practice questions, and practice tests to hone your skills, identify subject areas you need to work on a little more, and build your confidence for test day.

Like a personal guide, this book reveals the ins and outs of the GRE and secret passageways to reach your goal: admittance to the grad school of your choice and perhaps a scholarship to help pay your way. The purpose of this book is to help you learn what's necessary and useful for scoring high on the GRE. Period. No extra garbage is thrown in to fill space; no filler is added to make this book the fattest one on the market. If you need ***esoteric*** (hard to understand) or irrelevant material, go to the GRE shelf of your local library — you'll find plenty. If you need a fast, effective guide to acing the GRE, you're holding the right book.

About This Book

In *GRE For Dummies,* 7th Edition, I cover all the basic math and verbal concepts and introduce some actual GRE-type questions to practice with. I also show you how to approach each type of question, recognize the traps built into the questions, and master the tricks that help you avoid those traps.

To earn a top score on the GRE, you must achieve two goals, one primary and one secondary:

- **Primary goal: Master everything the test covers.** Read through the whole book. No matter how well you know a specific subject, you can improve, and you need to make sure you have the knowledge and skills to handle each section at GRE level. Believing you should work on only your weakest sections is a mistake. The GRE measures your overall and top skill levels, so building on your strengths is just as important as improving in your weakest subject areas.
- **Secondary goal: Strengthen your most challenging subject areas.** Turn to specific sections for targeted information and help. The organization of this book makes it very easy to find the type of math questions you always have trouble with, suggestions for answering Reading Comprehension questions without having finished the passage, and tricks for acing the sentence-based questions.

GRE For Dummies, 7th Edition, is not only simple and straightforward enough for those who are very rusty with the math and verbal, but also detailed and sophisticated enough to deliver to those same students the more complicated information necessary to get truly excellent scores.

Conventions Used in This Book

To help you through this book, I use the following conventions:

- All GRE vocabulary words appear like ***this.*** This special font indicates a vocab word that you may not know, followed directly by its meaning. (Here's a handy tip: Stamp these words in your memory by trying to use them in everyday life. Call your roommate or your children ***indolent, lethargic,*** and ***listless*** when they don't clean up after dinner, or promise your professor or boss you'll be ***diligent, meticulous,*** and ***painstaking*** in your next assignment.)
- All web addresses appear in `monofont`.
- Multiplication signs vary throughout the book, including the × symbol, as in $2 \times 2 = 4$; two side-by-side numbers or expressions each enclosed in parentheses, such as $(2)(5) = 10$; or occasionally a dot, as in $x \cdot x = x^2$. I use the dot in expressions that contain the variable x to ***preclude*** (prevent) any possible confusion with ×. Also, letters and numbers side-by-side without parentheses are multiplied: $2x$ means 2 times x.

What You're Not to Read

Everything in this book is helpful, but the sidebars are more for adding ***levity*** (light manner or attitude) than for sharpening your skills and aren't as essential as the other sections to your success on the GRE. If time is tight, you can skip the sidebars and still dramatically improve your exam score.

Foolish Assumptions

This book is intended to help you prepare for the GRE. I assume that you're in at least one of these three stages of your GRE planning:

- You've already scheduled the GRE, or are about to, and need some preparation before taking it.
- You have to take the GRE for acceptance into the graduate program at your preferred school.
- You're considering a graduate program or school that requires the GRE as part of the application process and want to know what the exam is all about.

How This Book Is Organized

This book is divided into six parts. Forming the core are three parts sort of in the middle, each of which tackles a different section of the GRE: Verbal, Math, and Analytical Writing. Part I provides everything you need to know to develop effective test-taking strategies. Part V features several practice exams to build your confidence. And Part VI provides some valuable bonus material. The following sections describe the contents of each part in greater detail.

Part I: Mastering the GRE Test-Taking Experience

Knowing what to expect on the test significantly improves your ability to perform well. The chapters in this part reveal what's on the test and how it's scored, test-taking strategies to improve your performance, and a checklist of everything you need to do to prepare for test day.

Part II: Tackling the Verbal Section One Word at a Time

The Verbal portion of the GRE challenges your reading comprehension and vocabulary skills. In this part, I show you how to tackle the two types of questions in the vocabulary section: Text Completion and Sentence Equivalence. I provide guidance on how to improve your reading comprehension and quickly pick out answers to questions by referring back to the reading passage. Finally, I explain various ways to expand your vocabulary to score even higher on the test.

Part III: High School Math and Beyond: Math You Thought You'd Never Need Again

GRE math, with little exception, is based very much on what you studied in high school. However, mastery of the math concepts alone won't get you a top math score. The GRE Math section challenges your ability to solve problems and recognize the underlying concepts. For example, the GRE expects you to know that squaring a proper fraction makes the number smaller, not larger, even if you don't know what the fraction actually is. In Part III, I review all these concepts with you, starting with basic arithmetic and covering geometry, algebra, word problems, charts and graphs, and quantitative comparisons, plus problem-solving strategies.

Part IV: Penning Powerful Analytical Essays

Your GRE experience begins with two essays. Your goal on the essays is twofold: Meet the requirements of the essay evaluators and write the essays without exhausting yourself. This second part is crucial so that you conserve enough brain power for the rest of the test. In Part IV, I show you an easy, step-by-step process for writing killer essays so you can meet the evaluators' requirements with minimal effort.

Part V: Taking Full-Length Practice GREs: It's All You

Not only do you need to master the skills used for the test, but you also need to be able to use these skills well in the test-taking environment. In other words, you need to be at your best for nearly four hours. Though all students can build their skills through full-length practice tests, those with test anxiety especially benefit from practice. The goal in Part V is to make the test-taking experience as familiar as possible so on test day, very little — if anything — surprises you.

Part VI: The Part of Tens

In the Part of Tens, I provide additional insights and tips to further improve your performance, including facts about the GRE, common mistakes to avoid, and good ways to warm up on test day. Though not specific to any one part of the GRE, Part VI is geared toward ensuring that you perform your absolute best on the day of the test.

Icons Used in This Book

Although everything included in this book is valuable, some tidbits call for special attention. Look for the following icons to quickly spot the most important information on the page.

This icon marks practice questions that are relevant to the subject matter being covered. After explaining a concept, I usually follow with an example question to show you how it's done.

This icon indicates little bits of wisdom to make your GRE experience go more smoothly and improve your success.

This icon marks key points to remember while working the GRE questions, especially anything that's likely to surprise you on the test. By knowing what to expect, you become better able to handle it.

This icon marks GRE traps and common student mistakes. Discovering these traps before test day is better than being ensnared in them when taking the test.

Where to Go from Here

Everything in this book is relevant to helping you get a firm understanding of the GRE. Whether you're strong or weak in any of the subject areas, you definitely want to practice the strategies and work the different question types of the entire test and, therefore, this entire book. Naturally, spend more time on your weak areas and try to go through this book from start to finish, especially the practice tests.

I've been helping GRE students beat the test for years, so not only do I know your common questions and mistakes, but I also know how to make the math and verbal questions easier for you to answer. This book distills my tricks and secrets, which I'm pleased to share with you. Your success, after all, is why we're both here.

Part I

Mastering the GRE Test-Taking Experience

"Watch this, Ruth. Steady ... steady ... calculate the volume of the stein first."

In this part . . .

Knowledge, skills, preparation, and practice are the four components for scoring well on any test, and the GRE is no different. Throughout this book, you acquire the knowledge, skills, and preparation required. The practice is up to you, but I provide the guidance to help you practice more effectively. This part helps you prepare for the GRE by providing the basics on what to expect on the test, how to study and build effective test-prep and test-taking strategies, and how to be ready both physically and mentally for test day. Though this part doesn't focus on any specific section of the GRE, knowing exactly what you're getting into is essential for scoring well.

Chapter 1

Knowing What to Expect with the GRE

In This Chapter

- Fitting the GRE into your schedule
- Deconstructing the GRE to better understand what's on it
- Grasping the scoring system
- Looking forward to intermissions

One of the easiest ways to reduce any test anxiety and optimize your performance on the GRE is to become familiar with it. Knowing what to expect gives you less to think about and fret over come test day, so you can focus on what really matters — the test itself.

In this chapter, I encourage you to sign up for the GRE early so you can get a time slot in line with your peak performance period of the day. I also reveal the GRE's structure and scoring system and clue you in on what to expect during the exam. With this guidance, you're better equipped to avoid any surprises that may throw you off your game.

Signing Up for the GRE

In most parts of the world, the GRE is a computer-based test, which makes it easier to administer to small groups of test-takers. Signing up in advance enables you to schedule the GRE for the day, time, and place that work best for you. If you're a morning person who's sharpest at sunrise, you can schedule the test for 8 a.m.; if you're a night owl who tends to sleep in, you can opt for an 11 a.m. or 2 p.m. time slot. Actual time slot availability varies according to the testing center, but you generally have more days and times to choose from than with paper-based tests, such as the SAT.

To sign up for the GRE, see the current *GRE Information and Registration Bulletin* (available through most college admissions offices), register online at `www.ets.org`, or register via phone by calling 800-473-2255. You can also check the GRE testing center locations and available time slots at `www.ets.org`.

To help you get in the right mindset, consider taking the practice tests at the same time of day you plan on taking the real thing. (Check out the practice tests in Chapters 16, 18, and 20. If you purchased the Premier edition, you can find two more tests on the CD at the back of this book.) I've had students employ this strategy to become accustomed to the effects that their *circadian rhythms* (hunger and nap patterns) have on their test-taking abilities. Neurotic? Maybe, but it's not a bad idea. As I discuss in greater detail throughout this book, one of your goals is to make the GRE as familiar as possible, or rather, make the test-taking experience as less *un*familiar as possible. (See Chapter 3 for info on how to prepare for the GRE.)

Because the computerized GRE is offered in small groups, testing centers tend to fill up quickly during the admission deadline months (April and November). If you're planning to take the GRE around these months (something you may need to do to get your test scores in on time), schedule your test early and secure your ideal time slot. You can always reschedule, but the last thing you need is an inconvenient time or location. One of my students had to drive from Phoenix to Tucson (approximately 120 miles) to take his GRE in order to get his scores in on time.

Breaking Down the GRE into Small Doses

Acronyms for standardized tests tend to convey a sense of gloom and doom. Telling someone you have to take the SAT, ACT, or GRE usually elicits the same facial expression as saying that you need to have your wisdom teeth pulled. However, breaking the GRE down into its component parts makes it much more manageable and much less threatening.

Table 1-1 provides a quick overview of what's on the GRE. The essays are always first, but the four multiple-choice sections may be in any order.

Table 1-1 GRE Breakdown by Section

Section	Number of Questions	Time Allotted
Analyze an Issue	1 essay	30 minutes
Analyze an Argument	1 essay	30 minutes
Verbal Section	20 questions	30 minutes
Math Section	20 questions	35 minutes
Verbal Section	20 questions	30 minutes
Math Section	20 questions	35 minutes
Unscored Hidden Math or Verbal Research Section	20 questions	30 or 35 minutes

At close to four hours long, the GRE challenges your stamina as much as your ability to answer the questions. No matter how solid your math and verbal skills are, you must maintain a high level of concentration for the duration of the test. You can achieve this through practicing in four-hour stretches and taking several practice tests.

The GRE includes an unscored Math or Verbal research section. You actually have three Math *or* three Verbal sections, meaning one section isn't scored. Unfortunately, you won't know which one it is. For more on unscored sections, see the "Unscored sections or questions" sidebar in this chapter.

Unlike other computer-based tests (such as the GMAT and TOEFL), the GRE allows you to skip questions and return to them later, as long as you're still in the section. When you reach the end of each section, the GRE displays a review screen that indicates any unanswered questions. If you have time remaining in the section, return to these questions and answer them as well as you can. This feature is nice because you can knock out all the easy questions before spending time on the hard ones. (See Chapter 2 for tips on managing your time during the GRE.)

In each section, the questions are worth the same amount of points, and they don't become more or less difficult based on your performance. Combined with the ability to go back to earlier questions, the format of the GRE is more like that of a paper-based test than some other computer-based tests, such as the adaptive GMAT. However, your performance on the Math or Verbal section determines the overall difficulty level of the *next* Math or Verbal section. For example, if you do extremely well on the first Math section, the GRE places you in high esteem and makes the second Math section harder. Even if you don't get as many questions right in the second Math section as you did in the first, the GRE considers that the questions are harder and gives you a higher score.

So exactly what types of questions and how many of each type can you expect to run into on the GRE? Check out Table 1-2 for the answers.

Table 1-2 GRE Breakdown by Question Type

Type of Question	*Approximate Number of Questions*
Per Math Section (20 questions each)	
Multiple choice with exactly one correct answer	6
Multiple choice with two or more correct answers	2
Fill in the blank with the correct answer	2
Data Interpretation (based on graphs)	3
Quantitative Comparisons	7
Per Verbal Section (20 questions each)	
Text Completion	6
Sentence Equivalence	4
Argument Analysis	2
Reading Comprehension	8

These question types are mixed throughout their respective sections, so you may encounter them in any order. Sometimes the software groups like questions at the beginning or the end. For example, if you're halfway through a Verbal section and haven't seen a Text Completion question, you soon will.

Unscored sections or questions

Although most questions on the GRE affect your score, some may not. The GRE may include an unscored section or unscored questions within scored sections. These unscored questions or sections neither help nor hurt your score. Unless your test specifically states that a section is optional and will not be scored, you have no way to distinguish between scored and unscored questions, so answer all questions to the best of your ability.

The GRE developers don't want you to know which questions are unscored because they want you to try your best in answering them.

On rare occasions, the test may include an identified unscored section at the end that you have the option of taking. If you feel like playing with the computer and helping out the Educational Testing Service (the organization that creates and administers the GRE), you can go ahead and answer the questions, but you aren't obligated to do so.

Scoring Max: 340 and 6

With the GRE, you receive three separate scores: Verbal, Math, and Analytical Writing. Although you get your unofficial Verbal and Math scores immediately after taking the test (as explained in the following section), you must wait 10 to 15 days to get your Analytical Writing score in the mail. The following sections explain in more depth some important scoring tidbits you may want to know.

Knowing how the scoring breaks down

On the GRE, you can score a maximum of 340 points on the multiple choice and 6 points on the essays. Here's the scoring range for each of the three sections:

- **Verbal:** The Verbal score ranges from 130 to 170 in 1-point increments. You get 130 points for just showing up, which accounts for about 80 percent of a job well done. It doesn't help much, though: You need to score as well as or better than most of the other people who took the test. Refer to the chapters in Part II for the lowdown on the Verbal sections.
- **Math:** The Math score also ranges from 130 to 170 in 1-point increments. Head to the chapters in Part III for more on the Math sections.
- **Analytical Writing:** You get 1 to 6 points per essay, with 6 being the highest. Two essay evaluators grade each essay, and your score per essay is the average of the two. If the two evaluators score your essay very differently (more than one point apart), then another grader steps in, and your essay score is the average of the three. Finally, the two essay scores are averaged for your Analytical Writing score of 1 to 6. Essay responses that are blank or filled with typed nonsense receive a score of 0. You can discover more information about the essays in Part IV.

So in essence, if you perfectly ace the Verbal and Math sections, you get 170 points for each, or a total of 340. If you're perfect on the two essays, you can get an essay score of 6. The three scores are separate: You get a Math score and a Verbal score, each from 130 to 170 in one-point increments, and an Analytical Writing score of 0 to 6, in half-point increments.

On the multiple-choice questions, you earn points only for completely correct answers. Answer incorrectly, and you don't get the points, but you don't lose any points, so guessing behooves you. If the question requires two or more answers, you have to get all the answers correct; you don't get partial credit for a partially correct answer. See "Playing the guessing game," later in this chapter, for more on this.

Calculating your score

Each question in each section counts exactly the same toward your score, regardless of the difficulty of the question. Because you can move back and forth within each section, a good strategy is to skip around and answer all the easy questions first and then go back and work the hard questions. Also, the more questions you get right, the higher your score — not the case with the old, adaptive-style GRE, where each section's score was mostly determined by the first 15 questions.

When you take a practice test, you can easily approximate your Math and Verbal scores. For the Math score, count the math questions you answered correctly and then add 130 to that number. Because the GRE has 40 math questions (two sections with 20 questions each), this method gives you a score from 130 to 170. You can find your Verbal score the exact same way, because the GRE also has 40 verbal questions.

The way that the actual GRE calculates your scores is slightly more complicated. It takes into account the difficulty levels of the second Math and Verbal sections, weighing the scores accordingly. A more difficult section results in a higher score, which is important. For example, if you do very well on the first Math section, the second Math section will be more difficult. Regardless of the section's difficulty level, each question within that section counts exactly the same toward your score. Short of this fine detail, however, you can closely approximate your practice-GRE scores using this scoring method.

Knowing how your scores measure up

If you score a perfect 340 or something close to it, you know you did well. If you score a 260, you know you bombed. But what if you score something in between? Did you pass? Did you fail? What do you make of your score? Well, you can't really tell much about your score out of context. There's no pass or fail; no A, B, C, D, F; and no percentile ranking just yet. Because I'm writing this in the first year of the new-and-improved GRE, I don't have *median scores* from the previous year — scores that half the people taking the test scored above and half scored below.

How well you did is relative to how well the other people taking the test performed and the requirements of the graduate program you're applying to. What's most important is that you score high enough to get accepted into the program you have your heart set on.

Your GRE score is only one part of the total application package. If you have a good undergraduate GPA, a strong résumé, and relevant work experience, you may not need as high of a GRE score. On the other hand, if the converse is true, then a stellar GRE score can compensate for your weak areas.

Playing the guessing game

The GRE doesn't penalize you extra for guessing. Sure, if you guess wrong, you don't get the points you would've gotten for answering correctly, but the GRE doesn't deduct extra points for incorrect answers, so

- If you don't know the answer, rule out as many obviously incorrect choices as possible and then guess from the remaining choices.
- Finish the section, even if you must take wild guesses near the end. Wrong answers count the same as not answering a question, so you may as well guess.

Seeing or cancelling your scores

When you finish the GRE, you have the option of either seeing or cancelling your Verbal and Math scores. Unfortunately, you don't get to see your scores before deciding whether to cancel them. If you *think* you had a bad day, you can cancel, and your scores are neither reported to the schools nor shown to you. However, the schools are notified that you cancelled your test. If you choose to see your score, you get it — minus the essay scores — right away.

How much do the schools care about cancelled scores? Probably not much, especially if a top GRE score (from when you retake the test 60 days later) is next to the original cancelled score on your file. If you really want to know the impact of a cancelled score, check with the admissions office of your target school. Each school weighs cancelled scores differently. See Chapter 2 for more about what to do after cancelling your GRE score.

Gimme a Break! GRE Intermissions

You have the option of taking a ten-minute break after the third section of the GRE. However, don't expect to have the entire ten minutes to yourself: Part of that time is for checking in and out while the proctors go through their security procedures to ensure you're not bringing in any materials to cheat with. The ten-minute intermission is timed by the computer, which resumes the test whether you're seated or not. You probably have five minutes to do your business, which leaves little time to grab a bite if you're hungry. Plan accordingly with snacks and water in your locker, so during your actual five minutes, you can refresh yourself without having to scramble.

Make sure your packed snacks are light and nutritious. Sugar makes you high for a few minutes and then brings you way down. Something heavy, like beef jerky, makes you drowsy. You don't want to crash right in the middle of a quadratic equation. Take a handful of peanuts, some trail mix, or anything else light that isn't going to send all the blood from your brain down to your stomach for digestion.

Between other sections of the test, you get a one-minute break — just enough time to stand up and stretch a bit. You don't have time to leave your seat and come back before the test resumes. If you absolutely, positively must use the restroom and leave the computer during the test, just remember that the clock keeps ticking.

Preparing for the test

Stories abound about how someone's friend's second cousin's roommate took the GRE cold (with no preparation) and aced it. This story may be true on a very rare occasion, but you hear only the success stories. Those test-takers who took the test unprepared and bombed it don't brag about the outcome. As an instructor, however, I hear those other stories all the time.

The GRE doesn't test your intelligence; it tests how prepared you are for the test. I'd put my money on a prepared dunce over an unprepared genius every single time. Dramatically raising a test-taker's score, say from the 30th-percentile to the 90th-percentile ranking, is something that I do every day before breakfast, and it's something I do for you through this book. Being prepared includes being familiar with the test and the questions, which means that the first time you calculate a fraction of a circle had better not be on the actual GRE. Make your mistakes *here,* in practice, *not* on the test.

Chapter 2

Owning the GRE: Strategies for Success

In This Chapter

- Managing your time before and during the test
- Deciding whether to retake the GRE
- Taking action if the test isn't administered properly
- Using scores up to five years old

The GRE isn't an IQ test. Nor is it a measure of your worth as a human being or a predictor of your ultimate success in life. The GRE is designed to determine your ability to excel in grad school by sizing you up in three areas:

- **Work ethic:** How hard you're willing and able to work to achieve an academic goal — in this case, performing well on the GRE — determines your work ethic. Grad schools consider this to be a measure of how hard you'll work in their program.
- **Study skills:** To do well on the GRE, you must master some basic study skills and be able to process and retain new information.
- **Test-taking ability:** Your test-taking ability is your ability to perform well on a test under pressure, which is separate from your ability to answer the questions. Exams are an essential part of grad school, so you need to prove that you can take a test without folding under pressure.

This book can't help you in the first area; that's all you. As a study guide, however, this book shapes you up in the second and third areas, enabling you to study more effectively and efficiently and improve your overall test-taking skills. By knowing the material and taking the practice tests, you establish a firm foundation for doing well on the GRE.

This chapter is designed to take your study skills and test-taking ability to the next level. To beat the GRE at its game, you need to maximize the use of your time, focus on key areas, and apply strategies to answer the questions quickly and correctly. This chapter shows you how to do all these things and provides you with a Plan B — how to proceed in the event that you don't do so well the first time.

Making the Best Use of Your Time

As soon as you decide to take the GRE, the clock starts ticking. You have only so much time to study, so much time to practice, and so little time to answer each question. Squander your time, and you reduce your chances of success. The good news: If you manage your time well and make the necessary preparations, you can improve your chances of doing well on the test. The following sections show you how to optimize your study and practice time and answer test questions more efficiently.

Budgeting your time for studying

As an undergrad, you may have mastered the fine art of cramming the night before an exam, but that doesn't work on the GRE. This test is based not on memorization, but rather on skills, which take time to develop. Give yourself plenty of time to absorb all the material you need to study. Here's what I recommend in terms of total time, the amount of that time you spend working through this book, and the amount of time to set aside per day:

- **Six to 12 weeks total preparation:** Give yourself plenty of time to work through this book, take practice tests, and review areas where you need extra preparation. Six to eight weeks works well for most people, but more time is generally better. At 12 weeks, you can do extremely well, but after 12 weeks, most people get burned out or lose interest, and their skills start to get rusty.
- **Three to four weeks on this book:** Working through this book takes about three weeks, not including the practice tests. The practice tests should each take 2½ hours (no essays) or 3½ hours (with essays), plus another hour or two to review the answer explanations.
- **One to three hours per day, five or six days per week:** Pace yourself. I've seen too many students burn themselves out from trying to master the whole test in three days. Your brain needs time to process all this new information and be ready to absorb more.

If you have only a couple weeks to study, mark your weakest subject areas in the table of contents at the beginning of this book and work through those chapters or sections first. If you're not sure about your weakest subject areas, take one of the practice tests in the book or on the CD to find out.

This book provides broad coverage of everything you're likely to encounter on the test, but if taking the practice tests reveals weaknesses in certain areas, you may need to consult additional resources to improve your understanding and skills.

Prioritize your study time and schedule daily sessions. Otherwise, other activities and responsibilities are likely to clutter your day to the point of pushing study time off your to-do list.

Budgeting your time for practicing

Just because you know a subject inside and out doesn't mean you can ace a test on it. Test-taking requires a completely separate skill set. Start taking practice tests at least two weeks prior to your scheduled GRE, so you have time to hone your skills, learn from your mistakes, and strengthen your weak areas.

Your proficiency with the test itself is as important as your math and verbal skills for attaining a top GRE score. As you take the practice tests, don't focus exclusively on errors you made in answering specific questions. Spend time evaluating test-taking mistakes. What kinds of mistakes do you make two hours into the exam? Do you still try as hard at the end as you do in the beginning? Do you misread the questions or make simple math mistakes? Do you fall for traps?

In addition to working the practice tests in this book, I recommend working the free computer-based practice tests that Educational Testing Services (ETS) provides at `www.ets.org`. See Chapter 3 for details.

Beating the clock: Time management tips

Taking the GRE is a little like playing *Beat the Clock.* The computer provides you with a stopwatch — an on-screen clock — to time each section. Your goal is to answer as many questions correctly as quickly as possible before the clock ticks down to 0:00. You have the option of removing the clock from the screen, but I don't recommend doing that. Instead, make the timer familiar and comfortable (or rather, less *un*comfortable) by using a timer while doing homework and practice tests. Practicing with a timer is part of preparing for the test-taking experience.

The clock changes from hours:minutes to minutes:seconds during the last five minutes; this, of course, means hustle time.

Don't obsess over giving each question a specific number of seconds, but know when to give up and come back to a question later. As long as you haven't exited a section, you can return to questions in that section. Simply click Review, click the question you want to return to, and then click Go to Question. You can also mark a question for review so it's flagged in the Review Screen. Just keep in mind that while you're reviewing questions and answers, the clock continues to tick. (See Chapter 3 for more about the computerized test.)

No question carries greater weight than any other question; easier ones are worth just as much as harder ones. A good strategy is to make a note on your scratch paper of any question that you can't answer quickly so that you can answer as many of the easy questions as possible and review the harder ones at the end.

Answer *every* question, even if you have to make a wild guess. Although you don't earn points for incorrect answers, you don't lose points, either; by guessing, at least you have a chance to earn the points. See Chapter 1 for details.

Repeating the Test

As I explain in Chapter 1, upon completion of the test, you have the option of accepting and seeing your scores immediately or cancelling the results if you're convinced you did poorly. If you cancel the results, you have two choices: Retake the test or choose another career path. If you accept your scores and end up with subpar results, you have a third option — stick with what you got.

If you wonder whether you should repeat the test, ask yourself the following questions before making that decision:

- **Am I repeating the test to get a certain minimum qualifying score?** If you have your heart set on a particular graduate school that requires a minimum GRE score, you may not need to take the test again and again until you get that score. Talk to the admissions folks at the school you want to attend. They weigh the GRE score along with your GPA, résumé, and personal interests and have some flexibility when making their decision; if your score is close to the target, they may just let you in. I see it happen all the time.
- **Am I willing to study twice as hard, or am I already burned out?** If you put your heart and soul into studying for the exam the first time, you may be too burned out (or ***enervated***) to take on another round of study and practice. After all, scores don't magically go up by themselves; improvement requires effort.

- **What types of mistakes did I make on the first test?** If you made mistakes because of a lack of familiarity with either the test format (you didn't understand what to do when faced with a Quantitative Comparison question) or substance (you didn't know the vocabulary words or were baffled by the geometry problems), you're a good candidate for repeating the test. If you know what you did wrong, you can mend your ways and improve your score.

  However, if you have no idea where you fell short or your mistakes were due to carelessness or a lack of concentration, you're very likely to make those same types of mistakes again. If you truly, honestly, sincerely, and without ***dissembling*** (lying) feel that you can stay focused and avoid making the same mistakes, go for it! But chances are, if you're the type of test-taker who *always* makes a lot of careless mistakes or *rarely* makes them, you're not going to change your whole test-taking style overnight. This, by the way, is one purpose for taking and reviewing the practice tests.

  After taking the actual GRE, you don't get to review the correct and incorrect answer choices. However, you can get a good sense of the types of mistakes that you're likely to make by going through the practice tests in this book and reviewing your wrong answers afterward.

- **Were there *extenuating* (underestimated) circumstances beyond my control?** Maybe your nerves were acting up on the first exam, you were feeling ill, or you didn't get enough sleep the night before. In that case, by all means repeat the exam. You're bound to feel better the next time. In addition, if the test was administered poorly or in a room full of distractions, you really should consider a retake. (See the section "Reporting Test Administration Abnormalities" for details.)

- **Did I choke?** This happens all the time, especially on the essay questions at the beginning. Or you could panic on a thorny math question, spending several minutes and frazzling yourself for the rest of the test. Fortunately, recovering from this slip-up is easy. Almost every test-taker I've seen choke does phenomenally better on the next try.

- **Did I run out of steam?** Stamina is a key factor of success on the four-hour GRE. If you don't practice writing the essays when taking the practice tests, you won't be prepared for the extra hour of work before the Math and Verbal sections. Also, because you're amped on test day, you're likely to run out of steam faster than usual. Knowing what to expect and preparing for it could boost your score on a retest.

- **Am I eligible to retake the GRE?** You can take the GRE only once per 60-day period and no more than five times per rolling 12 months. If you try to take the test more often than that, you won't be stopped from registering for or taking the test, but your scores won't be reported.

Can repeating the exam hurt you? Typically, no. Most schools look only at your highest score. Find out from the individual schools you're interested in whether that's their policy; it isn't the same for every school. If you're on the borderline, or if several students are vying for one spot, sometimes having taken the exam repeatedly can hurt you (especially if your most recent score took a nosedive). On the other hand, an admissions counselor who sees several exams with ascending scores may be impressed that you stuck to it and kept trying, even if your score rose just a little bit. In general, if you're willing to invest the study time and effort and take the repeat exam seriously, go for it.

All the scores you obtain for five years are part of your record and are sent to the schools you designate. You can't send scores from only one exam date. For example, if you do great in October then take the exam again in April and blow it big time, you can't tell ETS to ignore the April ***debacle*** (a sudden collapse, a rout) and send just the October scores.

Reporting Test Administration Abnormalities

Your test isn't actually administered by ETS. Companies licensed by ETS administer the GRE in your area, and they're required to adhere to certain standards. If something irregular occurred during the test that you believe reduced your score, call the ETS complaint line at 866-756-7346. You have seven days to register a complaint.

One of my students was seated and ready to begin the GRE only to have the test start time delayed an hour! On top of that, a lot of noise was coming from the next room — definitely an unwarranted distraction. If something like this happens to you, you can petition to have your score withheld and for the opportunity to take the GRE again at no charge.

Using Ancient Scores

What if you took the GRE a long time ago when you thought you were going to grad school and then opted to take a job or start a family instead? Well, if it was five years ago or less, you're in luck (assuming you scored well). The GRE folks make the scores reportable for up to five years. That means that if you're pleased with your old score, you can send it right along to the school of your choice and say adios to us right here and now. However, if you took the test more than five years ago, you have to take it again.

You can retake the test and perhaps improve your score, but until that score's fifth birthday, it remains part of your GRE record.

Chapter 3

Gearing Up for Test Day

In This Chapter

- Having everything you need for test day
- Brushing up on the testing center's rules and regulations
- Staying in tiptop test-taking shape
- Rehearsing with a computerized sample test

On test day, there's no such thing as a pleasant surprise. Any surprise you happen to experience is just going to throw you off your game, stress you out, deplete your energy, and draw your focus away from what really matters — performing your best on the GRE. Surprises can also make you so late that you actually miss your scheduled test time.

The goal of this chapter is to help you avoid nasty surprises so you know exactly what to expect on the day of the test and can focus on taking the GRE in a more relaxed and confident frame of mind.

Gathering Your Stuff before Test Day

Save yourself some time on the morning of the GRE by getting together everything you need the night before. The test is stressful in itself, and the last thing you need is to arrive at the testing center flustered because you were scrambling to find some paperwork (or the testing center) at the last minute.

Here's what you need:

- **Authorization voucher from Educational Testing Services (ETS):** You need to bring proof that you're signed up for the test. This evidence can take the form of an *authorization voucher,* which is proof directly from ETS that you registered for the test. The authorization voucher contains your confirmation number, reporting time, and the testing center's address. You can request that ETS mail, fax, or e-mail a voucher to you when you register for the test.
- **Comfortable clothes:** Dress in layers. Testing centers can be warm or, more typically, cold. Sitting there for hours shivering or sweating won't help your performance. Dress in layers and be prepared for anything.
- **Map or directions:** Know in advance how to get to the testing center. Drive there a few days prior to your scheduled test day to check out how long the drive is, where to park, how much parking costs, and so on. If you're taking public transportation, find out where and when you need to board the bus or train, how long the ride is, how much it costs, and where you get off.

One student had to take the test at a center in the middle of a downtown area. On the day of the test, she couldn't find any parking and became totally stressed out before she arrived at the testing center. It would have helped if she'd scoped out the area ahead of time and found different places to park.

- **Photo ID:** You must have identification with three key elements:
  - A recognizable photo
  - The name you registered for the test under
  - Your signature

  Usually, a driver's license, passport, employee ID, or military ID does the trick. A student ID alone isn't enough (although it works as a second form of ID in case something's unclear on your first form of ID). Note that a Social Security card or a credit card isn't acceptable identification.
- **Water and a snack:** Bring a bottle of water and a light snack, such as a fitness bar or granola bar. Avoid anything that's high in sugar, simple carbohydrates, or fats.

If you're wondering whether you need to bring scratch paper, pencils, a calculator, or anything like that, proceed to the next section.

Knowing What Not to Bring

Just as important as knowing what to bring to the testing center is knowing what not to bring. Leave the following items at home, in your car, or at the door:

- **Books and notes:** Forget about last-minute studying. You aren't allowed to take books or notes into the testing center. Besides, if you don't know the material by that time, you never will. (One of my students almost had his test score nullified because during his break, he picked up his test-prep book that was in his testing center locker. Fortunately, he didn't *open* the book, so he was allowed to keep his test score.)
- **Calculator:** You aren't allowed to use your own calculator, but an on-screen calculator is available during the Math sections of the exam. One nice thing about the on-screen calculator is that it features a button that transfers the number from the calculator field to the answer space. Your handheld calculator won't do that.
- **Friends for support:** Leave your friends at home. The ETS frowns on visitors. Having a friend drop you off and pick you up isn't a bad idea, though, especially if parking is likely to be a problem — like at a downtown testing center.
- **Phones and other electronics:** Radios, iPods, MP3 players, cellphones, and other mobile electronic devices are strictly prohibited. You can bring these electronics to the testing center, but they must stay in the locker while you're taking the GRE. And because you can't use these devices during the test, don't use them when completing practice tests.
- **Scratch paper:** You aren't allowed to bring in your own scratch paper; the testing center provides it for you. If you run low during the test, request more from the proctor during the one-minute breaks between sections. Although you have plenty of room to do calculations and scribbling, your scratch paper stays at the testing center when you're done.

The testing center provides lockers for test-takers to store their belongings, so if you bring a purse or backpack, you'll have a secure place to keep it.

Handling unique circumstances or needs

If you have a special circumstance or need, the GRE powers-that-be are usually very accommodating, as long as you give them a heads-up. For example, if you have a learning disability, you may be able to get additional testing time. Following is a brief list of special circumstances and how to obtain assistance for each:

- **Learning disabilities:** These disabilities refer to attention deficit hyperactivity disorder (ADHD), dyslexia, and other related or similar conditions. To find out whether you qualify for a disabilities waiver of any sort, contact the ETS Disability Services, Educational Testing Service, P.O. Box 6054, Princeton, NJ 08541-6054; phone 866-387-8602 (toll free) or 609-771-7780 (Monday–Friday 8:30 a.m. to 4:30 p.m. Eastern Time), TTY 609-771-7714, fax 609-771-7165; website `www.ets.org`, e-mail `stassd@ets.org`.
- **Physical disabilities:** ETS tries very hard to accommodate everyone. Folks who need special arrangements can get Braille or large-print exams, have test readers or recorders, work with interpreters, and so on. You can get the scoop about what the ETS considers to be disabilities and how the disabilities can change the way you take the GRE in the *Supplement for Test Takers with Disabilities.* This publication contains information, registration procedures, and other useful forms for individuals with physical disabilities. To get this publication, send a request to ETS Disability Services, P.O. Box 6054, Princeton, NJ 08541-6054. Or better yet, head to `www.ets.org/gre` and click the Test Takers with Disabilities or Health-Related Needs link. Voilà! All the info you need to know, along with contact information if you have questions or concerns.
- **Financial difficulties:** Until you ace the GRE, get into a top-notch graduate school, and come out ready to make your first million, you may have a rough time paying for the GRE. However, fee waivers are available. Note that the waiver applies only to the actual GRE fee, not to miscellaneous fees such as the test-disclosure service, hand-grading service, and so on. Your college counselor can help you obtain and fill out the appropriate request forms. (If you're not currently in college, a counselor or financial aid specialist at a nearby college or university may still be glad to help you. Just call for an appointment.)

Training Physically and Mentally for Test Day

Taking an intense four-hour exam is challenging both mentally and physically. Most people aren't used to concentrating at this level for such a long time. To meet the challenge, your brain needs a good supply of oxygen and other nutrients, and it gets those from an active, healthy, and alert body that consumes nutritious foods and beverages. The following sections provide guidance on whipping your body into shape for test day.

Staying active

You can't just be a bookworm for the year before the exam. You need to stay active. Exercise helps all parts of the body and leads to clearer thinking by increasing oxygen to the brain, so get moving! You don't need to train for a marathon. Walking, swimming, jogging, yoga, Pilates, and even *exergaming* with video games like Wii Fit gets your body in motion and increases overall health and circulation.

Eating well

Certain foods and beverages affect your cognitive ability, so avoid highly processed foods and foods high in processed sugars, starch, or fat. These foods tend to make you feel sluggish or result in brief highs followed by prolonged crashes. Lean more toward veggies and foods that are high in protein. When it comes to carbohydrates, opt for complex over simple. Complex carbohydrates are typically in fresh fruits, veggies, and whole-grain products. Simple carbohydrates are in candy, soda, anything made with white flour, and most junk foods. And forget those energy drinks that combine huge amounts of caffeine and sugar to get you to a state of heightened tension.

If you plan on taking an energy drink, or anything unusual, on the day of the test, here's the best advice I can offer: *Try it out on a practice test first.* If the drink gives you the jitters or upsets your stomach, you won't want to discover this on the day of the test.

Relaxing

Relaxation comes in many different forms for all kinds of people. Some folks are relaxed when they're with friends; some read books and play music; and some do yoga, meditate, or paint. The only requirement when choosing what relaxation tool to use is making sure your brain isn't running 100 miles an hour. The whole purpose of relaxation is to give your brain a rest. So find a relaxing activity you enjoy, thank your brain by telling it to take some time off, and recharge.

Relaxation isn't a luxury — it's a requirement for both a well-balanced life and success on the GRE. You're a multifaceted human, not a work-and-study automaton. Refer to Chapter 24 for some hands-on ways you can relax before the test.

I've seen students who are so overextended and overachieving that they stress themselves out for the test. They have trouble concentrating, get panic attacks, and generally exhaust themselves. One sure sign of panic that I see occasionally is the tendency to overanalyze simple questions. If you can't accept a simple, correct answer because you're sure there must be more to it, then this has happened to you, and it's time to take a break in your studying.

Test-Driving the Computerized Version

You take the GRE entirely on the computer. But even the most basic software has a learning curve, and you don't want to climb that learning curve on test day. Nor do you want to risk making a silly computer error that messes up your score — like clicking a button that deletes your entire essay.

To gain some experience with the computerized GRE, take it for a test-drive using the free Powerprep software that ETS offers. The Powerprep software features an actual GRE computer-based practice test for you to become accustomed to the format of the computer-based test. (The software works only with PC-compatible desktop and laptop computers running a version of Windows 7, VISTA, XP, or 2000.) Make sure you're using the newest version of the Powerprep software available from `www.ets.org`. Earlier versions of this software may be for the older formats of the GRE. Also, ETS tends to number their versions of Powerprep: The current version is Powerprep II.

If you purchased the Premier version of *GRE For Dummies,* 7th Edition, you can also check out the CD at the back of this book for hands-on practice with simulated computerized versions of the test.

To download and install the Powerprep software, go to `www.ets.org/gre` and search for Powerprep. Carefully follow the on-screen directions to locate, download, and install the software.

If you have trouble with the installation, return to the GRE site, click the link to view frequently asked questions about the Powerprep software, and then click the Downloading/Installation link. This takes you to a page with solutions to the most common problems.

To run the Powerprep software, open the Windows Start menu, click All Programs, click POWERPREP, and then click Launch POWERPREP. This displays the Introduction to the Computer-based GRE revised General Test page in your default web browser. This opening page contains several tabs for accessing an overview of the test, guidance on preparing for the test, details about the Analytical Writing, Verbal Reasoning, and Quantitative Reasoning sections of the test, and details about test scores.

For now, scroll down to the section "Practicing for the Test," click the Start Practicing Now button, and then scroll to the bottom of the resulting page and click Continue. This launches the practice test, which gives you access to a test preview tool and a timed and untimed practice test. Choose the desired practice test option and click Start Test.

The test appears just as it will on test day, with a title page and introduction. Keep clicking Continue, in the upper right corner of the screen, until you reach the General Test Information. Read the information and click Continue to proceed. Use the buttons in the upper right corner of the screen to navigate the test. Most of the buttons are self-explanatory, but the following ones deserve special attention:

- **Mark:** Enables you to choose a tentative answer and then flag the question. The Review screen shows marked questions with a checkmark next to them, so you can easily pick them out from the rest of the questions in the list.
- **Review:** Displays a list of questions you can return to. Click the question you want to go back to and then click the Go To Question button. You can then review the question and change your answer if desired.
- **Exit Section:** Ends this section and saves your essay or answers so you can proceed to the next section. After you click this button, you can't go back to review answers or return to unanswered questions in the section.
- **Quit Test:** Ends the test prematurely, cancelling your scores. You usually want to avoid this button, especially during the actual test — unless, of course, you really want to stop and cancel out your scores.

Take the computerized sample test not only to get a feel for the content and format of the questions but also to become accustomed to selecting answers and using the buttons to navigate. A day or two prior to the actual test, take the computerized practice test again to reorient yourself with the buttons.

Bringing the GRE into Your Comfort Zone

Panicking about the GRE is counterproductive. You want to enter the testing center feeling confident and relaxed. That means bringing the GRE into your comfort zone. Working through this book and taking the practice tests, both on paper and on a computer, can bring you very close to that goal, but having the right mindset is also useful. The following sections put the GRE in the proper perspective and serve to remind you of just how prepared you really are.

Getting familiar with subject matter and questions

The GRE focuses on a specific range of core concepts and presents questions in a fairly predictable format. Surprises are rare to non-existent. After you've successfully completed this book, you will have the knowledge and experience you need to perform well on the test. You gain even more familiarity with the test questions and format by taking the computerized GRE sample tests.

Reminding yourself of how fully prepared you are

A little self-affirmation goes a long way. In the days leading up to the test and on test day, remind yourself just how fully prepared you are. You've done all you can to prepare for the test. The hard part is over. Taking the GRE is an opportunity to prove yourself and finally take advantage of all the time and effort you invested in preparing for the challenge.

Understanding that the GRE is only one of many admissions requirements

Although your performance on the GRE is an important qualification for admission into the graduate school and program of your choice, it's not the only factor that admissions departments consider. Your work experience, GPA, extracurricular activities, and other factors that define who you are (including volunteer work) are just as important. Of course, you should do your very best on the test, but remind yourself that this isn't an all-or-nothing situation.

Part II

Tackling the Verbal Section One Word at a Time

"Your buddy says the two of you were peripheral to the incident in question. You just said you were superficial to the incident. Now which is it, peripheral or superficial?!"

In this part . . .

One of the sections on the GRE is the Verbal section. (*Verbal* is just a fancy name for "written or spoken word.") The questions within come in four styles: Text Completion, Sentence Equivalence, Argument Analysis, and Reading Comprehension. This part devotes one chapter to each question type (though Text Completion and Sentence Equivalence questions are similar enough to share a chapter). In each chapter, you discover the format of each question (what it looks like), an approach to the question (where to begin and an organized plan of attack), and the various tricks and traps built into the questions (with, of course, suggestions for recognizing and avoiding these traps). Each chapter also includes some challenging practice questions and detailed answer explanations.

The GRE Verbal section is legendary for using obscure English vocabulary. Therefore, this part also devotes one chapter to brushing up on your vocabulary and recognizing roots, prefixes, and suffixes.

Chapter 4

Text Completion and Sentence Equivalence: The Easiest Verbal Questions

In This Chapter

- Learning about the Text Completion and Sentence Equivalence questions
- Establishing an effective strategy for identifying the correct answer
- Attacking questions confidently with a three-step approach
- Tackling more challenging questions

Text Completion and Sentence Equivalence questions are the gimmies of the GRE because the questions and possible answers hold all the clues you need to answer these questions correctly. By using key strategies and avoiding common mistakes as described in this chapter, you can breeze through these questions and rack up points in a hurry. If you find the vocabulary is slowing you down, turn to Chapter 7 for words you're likely to encounter and their definitions.

Grasping Text Completion and Sentence Equivalence Questions

Because Text Completion and Sentence Equivalence questions are so similar, the strategy is the same for both, and it makes sense to cover them both in one chapter:

- **Text Completion:** A Text Completion question consists of a sentence or paragraph with one, two, or three blank spaces for a missing word(s) or phrase(s). Following the sentence or paragraph are choices for filling in the blank(s): five choices if the sentence has only one blank or three choices for each blank if the sentence has two or three blanks. Your job is to choose the most suitable word or words. Although all the answers may sound okay in the sentence, only one is correct for each blank.
- **Sentence Equivalence:** A Sentence Equivalence question consists of a single sentence with exactly one word missing and six answer choices. You're required to select the two words that fit the sentence and mean the same thing, and you don't get partial credit for choosing only one of the correct words.

The following at-a-glance table shows you what to expect from the variations of Text Completion and Sentence Equivalence questions. Don't worry about mixing this up: On the GRE, the number of blanks and choices for the Text Completion questions are obvious, and Sentence Equivalence questions with too few or two many answers selected are marked "Incomplete" in the review screen following the Verbal section, which means you can go back and correct them with the time remaining on the section.

Question Type	*Blanks*	*Choices per Blank*	*Choose Total*
Text Completion	3	3	3
	2	3	2
	1	5	1
Sentence Equivalence	1	6	2

The questions are always preceded by directions, such as "For each blank, select one entry" or "Select two answer choices." Also, the one-answer questions allow you to select only one answer, and the two-answer questions allow you to select more than one.

The following example of a Text Completion question shows how all answer choices appear to fit perfectly, but only two specific words actually make logical sense.

Directions: For each blank, select one entry from the corresponding column of choices. Fill all blanks in the way that best completes the text.

Frustrated at having to spend the entire weekend studying for the GRE instead of going hang gliding, Faye (i)_____ her book out the window with such (ii)_____ that it soared high into the sky, prompting three of her neighbors to capture it on video with their cellphones.

Blank (i)	***Blank (ii)***
Ⓐ tossed	Ⓓ ferocity
Ⓑ hurled	Ⓔ glee
Ⓒ pitched	Ⓕ gentleness

The keyword in this example is *frustrated,* which conveys a strong negative emotion. Choices **(B)** and **(D),** *hurled* and *ferocity,* are the only choices that support such a negative emotion. Note that this is a single, two-part question. You may select any of the three answer choices for each blank, but you must choose *both* correct answers to earn credit for the question.

The following example of a Sentence Equivalence question shows how all six answer choices appear to fit within the sentence structure, but only two answers actually support the meaning of the sentence.

Directions: Select the two answer choices that, when used to complete the sentence, fit the meaning of the sentence as a whole and produce two completed sentences that are alike in meaning.

Well-prepared and ready to take on the GRE, Billy _____ the test and made his family proud.

[A] aced

[B] missed

[C] passed

[D] held

[E] took

[F] knew

The sentence suggests that Billy did very well on the GRE. The best words to convey GRE success are *aced* and *passed,* making Choices **(A)** and **(C)** the correct answers. Again, you must select both of these correct answers to earn credit for the question.

Developing Your Skills for Finding the Correct Answers

Text Completion and Sentence Equivalence questions are designed to measure three core proficiencies of the test-taker (you): interpreting the sentence; using vocabulary properly; and recognizing irony, figures of speech, and formal diction. By understanding what the test-makers are testing for, you significantly improve your chances of correctly answering their questions.

The following sections give you an overview of these three proficiencies and how you can spot the correct answers. These proficiencies always lead you to the correct answer and, with practice, are very easy to apply.

Interpreting the sentence

Interpreting a sentence consists of determining its meaning in the absence of the missing words. By knowing the meaning of the sentence prior to looking at the possible answers, you can quickly eliminate choices that don't make sense. This technique is the single most important skill for working these verbal questions, and the GRE-makers have fun trying to trick you. No worries, though, this section (and the rest of the chapter) is packed with methods for interpreting sentences.

To interpret a sentence, read it carefully, using keywords to understand the *gist* of it — the overall meaning the sentence conveys. Check out the following Sentence Equivalence example to see what I mean.

Directions: Select the two answer choices that, when used to complete the sentence, fit the meaning as a whole and produce two completed sentences that are alike in meaning.

The bags were so heavy, we could _____ lift them.

A easily

B hardly

C fully

D nearly

E barely

F effortlessly

Even without the missing word, you can construe the meaning of the sentence. The phrase *so heavy* clues you in that these bags are difficult or impossible to lift. After realizing this, you can immediately eliminate *easily* and *effortlessly*. The words *fully* and *nearly* are a little tougher to ignore, but they really don't make sense either. The correct answers are Choices **(B)**, *hardly*, and **(E)**, *barely*.

Using vocabulary properly

After interpreting the sentence, the next step is to pick the right word. Proper usage helps determine the right word. (*Usage* is the customary manner of using particular words.)

To pick the correct word, think of how each answer choice sounds in the context of the sentence, as if you're speaking the sentence. Consider whether the word in the sentence makes sense or sounds a little odd. (To brush up on vocabulary and strategies for approaching unknown words, check out Chapter 7.)

Directions: For each blank, select one entry from the corresponding column of choices. Fill all blanks in the way that best completes the text.

The lights _____ when the engineer hit the kill switch.

Ⓐ died
Ⓑ went out
Ⓒ discontinued
Ⓓ ended
Ⓔ stopped

Each word choice supports the sentence meaning, but only *one* is properly used. Although the sentence does use the word *kill,* lights don't die, stop, discontinue, or end — they go out. The correct answer is Choice **(B).**

Recognizing irony, figures of speech, and formal diction

Even if the answer choices support the sentence meaning, subtle nuances in the meaning of words can separate wrong answers from right ones. Examine answer choices for skepticism, doubt, uncertainty, and emotional connotations that just don't fit.

Consider the tone of the sentence: Is it positive or negative? Pleased or disappointed? This high-level perspective can help you find words that convey the correct meaning.

Directions: Select the two answer choices that, when used to complete the sentence, fit the meaning of the sentence as a whole and produce two completed sentences that are alike in meaning.

I'm _____ at how good your GRE score is — I knew you could do it!

- [A] ecstatic
- [B] stunned
- [C] thrilled
- [D] shocked
- [E] dumbfounded
- [F] amazed

All the choices convey surprise, but *stunned, shocked, dumbfounded,* and *amazed* sound as if the person speaking doubted your abilities. Because the second half of the sentence doesn't convey any doubt ("I knew you could do it!"), the correct answers are Choices **(A)** and **(C).**

Attacking the Question Head-On

Whether you're faced with Text Completion or Sentence Equivalence questions, your battle plan is the same: Attack each question with confidence. Hesitation and doubt can waste time and make you talk yourself out of the right answer. Instead, use this three-step strategy:

1. **Read and interpret the sentence while covering the answer choices.**
2. **Fill the blanks with your own words.**
3. **Eliminate answer choices that don't match your words.**

The following sections explain these steps in detail.

Read and interpret the sentence while covering the answer choices

When working Text Completion and Sentence Equivalence questions, your first step is to interpret the sentence for its meaning. If you know what the sentence is saying, then you have a better understanding of which words best fill in the blanks. Althought that seems obvious, many test-takers skip this step.

While interpreting the sentence, don't look at the answer choices! Each puzzling answer choice not only completes the meaning of the sentence but also gives the sentence a very different meaning. Trying out answer choices before interpreting the sentence turns an easy question into a hard one and shifts your focus away from the sentence itself. Instead, read the sentence carefully and figure out what it's trying to say.

To avoid involuntarily glancing at the answer choices, hide them with the scratch paper provided. Doing so allows you to ponder the sentence's meaning without being distracted by the answer choices. Right there, your Verbal score just jumped 20 points. This tip applies to the computerized version, too. Hold the scratch paper right up on the computer screen. Silly? Yes. Effective? Absolutely. I have my students do it, and they tell me it's a lifesaver.

The following example illustrates the different meanings that a sentence can convey, using different words in the blanks. If you first try out all the answer choices, it becomes impossible to tell what the sentence is actually saying, so they're not shown here yet.

Having been coerced by her mother into accepting a blind date, Mitzi was (i)_____, although Marty, surprisingly, turned out to be (ii)_____.

First, interpret what the sentence is trying to say. The word *although* in the middle of the sentence tells you that the two phrases have different meanings. Therefore, the words in those blanks should be *antonyms* — words with opposite meanings — or nearly antonyms. They may not need to be opposites, but they certainly shouldn't mean the same thing. *Although* is an example of a transition word, which can function as a valuable clue. (See the later section "Identify transition words and use them to get the gist of the phrases" for more on transition words.)

Ask yourself the following questions: Was Mitzi pleased or disappointed? Was Marty, her date, surprisingly handsome or unremarkable? One key skill to doing well on the Text Completion questions is the ability to interpret sentences that are missing keywords.

A mother's coercive date suggestion (sorry, Mom) is probably lame, so it'd be surprising if the date were attractive. That's how you know what the sentence is trying to say.

Fill the blanks with your own words

The next step to solving the Text Completion and Sentence Equivalence problems is to think of your own words to fill in the blanks. Your words don't have to be perfect — you're not writing the sentence — but they do have to support the meaning of the sentence and, by extension, the meanings of the blank words themselves. By using this technique, you know exactly what to look for and can eliminate some answer choices (which is the next step). Right now, you're still covering up the answer choices with your scratch paper.

Pretend you're saying this sentence to someone in a conversation. Even though you may arrange the sentence differently, your keywords will match the missing words in the question.

> Having been coerced by her mother into accepting a blind date, Mitzi was *uninterested,* although Marty, surprisingly, turned out to be *good looking.*

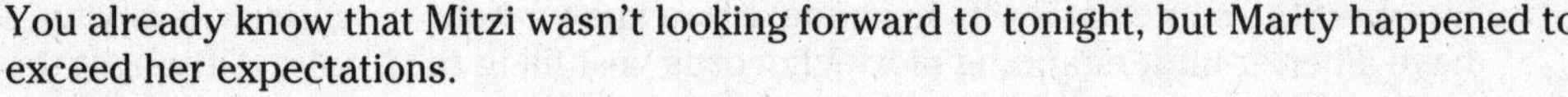

You already know that Mitzi wasn't looking forward to tonight, but Marty happened to exceed her expectations.

Your fill-in-the-blank word choice doesn't have to fit perfectly; it just needs to convey the meaning.

Eliminate answer choices that don't match your words

The last step to answering Text Completion and Sentence Equivalence questions is to go ahead and look at the answer choices. Knowing what the sentence is saying makes the right answer obvious.

Here's the example question again, this time with the answer choices provided.

Directions: For each blank, select one entry from the corresponding column of choices. Fill all blanks in the way that best completes the text.

Having been coerced by her mother into accepting a blind date, Mitzi was (i)_____, although Marty, surprisingly, turned out to be (ii)_____.

Blank (i)	***Blank (ii)***
Ⓐ dignified	Ⓓ gorgeous
Ⓑ ecstatic	Ⓔ boorish
Ⓒ noncommittal	Ⓕ mediocre

Compare the answer choices, one at a time, to the words you already came up with on your own (*uninterested* and *good looking*). Cross *dignified* off the list, because it has nothing to do with disinterest. Similarly, *boorish* has nothing positive about it. Mitzi couldn't possibly be ecstatic about having been coerced and the word *although* tells you that Marty's mediocrity wouldn't be a pleasant surprise, so eliminate these answers. The correct answers are Choices **(C)**, *noncommittal,* and **(D)**, *gorgeous.* Both closely fit the predictions and make sense when you read them back into the sentence.

Text Completion and Sentence Equivalence questions can be very challenging, so if you get stuck, don't use up a lot of time and energy trying to arrive at the right answers. Instead, cut your losses: Eliminate obviously wrong answer choices, make an educated guess, mark it for review (so you can return to it later if you have time), and move on.

These verbal questions should take you less than a minute each, saving you valuable time for the more time-consuming Reading Comprehension questions. (For more on the GRE Reading Comprehension questions, head over to Chapter 5.)

Overcoming Tricky Sentences

If solving every Text Completion and Sentence Equivalence question were as easy as the questions in the preceding section, every test-taker would get a perfect 170 on the Verbal section (those test-takers who read this book, anyway). However, these questions can be difficult to interpret. When you come across trickier sentences, you want to utilize the three basic strategies mentioned in the preceding section and build on them with the following three steps:

1. **Identify transition words and use them to get the gist of the phrases.**
2. **Break the sentence into smaller pieces.**
3. **Check one word blank at a time to eliminate answer choices.**

The following sections delve further into these steps.

Identify transition words and use them to get the gist of the phrases

Transition words exist in almost all GRE Text Completion and Sentence Equivalence questions and serve as valuable clues to interpreting the meaning of a sentence. (*Transition words* connect two ideas in a sentence or paragraph and tell you whether the two ideas in the sentence agree or contradict one another.) Understanding just how significantly a transition word can affect the meaning of a sentence enables you to use these words to decipher the meaning of a sentence in the absence of certain words.

For example, changing the transition word in the following sentence completely alters its meaning.

> *Although* he ran as fast as he could, Eric _____ the bus.

The transition word *although,* indicating contrast, tells you that Eric missed the bus. Consider the same sentence with a different transition word:

> *Because* he ran as fast as he could, Eric _____ the bus.

The transition word *because,* indicating cause and effect, tells you that Eric caught the bus.

With a little practice, transition words become easy to identify and use to your advantage. They're helpful when breaking the sentence into pieces (which is the next step) and are used frequently in the Analytical Writing portion of the GRE. (See the chapters in Part IV for more on the Analytical Writing essays.)

Common transition words include the following:

although	and	because	but
despite	either/or	however	in spite of
moreover	nonetheless	therefore	or

In the previous example sentence, changing the transition word *although* to *because* changes the entire meaning of the sentence. Note that the transition word isn't always between the phrases. In this next example, use the transition word to help interpret the sentence.

Although she usually was of a (i)_____ nature, Patty was (ii)_____ when she heard the history professor assign a paper due the first day back after spring break.

The transition word *although* tells you that Patty's usual nature is different from the way she felt when receiving her assignment.

Don't go through the answer choices first — that's why I don't show them here yet. On the real GRE, which you take on a computer (in most places), hold your scratch paper up to the screen to cover the answer choices.

Break the sentence into smaller pieces

Sometimes the sentences are so long and convoluted that you can't make much sense of them. To handle tricky questions, break the sentence into pieces to simplify the interpretation before adding your own words. The simplest way to do this is to separate the phrases, usually indicated by commas.

Continuing with the example from the previous section, break the sentence into the two following parts:

> Patty was _____ when she heard the history professor assign a paper.
>
> *and*
>
> Although she usually was of a _____ nature,

In smaller pieces, the gist of this sentence is easier to discern. One phrase describes how Patty felt when receiving the assignment, and the other phrase describes how she usually feels. You know from the transition word *although* that the words are probably dissimilar in meaning. You can also figure out that the first blank needs a word like *happy,* and the second blank, with an opposite meaning indicated by *although,* needs a word like *sad.*

Check one word blank at a time to eliminate answer choices

Although many of these types of questions feature only one word blank, some Text Completion questions have two or three blanks. You may not always be able to match all the blanks, especially on the more difficult questions. After you think of your own words to go in the blanks, the best strategy is to eliminate the answer choices one word at a time. So even if you're unable to match all the words, you can still eliminate a few wrong answer choices and select from a smaller group of answers.

Directions: For each blank, select one entry from the corresponding column of choices. Fill all blanks in the way that best completes the text.

Although she usually was of a (i)_____ nature, Patty was (ii)_____ when she heard the history professor assign a paper that would be due the first day back after spring break.

Blank (i)	***Blank (ii)***
Ⓐ frugal	Ⓓ enigmatic
Ⓑ keen	Ⓔ lugubrious
Ⓒ cheerful	Ⓕ ebullient

Now look at the answer choices and eliminate those that don't match the words you used to fill the blanks (*happy* and *sad*). Start with the first blank.

Using your first word clue, *happy,* which word from the first column of choices best describes Patty's nature? ***Frugal*** doesn't fit based solely on its meaning (economical), and it has no opposite in the second column. *Keen* really doesn't fit based simply on usage (described in the earlier section "Using vocabulary properly"). *Cheerful* seems to be the right choice for the first blank. In the second column, ***enigmatic*** means mysterious or cryptic, which really doesn't fit. If you don't know what *lugubrious* or *ebullient* means, you can make a pretty good guess that ***lugubrious*** is heavy and ***ebullient*** is upbeat, based on how the words sound. If that's the case, the transition word *although* rules out *ebullient* because the two words (*cheerful* and *ebullient*) are too similar. So *lugubrious* is the best choice. The correct answers are Choices **(C)** and **(E).**

If you know the definition of the second word, you can use it to support your answer choice: ***Ebullient*** means very happy, ***lugubrious*** means sad, and ***enigmatic*** means mysterious. (Flip to Chapter 7 for a lot more vocabulary.)

Getting Your Hands Dirty with Practice Questions

You're ready to tackle some practice Text Completion and Sentence Equivalence questions to get a better grasp of how to solve them on your own by using all the tools described in this chapter.

Text Completion questions

Directions: For each blank, select one entry from the corresponding column of choices. Fill all blanks in the way that best completes the text.

1. As a public relations specialist, Susan realizes the importance of kindness and _____ when dealing with even the most exasperating tourists.

Ⓐ etiquette
Ⓑ realism
Ⓒ patience
Ⓓ compassion
Ⓔ honesty

First, ask yourself: What's important when dealing with exasperated tourists? A public relations specialist would need to be polite. The first word choice, *etiquette,* looks good, but you don't treat someone with etiquette. (*Etiquette* is a system of rules for manners.) Check that word off the list. You don't show exasperated tourists *compassion,* either. Gone. *Honesty* won't help. Gone! *Realism* isn't even close. Gone! Through logic and elimination, the correct answer is Choice **(C)**.

2. Enabled by his (i)_____ and unimpeded by any sense of (ii)_____, Henry reached the end of the Ironman Triathlon.

Blank (i)	***Blank (ii)***
Ⓐ knowhow	Ⓓ weariness
Ⓑ appetite	Ⓔ courage
Ⓒ stamina	Ⓕ power

What's one thing that helps and another that hinders a triathlete? *Strength* and *fatigue* are good choices. In the first column, you can rule out *knowhow.* Either of the remaining words, *appetite* (in the sense of desire) and *stamina,* could fit, but stamina is more closely related to strength. In the second blank, you look for a word like *fatigue,* and *weariness* is clearly the closest match. Correct answers: Choices **(C)** and **(D)**.

3. Although dismayed by the pejorative comments made about her inappropriate dress at the diplomatic function, Judy (i)_____ her tears and showed only the most calm and (ii)_____ visage to her critics.

Blank (i)	***Blank (ii)***
Ⓐ suppressed	Ⓓ incensed
Ⓑ monitored	Ⓔ articulate
Ⓒ succumbed to	Ⓕ placid

If Judy had a calm and (something) ***visage*** (a form of the word *vision;* a countenance, or facial expression), the (something) must go hand in hand with calm. Although it doesn't have to be an exact synonym, the second word can't be an antonym either. Look for a word that means calm. ***Placid*** means calm and tranquil, as you know from the root *plac,* meaning peace (as in *placate*). Check the remaining two choices in the second column: ***Incensed*** means upset, burning mad (think of burning incense); ***articulate*** means well-spoken. Her visage (or facial expression) wouldn't be well-spoken, although Judy herself may be. *Placid* is best for the second word, so now find something suitable for the first word. *Monitoring* or *succumbing to* (giving in) her tears is unlikely to make Judy appear calm and placid, but *suppressing* her tears will. The correct answers are Choices **(A)** and **(F).**

4. There are those writers who carp and (i)_____ about the current depressed state of our economy. However, many people insist that such writers don't speak for the common man (or woman) who believes in the (ii)_____ of the nation and the (iii)_____ of its future.

Blank (i)	*Blank (ii)*	*Blank (iii)*
Ⓐ laud	Ⓓ resilience	Ⓖ morbidity
Ⓑ grouse	Ⓔ chaos	Ⓗ security
Ⓒ ponder	Ⓕ generosity	Ⓘ lampoon

Try to predict the words that fit into the blanks. Here, you can predict that the first word must be something bad (because the writers are ***carping,*** or griping, about a depressed economy). The word *however* cues you that the next two words are going to be more optimistic. In the first column, look for a word with a negative connotation; neither ***laud*** (to praise, as in app*laud*) nor ***ponder*** (as in *wonder*) meet that requirement. Only ***grouse*** (meaning to complain or grumble) fits with carp. In the second column, you can rule out ***chaos*** (confusion and disorganization) because it's not positive and ***generosity*** (charitableness) because that's not necessarily going to help turn around a depressed economy. ***Resilience*** (the ability to recover) is the best choice there. As for the third word, ***lampoon*** means to ridicule (think of the satirical magazine *National Lampoon*), and ***morbidity*** (desperation) conveys a very negative tone, so you can eliminate both of those choices and choose ***security,*** which describes a positive state for a future. Correct answers are Choices **(B), (D),** and **(H).**

5. Although often writing of (i)_____ activities, Emily Dickinson possessed the faculty of creating an eclectic group of characters ranging from the reticent to the epitome of (ii)_____.

Blank (i)	*Blank (ii)*
Ⓐ mundane	Ⓓ stoicism
Ⓑ egregious	Ⓔ effrontery
Ⓒ commensurate	Ⓕ taciturnity

If you know that ***reticent*** means shy and holding back, you can predict that the second blank must be the opposite of that, something bold and forward. ***Effrontery*** is shameless boldness and audacity. You have effrontery when you ask your boss for a raise right after he or she chews you out for bungling a project and costing the company money. *Effrontery* is the only word that fits the second blank. ***Taciturnity*** is the noun form of the word *taciturn,* meaning quiet, not talkative, not forward. ***Stoicism*** is not showing feelings or pain.

The transition word *although* tells you that the first blank must be the opposite of ***eclectic,*** which means from multiple sources, or in this case, diverse. ***Mundane*** means common, which is a good opposite of eclectic. Mundane activities are day-to-day tasks, nothing exciting like winning a lottery or visiting Antarctica. ***Egregious*** means terrible or flagrant. An egregious mistake is right out there for the world to see, not nearly the opposite of eclectic, so you can eliminate it. ***Commensurate*** means equivalent to or proportionate (your score on this section is commensurate with your vocabulary); again, this word isn't an opposite of eclectic, so cross it off the list. The correct answers are Choices **(A)** and **(E)**.

6. Unwilling to be labeled _____, Gwenette slowly and meticulously double-checked each fact before expounding upon her theory to her colleagues at the convention.

Ⓐ precipitate
Ⓑ meticulous
Ⓒ loquacious
Ⓓ efficacious
Ⓔ painstaking

First, break the sentence into two parts at the comma. Using the word *unwilling* in the first part, you know that the second part is going to be the opposite meaning of the word required to complete the first part. Now work from the second part back. The gist of the second part is that Gwenette is being careful, so now all you need to do is find the one word in the list that's closest to meaning careless.

The key here is pure vocabulary, but if you don't have a clue what any of the words mean, don't get stuck on it — just guess and go.

Precipitate means overly quick, leaping before looking. This word is a perfect fit. Correct answer: Choice **(A)**.

If you don't want to be labeled precipitate, confirm your answer by eliminating the four other choices. ***Loquacious*** means overly talkative, something Gwenette doesn't want to be labeled as but has little relevance to preparing her theory. ***Meticulous*** and ***painstaking*** mean careful with detail, paying close attention, so they're both the opposite of what you're looking for. ***Efficacious*** means efficient and effective; all of which Gwenette *does* want to be labeled.

Even if you don't know the exact meaning of the words, you can judge whether they generally fit. If you're not sure of an answer choice, confirm it after eliminating the other answer choices.

Sentence Equivalence questions

Directions: Select the two answer choices that, when used to complete the sentence, fit the meaning as a whole and produce two completed sentences that are alike in meaning.

7. A successful business-process _____designed to streamline existing operations will, by its nature, also support the company's strategic planning.

   A reaction

   B management

   C plan

   D initiative

   E supply chain

   F method

   Is this business-process thing a new event or ongoing? That it affects "existing operations" tells you that it doesn't currently exist and is, therefore, new. Look for words that suggest an early phase of development. *Reaction* obviously doesn't fit. *Management* and *supply chain* are business-sounding words that don't suggest anything new. *Method* also isn't distinctly new (a method could have been around for a while). The words *plan* and *initiative* suggest something in the early stages of development. Correct answers are Choices **(C)** and **(D).**

8. The sea tortoise, though lumbering and slow on land, can move with _____ speed and agility in water.

   A surprising

   B actual

   C according

   D defiant

   E unexpected

   F unequivocal

   If the tortoise is lumbering and slow on land, wouldn't you expect it to be slow in water, too? The crocodile, for example, is fast and nimble in either medium. In this sentence, however, the transition word *though* tells us that the tortoise's speed and agility in water is a surprise. The words *actual, according, defiant,* and *unequivocal* don't suggest any sort of surprise. The correct answers are Choices **(A)** and **(E).**

9. The speaker, ironically, _____ the very point he had stood up to make, and hurriedly sat down, hoping no one had caught his solecism.

   A prognosticated

   B divulged

   C refuted

   D countered

   E duplicated

   F ferreted out

   A ***solecism*** is an inconsistency, such as a mistake. From the context of the sentence, you can gather that a solecism is something negative because the speaker hoped no one had noticed it.

   To ***refute*** is to disprove or show to be false. To ***counter*** is to contradict. It'd be ***ironic*** (the opposite of what's expected) if the speaker disproved or contradicted the very point he stood up to make. Therefore, the correct answers are Choices **(C)** and **(D).**

Take a moment to go through the other words to increase your vocabulary. To ***prognosticate*** is to predict. *Pro-* means before, *gnos* means knowledge, and *-ate* means to make. To prognosticate is to "make knowledge before," to predict.

If you picked *prognosticated,* you probably fell for the trap of looking only at the answer choices and not inserting them into the sentence. Yes, something ironic is the opposite of what's expected, and a prognostication is nearly opposite of a summation, but that answer doesn't fit when inserted into the sentence. Be sure to take your time and look at the sentence with each answer choice. The Sentence Equivalence section isn't a place to try to save a few seconds.

The second choice, ***divulge,*** is to reveal. Though this word seems to fit, it doesn't support the intended meaning of the sentence. To divulge the very information you stand up to say isn't ironic, it's normal.

The second to last choice, *duplicity,* is an interesting word. The root *dup* means double, but duplicity isn't "doubleness" in the sense of two of something. ***Duplicity*** is deception, being two-faced. A traitor is noted for his or her duplicity. And to ***ferret out*** is to search diligently, as a detective ferrets out clues to help his client. You ferret out the tips and traps scattered throughout these explanations to remember them.

10. Dismayed by the _____ evidence available to her, the defense attorney spent her own money to hire a private investigator to acquire additional evidence.

A dearth of

B scanty

C vestigial

D immense

E concrete

F impartial

Predict words to fit in the blanks. If the attorney is dismayed by evidence and hires an investigator to get *more* evidence, she must not have had much evidence to begin with. You can predict that the first word means not very much. ***Scanty*** means barely sufficient and a ***dearth of*** is a lack of, which are the only two words that fit the blank. So the correct answers are Choices **(A)** and **(B).**

As for the remaining words, ***vestigial*** means functionless, after much of the original has disappeared; for example, the tailbone of humans is a vestigial tail. ***Immense*** means large, just the opposite of what you want. ***Concrete,*** in this context, means irrefutable; again, the opposite of what you want. ***Impartial*** evidence is neutral, neither good nor bad, which has nothing to do with the amount of evidence.

11. Rather than be decadent, the actor adopted an _____ lifestyle to help him focus on the professional side of his work.

A abstemious

B anachronous

C ascetic

D assiduous

E austere

F avarice

The actor could have adopted any kind of lifestyle, but look for words that indicate the opposite of decadent. ***Abstemious*** and ***ascetic*** both describe one who practices self-denial, so these words fit. The correct answers are Choices **(A)** and **(C)**.

As for the remaining words, ***anachronous*** describes something out of the proper time, such as if Robin Hood had had a flashlight. ***Avarice*** refers to a desire to hoard wealth, so that's definitely out. ***Assiduous*** means hardworking, which may also describe the actor, but you need a word that's the opposite of decadent. ***Austere*** means stern or unadorned, which isn't quite the opposite of decadent.

12. One who postures as completely fearless is unsurprisingly likely to drop the pretense and show a(n) _____ face.

[A] artless

[B] contentious

[C] craven

[D] deferent

[E] mealy-mouthed

[F] pusillanimous

If someone has a pretense of fearlessness, then behind it is a sense of cowardice. The words ***craven*** and ***pusillanimous*** both mean cowardly, so the correct answers are Choices **(C)** and **(F)**.

Artless means honest and natural, which may be the face behind a pretense, but the sentence describes fearlessness. ***Contentious*** describes someone willing to stand up for himself, which may be this posturing person, but it, too, wouldn't be behind a pretense of fearlessness. ***Deferent*** means giving in out of respect for another, and ***mealy-mouthed*** means insincere, which may refer to the pretense but wouldn't be behind it.

13. Inspired by their leader's tirade, the protestors took it upon themselves to continue the _____.

[A] diatribe

[B] diffidence

[C] harangue

[D] hyperbole

[E] euphemism

[F] equivocation

A ***tirade*** is a bitter verbal attack, so the protestors could only continue with their own tirades. ***Diatribe*** and ***harangue*** are synonyms for tirade, making the correct answers Choices **(A)** and **(C)**.

Diffidence refers to a lack of confidence. ***Hyperbole*** is an exaggeration, ***euphemism*** is the use of agreeable words in place of offensive language, and ***equivocation*** is the use of intentionally vague language.

14. The welfare system, designed to help those who are _____, is in need of reform.

A indigent

B mendacious

C mendicant

D misanthropic

E morose

F quiescent

The welfare system was designed to help those who are poor or destitute. ***Indigent*** and ***mendicant*** are synonyms for destitute, making the correct answers Choices **(A)** and **(C).**

Mendacious means dishonest, ***misanthropic*** means antisocial, ***morose*** means sullen, and ***quiescent*** means at rest.

15. As a rule, the company hires only _____ engineers, believing years of experience tend to jade engineers, blinding them to new ideas.

A felicitous

B fledgling

C gregarious

D insensible

E ingenuous

F neophyte

If the company wants only inexperienced engineers, then the engineers would have to be beginners or novices. ***Fledgling*** and ***neophyte*** fit this meaning, making the correct answers Choices **(B)** and **(F).**

Felicitous means suitable or appropriate, which may be true of the desired engineers but doesn't support the sentence's purpose of hiring novices. ***Gregarious*** means sociable and outgoing, which is also possibly true of the new hires but doesn't support the sentence's purpose. ***Insensible*** means unresponsive. ***Ingenuous*** means naive and trusting, which is close, but a company wouldn't necessarily look to hire someone who is naive.

16. Many _____ bloggers continue to aver countless half-truths, despite ample evidence to the contrary.

A dissonant

B doctrinaire

C dogmatic

D ebullient

E eclectic

F erudite

Aver means to declare something to be true. If bloggers declare half-truths to be true despite the contrary evidence, then they're ignoring the evidence. ***Doctrinaire*** and ***dogmatic*** fit this meaning, making the correct answers Choices **(B)** and **(C).**

Dissonant means ill-fitting, which may be true of the bloggers but doesn't address their aversion to the evidence. ***Ebullient*** means buoyant in disposition, which also doesn't fit. ***Eclectic*** means derived from various sources, and ***erudite*** means educated.

17. The buffalo, once _____ to this area, has been hunted nearly to extinction.

A endemic

B indigenous

C quintessential

D truculent

E veracious

F viable

The buffalo must have originated and lived in the area. ***Endemic*** and ***indigenous*** fit this meaning, making the correct answers Choices **(A)** and **(B).**

Quintessential refers to a perfect state, ***truculent*** means poor behavior, ***veracious*** means truthful and accurate, and ***viable*** means practical.

18. The _____ is one who spares no time for conciliatory gestures.

A churl

B cohort

C consummate

D contrite

E coy

F curmudgeon

Conciliatory refers to an effort to bring peace, as in the word ***reconcile.*** The sentence is talking about a person, because the pronoun *who* can only refer to a person — never a thing.

What kind of person would be too impatient to reconcile with those around him? One who is ill-tempered, such as a ***churl*** or a ***curmudgeon.*** The correct answers are Choices **(A)** and **(F).**

A ***cohort*** is a group of people with something in common. ***Consummate*** means complete and perfect, certainly not the case here. ***Contrite*** refers to one who is filled with sorrow for a wrongdoing, and ***coy*** means shy or modest.

19. A talent for easy conversation can help one build relationships, but too much can make one appear _____ and have the opposite effect.

A abstruse

B garrulous

C loquacious

D lugubrious

E ponderous

F recondite

If too much conversation can be bad, then find words that mean too talkative. ***Garrulous*** and ***loquacious*** refer to one who talks to the point of being meddlesome, so Choices **(B)** and **(C)** are the correct answers.

Abstruse and ***recondite*** refer to one who isn't easily understood, and they wouldn't necessarily be the bad effect of talking too much. ***Lugubrious*** means sad and mournful, which is certainly not the case here. ***Ponderous*** refers to one who is dull or moves slowly.

20. Beneath the _____, the man is something else entirely.

A disingenuousness

B divergence

C exculpation

D superciliousness

E superfluousness

F veneer

If the man puts up a false front, ***disingenuousness*** and ***veneer*** both accurately describe this person. The correct answers are Choices **(A)** and **(E).**

Divergence refers to straying away from the main point of a discussion. ***Exculpation*** means no longer considered guilty. ***Superciliousness*** would be on one who is disdained and scorned. ***Superfluousness*** refers to someone or something that's extraneous.

Chapter 5

Making Sense of What You Read: Reading Comprehension

In This Chapter

- Approaching the Reading Comprehension passages
- Learning tips and tricks designed to save you time

Reading Comprehension questions on the GRE comprise almost half of the Verbal questions. The actual number may vary slightly, but close to half of your Verbal score is determined by these questions. Each question consists of a single passage, sort of like a graduate-level journal article, on a science, social science, or humanities topic that you've probably never considered before and never will again.

The Verbal section of the GRE contains about four Reading Comprehension passages. For each passage, you must answer one to four questions. The computer screen is split with the passage on the left and a question on the right. You get the questions one at a time; if more than one question references a passage, each question appears separately on the right side of the screen while the passage stays on the left.

This chapter introduces the three question formats you'll encounter on the test, presents strategies for identifying the correct answers quickly, and provides some sample passages along with questions and their answers so you know what to expect on the test.

All Reading Comprehension questions are based directly on what's in the passage. You don't need to know anything about the subject outside the passage to answer the questions. In fact, if you're familiar with the subject, be careful not to mix your own knowledge with what's in the passage.

Recognizing the Three Reading Comprehension Question Formats

Being familiar with the question formats for the Reading Comprehension section enables you to field the questions more confidently, because you know what to expect. The GRE presents each question in one of the following three formats:

- **Multiple-choice questions:** Choose one answer.
- **Multiple-choice questions:** Choose one or more answers.
- **Sentence-selection questions:** Choose a sentence from the passage.

The following sections describe each question format in greater detail and provide an example of each format based on the following short passage from *Food Allergies For Dummies* by Robert A. Wood, MD, with Joe Kraynak (Wiley):

> In children and young adults, anaphylactic shock is relatively uncommon even with the most severe reactions, because their cardiovascular system is so resilient. This does not mean, however, that younger people are immune to severe anaphylaxis. Anaphylaxis in younger people typically results in breathing difficulty — a constricted or blocked airway that causes the fatal and near fatal reaction. In a fatal reaction, the heart stops only because the body eventually runs out of oxygen.

Multiple-choice questions: Choose one answer

The following format is the traditional multiple-choice question. You get five answers to pick from, and only one is the correct answer.

Based on the passage, how common is anaphylactic shock in older adults?

Ⓐ Very common

Ⓑ Relatively uncommon

Ⓒ About as frequent as in the general population

Ⓓ Nonexistent

Ⓔ Not stated in the passage

You pick one and only one answer. In this case, the correct answer is Choice **(E),** because the passage doesn't even mention older adults.

Multiple-choice questions: Choose one or more answers

The next question format is a spin on the traditional multiple-choice question. Three choices follow the question and one, two, or all three of them are correct. You must pick *all* of the correct choices and no incorrect choices to receive credit for your answer. You don't receive partial credit for picking only some of the correct answers. The GRE treats a partially answered question as a wrong answer.

When anaphylactic shock in a child or young adult is fatal, what happens? Consider each of the three choices separately and select all that apply.

[A] Heart stops.

[B] Airway is blocked or constricted.

[C] Body runs out of oxygen.

You pick all answers that are correct. In this case, all the answer choices — Choices **(A), (B),** and **(C)** — are correct.

You can quickly tell whether to select only one answer or up to three answers by looking at the instruction that accompanies the question: The GRE always instructs you whether to choose *one* or *all answers that apply.*

Sentence-selection questions: Choose a sentence from the passage

In the sentence-selection questions, the GRE presents a description or question followed by instructions to click the sentence in the passage that most closely matches the description or answers the question. Clicking any part of the sentence selects the entire sentence.

Choose the sentence in the passage that parents of young children are likely to find most reassuring.

In the sample passage provided earlier, you would click the sentence, "In children and young adults, anaphylactic shock is relatively uncommon even with the most severe reactions, because their cardiovascular system is so resilient."

Developing Strategies for Success

Reading Comprehension questions can be the most time-consuming questions of the Verbal section. The best way to ace these questions is to master and use strategies for quickly reading the passages, identifying key facts called for in the questions, and drawing inferences based on subtle implications. The following sections explain four useful strategies for arriving at the correct answers (and avoiding incorrect answers) more efficiently and effectively.

Using the context as your road map

When reading a science or humanities passage, you first want to get a mental grid of where all the key information is. Skim the passage as you would scan a room upon first entering it to get a general idea of where everything is located. Doing so can help you figure out where the information is as you begin to answer questions. Remember: Don't sweat the details. As you read each question, you can then quickly revisit the passage to locate the details for answering each question correctly.

Usually the first paragraph is an introduction, telling you what the passage is about (the main idea). Subsequent paragraphs (the body of the passage) provide details to support or develop the topic stated in the first paragraph. As you read each body paragraph, ask yourself what its purpose is and how it supports the main idea. Asking these questions gives you a clearer idea of what the related details are and where they're located in the passage.

The exceptions to this strategy are the social sciences questions, which tend to be based less on facts and more on what can be determined from the facts. As explained later in the section "The social sciences passage," you want to read these passages more carefully, so your brain has all the information it needs to draw correct inferences.

Sometimes an entire passage can be one giant paragraph. Don't let these types of passages discourage you from mapping the details — look for where one idea ends and another begins and make a mental note of where paragraphs should be separated. Creating these mental paragraph breaks can help you map the passage details as you would for a passage that is already broken into separate paragraphs.

Grasping the gist of the passage

Understanding the main idea of the passage is key to establishing the context of the paragraphs within. The main idea is also usually the basis of one of the questions, typically an early question. If you can briefly sum up the gist of the passage, then you not only develop a contextual understanding of the passage but also answer one of the questions.

Using keywords strategically

Reading Comprehension passages and questions often contain keywords that act as valuable clues in identifying correct answers and eliminating wrong ones. For example, say a particular passage is all about successful international adoption; you're asked to choose the best title for the passage from the following choices:

Ⓐ Trends in International Adoption

Ⓑ Children at Risk

Ⓒ Analyzing the Child Psyche

Ⓓ Overcoming the Challenges of International Adoptions

Ⓔ What Makes a Good Parent

In this case, both Choices (A) and (D) mention international adoption, but of these two answers, only Choice **(D)** suggests a title leading to a *successful* adoption.

Avoiding traps

The people who write the GRE are a tricky lot. They dangle wrong but tempting answers in front of you, hoping you take the bait. By recognizing the most common traps (and the human mind's tendencies toward making assumptions), you have a better chance of avoiding them:

- **Facts:** Answer choices may contain facts that aren't mentioned in the passage. The answer strikes you as correct because it's a true statement, but if that fact isn't mentioned in the passage, it's not a correct answer.
- **Half-truths:** Answer choices may contain information that's part accurate and part inaccurate or not even mentioned in the passage. Before choosing an answer, make sure what the answer states is 100 percent accurate based on the passage.
- **Your own knowledge:** If you're like most people, you add detail based on your own knowledge and expertise to things that you read. Sometimes, these details tempt you to choose an answer that's correct based on what you know but incorrect according to the passage. Be careful not to fill in the blanks with what you know beyond what's in the passage.
- **Subtle distinctions:** When a question includes words like *mostly, best, primarily,* or *primary,* watch out. Most of the answers are probably correct to some degree, but only one answer is the *most* correct.
- **Judgment statements:** A judgment statement declares something right or wrong or better or worse, such as "Cats make better pets than dogs" or "People should stay out of other people's business." These value judgments may be tempting choices, because the human mind likes to draw its own conclusions from what it reads. However, value judgments are almost never correct answers.

Acing the Three Commonly Tested Reading Comprehension Passages

Reading Comprehension passages are based on biological or physical sciences, social sciences, and humanities. Each of the following sections explains one of the passage types; presents a passage of that type along with sample questions, answers, and explanations to get you up to speed; and provides additional guidance and tips for successfully answering each question.

The biological and physical science passage

A biological or physical science passage is straightforward, giving you the scoop on how laser beams work, how to build a suspension bridge, how molecular theory applies, and so on. Although the passage itself may be difficult to get through (because it's full of facts and data from an unfamiliar subject), this type of passage is often the easiest because it has so few traps and tricks.

When approaching biological and physical science passages, don't get hung up on the scientific terminology. You usually don't need to know the meaning of all the scientific terms a passage throws at you in order to answer the questions correctly. However, these terms may function as keywords to help you locate the answers inside the passage, even if you don't know what the terms mean.

You can answer most biological or physical science questions directly from the facts provided in the passage itself.

Here's a science passage for you to practice. Don't forget to check the introduction paragraph for the overall gist of the passage and look for the high-level contribution of each paragraph. If you know what each paragraph's purpose is, you'll be able to quickly find the details when you need them.

Microbiological activity clearly affects the mechanical strength of leaves. Although it cannot be denied that with most species the loss of mechanical strength is the result of both invertebrate feeding and microbiological breakdown, the example of *Fagus sylvatica* illustrates loss without any sign of invertebrate attack being evident. *Fagus* shows little sign of invertebrate attack even after being exposed for eight months in either a lake or stream environment, but results of the rolling fragmentation experiment show that loss of mechanical strength, even in this apparently resistant species, is considerable.

Most species appear to exhibit a higher rate of degradation in the stream environment than in the lake. This is perhaps most clearly shown in the case of *Alnus.* Examination of the type of destruction suggests that the cause for the greater loss of material in the stream-processed leaves is a combination of both biological and mechanical degradation. The leaves exhibit an angular fragmentation, which is characteristic of mechanical damage, rather than the rounded holes typical of the attack by large particle feeders or the skeletal vein pattern produced by microbial degradation and small particle feeders. As the leaves become less strong, the fluid forces acting on the stream nylon cages cause successively greater fragmentation.

Mechanical fragmentation, like biological breakdown, is to some extent influenced by leaf structure and form. In some leaves with a strong midrib, the lamina break up, but the pieces remain attached by means of the midrib. One type of leaf may break cleanly whereas another tears off and is easily destroyed after the tissues are weakened by microbial attack.

In most species, the mechanical breakdown will take the form of gradual attrition at the margins. If the energy of the environment is sufficiently high, brittle species may be broken across the midrib, something that rarely happens with more pliable leaves. The result of attrition is that where the areas of the whole leaves follow a normal distribution, a bimodal distribution is produced; one peak is composed mainly of the fragmented pieces, the other of the larger remains.

To test the theory that a thin leaf has only half the chance of a thick one for entering the fossil record, all other things being equal, Ferguson (1971) cut discs of fresh leaves from 11 species of leaves, each with a different thickness, and rotated them with sand and water in a revolving drum. Each run lasted 100 hours and was repeated three times, but even after this treatment, all species showed little sign of wear. It therefore seems unlikely that leaf thickness alone, without substantial microbial preconditioning, contributes much to the probability that a leaf will enter a depositional environment in a recognizable form. The results of experiments with whole fresh leaves show that they are more resistant to fragmentation than leaves exposed to microbiological attack. Unless the leaf is exceptionally large or small, leaf size and thickness are not likely to be as critical in determining the preservation potential of a leaf type as the rate of microbiological degradation.

1. Which of the following would be the best title for the passage?

Ⓐ Why Leaves Disintegrate

Ⓑ An Analysis of Leaf Structure and Composition

Ⓒ Comparing Lakes and Streams

Ⓓ The Purpose of Particle Feeders

Ⓔ How Leaves' Mechanical Strength Is Affected by Microbiological Activity

Note that because the passage is talking primarily about leaves, that word needs to be in the title, which eliminates Choices (C) and (D) right off. Choice (A) is too broad; other causes of disintegration may exist that the passage doesn't mention. Choice (B) is too specific. The passage mentions leaf structure, but that topic isn't its primary focus. Correct answer: Choice **(E).**

2. Which of the following is mentioned as a reason for leaf degradation in streams? Consider each of the three choices separately and select all that apply.

[A] Mechanical damage

[B] Biological degradation

[C] Large particle feeders

The second paragraph of the passage tells you that ". . . loss of material in stream-processed leaves is a combination of biological and mechanical degradation." Choice (C) is incorrect, because the passage specifically states that the pattern of holes is contrary to that of large particle feeders. The correct answers are Choices **(A)** and **(B).**

3. The conclusion the author reached from Ferguson's revolving drum experiment was that

Ⓐ Leaf thickness is only a contributing factor to leaf fragmentation.

Ⓑ Leaves submersed in water degrade more rapidly than leaves deposited in mud or silt.

Ⓒ Leaves with a strong midrib deteriorate less than leaves without such a midrib.

Ⓓ Microbial attack is exacerbated by high temperatures.

Ⓔ Bimodal distribution reduces leaf attrition.

The middle of the last paragraph tells you that leaf thickness *alone* is unlikely to affect the final form of the leaf. You probably need to reread that sentence a few times to understand it, but a detail or fact question is the type of question you should be sure to answer correctly. Choice (B) introduces facts not discussed in the passage; the passage didn't talk of leaves in mud or silt. Choice (C) is mentioned in the passage but not in Ferguson's experiments.

Nothing appears in the passage about high temperatures, which eliminates Choice (D). (***Exacerbated*** means made worse.) Choice (E) sounds pretentious and pompous — and nice and scientific — but again has nothing to do with Ferguson. To answer this question correctly, you need to return to the passage to look up Ferguson specifically, not merely rely on your memory of the passage as a whole. Correct answer: Choice **(A).**

Be careful to answer *only* what the question is asking. Answer-choice traps include statements that are true but don't answer the question.

4. The tone of the passage is

Ⓐ Persuasive

Ⓑ Biased

Ⓒ Objective

Ⓓ Argumentative

Ⓔ Disparaging

Although you can make a case that the passage is persuasive, it isn't really trying to change the reader's opinion on an issue. It objectively presents scientific facts and experimental evidence. Because you know the gist of the passage and the context of each paragraph, the answer is obvious. Correct answer: Choice **(C).**

5. Select the sentence that explains the form of mechanical breakdown of most species of leaves.

Keywords come in handy in answering this question. The first and only place *mechanical breakdown* is mentioned is in the first sentence of the fourth paragraph. Correct answer: "In most species, the mechanical breakdown will take the form of gradual attrition at the margins."

6. The author is most likely addressing this passage to

Ⓐ Gardeners

Ⓑ Botanists

Ⓒ Paleontologists

Ⓓ Biologists

Ⓔ Epidemiologists

The most important clue in the question is *most likely.* You know the passage is about plants, so you can eliminate Choice (E), epidemiologists (people who study transmittable diseases). You can also eliminate Choice (A), gardeners, because they're more interested in growing plants than in watching them decompose. Choice (D) is tempting because biologists study life, but they study both plant and animal life. Botanists (Choice [B]), who focus exclusively on plants in any sort of scientific way, are a good choice, but they tend to focus more on living plants and species than plant decomposition. Paleontologists, who study plant fossils, are *most likely* to read this passage. The correct answer is Choice **(C).**

The social sciences passage

The GRE usually includes one social sciences passage. It may be about history, psychology, business, or a variety of other topics. In other words, the term *social sciences* is broad enough to include whatever the test-makers want it to include. Because social sciences passages offer a perspective of a subject that you may already be familiar with, such as history, psychology, or sociology, you can use your understanding of the subject as a backdrop to make the passage easier to read and understand.

Be sure not to use your own knowledge of the subject to answer the questions. *Everything* you need to answer the questions is in the passage, and your outside knowledge may differ from what the questions ask.

In many ways, a social sciences passage is nearly the opposite of a biological or physical science passage. The questions deal more with inferences and less with explicitly stated facts. Therefore, you must read the passage carefully, trying to understand not only what's stated but also what's implied. Take some time to think about what you're reading.

The questions that follow a social sciences passage may not be as straightforward as those for a biological or physical science passage. You may not be able to go back to a specific line and pick out a single fact. Instead, these questions require that you understand the big picture or comprehend what the author meant but didn't come right out and say. You may be asked why an author included a particular example or explanation.

Here's a social sciences passage for you to practice. Though you need to read the passage more carefully, the underlying strategy is the same: Look for the gist of the passage, usually in the first paragraph, and identify the purpose of each paragraph thereafter. You'll still need to revisit these paragraphs to find details, so knowing where the details are located is easier and more useful than memorizing them.

Multinational corporations frequently encounter impediments in their attempts to explain to politicians, human rights groups, and (perhaps most importantly) their consumer base why they do business with, and even seek closer business ties to, countries whose human rights records are considered heinous by United States standards. The CEOs propound that in the business trenches the issue of human rights must effectively be detached from the wider spectrum of free trade. Discussion of the uneasy alliance between trade and human rights has trickled down from the boardrooms of large multinational corporations to the consumer on the street who, given the wide variety of products available to him, is eager to show support for human rights by boycotting the products of a company he feels does not do enough to help its overseas workers. International human rights organizations also are pressuring the multinationals to push for more humane working conditions in other countries and to, in effect, develop a code of business conduct that must be adhered to if the American company is to continue working with the overseas partner.

The president, in drawing up a plan for what he calls the "economic architecture of our times," wants economists, business leaders, and human rights groups to work together to develop a set of principles that the foreign partners of United States corporations will voluntarily embrace. Human rights activists, incensed at the nebulous plans for implementing such rules, charge that their agenda is being given low priority by the State Department. The president vociferously denies their charges, arguing that each situation is approached on its merits without prejudice, and hopes that all the groups can work together to develop principles based on empirical research rather than political fiat, emphasizing that the businesses with experience in the field must initiate the process of developing such guidelines. Business leaders, while paying lip service to the concept of these principles, fight stealthily against their formal endorsement because they fear such "voluntary" concepts may someday be given the force of law. Few business leaders have forgotten the Sullivan Principles, in which a set of voluntary rules regarding business conduct with South Africa (giving benefits to workers and banning apartheid in the companies that worked with U.S. partners) became legislation.

7. Which of the following best states the central idea of the passage?

Ⓐ Politicians are quixotic in their assessment of the priorities of the State Department.

Ⓑ Multinational corporations have little if any influence on the domestic policies of their overseas partners.

Ⓒ Voluntary principles that are turned into law are unconstitutional.

Ⓓ Disagreement exists between the desires of human rights activists to improve the working conditions of overseas workers and the pragmatic approach taken by the corporations.

Ⓔ It is inappropriate to expect foreign corporations to adhere to American standards.

In Choice (A), the word ***quixotic*** means idealistic or impractical. The word comes from the fictional character Don Quixote who tilted at windmills. (***Tilting*** refers to a knight on horseback tilting his joust toward a target for the purpose of attack.) Although the president in this passage may not be realistic in his assessment of State Department policies, his belief isn't the main idea of the passage.

Choice (E) is a value judgment. An answer that passes judgment, saying something is right or wrong, better or worse, or more or less appropriate (as in this case), is almost never the correct answer.

The main idea of any passage is usually stated in the first sentence or two. The first sentence of this passage touches on the difficulties that corporations have explaining their business ties with certain countries to politicians, human rights groups, and consumers. From this statement, you may infer that those groups disagree with the policies of the corporations. Correct answer: Choice **(D).**

Just because a statement is true doesn't necessarily mean it's the correct answer to the question, especially a main idea question. The answer choices are often true statements, or at least plausible ones, but this doesn't make them "best state the *central idea* of the passage."

8. According to the passage, the president wants the voluntary principles to be initiated by businesses rather than by politicians or human rights activists because

Ⓐ Businesses have empirical experience in the field and thus know what the conditions are and how they may/should be remedied.

Ⓑ Businesses make profits from the labor of the workers and thus have a moral obligation to improve their employees' working conditions.

Ⓒ Workers will not accept principles drawn up by politicians whom they distrust but may agree to principles created by the corporations that pay them.

Ⓓ Foreign nations are distrustful of U.S. political intervention and are more likely to accept suggestions from multinational corporations.

Ⓔ Political activist groups have concerns that are too dramatically different from those of the corporations for the groups to be able to work together.

Choices (B), (C), (D), and (E) assume facts not in evidence, as the lawyers say. Although you personally may believe the statements in these answer choices to be true, they don't answer the specific question.

When a question begins with the words *according to the passage,* you need to go back to the passage and find the answer. The word *empirical* is a keyword here, and it's buried in the middle of the second paragraph.

Find the word, read the sentence, and you've found the answer: "The president vociferously denies their charges, arguing that each situation is approached on its merits without prejudice, and hopes that all the groups can work together to develop principles based on *empirical research* rather than political fiat, emphasizing that the *businesses with experience in the field must initiate the process* of developing such guidelines." You don't even need to know what *empirical* means. Correct answer: Choice **(A).**

9. Select the sentence that describes the human rights activists' response to the president's plan.

The passage contains only one mention of *human rights activists,* and it appears in the second sentence of the first paragraph. So the correct answer is, "Human rights activists, incensed at the nebulous plans for implementing such rules, charge that their agenda is being given low priority by the State Department."

10. Which of the following is a reason the author mentions the boycott of a corporation's products by its customers? Consider each of the three choices separately and select all that apply.

A To show the difficulties that arise when corporations attempt to become involved in politics

B To suggest the possibility of failure of any plan that does not account for the customer's perspective

C To indicate the pressures that are on the multinational corporations

Choice (A) makes a valid point. Difficulties may arise when corporations attempt to become involved in politics. However, the passage doesn't give that as a reason for a boycott, so Choice (A) is wrong. Choice (B) seems logical, because a company that ignores its customers will probably fail. The passage mentions corporate communications with customers in the first sentence but not the customer's perspective, so Choice (B) is wrong. Choice (C) is also true, because according to the passage, multinational corporations run the risk of alienating any group and thus inciting a boycott, which is a reason given by the passage. Correct answer: Choice **(C).**

If you're an expert in international marketing or international politics, don't let your knowledge of the subject interfere with your ability to answer the questions. If you know firsthand that the passage is wrong, it doesn't matter: Go with what the passage says.

11. Which of the following statements about the Sullivan Principles can best be inferred from the passage?

Ⓐ They had a detrimental effect on the profits of those corporations doing business with South Africa.

Ⓑ They represented an improper alliance between political and business groups.

Ⓒ They placed the needs of the foreign workers over those of the domestic workers whose jobs would therefore be in jeopardy.

Ⓓ They will be used as a model to create future voluntary business guidelines.

Ⓔ They will have a chilling effect on future adoption of voluntary guidelines.

Choice (A) is the major trap here. Perhaps you assumed that because the companies seem to dislike the Sullivan Principles, they hurt company profits. However, nothing was said in the passage about profits. Maybe the companies still made good profits but objected to the Sullivan Principles, well, on principle. The companies just may not have wanted governmental intervention, even if profits weren't decreased.

Two keywords/phrases can help you answer this question: *Sullivan Principles* tells you to look at the end of the final paragraph where these principles are first mentioned. The word *chilling* in Choice (E) means "to cause fear." The second to last sentence, just before the sentence about the Sullivan Principles, states that ". . . they [business leaders] *fear* such 'voluntary' concepts may someday be given the force of law." Because business leaders fear that the adoption of voluntary guidelines will lead to forced legislation, the Sullivan Principles will have a chilling effect on the future adoption of voluntary guidelines. The correct answer is Choice **(E)**.

To answer this question correctly, you really need to understand not only the sentence about the Sullivan Principles but also the sentence before it. An inference question like this one usually means you have to read at least two statements and make a conclusion from them; you can't just go back to one specific sentence or phrase of the passage and get the answer.

The humanities passage

Humanities passages may be about art, music, philosophy, drama, or literature. The passages are usually positive, especially if they talk about a person who was a pioneer in his or her field, such as the first African American astronaut or the first female doctor. Use this to your advantage: If someone is worthy of mention historically or in a Reading Comprehension passage, then he or she must have been an amazing person or done something truly noteworthy. This sense of admiration helps you create the context in which to frame the passage.

The humanities passages seem to be the most down-to-earth of the lot. They're easy to read, informative, and can even be enjoyable. The approach is the same, though: Look for the gist of the passage in a few words and establish a context for the whole story and each paragraph. You can always go back for the details later.

Although the humanities passages don't require meticulous reading, the questions are another matter. The questions following a humanities passage often require you to get into the mind of the author in order to read between the lines and make inferences. While you're reading a passage about a particular person, for example, you're supposed to ascertain not just what the person accomplished but why she worked toward her goals and what mark she hoped to leave on the world.

Here's an example of a typical humanities passage, taken from *LSAT For Dummies* by Amy Hackney Blackwell (Wiley), about someone you've probably never heard of before but will still enjoy reading about.

Junzaburou Nishiwaki, a 20th-century Japanese poet, scholar, and translator, spent his career working to introduce Japanese readers to European and American writing and to break his country out of its literary insularity. He was interested in European culture all of his life. Born to a wealthy family in rural Niigata prefecture in 1894, Nishiwaki spent his youth aspiring to be a painter, and traveled to Tokyo in 1911 to study fused Japanese and European artistic traditions. After his father died in 1913, Nishiwaki studied economics at Keio University, but his real love was English literature. After graduating, he worked for several years as a reporter at the English-language *Japan Times* and as a teacher at Keio University.

Nishiwaki finally received the opportunity to concentrate on English literature in 1922, when Keio University sent him to Oxford University for three years. He spent this time reading literature in Old and Middle English and classical Greek and Latin. He became fluent in English, French, German, Latin, and Greek. While he was in England, Roaring Twenties modernism caught his eye, and the works of writers such as James Joyce, Ezra Pound, and T.S. Eliot were crucially important to his literary development. In 1925, Nishiwaki published his first book, *Spectrum,* a volume of poems written in English. He explained that English offered him much more freedom of expression than traditional Japanese poetic language.

Nishiwaki returned to Keio University in 1925 and became a professor of English literature, teaching linguistics, Old and Middle English, and the history of English literature. He remained active in modernist and avant-garde literary circles. In 1933 he published *Ambarvalia,* his first volume of poetry written in Japanese; this collection of surrealist verse ranged far and wide through European geography and history, and included Japanese translations of Catullus, Sophocles, and Shakespeare. Angered by the Japanese government's fascist policies, Nishiwaki refused to write poetry during the Second World War. He spent the war years writing a dissertation on ancient Germanic literature.

After the war, Nishiwaki resumed his poetic pursuits and in 1947 published *Tabibito kaerazu,* in which he abandoned modernist language and returned to a classical Japanese poetic style, but with his own postmodernist touch, incorporating both Eastern and Western literary traditions. In 1953, Nishiwaki published *Kindai no guuwa,* which critics consider his most poetically mature work. He spent his last years producing works of such writers as D.H. Lawrence, James Joyce, T.S. Eliot, Stéphane Mallarmé, Shakespeare, and Chaucer. Nishiwaki retired from Keio University in 1962, though he continued to teach and write poetry. Before his death in 1982, he received numerous honors and awards; he was appointed to the Japanese Academy of Arts and Sciences, named a Person of Cultural Merit, and nominated for the Nobel Prize by Ezra Pound. Critics today consider Nishiwaki to have exercised more influence on younger poets than any other Japanese poet since 1945.

12. Which one of the following most accurately states the main idea of the passage?

Ⓐ Nishiwaki was a Japanese poet who rebelled against the strictures of his country's government and protested its policies toward Europe during World War II.

Ⓑ Nishiwaki was a Japanese poet and literary critic who embraced European literature as a way of rebelling against the constraints of his family and traditional Japanese culture.

Ⓒ Nishiwaki was a Japanese poet and professor who spent his life trying to convince young Japanese students that European literary forms were superior to Japanese poetic styles.

Ⓓ Nishiwaki was a Japanese poet and linguist who throughout his life chose to write in English rather than Japanese.

Ⓔ Nishiwaki was a Japanese poet and scholar who spent his life specializing in European literature, which proved tremendously influential to his own work.

A process of elimination reveals the correct answer. Choice (A) is wrong: Though Nishiwaki did protest against his country's fascist policies during World War II, this fact isn't the main idea of the passage. Choice (B) is flat out wrong: Although the first paragraph discusses Nishiwaki's departure from family and his country's literary insularity, the word *rebelling* is too harsh. Choice (C) is also wrong: The passage doesn't say that he tried to convince his students one way or the other. Choice (D) is wrong: The passage states only that his first book was in English and many others were in Japanese. Correct answer: Choice **(E).**

13. The author's attitude toward Nishiwaki's life and career can be best described as

Ⓐ Scholarly interest in the life and works of a significant literary figure

Ⓑ Mild surprise at Nishiwaki's choosing to write poetry in a language foreign to him

Ⓒ Open admiration for Nishiwaki's ability to function in several languages

Ⓓ Skepticism toward Nishiwaki's motives in refusing to write poetry during the Second World War

Ⓔ Envy of Nishiwaki's success in publishing and academia

Choices (B), (D), and (E) are wrong because the passage doesn't reflect surprise, skepticism, or envy. Choices (A) and (C) remain, but you can eliminate Choice (C): The passage is objective, not admiring, and Nishiwaki's multilingual abilities is a supporting detail to his accomplishments. The correct answer is Choice **(A).**

14. The primary function of the first paragraph is to

Ⓐ Describe Nishiwaki's brief study of painting.

Ⓑ Introduce Nishiwaki and his lifelong interest in European culture.

Ⓒ Summarize Nishiwaki's contribution to Japanese literature.

Ⓓ Explain why a Japanese man chose to specialize in English literature.

Ⓔ Analyze European contributions to Japanese culture at the start of the 20th century.

After rereading the first paragraph, you know that in a nutshell it introduces Nishiwaki as one who worked to bridge the literature gap separating Japan from Europe and America. It also summarizes Nishiwaki's interest in art through college and his early career years afterward. Most importantly, the first paragraph sets the stage for the rest of the essay. Armed with this perspective, only one possible answer remains: Choice **(B).**

15. Select the sentence in the passage that explains why Nishiwaki stopped writing poetry during World War II.

Like most select-a-sentence questions, as long as you can spot the correct sentence buried in the passage, this one's a gimme. Correct answer: "Angered by the Japanese government's fascist policies, Nishiwaki refused to write poetry during the Second World War."

16. The passage is primarily concerned with

Ⓐ Comparing Nishiwaki's poetry to that of other Japanese poets of the 20th century

Ⓑ Discussing the role of the avant-garde movement in Nishiwaki's writing

Ⓒ Providing a brief biography of Nishiwaki that explains the significance of his work

Ⓓ Explaining why writers can benefit from studying literature from other countries

Ⓔ Describing the transformation in Japanese poetic style during the post-war period

The keywords in this question are *primarily concerned with.* The passage may suggest some of the points listed, but its *primary concern* is more explicit. Choice (A) is wrong because the author doesn't mention the work of other Japanese poets. Choice (B) is wrong because although the avant-garde movement was influential to Nishiwaki's writing, this point is hardly the primary concern. Choice (C) looks about right, but check the others just in case. Choice (D) is wrong because the author doesn't mention the benefits of studying foreign literature. Choice (E) is wrong because the passage doesn't mention changes in Japanese poetic style after the war. Correct answer: Choice **(C).**

17. According to the passage, which one of the following types of literature did *not* greatly interest Nishiwaki? Consider each of the three choices separately and select all that apply.

🄰 Old and Middle English literature such as *Beowulf* and *The Canterbury Tales*

🄱 Classical Greek works such as *Antigone*

🄲 Classical Japanese literature such as *The Tale of Genji*

From the first paragraph, you know that Nishiwaki's real love was English literature. From the second paragraph, you know that Nishiwaki spent his time at Oxford reading Old and Middle English and classical Greek and Latin. However, even though he may have had some interest in Japanese literature, it didn't *greatly* interest him as the question states. Only one correct answer: Choice **(C)**.

18. Select the sentence that explains why Nishiwaki chose to write his first published poems in English.

 Though many sentences in the passage mention Nishiwaki's interest in English literature, in only one sentence does the passage provide Nishiwaki's explanation of why he chose to write his first published poems in English. Correct answer: "He explained that English offered him much more freedom of expression than traditional Japanese poetic language."

Chapter 6

Analyzing the Argument Questions

In This Chapter

- Tackling Argument Analysis questions step-by-step
- Reading the passage analytically
- Discovering what the question is asking for
- Thinking up your own answer before choosing one
- Picking the correct answer by the process of elimination

You've probably heard the old expression, "You can't believe everything you hear." That's what argument analysis is all about — questioning arguments you read in books, magazines, newspapers, and on the web; assertions made on the nightly news; claims made by politicians; advertising pitches; and so on. Graduate schools expect you not only to read with understanding but also to scrutinize information and arguments and sort out what's true and reasonable from what's not.

An *Argument Analysis question* challenges you to identify the author's stance on a particular issue and determine whether the author has done a sufficient job of presenting and supporting his position. This chapter reveals what to look for in the argument and the question and answer choices that follow it. This chapter also explains how to deconstruct an argument to determine whether it's logically sound and well supported.

When taking the GRE, expect two Argument Analysis questions in each Verbal section. Each question consists of a short argument followed by one question and five answer choices. These arguments are easy to spot because they always present a plan or a conclusion based on a set of facts. In this chapter, you learn how to deconstruct the argument based on the facts given.

Use this five-step approach to tackle an Argument Analysis question:

1. **Cover the answer choices with your scratch paper.**
2. **Read the question and understand what it's asking you to do.**
3. **Read the passage, keeping an eye out for information you need to answer the question.**
4. **Answer the question in your own words.**
5. **Eliminate wrong answer choices to reveal the right one.**

This chapter leads you through this five-step process and transforms you into a critical thinker, if you're not one already.

Covering the Answer Choices

First, cover the answer choices with your scrap paper. Although doing so may look peculiar to your fellow examinees, using this strategy improves your GRE score and can give you a higher score than theirs. Doing this also improves your chances of answering the questions correctly, because the answer choices clutter your brain and muddle your thinking with ***superfluous*** (nonessential) information.

By covering the answers, you can focus on establishing the gist of the argument before looking over the answer choices. With a solid understanding of the argument, any irrelevant answer choices become more obvious and easier to rule out.

Knowing What to Look for in the Question

While keeping the answer choices covered, read and understand what the question asks, so you know what to look for as you read the answer choices. Each question typically asks you to pick the choice that does one of the following:

- Most seriously weakens the argument or something in it
- Adds the best support to strengthen the argument or something in it
- Draws the most reasonable conclusion from the passage
- Identifies the assumption that must be true for the argument to be true
- Most accurately represents the premise on which the argument is based

The questions may not use the actual wording provided here; for example, instead of asking which choice most seriously *weakens* the argument, a question may ask which choice most effectively *undermines* the argument. Don't get caught up in semantics. Just realize that questions may be worded differently, so be sure you understand what the question is asking.

Reading the Passage with a Critical Eye

By knowing what the question is asking, as explained in the previous section, you're better equipped to play the role of *active reader* — one who reads with a purpose. Instead of just reading the words, active and critical readers go in asking questions, such as "What's the main idea?" "What would strengthen this argument?" "What would weaken this argument?" and "What's this passage implying?" Reading the question first, as I discuss in the preceding section, guides this critical reading step by suggesting what you should be asking.

When you read actively, you ask these questions and more, which help you gain a deeper understanding of the material and improve your retention of it. On the GRE, however, active reading is guided, because the exam gives you the *one* question you need to answer, and you read it before reading the argument.

The following sections provide guidance on what to look for in a passage to answer different types of Argument Analysis questions.

Identifying the premise and conclusion

Think of a logical argument as an if-then statement: The *if* part is the premise, and the *then* part is the conclusion. When a question asks you to identify the conclusion or choose a statement that most effectively challenges or supports the argument, break it down into premise and conclusion.

Officially, the premise and conclusion are as follows:

- **Premise:** The premise (the *if* part) is facts or reasons that support the conclusion, including observations, statistics, reasonable generalizations, or anecdotes.
- **Conclusion:** The conclusion (the *then* part) is the argument's or author's main point, assertion, or opinion.

After identifying the premise and conclusion, you have what you need to begin your argument analysis, as explained in the next few sections.

A strong selling point for charter schools has been their lower cost. Because charter schools receive no public funding for building schools, they cannot afford to build expensive facilities of their own. Instead, they have had to develop cost-effective classroom solutions, such as renting office space and storefronts. The current bill would make public funding available to charter schools for capital investments. Therefore, if the bill passes, charter schools will be able to start using public funding for building facilities, making them much less cost-effective.

To reduce this argument to an if-then statement, you may come up with something like this:

> If public funding is made available to charter schools, then they will no longer be cost-effective.

This single, simple restatement of the argument helps you evaluate the answer choices without having to reread the entire passage. If the question asks something about the conclusion or the main point that the passage makes, look to the *then* part of the statement. If the question asks you to choose a statement that challenges or supports the argument, try each answer choice until you find the one that most effectively challenges or supports the *if* part of the statement.

Look for the following words to identify the conclusion: *then, therefore, thus, hence, so, consequently, as a result,* and *in conclusion.* However, don't rely solely on these words; they may be implied rather than stated.

Finding the hidden assumption

An *assumption* is a claim the passage makes without stating it directly. The assumption either plugs a gap in logic between the premise and conclusion or narrows the gap so you can reach only one reasonable conclusion. When asked to identify an assumption, look for the answer choice that *must* be true for the argument to be true. When reading each answer choice, ask yourself, "Could the argument still be true if this were false?" If your answer is no, you most likely found the right choice, but read through the other choices, as explained later in this chapter, just to be sure.

Unfortunately, identifying an assumption by just looking at the passage is difficult, because you're trying to see what's missing — what's *not* there. So if you encounter a question that looks something like one of the following, look for a logical gap in the passage, which typically stands between the premise and the conclusion:

- Which of the following is an assumption . . . ?
- . . . relies on which of the following assumptions?
- . . . is based on which of the following assumptions?

Here's an example for finding a hidden assumption in a passage:

Women have been fighting for equal employment opportunities and pay for decades now, but have yet to achieve parity in the workplace. To achieve gender parity in the workplace, hiring quotas must be enacted and strictly enforced.

First, identify the premise and conclusion, the if-then statement:

- **Premise:** Women have been fighting for equal opportunities and pay without results.
- **Conclusion:** Hiring quotas are needed.

Between the premise and the conclusion is the assumption that gender bias exists in the workplace. The assumption isn't stated in the passage, but you can infer it from the premise and conclusion. The assumption also passes the test for qualifying as a bona fide assumption, because if it were false, the argument would be false, too.

Spotting weaknesses in supporting details

Arguments contain supporting details, usually facts, statistics, examples, or expert opinions. When you encounter a question that asks you to identify which statement, if true, undermines or supports the argument, you probably need to evaluate supporting details both in the premise and in the answer choices. As you read the passage, pay special attention and look for weaknesses or inaccuracies in the supporting details as well as the conclusion drawn from them.

To choose the correct answer choice that weakens an argument, look for the choice that does one or both of the following:

- Contradicts or calls into question one of the supporting details in the passage
- Highlights the disconnect in the passage between the supporting details and the conclusion

According to the USDA, ethanol production will consume 40 percent of this year's corn harvest, meaning that about 5 billion bushels of corn will be used for fuel instead of food. With global drought and weather-related food shortages occurring in countries all over the world, prices for cereal, meat, and other staples are likely to soar in the U.S., while people in many poorer countries will go hungry. To make up for the shortfall in this year's harvest, lifting of the federal government's mandates on ethanol production has become a moral imperative.

When you read a passage like this that's packed with details, jot them down on your scratch paper followed by the conclusion:

- **Premises:** Forty percent of corn is used to produce fuel, not food; global drought; global food prices will rise.
- **Conclusion:** Federal mandates on ethanol production must be lifted.

If the question asks you to choose a statement that best undermines the argument, examine the choices to find the one that does the best job of contradicting a supporting detail or showing that one or more of the supporting details isn't responsible for what's stated in the conclusion. For example, if the global drought affected other foods but not corn, and a surplus of corn existed with enough for both the planned ethanol production *and* the existing food channels, then the plan to use 40 percent of corn for fuel wouldn't significantly affect the price of food.

On the other hand, if the question asks you to choose the statement that adds the best support for the argument, look for the choice that most effectively supports the conclusion that lifting the federal government's mandates on ethanol production would increase the availability of food for human consumption. For example, pointing out that the U.S. is responsible for nearly 70 percent of the world's corn exports and that ethanol production is likely to consume 20 percent of the total U.S. corn crop would be pretty solid evidence that ethanol production is likely to contribute to food shortages.

Exploring common logical fallacies

Arguments may seem logical and fair on the surface but actually be ***fallacious*** (erroneous, flawed). The following sections reveal some of the more common logical fallacies you're likely to find on the exam. By spotting such fallacies, you identify weaknesses in arguments and gather the knowledge required to determine which statements best support or refute the argument.

Circular reasoning

In *circular reasoning*, a premise supports a premise or a conclusion supports a conclusion. For example, a statement such as, "The United States is the greatest country in the world, because no other country comes close," is an example of circular reasoning — trying to support the conclusion with another conclusion. Another example is, "Most dentists prefer this toothpaste because four out of five dentists prefer it," which is supporting a premise with a premise; in this case, the conclusion merely restates the premise.

Watch out for circular reasoning in answer choices when the question asks you to choose a statement that supports an argument. Circular reasoning statements are easy to spot because they restate information that's already in the argument.

Erroneous cause-and-effect arguments

Erroneous cause-and-effect arguments come in several styles. The most common is often referred to in Latin as *post hoc ergo propter hoc,* meaning "after this, therefore because of this." You don't need to memorize the Latin terminology; however, do remember that just because one event follows another doesn't mean the first event caused the second event. For example, if a cigarette-tax increase were to be followed by a decrease in the per-capita rate of smoking, you can't assume that one caused the other. A third event may have also occurred that brought the outcome. If the cigarette-tax increase happened at the same time as the release of a new, shocking report detailing the dangers of smoking, then the report, not the tax increase, may have caused the reduction in smoking.

Sweeping generalizations

A *sweeping generalization* applies a general rule to a specific case, such as a plan that works in one context will certainly work in another. For example, someone may argue that because the addition of sharp-turn warning signs to roads in Town X reduced the rate of accidents, adding these signs to the roads in Town Y will surely have the same effect. This argument uses a sweeping generalization by assuming that the roads in the two towns are similar. To weaken this argument, the correct answer choice may suggest that Town X has lots of curvy mountain roads while Town Y has only straight, flat roads. Because sharp-turn warning signs don't make straight roads safer, this new information weakens the argument.

More logical fallacies

The GRE doesn't require an ability to identify logical fallacies (or the Latin names for them), but being aware of such fallacies and looking for them in real examples is a great way to exercise your brain and avoid being taken in by faulty logic. This chapter introduces a few of the most common logical fallacies you can expect to encounter on the test, but plenty more exist, including the following:

- **Ad hominem:** Latin for "against the man," an *ad hominem* argument attacks the person instead of what the person says. For example, if an investment advisor comes on the news and says that investors should buy gold as a hedge against inflation, and another analyst replies, "You don't even have a bachelor's degree in economics," the second analyst is arguing ad hominem by attacking the person and not the advice to buy gold.
- **Red herring:** A *red herring* is any attempt to stray from the issue. For example, suppose two people are discussing the pros and cons of nuclear energy, and one person says something like, "Sure, nuclear energy is a clean, efficient source of power, but the atomic bomb has the potential of wiping out entire cities." This red herring takes the debate in an entirely different direction, shifting the focus from nuclear power to nuclear warfare.
- **Straw man fallacy:** The *straw man fallacy* intentionally distorts the opponent's position and then attacks the distorted position instead of attacking what the person actually said. Suppose two politicians are discussing the state budget. The first politician says, "By combining these three health agencies, the state can save 25 percent in funding annually." The second politician replies, "Slashing funding for healthcare actually costs more money than it saves." The second politician has committed the straw man fallacy by misrepresenting the first politician's position and then attacking it.
- **Either/or fallacy:** The *either/or fallacy,* sometimes called a *false dilemma* or *black-and-white thinking,* presents two options as the only available ones, even though neither option may be correct and other options may exist. Suppose a committee is discussing the future of its parent-teacher organization, and one of the committee members says, "If we decide to stop fundraising, we may as well not have a parent-teacher organization." The either/or fallacy here is based on the premise that the sole function of a parent-teacher organization is to raise money for the schools, when in fact other functions exist, such as increasing levels of volunteerism and improving communication between parents and schools.

Answering the Question in Your Own Words

After you have a clear understanding of the argument's premise and conclusion, answer the question in your own words, giving the answer choices less power to lead you astray. Fortunately, the question serves as your focal point. For example, if the question asks you to identify the assumption, you needn't waste time considering whether the argument commits a logical fallacy or evaluating evidence that may support or undermine the argument — you focus solely on the assumption.

Following are the different question types and what you need to ask yourself and answer before looking at the answer choices:

- **Weaken the argument:** What new information that's not in the argument would weaken it? Does the argument commit a logical fallacy? If so, which one?
- **Strengthen the argument:** What new information that's not in the argument would strengthen it?
- **Identify the assumption:** What assumption does the author make that if you could prove untrue would prove the conclusion false?
- **Identify the inference:** Based on the supporting details, what point is the author trying to make?
- **Choose the best conclusion:** What is the author's stand on this issue?

Don't review the answer choices before answering the question in your own words. Just as with the Text Completion and Sentence Equivalence questions discussed in Chapter 4, if you read the choices first, they may muddle your understanding of the passage and the question.

Eliminating Wrong Answers to Find the Right One

Like the other verbal questions on the GRE, answering the Argument Analysis questions means eliminating the obviously wrong answers and working with what's left. After you've answered the question yourself, look at each answer choice and eliminate those that don't match your own answer. The following sections show you how to eliminate wrong answers and also highlight some common traps to avoid.

Leveraging the process of elimination

GRE developers are a tricky bunch. They seem to take pleasure in intentionally misleading test-takers. To defend yourself against this ***chicanery*** (trickery intended to deceive), brush up on the most common traps.

Beware of "always," "never," and other absolutes

Absolute answers — those containing the words *always, never, must, all,* or *none* — are almost always wrong, so you can red flag them for elimination more quickly than the other choices. You may not always be able to eliminate answer choices that contain absolutes, but this strategy works often enough to narrow your choices if you're stuck.

Dodge the decoys

On the GRE, an argument may contain information that's irrelevant to answering the question. When that occurs, chances are that at least one of the answer choices mentions that irrelevant information. Answering the question yourself before looking at the answer choices makes any of these irrelevant answers easier to spot.

Stay dispassionate

Correct answer choices are usually unbiased and tone neutral. If an answer choice seems emotional or opinionated, it's probably a prime candidate for elimination. If you can't eliminate the answer choice right off the bat, scrutinize it closely before choosing it.

Avoid picking an answer just because it's true

Don't choose an answer just because it's true. Plenty of answer choices are true, but they fail to address the question. When you see an answer choice that's true, make sure it answers the question and is supported in the passage before choosing it.

Don't be tempted by opposites

If the question asks you to choose an answer choice that most effectively weakens or adds support to the argument, the answer choices almost always contain at least one statement that does the exact opposite. It may make sense, because it contains the elements that you're looking for, but make sure it goes in the right direction; if you're strengthening an argument, for example, this wrong answer may seem to fit perfectly but actually weaken the argument.

Testing your skills

Here's a sample question to test your skills, followed by the best approach for choosing the right answer.

Recent test scores released by Washington D.C.'s department of education show a four-point drop in reading proficiency in its elementary schools from the previous year to 44.5 percent. Math proficiency dropped 5 points to 43.4 percent. Washington D.C.'s public school system is obviously failing in its mission to improve academic success.

The argument that Washington D.C.'s public school system is failing to improve academic success is based on which of the following assumptions?

Ⓐ Washington D.C.'s public school system doesn't have sufficient funding to improve test scores.

Ⓑ Proficiency rates are the same at the middle- and high-school levels.

Ⓒ Private schools and charter schools had significantly higher test scores.

Ⓓ Test scores are an accurate measure of academic success.

Ⓔ More students from lower socio-economic backgrounds took the test this time.

Based on the guidelines in this chapter, here's how to approach this question:

1. **Cover the answer choices with your scratch paper.**
2. **Read the question to discover your mission.**

   What's the assumption upon which the argument is based?
3. **Read the passage to identify the premise and conclusion (if-then).**

   If test scores have dropped, *then* Washington D.C.'s public school system is failing.
4. **Answer the question in your own words.**

   The assumption is necessary in making the argument true, so to make the argument false, you'd have to challenge either the fact that the test scores dropped or that they matter. Because you can't argue fact, the assumption is that the test scores accurately reflect a school system's success.
5. **Eliminate wrong answers to find the right one.**

   Choice (A) is wrong because funding is outside the scope of the argument.

   Choice (B) is wrong because this statement may strengthen the argument but isn't an assumption on which the argument is based.

   Choice (C) is wrong because the success of other schools has nothing to do with the failure of the school system in question.

   Choice (D) is correct because if test scores weren't an accurate indication of academic success, this argument would be false.

   Choice (E) is wrong because this statement may weaken the argument but isn't an assumption on which the argument is based.

The correct answer is Choice **(D)**.

Trying some other examples

Now that you know the overall approach, try your hand at a few more Argument Analysis questions.

For universal healthcare to become an affordable reality, the federal government first needs to implement cost control measures in the healthcare industry. Tort reform is the obvious place to start. The costs of medical malpractice insurance and lawsuits are skyrocketing, and medical professionals simply increase the cost of their services to keep pace. Tort reform would significantly reduce the number of frivolous malpractice claims, limit the damage awarded to plaintiffs, and reduce the cost of malpractice insurance. Healthcare providers could then pass the savings along to consumers. Until some sort of tort reform effectively addresses this issue, healthcare will continue to be unaffordable regardless of whether people are paying out of pocket or through a government-administered program.

1. Which of the following statements most accurately identifies the assumption that must be true for the argument to be true?

Ⓐ Universal healthcare will increase the cost of healthcare services.

Ⓑ Medical insurance costs are rising.

Ⓒ The costs of medical malpractice lawsuits and insurance represent a significant portion of healthcare costs.

Ⓓ Universal healthcare will decrease the cost of healthcare services.

Ⓔ Tort reform would reduce medical malpractice litigation and limit damages awarded to plaintiffs.

The question asks for the assumption on which the argument is based, and the assumption lies between the premise and the conclusion. Rephrase the argument as an if-then statement, and you get something like this: "If we have tort reform, then health services will cost less." Examine the answer choices to find the one that lies between the premise and conclusion. You can instantly rule out Choice (E), because it merely repeats the definition of tort reform from the passage. Rule out Choices (A) and (D), because nothing in the passage touches on universal healthcare having an effect on the cost of healthcare services. Rule out Choice (B), which may be true but doesn't touch on the premise. That leaves Choice (C), the assumption that medical malpractice lawsuits and insurance contribute significantly to the cost of health services. If this isn't true, then tort reform is unlikely to significantly reduce costs for consumers. Correct answer: Choice **(C).**

While many government reformists seek to curb the influence of corporate lobbying on Capitol Hill, the issue of insider trading continues to fly under the radar. Currently, no law limits members of Congress from trading shares of stock based on what they know about legislative acts that could benefit or harm any given industry or company. Likewise, no law prevents a member of Congress from voting on legislation that would likely affect the share price of a company in which the member is currently invested. As a result, votes may be influenced less by what is right and best for the country and more by the potential effect those votes may have on the performance of a Congress member's investment portfolio. To encourage Congress to do what's best for constituents rather than what's best for their investment portfolios, Congress needs to close the loopholes that exempt members of Congress from the insider trading rules and regulations that everyone else is required to follow.

2. Which of the following statements, if true, most supports the position that Congress needs to close the insider-trading loopholes that provide an unfair advantage to politicians and members of their staff?

Choose all that apply.

- A In two months, a top energy-policy adviser nearly doubled his $3,500 investment in a renewable-energy firm after the senator for whom he worked helped pass a 30 percent tax credit for companies in the solar-energy business.
- B Three members of Congress introduced the Stop Trading on Congressional Knowledge Act, or STOCK Act (H.R. 682), in March 2009, to bar federal employees, including members of Congress and their staff, from cashing in on non-public information they receive in their official capacities.
- C A 2004 study revealed that U.S. Senators' stock trades performed, on average, 12.3 percent better than the market average and 6 percent better than professional investment portfolio manager averages.

Choice (A) provides reasonable support for this claim: An investment having a 100 percent return after two months is rare, and that the investment was in the industry affected by the staffer's boss is too much of a coincidence. You can rule out Choice (B), because an Act to prohibit an action isn't proof that the action has occurred. You can also rule out Choice (C), because other reasons for the U.S. Senators' good performance are possible. It's possible that senators are savvier investors or can afford the top portfolio managers. Correct answer: Choice **(A).**

Chapter 7

Expanding Your Vocabulary to Boost Your Score

In This Chapter

- Looking for clues in prefixes, suffixes, and roots
- Reviewing vocabulary words found on the GRE

You can't get around it — you absolutely *must* know vocabulary to do well on the GRE. Regardless of your conversational expertise, the GRE is more concerned that you can communicate on an academic level. Many of the words used on the GRE probably aren't words you use on a daily basis, but you've most likely heard them somewhere before. You can't know for certain which words are going to appear on the test, but the odds are good that you'll see some of the ones presented in this chapter.

Mastering new vocabulary words is more than just reading this chapter. You need to make it part of your daily practice. Study daily. Revisit the words you think you already know. Knowing as many vocabulary words as possible helps immensely with the Verbal section. You can also improve your vocabulary by reading novels, articles, and so on.

This chapter helps you get a firmer grasp on vocabulary words used on the GRE. I provide a detailed discussion on prefixes, suffixes, and roots, which can help you significantly improve your vocabulary. I also provide a long list of common vocabulary words that you need to know. If you purchased the *GRE For Dummies,* Premier 7th Edition, pop in the accompanying CD for additional vocabulary words in flashcard format.

Brushing Up on Prefixes, Suffixes, and Roots

Mastering prefixes, suffixes, and roots can bump up your Verbal score significantly. Although prefixes and suffixes abound, the ones in the following sections are the most common, with examples of each. Take the time and memorize them.

If English isn't your first language, vocabulary may be the hardest part of the exam for you. Using roots, prefixes, and suffixes to determine a word's meaning can help you greatly.

Eponymous words

An *eponym* is a word derived from the name of a person. For example, the cardigan sweater got its name from the Earl of Cardigan. Here are a few eponyms to add to your GRE vocabulary:

- ***bowdlerize:*** To omit indecent words or phrases in a book or piece of writing (you bowdlerize a love letter before you let your roommate read it). In 1818, Dr. Thomas Bowdler, an English physician, published a ten-volume edition of Shakespeare's plays called *The Family Shakespeare.* He left out all the dirty parts. For example, instead of "Out, damn'd spot!" the line reads, "Out, crimson spot!"
- ***boycott:*** You'd think that Mr. Boycott started the practice of boycotting, wouldn't you? Just the opposite: He was the victim of the first boycott. Charles Boycott was a retired English army captain who refused to lower rents to his farmer tenants after a few bad harvests and was accused of exploiting the poor. The locals harassed him, stealing his crops and refusing to sell his products in their stores, until he was hounded out of the county. Today, when you refuse to have anything to do with someone, you're said to boycott him or her.
- ***draconian:*** Extremely harsh and severe. When you tell your professor that dropping your grade one whole letter just because you turned in a report one day late is truly draconian, you're harking all the way back to about 620 BC. Draco was an Athenian who wrote a code of laws that made nearly every crime punishable by death, even laziness and, uh, urinating in public. The word *draconian* came to apply to any laws that were just too darn cruel or strict.
- ***maverick:*** An individualist; an unconventional person. Samuel Maverick, who lived during the 1800s, was a Texas rancher whose unbranded cattle roamed free. Maverick's neighbors refused to hand back his strays, claiming that because they were unbranded, he had no proof they were his. The word eventually evolved into meaning anything without a brand, or unusual or unique.
- ***quisling:*** A traitor. Vidkun Quisling was a Norwegian politician who turned traitor in World War II, siding with Hitler. He was executed by a firing squad at the end of the war, but his name lives on to torment GRE-takers.
- ***simony:*** The buying or selling of religious or sacred objects or privileges. Simon Magus (who's often described as a reformed wizard — great job description!) offered St. Peter and St. John money to give him their religious abilities. The word *simony* was especially popular in the Middle Ages, when people sold pardons, indulgences, and the like.

Bonus! You probably already know the following words, but did you know they're also eponyms?

- ***diesel:*** A type of engine, named for Rudolf Diesel, a German engineer.
- ***mausoleum:*** A large tomb or memorial, named for King Mausolus, King of Calia in ancient Greece about 370 BC.
- ***nicotine:*** The addictive stuff in tobacco, named for French diplomat Jean Nicot.
- ***saxophone:*** A musical instrument, invented by and named after Adolphe Sax, a Belgian musician of the early to mid-1800s.
- ***shrapnel:*** Fragments thrown out by a shell or a bomb, invented in 1802 by Lieutenant General Henry Shrapnel, an English army officer.
- ***silhouette:*** Profile or shadow of a face, named after Étienne de Silhouette (1709–1767), a French finance minister.

Prefixes

A *prefix* is one or more letters at the beginning of a word that alters its meaning. For example, if a feat is ***possible,*** then you can do it. With a simple prefix, you can change that feat to *im*possible, and you can't do it. Knowing that *im-* means can't, you can narrow down the possible meanings of a word starting with *im-*, such as *impermeable.* Whatever the word is, the *im-* refers to something that can't be done. (Because *permeate* means to pass through, ***impermeable*** means cannot be penetrated.) Following are the most common prefixes you need to know with several related examples:

- ***a-*** **= not or without:** Someone *amoral* is without morals or conscience; someone *atypical* isn't typical or normal. Someone *apathetic* is uncaring or without feeling, like most test-takers by the time they finish the GRE and are leaving the exam room. ("The world is going to end tomorrow? Who cares? I'm going to bed.")
- ***an-*** **= not or without:** An *anaerobic* environment is without oxygen (like the testing center feels when a killer question leaves you gasping for air). *Anarchy* is without rule or government (like a classroom when a substitute teacher is in for the day).
- ***eu-*** **= good:** A *eulogy* is a good speech, usually given for the dearly departed at a funeral. A *euphemism* is a good way of saying something or a polite expression, like saying that someone has passed away rather than calling her worm meat.
- ***ben-/bon-*** **= good:** A *benefit* is something that has a good result, an advantage. Someone *benevolent* is good and kind; when you have a date, a benevolent father lets you take his new car rather than your old clunker. *Bon voyage* means have a good voyage; a *bon vivant* is a person who lives the good life.
- ***caco-*** **= bad:** Something *cacophonous* is bad sounding, such as fingernails on a chalkboard.
- ***de*** **= down from, away from (to put down):** To *de*scend or *de*part is to go down from or away from. To *de*nounce is to put down or to speak badly of, as in *de*nouncing those hogs who chow down all the pizza before you get to the party.

  Many unknown words on the GRE that start with *de* mean to put down in the sense of to criticize or bad-mouth. Here are just a few: demean, denounce, denigrate, derogate, deprecate, and decry.
- ***ex*** **= out of, away from:** An *ex*it is literally out of or away from *it* — *ex*-it. (The word *exit* is probably one of the most logical words around.) To *ex*tricate is to get out of something. You can extricate yourself from an argument by pretending to faint, basking in all the sympathy as you're carried away. To *ex*culpate is to get off the hook — literally to make away from guilt. *Culp* means guilt. When the president of the Hellenic Council wants to know who TP'd the dean's house, you can claim that you and your sorority sisters aren't *culpable*.
- ***ne-/mal-*** **= bad:** Something *negative* is bad, like a negative attitude. Someone ***nefarious*** is full of bad, or wicked and evil, such as a nefarious wizard in a fantasy novel. Something *malicious* also is full of bad, or wicked and harmful, such as a malicious rumor.
- ***im-*** **= not:** Something *impossible* isn't possible — it just can't happen. Someone *immortal* isn't going to die but will live forever because *mortal* means able to die. Someone *implacable* isn't able to be calmed down, because ***placate*** means to ease one's anger.

  Notice that *im-* can also mean inside (*immerse* means to put into), but that meaning isn't as common on the GRE. First, think of *im-* as meaning not; if that doesn't seem appropriate, switch to Plan B and see whether *im-* can mean inside within the context of the question.
- ***in-*** **= not:** Something *inappropriate* isn't appropriate, because *appropriate* means proper. Someone *inept* isn't adept, meaning she's not skillful. Someone who's *insolvent* has no money and is bankrupt, like most students after four years of college.

  In- can also mean inside (*innate* means something born inside of you) or beginning (the *initial* letters of your name are the beginning letters). However, the most common meaning of *in-* is not. Think of that one first; if it doesn't seem to work in a particular question, try the other meaning.
- ***ante-*** **= before:** When the clock reads 5 a.m., the *a.m.* stands for *ante meridiem,* which means before the middle or first half of the day. *Antebellum* means before the war. Tara in *Gone with the Wind* was an antebellum mansion, built before the Civil War. *Antediluvian* literally means before the flood, before Noah's deluge. Figuratively, it

means very old; if you call your mother antediluvian, you mean that she's been around since before the flood. (It's a great word to use as an insult because almost no one knows what it means and you can get away with it.)

- ***post-*** **= after:** When the clock reads 5 p.m., the *p.m.* stands for *post meridiem,* which means after the middle or second half of the day. Something *postmortem* occurs after death. A postmortem exam is an autopsy.

Suffixes

A *suffix* is three or four letters at the end of a word that gives the word a specific inflection or changes its type, such as from an adjective to a noun. For example, if you encounter the word *studious,* you know it refers to one who *studies.* The word *study* changes from a verb to an adjective, and from an action to a tendency, with the suffix *-ous.* Following are the most common suffixes you need to know with several related examples:

- ***-ette*** **= little:** A *cigarette* is a little cigar. A *dinette* table is a little dining table. A *coquette* is a little flirt (literally, a little chicken, but that doesn't sound as pretty).
- ***-illo*** **= little:** An *armadillo* is a little armored animal. A *peccadillo* is a little sin. (Do you speak Spanish? If so, then you probably know that *pecar* translates as "to sin" in English.)
- ***-ous*** **= full of (very):** Someone *joyous* is full of joy. Someone *amorous* is full of *amour,* or love. Someone *pulchritudinous* is full of beauty and, therefore, beautiful.
- ***-ist*** **= a person:** A *typist* is a person who types. A *pugilist* is a person who fights (*pug* means war or fight), a boxer. A *pacifist* is a person who believes in peace, a noncombatant (*pac* means peace or calm).
- ***-ify (-efy)*** **= to make:** To *beautify* is to make beautiful. To *ossify* is to make bone. (If you break your wrist, it takes weeks to ossify again, or for the bone to regenerate.) To *deify* is to make into a deity, a god. To *liquefy* is to turn a solid into a liquid.
- ***-ize*** **= to make:** To *alphabetize* is to make alphabetical. To *immunize* is to make immune. To *ostracize* is to make separate from the group, or to shun.
- ***-ate*** **= to make:** To *duplicate* is to make double. To *renovate* is to make new again (*nov* means new). To ***placate*** is to make peaceful or calm (*plac* means peace or calm).
- ***-ity*** **= a noun suffix that doesn't actually mean anything; it just turns a word into a noun:** *Jollity* is the noun form of jolly. *Serenity* is the noun form of serene. *Timidity* is the noun form of timid.

Roots

A *root* is the core part of a word that gives the word its basic meaning. Recognizing a common root helps you discern the meaning of an unfamiliar word. For example, knowing that *ver* means truth, as in *verify,* you can recognize that the unfamiliar word *aver* has something to do with truth. ***Aver*** means to hold true or affirm the truth. Following are the most common roots that you need to know with several related examples:

- ***ambu*** **= walk, move:** In a hospital, patients are either bedridden (they can't move) or *ambu*latory (they can walk and move about). A somn*ambu*list is a sleepwalker. *Som-* means sleep, *-ist* is a person, and *ambu* is to walk or move.
- ***andro*** **= man:** An *andro*id is a robot shaped like a man. Someone *androgynous* exhibits both male *(andro)* and female *(gyn)* characteristics (literally, he/she is full of man and woman).

- ***anthro*** = **human or mankind:** *Anthro*pology is the study of humans (not just a particular gender but humans in general). A mis*anthro*pe hates humans. (An equal-opportunity hater: He or she hates both men and women alike.)
- ***bellu, belli*** = **war, fight:** If you're *belli*gerent, you're ready to fight — in fact, you're downright hostile. An ante*bellu*m mansion is one that was created before the Civil War. (Remember that *ante-* means before. You can find this word in the list of prefixes earlier in this chapter.)
- ***cred*** = **trust or belief:** Something in*cred*ible is unbelievable, such as the excuse, "I would've picked you up on time, sweetheart, but there was a 75-car pileup on the freeway." If you're *cred*ulous, you're trusting and *naive* (literally, full of trust). In fact, if you're credulous, you probably actually feel sorry for your honey being stuck in traffic.

Be careful not to confuse the words *credible* and *credulous.* Something *credible* is trustable or believable. A credible excuse can get you out of trouble if you turn a paper in late. *Credulous,* on the other hand, means full of trust, naive, or gullible. The more credulous your professor is, the less credible that excuse needs to be. Furthermore, if you're in*credulous,* then you doubt something is true.

- ***gnos*** = **knowledge:** A doctor shows his or her knowledge by making a dia*gnos*is (analysis of the situation) or a pro*gnos*is (prediction about the future of the illness). An a*gnos*tic is a person who doesn't know whether a god exists. Differentiate an agnostic from an atheist: An *atheist* is literally without god, a person who believes there's no god. An *agnostic* is without knowledge, believing a god may or may not exist.
- ***greg*** = **group, herd:** A con*greg*ation is a group or herd of people. A *greg*arious person likes to be part of a group — he or she is sociable. To se*greg*ate is literally to make away from the group. (*Se-* means apart or away from, as in *separate, sever, sequester,* and *seclusion.*)
- ***gyn*** = **woman:** A *gyn*ecologist is a physician who treats women. A miso*gyn*ist is a person who hates women.
- ***loq, log, loc, lix*** = **speech or talk:** Someone *loq*uacious talks a lot. (That person is literally full of talk.) A dia*log*ue is talk or conversation between two people. E*loc*ution is proper speech. A pro*lix* person is very talkative. (Literally, he or she engages in big, or much, talk.)
- ***luc, lum, lus*** = **light, clear:** Something *lum*inous is shiny and full of light. Ask the teacher to e*luc*idate something you don't understand (literally, to make clear). *Lus*trous hair reflects the light and is sleek and glossy.
- ***meta*** = **beyond, after:** A *meta*morphosis is a change of shape beyond the present shape.
- ***morph*** = **shape:** Something a*morph*ous is without shape. *Morph*ology is the study of shape. ("Yes, of course, I take my studies seriously. I spent all weekend on *morph*ology at the beach.")
- ***mut*** = **change:** The Teenage *Mut*ant Ninja Turtles *mut*ated, or changed, from mild-mannered turtles to pizza-gobbling crime fighters. Something im*mut*able isn't changeable; it remains constant. Don't confuse *mut* (change) with *mute* (silent).
- ***pac*** = **peace, calm:** Why do you give a baby a *pac*ifier? To calm him or her down. To get its name, the *Pac*ific Ocean must have appeared calm at the time it was discovered.
- ***path*** = **feeling:** Something *path*etic arouses feeling or pity. To sym*path*ize is to share the feelings (literally, to make the same feeling). Anti*path*y is a dislike — literally, a feeling against. For example, no matter how much the moron apologizes, you still may harbor antipathy toward the jerk who parked right behind you and blocked you in, making you late for a date and causing all sorts of unfortunate romantic repercussions.
- ***phon*** = **sound:** *Phon*ics helps you to sound out words. Caco*phon*y is bad sound; eu*phon*y is good sound. Homo*phon*es are words that sound the same, such as *red* and *read.*

All in a day's work, labor, toil, pursuit, grind . . .

One way you can improve your vocabulary quickly is to group words with similar meanings — remembering five or ten for the price of one. If you can remember *harbinger,* you can remember *prescient.*

- I'm *looking forward* to this:

auguries	presage
bode	prescient
harbinger	prognosis
portent	prognosticate

- You have to keep your sense of *humor:*

badinage	mirth
japing	puckish
jocose	ribald
jocular	risible
jollity	twit
levity	wag

- It's a *sad* day when you don't know your vocabulary:

bereft	lugubrious
despondent	plaintive
doleful	maudlin
dour	melancholic
jeremiad	saturnine
lachrymose	Weltschmerz

- That's easy for you to *say:*

declaim	prolix
exhort	raconteur
persiflage	stentorian
philippic	tergiversate
pontificate	voluble

- Just how *boring* is this vocabulary?

banalprosaic	
bromide	somniferous
ennui	soporific
hackneyed	tedious
listless	trite
platitude	vapid

- It takes a lot of *guts* to know these words:

audacity	intrepid
doughty	redoubtable
effrontery	uncowed
impudent	undaunted

- Hip, hip, hooray! Words of *praise:*

accolade	obsequious
encomium	paean
eulogy	panegyric
extol	plaudits
kudos	sycophant
laud toady	

- Are you sick to *death* of vocabulary?

cadaver	morbid
demise	noxious
dirge	obsequies
elegy	valetudinarian
insalubrious	wan

- ***plac* = peace, calm:** To *plac*ate someone is to calm him or her down or to make peace with that person. You placate your irate sweetheart, for example, by sending a dozen roses (hint, hint). Someone im*plac*able is someone you aren't able to calm down — or someone really stubborn. If those roses don't do the trick, for example, your sweetheart is too implacable to placate.
- ***pro* = big, much:** *Pro*fuse apologies are big, or much — in essence, a *lot* of apologies. A *pro*lific writer produces a great deal of written material.

Pro has two additional meanings less commonly used on the GRE. It can mean before, as in "A *pro*logue comes before a play." Similarly, to *prog*nosticate is to make knowledge before or to predict. A *prog*nosticator is a fortune-teller. *Pro* can also mean *for*. Someone who is *pro* freedom of speech is in favor of freedom of speech. Someone with a *pro*clivity toward a certain activity is for that activity, or has a natural tendency toward it.

- ***pug* = war, fight:** Someone *pug*nacious is ready to fight. A *pug*ilist is a person who likes to fight — such as a professional boxer. (Did you ever see those big sticks that marines train with in hand-to-hand combat — the ones that look like cotton swabs with a thyroid condition? Those are called *pug*il sticks.)
- ***scien* = knowledge:** A *scien*tist is a person with knowledge. Someone pre*scien*t has forethought or knowledge ahead of time — for example, a prognosticator. (A fortune-teller, remember?) After you study these roots, you'll be closer to being omni*scien*t — all knowing.
- ***som* = sleep:** If you have in*som*nia, you can't sleep. (The prefix *in-* means not.)
- ***son* = sound:** A *son*ic boom breaks the sound barrier. Dis*son*ance is clashing sounds. A *son*orous voice has a good sound.
- ***sop* = sleep:** A glass of warm milk is a *sop*orific. So is a boring professor.

Memorizing the GRE's Most Common Vocabulary Words

This section features the most commonly occurring words on the GRE. Besides reviewing the words and their definitions in this section, I recommend using a dictionary or a dictionary website while practicing the Verbal section of the GRE. When you get stuck on a word, you can look it up. After that, you'll never forget it!

As you review these words, pay attention to the word parts (prefixes, suffixes, and roots) from the lists earlier in this chapter. Try covering up the definitions and discerning the word meanings from these parts. You can also make notecards and highlight the word parts. With practice, interpreting new words becomes much easier.

- ***aberrant:*** Abnormal; different from the accepted norm
- ***abeyance:*** State of suspension; temporary inaction
- ***abstemious:*** Characterized by a state of self-denial, particularly in the area of food or drink
- ***acquiescent:*** Agreeing without protest
- ***acrid:*** Bitter; harsh
- ***acrimonious:*** Bitter in temper, manner, and speech
- ***acumen:*** Keenness; quickness of intellectual insight
- ***admonition:*** A gentle reproof
- ***affront:*** To offend, as with a gesture
- ***aggrandize:*** To widen in scope or make bigger
- ***aggregate:*** Amounting to a whole
- ***allay:*** To reduce the intensity of

- ***amalgamate:*** To mix or blend together in a homogenous body
- ***ameliorate:*** To make better or improve
- ***anecdote:*** A short account of an interesting incident
- ***archipelago:*** A large group of islands
- ***artifice:*** Cleverness or skill
- ***ascetic:*** Given to severe self-denial; practicing excessive abstinence
- ***assiduous:*** Persistent, unceasing
- ***astute:*** Keen; wise
- ***audacious:*** Fearless
- ***austere:*** Unadorned; severely simple
- ***aver:*** To avouch, justify, or prove
- ***banal:*** Trite; commonplace
- ***base:*** The underlying concept of a system or theory
- ***beset:*** To surround, as in an attack
- ***blatant:*** Offensively loud
- ***bolster:*** To support; to reinforce
- ***bombastic:*** Using inflated language; pompous
- ***boon:*** A timely benefit
- ***brevity:*** Briefness or conciseness
- ***browbeat:*** To intimidate in an overbearing manner
- ***bumptious:*** Offensively self-assertive; pushy
- ***bungle:*** To perform clumsily or inadequately; botch
- ***burgeon:*** To grow forth; to send out buds
- ***cacophony:*** A disagreeable, harsh, or discordant sound or tone
- ***callous:*** Insensitive; indifferent
- ***calumniate:*** To make false and malicious statements about
- ***candor:*** To be open and sincere
- ***chicanery:*** Use of trickery to deceive
- ***churl:*** A rude, boorish, or surly person
- ***coda:*** Concluding section of a musical or literary piece; something that summarizes
- ***cognizant:*** Aware; taking notice
- ***colloquial:*** Pertaining to common speech
- ***complacency:*** A feeling of quiet security
- ***confidante:*** One to whom secrets are confided
- ***congruous:*** Appropriate or fitting
- ***consternation:*** Panic
- ***contentious:*** Quarrelsome
- ***contrite:*** Penitent
- ***contumacious:*** Rebellious
- ***corroborate:*** To make more certain; confirm

- ***countenance:*** Appearance, especially the look or expression of the face
- ***counterpart:*** A person or thing resembling or complementing another
- ***craven:*** Cowardly
- ***credulity:*** Willingness to behave or trust too readily
- ***cronyism:*** The practice of favoring one's friends, especially in political appointments
- ***cursory:*** Hasty, superficial, as of a review of something
- ***dearth:*** An inadequate supply; scarcity; lack
- ***decorum:*** Orderliness and good taste in manners
- ***deleterious:*** Hurtful, morally or physically
- ***delineate:*** To represent by sketch or diagram
- ***depravity:*** The state of being morally bad or evil
- ***deride:*** To ridicule; to make fun of
- ***derision:*** Ridicule
- ***derivative:*** Something obtained from a source
- ***desultory:*** Aimless; haphazard
- ***diatribe:*** Bitter or malicious criticism
- ***didactic:*** Pertaining to teaching
- ***dilatory:*** Causing delay
- ***disconcert:*** To disturb the composure of
- ***discretion:*** The power to act according to one's own judgment; the quality of being discreet
- ***disquiet:*** Lack of calm, peace, or ease
- ***dissemble:*** To disguise or pretend
- ***dissolution:*** Breaking up of a union of persons
- ***divest:*** To strip; to deprive
- ***divulge:*** To tell or make known, generally of something secret or private
- ***doldrums:*** A state of inactivity or low spirits
- ***dubious:*** Doubtful
- ***dupe:*** Someone easily fooled
- ***ebullient:*** Showing great enthusiasm or exhilaration
- ***efficacy:*** Power to produce an intended effect
- ***effrontery:*** Shameless boldness; impudence
- ***egress:*** Exit
- ***elegy:*** A poem lamenting the dead
- ***elicit:*** To extract without violence; to learn through discussion
- ***elitism:*** Consciousness or pride in belonging to a select group
- ***embellish:*** To add attractive and ornamental features
- ***emulate:*** Imitate
- ***enervate:*** To weaken
- ***engender:*** To produce

- ***ennui:*** Boredom
- ***ephemeral:*** Short-lived; fleeting
- ***equable:*** Free from many changes or variations
- ***equanimity:*** Evenness of mind or temper
- ***equivocal:*** Ambiguous
- ***equivocate:*** To use ambiguous or unclear expressions, usually to avoid commitment or to mislead
- ***eradicate:*** To destroy completely
- ***erudite:*** Very learned
- ***eschew:*** To keep clear of
- ***esoteric:*** Hard to understand; known only by a few
- ***exacerbate:*** To make more sharp or severe; to make worse
- ***exculpate:*** To free from blame
- ***exigency:*** Urgent situation
- ***expatiate:*** To speak or write at some length
- ***expiation:*** The means by which atonement or reparation is made
- ***extirpate:*** To root out; to eradicate
- ***extrapolation:*** To infer an unknown from something that is known
- ***facetious:*** Amusing
- ***fallacious:*** Illogical
- ***fatuous:*** Idiotic
- ***fervor:*** Ardor or intensity of feeling
- ***fledgling:*** Inexperienced
- ***foment:*** To nurse to life; to encourage
- ***forestall:*** To prevent by taking action in advance
- ***fortification:*** The act of strengthening or protecting
- ***frugal:*** Economical
- ***fulminate:*** To cause to explode
- ***fumble:*** To feel or grope about clumsily
- ***gaffe:*** A social blunder; faux pas
- ***gainsay:*** To contradict; to deny
- ***garrulous:*** Prone to trivial talking
- ***germane:*** Relevant
- ***goad:*** To urge on
- ***grandiloquent:*** Pompous; bombastic
- ***grandstand:*** To conduct oneself or perform showily in an attempt to impress onlookers
- ***gregarious:*** Sociable; outgoing
- ***guileless:*** Without deceit
- ***gullible:*** Easily deceived
- ***halcyon:*** Calm

- ***haphazard:*** Characterized by a lack of order or planning
- ***harangue:*** A tirade
- ***harbinger:*** One who foreruns and announces the coming of a person or thing
- ***hedge:*** A barrier or boundary; an act of preventing complete loss of a bet or investment
- ***heresy:*** Opinion or doctrine subversive of settled or accepted beliefs
- ***homogeneous:*** Of the same kind
- ***hyperbole:*** Exaggeration or overstatement
- ***iconoclast:*** An image-breaker
- ***ignominious:*** Shameful
- ***impecunious:*** Having no money; broke
- ***impede:*** To hinder; to block
- ***impenitent:*** Not feeling regret about one's sins
- ***imperious:*** Insisting on obedience
- ***imperturbable:*** Calm
- ***impervious:*** Impenetrable
- ***impetuous:*** Impulsive
- ***implicit:*** Implied
- ***importune:*** To harass with persistent demands
- ***impugn:*** To assail with arguments or accusations
- ***inadvertently:*** Unintentionally
- ***inane:*** Silly
- ***inchoate:*** Recently begun
- ***inconstant:*** Changeable; fickle; variable
- ***indolence:*** Laziness
- ***ineffable:*** Unutterable
- ***inert:*** Inactive; lacking power to move
- ***inexorable:*** Unrelenting
- ***ingratiating:*** Charming, agreeable
- ***innocuous:*** Harmless
- ***insinuate:*** To suggest or hint slyly
- ***insipid:*** Bland
- ***insouciant:*** Nonchalant
- ***intimation:*** Something indicated or made known indirectly
- ***intrepid:*** Fearless and bold
- ***inure:*** To harden or toughen by use, exercise, or exposure
- ***invidious:*** Showing or feeling envy
- ***irascible:*** Easily angered
- ***itinerant:*** Wandering
- ***jingoism:*** Professing one's patriotism loudly and excessively
- ***killjoy:*** A person who spoils the joy or pleasure of others

- ***laconic:*** Brief and to the point
- ***latent:*** Dormant
- ***laudable:*** Praiseworthy
- ***licentious:*** Wanton
- ***liken:*** To represent as similar to someone or something
- ***loquacious:*** Talkative
- ***lucid:*** Easily understood; clear
- ***magnanimity:*** Generosity
- ***malingerer:*** One who feigns illness to escape duty
- ***malleable:*** Pliant
- ***masticate:*** To chew or reduce to a pulp
- ***maverick:*** Rebel; nonconformist
- ***mediocrity:*** The state or quality of being mediocre
- ***mendacious:*** Untrue
- ***metamorphosis:*** Change of form
- ***meticulous:*** Overcautious
- ***misanthrope:*** One who hates mankind
- ***mitigate:*** To lessen in intensity; to appease
- ***modicum:*** A small amount
- ***mollify:*** To soothe
- ***mordant:*** Biting
- ***moribund:*** Near death or extinction
- ***morose:*** Ill-humored; sullen
- ***mundane:*** Ordinary; dull
- ***myopic:*** Shortsighted or narrow-minded
- ***narcissism:*** Excessive fascination with oneself
- ***nefarious:*** Extremely wicked
- ***negate:*** To cancel out; to nullify
- ***neophyte:*** Beginner
- ***nepotism:*** Favoritism shown on the basis of family relationship
- ***obdurate:*** Stubborn
- ***obfuscate:*** To darken
- ***obsequious:*** Servile; ready to serve
- ***obviate:*** To make unnecessary
- ***odious:*** Hateful
- ***officious:*** Meddlesome
- ***onus:*** Burden
- ***opprobrium:*** Infamy; vilification
- ***oscillate:*** To waver

- ***ostentation:*** A display of vanity; showiness
- ***palpable:*** Perceptible by feeling or touch
- ***panache:*** A grand or flamboyant manner or style
- ***parable:*** A short story designed to illustrate a lesson
- ***paragon:*** Model of perfection
- ***parsimonious:*** Sparing in spending of money
- ***partisan:*** One-sided; committed to one party
- ***pathos:*** Having a quality that rouses emotion or sympathy
- ***paucity:*** Fewness
- ***pejorative:*** Having a disparaging or derogatory effect
- ***penchant:*** Strong inclination
- ***penurious:*** Excessively sparing in the use of money; frugal
- ***perennial:*** Something long-lasting
- ***perfidy:*** Treachery
- ***permeable:*** Penetrable; porous
- ***pernicious:*** Tending to kill or hurt
- ***pervasive:*** Spread throughout
- ***phlegmatic:*** Not easily roused to feeling or emotion
- ***pious:*** Religious
- ***placate:*** To soothe; to bring from a hostile state to a calm one
- ***platitude:*** Trite or commonplace statement
- ***plethora:*** Excess; superabundance
- ***plumb:*** To make vertical
- ***polarize:*** To divide into sharply opposing factions
- ***pompous:*** Ostentatiously lofty or high-flown
- ***ponderous:*** Massive, awkward, unwieldy
- ***porous:*** Full of pores
- ***portend:*** Foretell
- ***poseur:*** A person who attempts to impress others by assuming a manner other than his true one
- ***pragmatic:*** Practical
- ***precarious:*** Perilous
- ***precipitate:*** Rash; premature
- ***precocious:*** Mature at a young age
- ***preeminent:*** Eminent above or before others
- ***prescience:*** Knowledge of events before they happen
- ***presentiment:*** A feeling or impression that something is about to happen
- ***prevaricate:*** To use ambiguous language for the purpose of deceiving
- ***proclivity:*** Natural inclination

- ***prodigal:*** Wasteful or lavish
- ***prodigious:*** Immense
- ***prodigy:*** A person, usually a child, having extraordinary talent
- ***profound:*** Deep; not superficial
- ***proliferate:*** To grow rapidly
- ***propensity:*** Natural inclination
- ***prophetic:*** Of the nature or containing a prophecy
- ***propitious:*** Indicative of favor
- ***prosaic:*** Commonplace or dull
- ***protean:*** Changeable in shape or form
- ***prudence:*** Caution
- ***puerile:*** Childish
- ***pugnacious:*** Quarrelsome
- ***pungent:*** Stinging; sharp in taste or smell
- ***pusillanimous:*** Cowardly; fainthearted
- ***qualms:*** Misgivings; uneasy fears
- ***quibble:*** Minor objection or complaint
- ***quiescence:*** Being quiet or still; inactivity
- ***quixotic:*** Idealistic; romantic to a ridiculous degree
- ***recant:*** To formally withdraw one's belief
- ***recidivism:*** The tendency toward repeated or habitual relapse
- ***recondite:*** Incomprehensible to one of ordinary understanding; profound
- ***redress:*** To set right by compensation or punishment
- ***refutation:*** An act of disproving a statement or charge
- ***repose:*** The state of being at rest
- ***reprobate:*** A sinful and depraved person
- ***repudiate:*** To refuse to have anything to do with
- ***rescind:*** To void by enacting authority
- ***respite:*** Interval of rest
- ***restive:*** Impatient or refusing to go forward
- ***reticent:*** Reserved; inclined to silence
- ***reverent:*** Respectful
- ***rhetoric:*** The art of effective communication
- ***rout:*** To drive out; to stampede
- ***rueful:*** Causing sorrow or pity
- ***ruminate:*** To chew over again; to think over
- ***sagacious:*** Wise
- ***salacious:*** Having strong sexual desires
- ***salubrious:*** Healthful

- ***sanction:*** To approve
- ***sanguine:*** Cheerfully confident; optimistic
- ***satiate:*** To satisfy or fulfill the appetite or desire of
- ***savor:*** To satisfy fully
- ***secrete:*** To hide away
- ***sedulous:*** Persevering in effort or endeavor
- ***seethe:*** To be disturbed
- ***seminal:*** Influencing future developments
- ***shard:*** Fragment
- ***shirk:*** To avoid
- ***shoddy:*** Not genuine; inferior
- ***sinuous:*** Curving in and out
- ***skeptic:*** Doubter
- ***skepticism:*** Doubt or disbelief
- ***skittish:*** Lively; frisky
- ***slander:*** Defamation
- ***slothful:*** Slow-moving, lazy
- ***solicitous:*** Worried; concerned
- ***sonorous:*** Resonant
- ***soporific:*** Causing sleep
- ***spate:*** A sudden, almost overwhelming outpouring
- ***specious:*** Seemingly reasonable but incorrect
- ***spendthrift:*** Someone who wastes money
- ***spurious:*** Not genuine
- ***stentorian:*** Extremely loud
- ***stigma:*** A token of disgrace
- ***stint:*** To be thrifty
- ***stipulate:*** To make express conditions
- ***stolid:*** Dull; impassive
- ***stratify:*** To form or place in layers
- ***striated:*** Marked with parallel bands
- ***strut:*** A pompous walk
- ***sublime:*** Supreme or outstanding; elevated
- ***subterfuge:*** Evasion
- ***supercilious:*** Showing careless contempt
- ***superfluous:*** More than what is needed
- ***supersede:*** To cause to be set back
- ***supine:*** Lying on the back
- ***sybarite:*** A person devoted to luxury and pleasure

- ***sycophant:*** A self-seeking, servile flatterer
- ***tacit:*** Understood
- ***taciturn:*** Stern; silent
- ***tangential:*** Digressing
- ***tantamount:*** Equivalent in effect or value
- ***tawdry:*** Cheap
- ***temerity:*** A foolish disregard of danger
- ***tempestuous:*** Stormy; impassioned
- ***tenacious:*** Holding fast
- ***tendentious:*** Having or showing a definite tendency, bias, or purpose
- ***tenuous:*** Thin; slim
- ***tepid:*** Lukewarm
- ***thrall:*** Slave; bondage
- ***thwart:*** To frustrate
- ***timidity:*** Lacking in self-assurance or courage
- ***titillate:*** To tickle
- ***titular:*** Pertaining to the nature of a title
- ***torpid:*** Dull; sluggish; inactive
- ***tortuous:*** Abounding in irregular bends or turns
- ***tractable:*** Docile
- ***transgression:*** Violation; sin
- ***transience:*** Being in a state of transition
- ***transmute:*** To change
- ***transparent:*** Easily detected
- ***transpire:*** To happen, to be revealed
- ***trepidation:*** Nervous feeling; fear
- ***truculence:*** Ferocity
- ***turgid:*** Inflated, overblown, or pompous
- ***tutelage:*** The act of training or being under instruction
- ***tyro:*** Beginner
- ***ubiquitous:*** Being present everywhere
- ***umbrage:*** Sense of injury
- ***unassuaged:*** Unsatisfied; not soothed
- ***uncouth:*** Clumsy; rude
- ***undermine:*** To weaken; to sap
- ***unerringly:*** Without fail
- ***ungainly:*** Awkward; clumsy
- ***unison:*** Complete accord

- ***unruly:*** Disobedient
- ***untenable:*** Indefensible
- ***upbraid:*** To reproach as deserving blame
- ***urbanity:*** Refined courtesy or politeness
- ***vacillate:*** To waver; to fluctuate
- ***vagabond:*** Wanderer
- ***vainglorious:*** Excessive; pretentious
- ***valorous:*** Courageous
- ***vantage:*** Position giving advantage
- ***vapid:*** Having lost quality and flavor; dull; lifeless
- ***variegated:*** Many colored
- ***vehement:*** Forceful
- ***venerate:*** To look upon with deep respect
- ***veracious:*** Truthful
- ***verbiage:*** Use of many words
- ***verbose:*** Wordy
- ***vestigial:*** Occurring or persisting as a rudimentary or degenerate structure
- ***vicissitude:*** Change of condition or circumstances, generally of fortune
- ***virtuosity:*** Having the character or ability of an expert
- ***virulence:*** Intense sharpness of anger; intensity
- ***viscous:*** Sticky; gluey
- ***vituperate:*** Overwhelm with wordy abuse
- ***vociferous:*** Making a loud outcry
- ***volatile:*** Changeable
- ***volition:*** A choice or decision made by the will
- ***voluble:*** Fluent; talkative
- ***warranted:*** Justified
- ***wary:*** Very cautious
- ***welter:*** Turmoil
- ***whet:*** To sharpen or stimulate
- ***whimsical:*** Fanciful
- ***whorl:*** Ring
- ***winsome:*** Attractive
- ***wreak:*** Inflict
- ***writhe:*** Twist
- ***yore:*** Time past
- ***zealot:*** Fanatic
- ***zeitgeist:*** Intellectual and moral tendencies of any age

Finding GRE vocab words in literature

Question: What do the GRE and *Moby Dick* have in common?

Answer: They both feature the following vocabulary words:

prodigious	fathom	ruefully
blunder	fastidious	tyro
antediluvian	wretched	omnipotent
voracious	incensed	cadge
heinous	precipice	descry
effulgent	inert	leviathan
floundering	disparaging	sagacious
depict	incredulous	superficial
conflagration	dogged	indiscriminate

Part III

High School Math and Beyond: Math You Thought You'd Never Need Again

In this part . . .

If you're fresh out of college with a degree in math or physics, you can probably skip this part, but chances are pretty good that the last time you cracked open a math book or tackled a word problem was back in high school. When that was over, you probably breathed a deep sigh of relief and said, "Thank goodness I'll never have to do *that* again!" Well, I hate to break it to you, but you're going to have to do that again.

The good news is that the chapters in this part quickly bring you up to speed on all the math you need for the GRE. In the following chapter, you brush up on basic math, including the order of operations, decimals, fractions, and percentages. In subsequent chapters, you review specific areas, including algebra and geometry, and sharpen your skills at solving word problems, reading tables and graphs, and answering Quantitative Comparison questions. Within each chapter are plenty of example problems to give you the hands-on experience you need to confront the GRE Math section with confidence.

Chapter 8

Brushing Up on Basic Arithmetic

In This Chapter

- Working with whole numbers, including factors, multiples, and prime numbers
- Using parts of numbers, including decimals, fractions, and percentages
- Mastering ratios
- Practicing a few simple math problems

You may feel like you're back in middle school with the material in this chapter. Although many of these concepts are fairly easy, you do need a firm grasp of them for answering questions on the GRE. The good news: This is stuff you know, and you just need a refresher.

This chapter covers most of the basic arithmetic concepts, including whole numbers, units of measurement, decimals, fractions, percentages, and ratios featured on the GRE. After reading this chapter and practicing the concepts described within, you'll be armed and ready for any basic math question the GRE throws at you.

Eyeing Integers, Factors, and Multiples

You must be familiar with the following types of numbers for the GRE. Many of the GRE math questions use these terms, and the GRE expects you to know what they are. For example, the question states, "x is an integer" or "x is a factor of 21."

- **Integers:** Any whole number, positive or negative, is an integer. Zero is neither positive nor negative, but it's considered an integer. Integers include –3, –2, –1, 0, 1, 2, and 3.
- **Real numbers:** Any number that goes on the number line is considered a real number. These numbers include all negative and positive fractions, decimals, whole numbers, and zero.
- **Non-real numbers:** Any number that can't exist in real math and, therefore, isn't on the number line is a non-real number. Mathematics has several types of non-real numbers, but you only need to worry about two for the GRE:
    - The square root of a negative number (see Chapter 9)
    - Any number divided by zero
- **Factors:** Any integer that you get from dividing another integer is a factor. For example, the factors of 36 are 1, 2, 3, 4, 6, 9, 12, 18, and 36. Note that every integer is a factor of itself and 1 is a factor of every number.
- **Multiples:** Any integer you get from multiplying another integer is a multiple. The multiples of 3 begin with 3, 6, 9, 12, and 15, but they go on infinitely. Like factors, every integer is a multiple of itself.
- **Prime numbers:** Any integer that has exactly two factors (1 and itself) is a prime number. I discuss prime numbers in greater detail in the next section.

Factoring in Prime Time: Prime and Composite Numbers

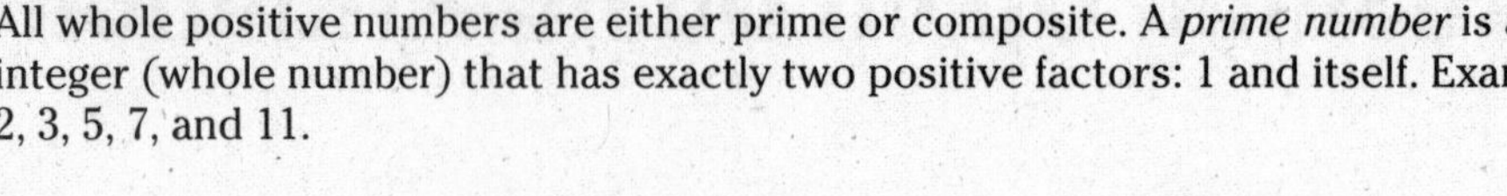

All whole positive numbers are either prime or composite. A *prime number* is a positive integer (whole number) that has exactly two positive factors: 1 and itself. Examples include 2, 3, 5, 7, and 11.

These little rules about prime numbers can help you better identify them:

- Zero isn't a prime number, because it's divisible by more than two factors. Anything times zero is zero.
- One isn't a prime number, because it has only one factor: itself.
- Two is the *only* even prime, because it's the only even number with exactly two factors: 1 and itself.

Meanwhile, *composite numbers* have more than two factors and can be divided by more than just 1 and themselves. Examples include 4, 6, 8, and 9.

A composite number can be broken down to its prime factors. For example, 36 can be broken down to $2 \times 2 \times 3 \times 3$; 84 can be broken down to $2 \times 2 \times 3 \times 7$; and 125 can be broken down to $5 \times 5 \times 5$.

Here's a GRE question example that challenges your grasp of prime numbers:

Quantity A	***Quantity B***
The number of prime numbers from 0 to 10 inclusive	The number of prime numbers from 11 to 20 inclusive

Ⓐ Quantity A is greater.

Ⓑ Quantity B is greater.

Ⓒ The two quantities are equal.

Ⓓ The relationship cannot be determined from the information given.

In Quantity A, the prime numbers from 0 to 10 inclusive are 2, 3, 5, and 7. In Quantity B, the prime numbers from 11 to 20 inclusive are 11, 13, 17, and 19. Both quantities have four prime numbers, but counting 0 and 1 as prime would lead you to choose Choice (A), which is incorrect. The correct answer is Choice **(C).**

Reading between the Lines: Absolute Value

The *absolute value,* indicated by two vertical parallel lines, is the positive form of a number. Technically, absolute value refers to the distance from zero on the number line. This means that because –7 is 7 units away from zero, the absolute value of –7, written as $|-7|$, is 7.

Here's the type of absolute value concept you may encounter on the GRE:

$$-|-3| = -+3 = -3$$

The answer may seem counterintuitive. Isn't a negative number times a negative number a positive number? Yes, but this problem is actually a negative times a positive. Because the absolute value of –3 is 3, you multiply positive 3 by the negative to get **–3.**

Here's a trickier example:

$-|-|-5|| =$

The official way to solve the problem is to work from the inside out. Say to yourself as you go along, "The absolute value of –5 is 5. Then the negative of that is –5. But the absolute value of –5 is 5. And finally, the negative of that is **–5.**"

Remembering the Order of Things: Putting PEMDAS to Use

When you encounter a problem on the GRE that includes several different operations, such as addition, subtraction, multiplication, division, squaring, and so on, you should do them in a particular order to reach the correct answer. Here is the order:

1. **Parentheses:** Solve what's in parentheses first. If you have parentheses inside other sets of parentheses, work from the inside out.
2. **Exponents:** Squaring, cubing, or using whatever other exponent is next.
3. **Multiplication or Division:** Work from left to right and solve.
4. **Addition or subtraction:** Again, solve from left to right.

The best way to remember the order of operations is to use the phrase "Please Excuse My Dear Aunt Sally" (PEMDAS), which stands for parentheses, exponents, multiplication, division, addition, and subtraction. Use PEMDAS for the following problem.

$10\ (3 - 5)^2$

Start with what's inside the parentheses: 3 – 5 = –2. Then move on to the exponents: –2 squared equals 4. Finally, do the multiplication: 4 × 10 = **40.**

The GRE tests your ability to approach these questions analytically, which means thinking outside the established methods. PEMDAS is a good rule, but blindly following any rule, including PEMDAS, could turn an easy question into a difficult question. Instead, take a high-level look at any math question before trying to solve it.

Say you have the following problem:

$\left(\frac{600}{5}\right)^0 =$

You could begin with dividing 600 by 5 before raising it to the 0 power. But wait a second — anything to the 0 power equals **1.** By taking a high-level look at the question before trying to solve it, you save yourself the effort of working the parentheses first.

Measuring Up: Units of Measurement

In conversion questions, the GRE always tells you the relationship between two units of measurement, *except* for units of time; for example, you won't be told that 60 seconds = 1 minute.

If you're asked how many ounces are in 5 pounds, the GRE includes the units of measurement (1 pound = 16 ounces). To solve it, do the following steps:

1. **Set the conversion equation up as fractions to avoid mixing up the multiplying and dividing.**

   $$\left(\frac{5\text{ lbs}}{1}\right)\left(\frac{16\text{ oz}}{1\text{ lb}}\right)$$

2. **Cancel the common terms.**

   In this example, you cancel the lb units:

   $$\left(\frac{5\text{ }\cancel{\text{lbs}}}{1}\right)\left(\frac{16\text{ oz}}{1\text{ }\cancel{\text{lb}}}\right)$$

3. **Multiply fractions.**

   $$\left(\frac{80\text{ oz}}{1}\right)=80\text{ oz}$$

When dealing with area and volume, always convert to the *smallest* unit in the question *before* calculating. For example, 2 yards by 2 yards might be 4 yards, but if converting to feet, you should convert *before* calculating. This way you get the correct answer of 36 square feet (from 6 feet by 6 feet) instead of the incorrect answer of 12 square feet (from 4 square yards).

If 12 inches are in a foot, then how many square inches are in a square foot? If you say 12, you've fallen for the trap. Why? Because 12 × 12 = 144, which is the actual number of square inches in a square foot.

Here's how you may fall for that trap in an otherwise easy problem:

Quantity A	***Quantity B***
Number of square inches in 3 square feet	36

Ⓐ Quantity A is greater.

Ⓑ Quantity B is greater.

Ⓒ The two quantities are equal.

Ⓓ The relationship cannot be determined from the information given.

Your first reaction is to think that the quantities are equal because there are 12 inches to a foot and 12 × 3 = 36. However, because a square foot has 144 square inches, and 144 × 3 is definitely greater than 36 (don't waste any time doing the math), the answer is Choice **(A).**

Bonus: How many cubic inches are in a cubic foot? Twelve inches per side cubed is 12^3, which equals 1,728 cubic inches. (For more on 3-D geometric shapes, turn to Chapter 10.)

Discovering the Point with Decimals

Working with decimals isn't overly difficult. All you have to do is remember a few key points:

- Line up the decimal points when adding or subtracting.
- Count the decimal places when multiplying.
- Move the decimal points of both numbers when dividing.

Though the GRE features an on-screen calculator, you really don't need it, even with decimal-based math problems. Figuring out how decimals work is easy. The following sections walk you through adding, subtracting, multiplying, and dividing decimals.

Reducing your reliance on the calculator is a sure way to boost your score. Not only can you work problems on scratch paper faster than in the calculator, but you also can make an unnoticed typo on the calculator, which can lead to a wrong answer.

Adding and subtracting decimals

To add or subtract decimals accurately, first line up the decimal points. Then add or subtract as usual, placing the decimal point in the answer right below where it falls in the original numbers.

$$\begin{array}{r} 41.6 \\ +0.12 \\ \hline 41.72 \end{array}$$

After you line up the decimals, you can add or subtract as usual.

Multiplying decimals

When multiplying decimals, you want to ensure the number of decimal places in the answer is the same as the *total* number of decimal places in all the numbers you're multiplying. Multiply the numbers first, and then count the decimal places.

$$0.06 \times 0.03 = 0.0018$$

You know that 6×3 is 18. But the 0.06 and the 0.03 each has two decimal places, for a total of four. Therefore, the final answer also has four decimal places.

Don't forget to include the zeros at the end when counting the decimal places. After you have your answer, you can drop the end zeros.

$$0.04 \times 0.05 = 0.0020 = 0.002$$

You know that 4×5 is 20, so be sure to include the entire 20 (two and zero) when counting the decimal places. After you have the decimal set correctly, you can drop the right-side zero.

Dividing decimals

Before dividing decimals, turn the decimals into integers by moving the decimal points of both numbers to the right the same number of spaces, until both numbers are whole numbers.

A tricky $0.032 \div 0.008$ becomes an easy $32 \div 8$ for a final answer of 4.

Facing Off with Fractions

You probably mastered fractions back in middle school. With some brushing off of the cobwebs, you can master them again. The following sections point out how to add, subtract, multiply, and divide fractions and how to handle mixed numbers.

Adding or subtracting fractions

You can add and subtract fractions only with a *common denominator* (the same bottom part of the fraction). After the fractions you're adding or subtracting have been modified to contain the same denominator, you add or subtract the *numerator* (the top part of the fraction).

To find a common denominator, you can multiply all the denominators. Doing so, however, doesn't give you the lowest common denominator. Check out this example:

$$\frac{2}{5}+\frac{3}{7}=$$

Here, 5 and 7 are different denominators, so you can't add these two fractions. However, make the denominators the same, and then you *can* add them.

$$\frac{2}{5}+\frac{3}{7}=\frac{2(7)}{5(7)}+\frac{3(5)}{7(5)}=\frac{14}{35}+\frac{15}{35}=\frac{29}{35}$$

Make sure to multiply the top and bottom of the fraction by the same number to avoid changing the value of the fraction. After the denominators are the same, you can add the fractions. The common denominator will carry over to the answer, but the numerators will add together (or subtract from each other) to give you the final answer.

$$\frac{1}{6}-\frac{1}{15}=$$

Here's how to find the lowest common denominator of 15 and 6: You can multiply 15×6, but that's not the *lowest* common denominator, and that would create a lot of extra work. Instead, count by 15s, because 15 is the larger of the two numbers.

Check each multiple of 15 for divisibility by 6. Does 15 work? No, 6 doesn't go into 15. How about 30? Yes, both 15 and 6 go into 30. There you have it: The lowest common denominator is 30.

$$\frac{1}{6}-\frac{1}{15}=\frac{1(5)}{6(5)}-\frac{1(2)}{15(2)}=\frac{5}{30}-\frac{2}{30}=\frac{3}{30}=\frac{1}{10}$$

Multiplying fractions

To multiply fractions, you just go straight across, multiplying the numerators with each other and the denominators with each other.

$$\frac{2}{5}\times\frac{3}{7}=\frac{(2\times3)}{(5\times7)}=\frac{6}{35}$$

Always check whether you can cancel out common factors between a numerator and a denominator before you begin multiplying in order to avoid dealing with big, awkward numbers and having to reduce fractions at the end. Canceling in advance just makes the numbers smaller and easier to work with.

For example, in these fractions, both the 6 and the 9 are divisible by 3. You can cancel those 3s from the numerator and denominator before multiplying the fractions.

$$\frac{6}{5}\times\frac{4}{9}=\frac{(3)(2)}{5}\times\frac{4}{(3)(3)}=\frac{(2)}{5}\times\frac{4}{(3)}=\frac{(2\times4)}{(5\times3)}=\frac{8}{15}$$

In this next example, the 4 and the 8 reduce (both are divisible by 4), and the 15 and the 5 reduce (both are divisible by 5), simplifying the problem:

$$\frac{4}{15}\times\frac{5}{8}=\frac{1}{3}\times\frac{1}{2}=\frac{(1\times 1)}{(3\times 2)}=\frac{1}{6}$$

Dividing fractions

To divide two fractions, you *invert* the second fraction (turning it upside down) and then multiply the two fractions. See this example:

$$\frac{1}{3}\div\frac{2}{5}=\frac{1}{3}\times\frac{5}{2}=\frac{(1\times 5)}{(3\times 2)}=\frac{5}{6}$$

Mixed numbers

A *mixed number* is a whole number with a fraction tagging along behind it, such as $2\frac{1}{3}$, $4\frac{2}{5}$, or $9\frac{1}{2}$. Before you can work with a mixed number (and then add, subtract, multiply, or divide by it), you first have to get it into fraction form. To do so, multiply the denominator (bottom number) by the whole number and add that to the numerator (top number). Then put the sum over the denominator.

$$2\frac{1}{3}:(3\times 2)+1=7\Rightarrow\frac{7}{3}$$

$$4\frac{2}{5}:(5\times 4)+2=22\Rightarrow\frac{22}{5}$$

$$9\frac{1}{2}:(2\times 9)+1=19\Rightarrow\frac{19}{2}$$

To convert an improper fraction back to a mixed number, count the number of times the denominator goes into the numerator, put that down as the whole number, and then the amount left over goes over the original denominator.

For example, to convert $\frac{22}{7}$ into a mixed number, here's what you do:

$$\frac{22}{7}=22\div 7=3+(1\div 7)=3\frac{1}{7}$$

Manipulating Percentages

Percentage-based questions are easy if you know how to work them. The GRE test writers will probably throw a couple percentage-related questions at you to make sure you know how to work them. This section shows you how to convert the percentages into easier forms to work with and how to use formulas to find the answers to the GRE questions.

Converting between percentages and decimals or fractions

When the GRE gives you a percentage-based math question, you don't have to work it as such. Converting the percentage to a decimal or fraction can make the question much easier to answer. You may need to convert back to a percentage to put the answer in the right form. Just do the following:

- **To convert a percentage to a decimal:** Move the decimal point two places to the left of the percentage and drop the % sign.

  35% = 0.35 6% = 0.06 50% = 0.5 3.33% = 0.0333

- **To convert a decimal to a percentage:** Move the decimal point two places to the right and add the % sign.

  0.32 = 32% 0.185 = 18.5% 0.05 = 5%

- **To convert a percentage to a fraction:** Place the number over 100, drop the % sign, and reduce if possible.

  $$50\% = \frac{50}{100} = \frac{1}{2}$$

  $$125\% = \frac{125}{100} = \frac{5}{4}$$

  $$4\% = \frac{4}{100} = \frac{1}{25}$$

- **To convert a fraction to a percentage:** Set the fraction equal to x over 100 and cross-multiply to find x. The x is your percentage.

  $\frac{27}{50}$ becomes $\frac{27}{50} = \frac{x}{100}$

  Cross-multiply to solve for x, which equals 54. Therefore, the fraction equals 54%.

Cross-multiplying can be done only with two fractions that equal each other. If you're missing part of one fraction, place an x where the part is missing, and cross-multiply to find out what x is. Multiply the numerator of the first fraction with the denominator of the second, and set that equal to the product of the denominator of the second fraction with the numerator of the first. It's simpler in practice than in explanation, as in the following example:

$$\frac{8}{x} = \frac{28}{7}$$

First, multiply the 8 and 7 and set that equal to the 28 times x, giving you

$$56 = 28x$$

Then divide both sides by 28 to find the value of x:

$$2 = x$$

Finding the percent of change

You may get a question asking you for a percent of change from an original amount. To find this, use this formula:

$$\text{Percent of change} = \frac{\text{Amount of change}}{\text{Original amount}}$$

Finding the percent of change requires two simple steps:

1. **Find the *number* (amount) that the item increased or decreased — that is, the amount of change.**

For example, if a baseball team won 25 games last year and 30 games this year, the amount of change is 5. If a salesperson earned \$10,000 last year and \$8,000 this year, the amount of change is 2,000.

2. **Place the amount of change over the original amount.**

   If the team won 25 games last year and 30 games this year, the original amount is 25. If the salesperson earned \$10,000 last year and \$8,000 this year, the original amount is \$10,000.

For the baseball team

$$\frac{5}{25}=\frac{1}{5}=20\%$$

(you divide 1 by 5 to get 0.20 and multiply by 100 to make it a percentage).

For the ***hapless*** (meaning unfortunate — think the opposite of *happy*) salesman,

$$\frac{2{,}000}{10{,}000}=\frac{20}{100}=20\%$$

(you again divide 20 by 100 to get 0.20 and multiply by 100 to make it a percentage).

In 2006, Coach Jamieson won 50 prizes at the county fair by tossing a basketball into a bushel basket. In 2007, he won 40 prizes. What was his percent decrease?

Ⓐ 10

Ⓑ 20

Ⓒ 30

Ⓓ 40

Ⓔ 50

The number by which Coach Jamieson's prizes decreased is 10 (from 50 to 40). Place the 10 over the original amount of 50 for a decrease of 20%. The correct answer is Choice **(B).**

Carissa has three quarters. Her father gives her three more. Carissa's wealth has increased by what percent?

Ⓐ 50

Ⓑ 100

Ⓒ 200

Ⓓ 300

Ⓔ 500

Did you fall for the trap answer, Choice (C)? Carissa's wealth has doubled, to be sure, but the percent increase is only 100. You can prove that with the percent of change formula. The number increase is 0.75 (she has three more quarters, or 75 cents), and her original whole was 0.75. So if you follow the formula, you get $\frac{75}{75}=100\%$. The right answer is Choice **(B).**

When you double something, you increase it by 100%, because you must subtract the original that you began with. When you triple something, you increase it by 200%, because you must subtract the original you began with. For example, if you had \$3 and you now have \$9, you've tripled your money, but you've increased it by only 200%.

Making Ratios More Rational

After you know the tricks, ratios are some of the easiest problems to answer quickly. A *ratio* is a proportional relationship between two similar numbers or quantities. A ratio is written as either A : B or $\frac{A}{B}$. For example,

The ratio *of* yachts *to* sailboats = yachts : sailboats

The ratio *of* umbrellas *to* people = $\frac{\text{umbrellas}}{\text{people}}$

The following sections look at two ways to solve simple ratios and the best way to handle combined ratios.

Considering the total number of items

Because ratios compare the amounts of two different things, the *total* number of items is a multiple of the sum of the numbers in the ratio. In other words, if the ratio is 3 dogs for every 2 cats, then the total number of dogs can't be 7 — it has to be 3, 6, or 9, or any multiple of 3. Same with the cats: The number has to be a multiple of 2. You first need to find the sum of the numbers in the ratio: 3 + 2 = 5. So the total number of animals has to be a multiple of 5, with 3 for the dogs and 2 for the cats.

You may encounter a problem like this on the GRE:

At a game, the ratio of your team's fans to the other team's fans is 4:5. Which of the following can be the total number of fans at the game?

To solve this ratio problem, you first add the numbers in the ratio: 4 + 5 = 9. The total number of fans must be a multiple of 9 (9, 18, 27, 36, and so on). The total number of fans must be divisible by 9. Can the total, for example, be 54? Yes, because 9 goes evenly into 54. Can it be 64? No, because 9 doesn't go evenly into 64.

While trying to get Willie to turn down his stereo, his downstairs neighbor pounds on the ceiling and shouts up to his bedroom. If she pounds 7 times for every 5 times she shouts, which of the following can be the total number of poundings and shouts?

Ⓐ 75

Ⓑ 57

Ⓒ 48

Ⓓ 35

Ⓔ 30

Add the numbers in the ratio: 7 + 5 = 12. The total must be a multiple of 12 (meaning it must be evenly divisible by 12). Only Choice (C), 48, is evenly divisible by 12. Choices (A), 75, and (B), 57, try to trick you by using the numbers 7 and 5 from the ratio. Choice (D) is a trap with the product of 7 and 5. The correct answer is Choice **(C).**

Notice how the questions ask which answers *can be* the possible totals (any multiple of the sums). They're not asking "which of the following *is* the total," in which case you'd need more information to answer the question.

Quantity A		*Quantity B*
	Ratio of CDs to tapes = 2:9	
Total of CDs and tapes		11

Ⓐ Quantity A is greater.

Ⓑ Quantity B is greater.

Ⓒ The two quantities are equal.

Ⓓ The relationship cannot be determined from the information given.

You know the total must be a multiple of 11, but it can be an infinite number of terms: 11, 22, 33, 44, 55, and so on. This trap has destroyed many overly confident test-takers through the years. The correct answer is Choice **(D).**

Finding the amount of a specific term

When you're given a ratio and a total and are asked to find the amount of a specific term, one way to solve the ratio is to do the following:

1. **Add the numbers in the ratio.**

   The total number of items is a multiple of this sum.
2. **Divide the total number of items by that sum.**
3. **Multiply that quotient by each term in the ratio.**
4. **Add the answers to double-check that they add up to the total.**

   Be sure to do this step to check your work.

It takes longer to explain these steps than it does to work them. With a little practice, the technique becomes second nature. Consider this example:

Congratulating the members of his team, which had just won 21 to 0, the ecstatic coach gestured to each member of the squad, calling everyone either a champ or a winner. If there were 3 champs for every 4 winners, and every member of the 28-man squad was either a champ or a winner, how many champs were there?

There are 3 champs for every 4 winners, so add the numbers in the ratio: $3 + 4 = 7$. Then divide that sum into the total number of players: $\frac{28}{7} = 4$. Now multiply that number by each term in the ratio: $3 \times 4 = 12$ champs; $4 \times 4 = 16$ winners. The question asks for the number of champs, so the correct answer is **12.** Finally, add the answers to double-check that they sum up to 28: $12 + 16 = 28$.

If the GRE math problem features an existing ratio, and you have to change the number of items while maintaining the ratio, you can easily calculate the number of items you need by setting up a *proportion,* which is two ratios (fractions) set equal to each other. Make the existing ratio (as a fraction) equal to the new items (also as a fraction), and cross-multiply to find the missing value.

Your college has to maintain its current ratio of 3 graduate assistants for every 40 students. If 240 new students are expected this fall, how many new graduate assistants should the school hire to maintain the ratio?

1. **Set up the existing ratio as a fraction.**

$$\frac{\text{Assistants}}{\text{Students}} = \frac{3}{40}$$

2. **Set up the new additions as a fraction, with x as the unknown value.**

$$\frac{\text{Needed Assistants}}{\text{New Students}} = \frac{x}{240}$$

3. **Set the fractions equal to each other.**

$$\frac{3}{40} = \frac{x}{240}$$

4. **Solve for x.**

Cross-multiply, multiplying the numerator of each fraction by the denominator of the other:

$$40x = 720$$
$$x = 18$$

Thus, **18** new graduate assistants are needed to maintain the ratio.

Combining two or more ratios

Sometimes the GRE provides you with two different ratios. However, one item is common in each of the ratios. For example, a jazz shop has 6 saxophones for every 5 drum kits and 2 drum kits for every 3 trombones. You can use the common item (drum kits) to combine the ratios for a single ratio of instruments at the jazz shop.

Combining ratios is a little like adding fractions. When adding fractions, you find the lowest common denominator. Ratios don't have numerators or denominators, but they do have something in common — in this case, drum kits. In order to combine ratios, follow these simple steps.

Sam's jazz shop has 6 saxophones for every 5 drum kits and 2 drum kits for every 3 trombones. What's the ratio of saxophones to trombones?

1. **Set up the ratios as A : B.**

Place the item that the ratios have in common (drum kits) into a column.

Saxes		Drums		'Bones
6	:	5		
		2	:	3

2. **Find a common multiple for the item that these ratios have in common.**

In this instance, both ratios include drum kits. The least common multiple of 5 and 2 (the numbers of drum kits) is 10.

3. **Multiply each term in the ratios so that the quantity of the item in common equals the common multiple (from Step 2).**

Now, if you were adding these as fractions, you'd write the drums as the denominators, and your work would start out like this:

$$\frac{6}{5} + \frac{3}{2} = \frac{6(2)}{2(2)} + \frac{3(5)}{2(5)} = \frac{12}{10} + \frac{15}{10}$$

Of course, you aren't adding fractions, but you treat the ratios the same way: Multiply both terms of each ratio by the same number, as though you're getting a common denominator. Here, you want the number of drum kits to equal 10. Multiply both terms in the first ratio by 2, and multiply both terms in the second ratio by 5:

Saxes		Drums		'Bones
6(2)	:	5(2)		
		2(5)	:	3(5)

Saxes		Drums		'Bones
12	:	10		
		10	:	15

4. **Write out a combined ratio.**

Saxes		Drums		'Bones
12	:	10		
		10	:	15
12	:	10	:	15

The combined ratio of saxophones to drum kits to trombones is 12:10:15. To answer the question, give only the ratio of saxophones to trombones, which is 12:15, or **4:5.**

Working the Numbers: Arithmetic Practice Problems

Now it's your turn. Each of these practice questions is based on at least one concept discussed earlier in this chapter. If you get stuck, don't hesitate to flip back a few pages to review some step-by-steps. The concepts in this chapter are central to the GRE Math section, so being able to solve and understand these practice problems is important.

1. After a rough hockey game, Bernie checks his uniform and finds 3 smudges for every 5 tears. Which of the following can be the total number of smudges and tears on Bernie's uniform?

Ⓐ 53

Ⓑ 45

Ⓒ 35

Ⓓ 33

Ⓔ 32

Add the numbers in the ratio: $3 + 5 = 8$. The total must be a multiple of 8 (or, looking at it another way, the total must be evenly divisible by 8). Only Choice (E) is a multiple of 8 ($8 \times 4 = 32$). The correct answer is Choice **(E).**

2. Banker's Credit Union has 7 call-center reps on hand for every 200 customers. With an aggressive marketing campaign, the bank just signed up an additional 1,400 customers. How many new reps should the bank hire in order to maintain this ratio?

Ⓐ 14

Ⓑ 20

Ⓒ 35

Ⓓ 49

Ⓔ 50

Set up the equation:

$$\frac{\text{Reps}}{\text{Customers}} = \frac{7}{200} = \frac{x}{1400}$$

Cross-multiply, and you find that $x = 49$. The correct answer is Choice **(D).**

3. A sports shop has 3 jerseys for every 2 helmets and 6 kneepads for every 5 jerseys. What's the ratio of helmets to kneepads?

Ⓐ 1:3

Ⓑ 4:9

Ⓒ 5:9

Ⓓ 2:3

Ⓔ 7:9

Set up the ratios:

Jerseys		Helmets		Kneepads
3	:	2		
5		:		6

Find a common multiple of jerseys. A common multiple of 3 and 5 is 15, so multiply each term of the first ratio by 5 and each term of the second by 3:

Jerseys		Helmets		Kneepads
15	:	10		
15		:		18

Write them out as a combined ratio:

Jerseys		Helmets		Kneepads
15	:	10		
15		:		18
15	:	10	:	18

The ratio of helmets to kneepads is 10:18, or 5:9, so the correct answer is Choice **(C).**

Chapter 9

Algebra: Finding What X Really Means

In This Chapter

- Working with bases and exponents
- Dealing with variables like x and y
- Solving for x and algebraic expressions
- Digging deep into roots and radicals
- Plotting points, lines, and slopes with coordinate geometry
- Manipulating functions and sequences

Algebra is a branch of mathematics that uses numbers, letters, and operations to represent the concepts and rules of mathematics. Through an understanding of these concepts and rules, you're often able to use what you know (the information a question provides) to determine what you don't know, such as the value of x. You've probably already solved lots of algebra questions in junior high and high school, and perhaps even in your college courses. You just need a refresher to get your head back in the game.

This chapter reveals everything you need to know about algebra to be fully prepared for the test. It starts slowly with bases, exponents, and variables like x and y and gradually moves on to complicated algebraic concepts. Although you're free to skip around, if you're rusty with these concepts, you may want to start at the very beginning.

Tapping the Powers of Bases and Exponents

Many GRE math questions require you to know how to work with bases and exponents. When you multiply a number repeatedly by itself, you raise that number to a certain power; for example, 3 to the power of 4, or 3^4, is $3 \times 3 \times 3 \times 3 = 81$. In this example, 3 is the base, and 4 is the exponent. The *exponent* simply tells you how many times to multiply the *base* (number) by itself. Here are a few more examples:

$10^2 = 10 \times 10 = 100$

$5^3 = 5 \times 5 \times 5 = 125$

$x^4 = x \times x \times x \times x$

Remember the following rules when working with bases and exponents:

1. **Any number to the zero power always equals 1.**

   $x^0 = 1$

   $5^0 = 1$

   $129^0 = 1$

2. **Any number to a negative exponent is the reciprocal of that number to its positive exponent.**

$$x^{-4} = \frac{1}{x^4}$$

$$5^{-3} = \frac{1}{5^3}$$

$$129^{-1} = \frac{1}{129}$$

A *number* with a negative exponent isn't negative. When you flip it, you get the reciprocal, and the negative goes away.

5^{-3} equals the reciprocal of 5^3: $\frac{1}{5^3} = \frac{1}{125}$

3. **When you raise 10 to a power, you get 1 followed by the number of zeros equal to that power.**

$10^2 = 100$ (two zeros)

$10^3 = 1{,}000$ (three zeros)

$10^4 = 10{,}000$ (four zeros)

Because $10^4 = 10{,}000$, then 5×10^4 is $5 \times 10{,}000$, which equals 50,000.

4. **To multiply like bases, add their exponents.**

$x^3 \times x^2 = x^{(3+2)} = x^5$

$5^3 \times 5^4 = 5^{(3+4)} = 5^7$

$129^2 \times 129^7 = 129^{(2+7)} = 129^9$

You can't multiply *different* bases.

$x^2 \times y^3$ stays $x^2 \times y^3$

$5^2 \times 129^3$ stays $5^2 \times 129^3$

5. **To divide like bases, subtract the exponents.**

$x^5 \div x^2 = x^{(5-2)} = x^3$

$5^9 \div 5^3 = 5^{(9-3)} = 5^6$

$129^4 \div 129^0 = 129^{(4-0)} = 129^4$

Did you look at the second example, $5^9 \div 5^3$, and think the answer was 5^3? Falling into the trap of dividing rather than subtracting is pretty easy, especially when you see numbers that just beg to be divided, like 9 and 3. Keep your guard up.

6. **Multiply the exponents of a base inside and outside of parentheses.**

$(x^2)^3 = x^{(2 \times 3)} = x^6$

$(5^3)^3 = 5^{(3 \times 3)} = 5^9$

$(129^0)^3 = 129^{(0 \times 3)} = 129^0 = 1$

7. **To add or subtract like bases with like powers, add or subtract the numerical coefficients of the bases.**

The *numerical coefficient* is the number to the left of the base; for example, in $31x^3$, 31 is the numerical coefficient.

$37x^3 + 10x^3 = 47x^3$

$15y^2 - 10y^2 = 5y^2$

You can't add or subtract like bases with *different* exponents. For example, $14x^3 - 9x^2$ isn't equal to $5x^3$, $5x^2$, or $5x$. It stays $14x^3 - 9x^2$. The bases *and* exponents must be the same for you to add or subtract the terms.

8. **You can't add or subtract the numerical coefficients of unlike bases.**

$$16x^2 - 4y^2 = 16x^2 - 4y^2 \text{ (}\textit{not } 12x^2, 12y^2, \text{ or } 12xy^2\text{)}$$

Time to try out a few Quantitative Comparison (QC) questions with bases and exponents! (In QC questions, you compare the contents in two columns. I explain all about QC questions in Chapter 13.)

For all QC questions on the GRE, you choose from the following answer choices:

Ⓐ Quantity A is greater.

Ⓑ Quantity B is greater.

Ⓒ The two quantities are equal.

Ⓓ The relationship cannot be determined from the information given.

Quantity A	***Quantity B***
x^3	$\frac{x^7}{x^4}$

Remember that when you divide, you subtract the exponents, so $x^{(7-4)} = x^3$, no matter what the value of x is. *Correct answer:* Choice **(C).**

Quantity A	***Quantity B***
$(x^3)^4$	x^{12}

Because you multiply exponents together when you take to a higher power, no matter what value x has, the two quantities are the same: $x^{12} = x^{12}$. *Correct answer:* Choice **(C).**

Quantity A	***Quantity B***
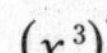 $(x^3)^4$	12

Because you don't know what the value of x is, you can't tell which quantity is greater. You may think that anything to the 12th power is a large number, making Choice (A) the correct answer, but you need to know more about x. If x were 2, then you'd be right. If x were $\frac{1}{2}$, you'd be wrong. This trap is really easy to fall for. See Chapter 13 for more on picking values for x to try different possibilities. *Correct answer:* Choice **(D).**

Quantity A	***Quantity B***
$16x^4 - 4x^3$	$12x$

Because you don't know what x is, as in the preceding question, try different values for x to get different answers. If you selected Choice (C), you fell for the trap. Again. *Correct answer:* Choice **(D).**

Quantity A	***Quantity B***
$10x^3 - 2y^3$	$8xy$

Because you don't know what x or y is, you can't tell which quantity is greater. *Correct answer:* Choice **(D).**

Working with Symbolism Problems

You may encounter questions based on symbols and functions on the GRE. Though the questions are different, the approach for either is exactly the same: substitute for the variable. Whether you're working a symbol or a function question, the math itself is always easy. The trick is knowing how to set up the equation. This section explains how to set up the equations to solve these types of problems and then do the math to arrive at the answer.

Substitute for the variable in the symbol question

You see a problem with a strange symbol. It may be a letter with a symbol, a triangle, a star, or a circle with a dot as in the following example. You've never seen it before, and you're not sure what it means. Don't worry — the GRE always tells you what the symbol means, and the meaning is always unique to the specific question.

The symbol is included in a short explanation that looks something like this:

$$a \odot b \odot c = \frac{(a+b)}{(b+c)}$$

A question always follows the explanation, which looks something like this:

$$3 \odot 4 \odot 5 =$$

Solve this problem by using the preceding explanation and following these steps:

1. **Substitute the variables in the explanation with the numbers provided in the question.**

   For the preceding explanation, substitute *a, b,* and *c,* with 3, 4, and 5 respectively.

   $$3 \odot 4 \odot 5 = \frac{(3+4)}{(4+5)}$$

2. **Simplify the fraction to get the answer.**

   $$\frac{(3+4)}{(4+5)} = \frac{7}{9}$$

$$[\![x]\!] = \frac{2x}{x+2}$$

$$[\![-4]\!] =$$

To solve, do the following:

1. **Substitute the variable in the explanation.**

   Substitute *x* with –4.

   $$[\![-4]\!] = \frac{2(-4)}{-4+2}$$

2. **Simplify the fraction for your answer.**

   $$\frac{2(-4)}{-4+2} = \frac{-8}{-2} = 4$$

Substitute for the variable in the function question

You can recognize a function question by the distinctive $f(x)$. The letters aren't always *f* and *x*, (for example, $g[h]$ is common,) but the setup is always the same, so you can recognize these questions regardless of the letters. You may see a problem like this:

$f(x) = (2x)^3$. Solve for $f(2)$.

Take the same actions you did in the previous section: Substitute the number for the *x* (or whichever letter is in the parentheses). In other words, just plug in the 2 where you see an *x* in the explanation.

$$f(2) = (2 \times 2)^3 = 4^3 = 64$$

Try another one:

$f(x) = x + x^2 + x^3$. Solve for $f(10)$.

Just plug the 10 in for the *x*: $f(10) = 10 + 10^2 + 10^3 = 10 + 100 + 1{,}000 = 1{,}110$.

Mastering the Fundamentals of Algebra

To correctly answer algebra questions on the GRE, you must be able to

- Solve for *x* in an equation.
- Use the FOIL method to multiply binomials. Refer to the later section "Multiplying with the FOIL method" for more in-depth information about FOIL.
- Factor down a quadratic equation and take an algebraic expression from its final form back to its original form of two sets of parentheses.

The following sections run down the important basics of algebra you need to know in order to handle what the GRE throws at you.

Solving for x

To solve for *x*, follow these steps:

1. **Isolate the variable.**

   In other words, get all the *x*'s on one side and all the numbers on the other side.

2. **Add or subtract all the x's on one side; add or subtract all the non-x's on the other side.**
3. **Divide both sides of the equation by the number in front of the x.**

Now try it with this equation:

$3x + 7 = 9x - 5$

1. **Isolate the variable.**

   Move the $3x$ to the right side of the equation, and *change the sign* to make it $-3x$. Move the -5 to the left, and *change the sign* to make it $+5$. You now have $7 + 5 = 9x - 3x$.

   Forgetting to change the sign is one of the most common, careless mistakes people make. The test-makers realize this tendency and often include trap answer choices. If you think of subtracting the same amount from both sides of the equation, you're less likely to make this common mistake.

2. **Add or subtract the x's on one side; add or subtract the non-x's on the other side.**

$$7+5=9x-3x$$
$$12=6x$$

3. **Divide both sides by the number next to the x.**

$$\frac{12}{6}=\frac{6x}{6}$$
$$x=2$$

To check your answer, plug the 2 back into the original equation to make sure it works:

$$3(2)+7=9(2)-5$$
$$6+7=18-5$$
$$13=13$$

Another option, though time-consuming, is to solve the problem by trial and error. When asked to solve for x and presented with a list of answer choices, try each answer choice until you find the one that works. Sticking with the example of $3x + 7 = 9x - 5$, suppose these are your answer choices:

Ⓐ 5

Ⓑ $3\frac{1}{2}$

Ⓒ 2

Ⓓ 0

Ⓔ −2

Keep life simple by starting with answer choices that are easy to figure in your head. In this case, the easiest answer choice is 0, because that would make $3x = 0$ and $9x = 0$, making $7 = -5$; scratch that one off the list of options. The choices 2, −2, and 5 are also easy to plug in. If none of the easy answers work, then you can go back and try $3\frac{1}{2}$. *Correct answer:* Choice **(C)**.

Multiplying with the FOIL method

When multiplying any number by a *binomial* (a value expressed as the sum or difference of two numbers), you use the *distributive property,* which tells you to multiply all the values inside the parentheses by the multiplier to the left of the parentheses. For example:

$9(3x + 2y) = (9 \times 3x) + (9 \times 2y) = 27x + 18y$

When multiplying two binomials, such as $(a + b)(a - b)$, you also use the distributive property. Basically, you multiply everything in one set of parentheses by everything in the other set of parentheses, and then add up all the results. This is also known as the FOIL method, which stands for *First, Outer, Inner, Last*. With the equation $(a + b)(a - b)$, you do the following:

1. **Multiply the *First* variables:** $a \times a = a^2$.
2. **Multiply the *Outer* variables:** $a \times (-b) = -ab$.
3. **Multiply the *Inner* variables:** $b \times a = ba$ (which is the same as ab).
4. **Multiply the *Last* variables:** $b \times (-b) = -b^2$.
5. **Combine like terms:** $a^2 - ab + ab - b^2 = a^2 - b^2$. (The $-ab + ab$ cancel each other out.)

Like terms are two or more terms with the same variable(s) and power(s). For example, you may combine $3x^3 - 1x^3$, because the two terms have the same variable raised to the same power, x^3. You can't, however, combine $3x^3$ and $1y^3$ or $1x^5$, because in the first case, the variables differ, and in the second case, the powers differ.

When multiplying, the order doesn't matter. This means $ab = ba$.

Try another one: $(3a + b)(a - 2b)$.

1. **Multiply the *First* terms:** $3a \times a = 3a^2$.
2. **Multiply the *Outer* terms:** $3a \times (-2b) = -6ab$.
3. **Multiply the *Inner* terms:** $b \times a = ba$ (which is the same as ab).
4. **Multiply the *Last* terms:** $b \times (-2b) = -2b^2$.
5. **Combine like terms ($-6ab + ab = -5ab$) to get the final answer:** $3a^2 - 5ab - 2b^2$.

Memorize the following three FOIL problems so that you don't have to bother working them out every time. Knowing these problems by heart can save you time and help you avoid careless mistakes on the actual exam.

1. **$(a + b)^2 = a^2 + 2ab + b^2$**

   You can prove this equation using FOIL: $(a + b)(a + b)$.

   a. **Multiply the *First* terms:** $a \times a = a^2$.

   b. **Multiply the *Outer* terms:** $a \times b = ab$.

   c. **Multiply the *Inner* terms:** $b \times a = ba$ (which is the same as ab).

   d. **Multiply the *Last* terms:** $b \times b = b^2$.

   e. **Combine like terms ($ab + ab = 2ab$) to get the final answer:** $a^2 + 2ab + b^2$.

2. **$(a - b)^2 = a^2 - 2ab + b^2$**

   You can also prove this equation using FOIL: $(a - b)(a - b)$.

   a. **Multiply the *First* terms:** $a \times a = a^2$.

   b. **Multiply the *Outer* terms:** $a \times (-b) = -ab$.

   c. **Multiply the *Inner* terms:** $(-b) \times a = -ba$ (which is the same as $-ab$).

   d. **Multiply the *Last* terms:** $(-b) \times (-b) = b^2$.

   e. **Combine like terms ($-ab - ab = -2ab$) to get the final answer:** $a^2 - 2ab + b^2$.

Be careful to note that the b^2 at the end is *positive,* not negative, because multiplying a negative times a negative produces a positive.

3. **$(a - b)(a + b) = a^2 - b^2$**

   You can also prove this equation with FOIL: $(a - b)(a + b)$.

   a. **Multiply the *First* terms:** $a \times a = a^2$.

   b. **Multiply the *Outer* terms:** $a \times b = ab$.

   c. **Multiply the *Inner* terms:** $(-b) \times a = -ba$ (which is the same as $-ab$).

   d. **Multiply the *Last* terms:** $(-b) \times b = -b^2$.

   e. **Combine like terms ($ab - ab = 0$) to get the final answer:** $a^2 - b^2$.

Unfoiling: Also known as factoring

As often as you foil terms on the GRE, you also *factor* them, which is the same as unfoiling. Factoring is the third algebraic trick you need to know for the GRE: taking an algebraic expression from its final form back to its original form of two binomials.

Given $x^2 + 13x + 42 = 0$, what are the two possible values for x? Work this question one step at a time:

1. **Draw two sets of parentheses.**

   $(\quad)(\quad) = 0$

2. **Fill in the *First* terms.**

   To get x^2, the *First* terms have to be x and x.

   $(x\quad)(x\quad) = 0$

3. **Look now at the *Last* terms.**

   You need two numbers that equal +42 when multiplied together. You have several possibilities: 42×1, 21×2, or 6×7. You can even have two negative numbers: -42×-1, -21×-2, or -6×-7. Because you aren't sure which one to choose yet, go on to the next step.

4. **Look at the *Inner* terms.**

   You have to add two values to get +13. What's the first one that springs to mind? Probably 6 + 7 — one of the possibilities in the preceding step. Plug it in and try it.

   $(x + 6)(x + 7) = x^2 + 7x + 6x + 42 = x^2 + 13x + 42$

Great work, but you're not finished yet. If the whole equation equals zero, then either $x + 6 = 0$ or $x + 7 = 0$, because the only way to make a product zero is to make one of the factors zero. Therefore, x can equal -6 or -7.

Note that x doesn't equal both -6 and -7; it equals one or the other, and you don't know which one. That's why the question is phrased, "What are the two *possible* values for x?"

With a multiple-choice problem, you can simply try the answer choices provided. Sometimes doing this is easier than factoring the expression, but it's good to have this skill down just in case.

Dealing with Roots and Radicals

You're likely to bump into at least a couple problems on the GRE that include roots or radicals. A *root* is a number that's multiplied a certain number of times by itself; for example, 3 is the square root of 9 ($3 \times 3 = 9$) and the cube root of 27 ($3 \times 3 \times 3 = 27$). A *radical* is another way of expressing a root; for example, the square root of 9 may be represented as $\sqrt{9}$.The cube root of 27 may be shown as $\sqrt[3]{27}$.

The following sections point out all types of problems you may encounter on the GRE related to roots and radicals. But first, you must acquire the all-important skill of simplifying roots and radicals.

Simplifying radicals and roots

When possible, simplify radicals to get rid of them. *Simplifying* basically means reducing the radical to its most manageable form, ideally getting rid of the radical altogether. To simplify a radical, you generally factor what's inside the radical and then pull out any squared factors. Here are a few examples where simplification removes the radical completely:

$$\sqrt{4} = \sqrt{2 \times 2} = 2$$
$$\sqrt{9} = \sqrt{3 \times 3} = 3$$
$$\sqrt{16} = \sqrt{4 \times 4} = 4$$
$$\sqrt{25} = \sqrt{5 \times 5} = 5$$

In some cases, removing the radical isn't such a neat and tidy operation, but you can still reduce it to make it easier to work with. In problems where you can't reduce the radical to a whole number, the GRE doesn't expect you to, and the correct answer choice will include a radical. Here's an example of a radical you can't reduce to an integer but can simplify:

$$\sqrt{104} = \sqrt{4 \times 26} = \sqrt{4} \times \sqrt{26} = 2\sqrt{26}$$

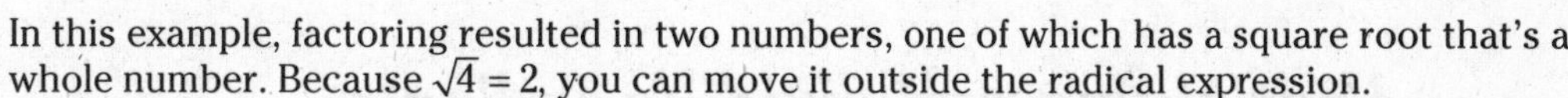

In this example, factoring resulted in two numbers, one of which has a square root that's a whole number. Because $\sqrt{4} = 2$, you can move it outside the radical expression.

Roots don't always equal whole numbers, such as 2, 3, 4, and 5. If you encounter $\sqrt{7}$, for example, look at the answer choices. Usually, the answer says $\sqrt{7}$, and you can leave it at that.

However, sometimes the question may ask for what "is approximately equal to" or "is closest to," and that means you have to estimate the radical, as explained next.

Estimating the radical

When asked to estimate $\sqrt{7}$, consider that it falls between $\sqrt{4}$ and $\sqrt{9}$. Because $\sqrt{4} = 2$ and $\sqrt{9} = 3$, $\sqrt{7}$ is roughly 2.5. Knowing the answer is between 2 and 3 is precise enough to answer the GRE question. You never have to estimate it more precisely than that.

Memorize $\sqrt{2} = 1.41$. Don't worry about memorizing any of the other radicals, but knowing the answer to $\sqrt{2}$ can get you out of a pinch.

Adding and subtracting radicals

To add and subtract radicals, adhere to the following two rules:

1. **To add or subtract *like* radicals, add or subtract the number in front of the radical (your old friend, the numerical coefficient).**

   $$2\sqrt{7}+5\sqrt{7}=7\sqrt{7}$$

   $$9\sqrt{13}-4\sqrt{13}=5\sqrt{13}$$

   The absence of a coefficient in front of a radical means the coefficient is 1, so $\sqrt{3}+\sqrt{3}+\sqrt{3}=3\sqrt{3}$.

2. **You *can't* add or subtract unlike radicals (just as you can't add or subtract unlike variables).**

   $6\sqrt{5}+4\sqrt{3}=6\sqrt{5}+4\sqrt{3}$ (You can't add the two and get $10\sqrt{8}$.)

Don't glance at a problem, see that the radicals aren't the same, and immediately assume that you can't add the two terms. You may be able to simplify one radical to make it match the radical in the other term.

$$\sqrt{52}+\sqrt{13}=$$
$$\sqrt{4\times 13}+\sqrt{13}=$$
$$2\sqrt{13}+\sqrt{13}=3\sqrt{13}$$

You can't add or subtract using the numbers contained under the radical:

$$\sqrt{64}+\sqrt{16}\neq\sqrt{80}$$

You have to calculate the root of the radical and then apply the operation:

$$\sqrt{64}+\sqrt{16}=$$
$$8+4=12$$

Multiplying and dividing radicals

To multiply and divide radicals, follow these two rules:

1. **When you multiply or divide radicals, put all the numbers inside one radical and then multiply or divide the numbers.**

   $$\sqrt{5}\times\sqrt{6}=\sqrt{5\times 6}=\sqrt{30}$$

   $$\sqrt{15}\div\sqrt{5}=\sqrt{15\div 5}=\sqrt{3}$$

2. **If you have numbers in front of the radicals, multiply or divide them as well.**

   Because the order doesn't matter when multiplying, move the pieces around to make them easier to multiply.

   $$\left(6\sqrt{3}\right)\left(4\sqrt{2}\right)=$$
   $$(6)(4)\left(\sqrt{3\times 2}\right)=$$
   $$(24)\left(\sqrt{6}\right)=24\sqrt{6}$$

   Of course, don't rearrange numbers when dividing.

$$6\sqrt{16} \div 2\sqrt{4} =$$
$$(6 \div 2)\left(\sqrt{16 \div 4}\right) =$$
$$(3)\left(\sqrt{4}\right) =$$
$$(3)(2) = 6$$

$37\sqrt{5} \times 3\sqrt{6}$

Ⓐ $40\sqrt{11}$

Ⓑ $40\sqrt{30}$

Ⓒ $111\sqrt{11}$

Ⓓ $111\sqrt{30}$

Ⓔ 1,221

You can easily figure out that $37 \times 3 = 90 + 21 = 111$ and that $\sqrt{5} \times \sqrt{6} = \sqrt{30}$, so the answer is $111\sqrt{30}$. That's just straightforward multiplication. *Correct answer:* Choice **(D).**

Working radicals from the inside out

When you see an operation under the radical, work it first, and then take the square root of the answer.

$$\sqrt{\frac{1}{3} + \frac{1}{9}}$$

First, solve for $\frac{1}{3} + \frac{1}{9}$. The common denominator is 9, making the numerators 1 and 3, resulting in $\frac{4}{9}$. *Now* take the square roots:

$$\sqrt{4} = 2$$
$$\sqrt{9} = 3$$

Your final answer is $\frac{2}{3}$.

Traversing the X and Y Axes with Coordinate Geometry

Coordinate geometry is where algebra and geometry meet — a method of describing points, lines, and shapes by using algebraic expressions. To begin to understand coordinate geometry, you first need to get your bearings on the coordinate plane.

The *coordinate plane* is a two-dimensional area defined by a horizontal *x*-axis and a vertical *y*-axis that intersect at a *point of origin* labeled (0, 0). Each point is labeled using an ordered pair (*x*, *y*) with the first number in the parentheses indicating how far to the right or left of (0, 0) the point is and the second number indicating how far above or below (0, 0) the point is.

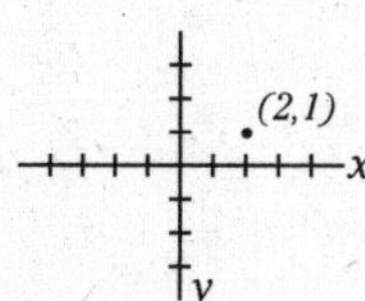

A line connecting points whose x- and y-coordinates are the same forms a 45-degree angle with each axis to the origin.

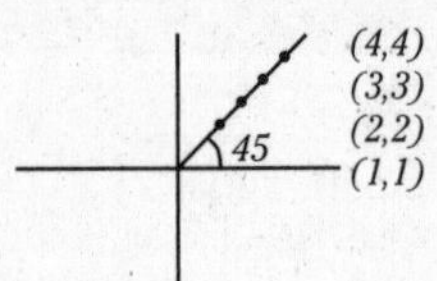

The following sections reveal need-to-know information about how to solve different coordinate geometry questions you may encounter on the GRE.

Using formulas to solve problems

To answer questions related to coordinate geometry, you need to know a few key formulas and how to use them.

Distance formula

If you're asked to find the distance between two points, you can use the *distance formula,* which is based on the Pythagorean theorem, as explained in Chapter 10. In a right triangle, using the lengths of the two shorter sides, you can determine the length of the longest side (the *hypotenuse*) or, as expressed as an equation, $a^2 + b^2 = c^2$ where a and b are the lengths of the shorter sides and c is the length of the longest side. Another way to write it is $c = \sqrt{a^2 + b^2}$.

In coordinate geometry, you use this formula along with the coordinates of two points to specify the length of the sides. Given two points, one with coordinates (x_1, y_1) and the other with coordinates (x_2, y_2), the length of one of the shorter sides is $x_2 - x_1$, and the length of the other shorter side is $y_2 - y_1$. Suppose you're asked to calculate the distance between two points with coordinates (1, 2) and (7, 10). On the coordinate system, the right triangle would look like so, and the length of one short side would be $x_2 - x_1 = 7 - 1 = 6$, and the length of the other short side would be $y_2 - y_1 = 10 - 2 = 8$.

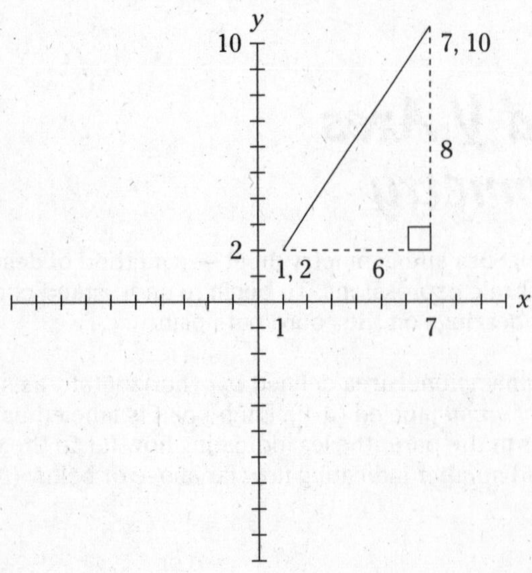

Knowing the coordinates of the two points, you can use the distance formula to calculate the length of the hypotenuse, which equals the distance between the two points:

$$\begin{aligned} distance &= \sqrt{(x_2 - x_1)^2 + (y_2 - y_1)^2} \\ &= \sqrt{(7-1)^2 + (10-2)^2} \\ &= \sqrt{6^2 + 8^2} \\ &= \sqrt{36+64} \\ &= \sqrt{100} \\ &= 10 \end{aligned}$$

You can memorize the formula or draw the grid and triangle and use the Pythagorean theorem — either way works!

Find the distance from (9, 4) to (8, 6).

$$\begin{aligned} distance &= \sqrt{(x_2 - x_1)^2 + (y_2 - y_1)^2} \\ &= \sqrt{(8-9)^2 + (6-4)^2} \\ &= \sqrt{-1^2 + 2^2} \\ &= \sqrt{1+4} \\ &= \sqrt{5} \end{aligned}$$

Slope formula

The *slope of a line* is defined as rise over run — the distance the line rises compared to its horizontal distance. To calculate the slope of a line, use the following formula:

$$slope = \frac{y_2 - y_1}{x_2 - x_1}$$

What is the slope connecting the two points L (–1, –2) and M (4, 6)?

$$slope = \frac{y_2 - y_1}{x_2 - x_1}$$

$$\begin{aligned} slope &= \frac{6-(-2)}{4-(-1)} \\ &= \frac{6+2}{4+1} \\ &= \frac{8}{5} \end{aligned}$$

Equation of a line

The *equation of a line* (also known as the *slope intercept form*) is $y = mx + b$, where x and y are coordinates of any point on the line, m is the slope, and b is the y-intercept (the point at which the line representing the equation intersects the y-axis). To find the y-intercept, either plug in zero for x or just look at the b.

Midpoint formula

If asked to find the midpoint of a line segment defined by two ordered pairs, use the following midpoint formula:

$$midpoint = \left(\frac{x_1 + x_2}{2}, \frac{y_1 + y_2}{2} \right)$$

Performing linear algebraic equations

Linear algebraic equations are in the form $Ax + By = C$, where neither A nor B is zero. The solution of the equation is any ordered pair that makes the result true. To solve these types of problems, you plug in values for x and y that make the expression true. For example, in the equation $2x + 3y = 24$, the following ordered pairs, to name a few, all make the result true: (0, 8), (6, 4), and (–3, 10).

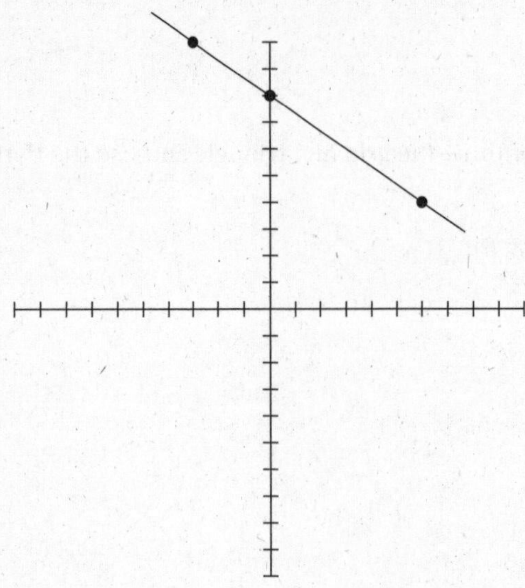

You may also encounter linear equations in a slightly different format; for example, instead of $2x + 3y = 24$, you may see $3y = 24 - 2x$ or $2x = 24 - 3y$. Regardless of how the equation is presented, you can usually find two points on the line by setting x to 0 and solving for y and then setting y to 0 and solving for x:

$$\begin{aligned} 2x+3y &= 24 \\ 2(0)+3y &= 24 \\ 3y &= 24 \\ y &= 8 \\ x,y &= (0,8) \\ 2x+3(0) &= 24 \\ 2x &= 24 \\ x &= 12 \\ x,y &= (12,0) \end{aligned}$$

If you need to determine which (x, y) coordinates make a linear equation true, substitute the coordinate pairs provided in the answers to identify pairs that work and exclude pairs that don't.

Identify all of the following that make the expression $5x + 3y = 27$ true.

Select all correct answers.

A (0, 9)

B (6, 1)

C (9, –6)

D (5, 2)

E (6, –1)

F (3, –2)

To solve this problem, substitute the coordinates provided into the equation:

$5(0) + 3(9) = 0 + 27 = 27$

$5(6) + 3(1) = 30 + 3 = 33$

$5(9) + 3(-6) = 45 - 18 = 27$

$5(5) + 3(2) = 25 + 6 = 31$

$5(6) + 3(-1) = 30 - 3 = 27$

$5(3) + 3(-2) = 15 - 6 = 9$

Correct answers: Choices **(A), (C),** and **(E).**

Solving simultaneous equations

Although linear equations have an infinite number of solutions, simultaneous equations have a single solution that makes both equations correct. The single solution is the intersection of the lines represented by the two equations. To solve simultaneous equations, use the method of addition or substitution, as explained in the following sections.

Method of addition

If one pair of coefficients is equal but opposite, such as $3y$ and $-3y$, then add the equations to cancel one unknown and solve for the other unknown.

$$\begin{aligned} 5x - 2y &= 4 \\ x + 2y &= 8 \end{aligned}$$

Because the equations include a pair of coefficients equal but opposite ($-2y$ and $2y$), first use the method of addition to solve for x:

$$\begin{aligned} 5x - 2y &= 4 \\ x + 2y &= 8 \\ \hline 6x + 0 &= 12 \\ x &= 2 \end{aligned}$$

To find the value for y, you can then substitute the value of x into either equation:

$$\begin{aligned}5(2)-2y&=4\\10-2y&=4\\-2y&=4-10\\-2y&=-6\\y&=3\end{aligned}$$

If you were to graph the equations, you would see that the ordered pair (2, 3) is the point where the two lines intersect.

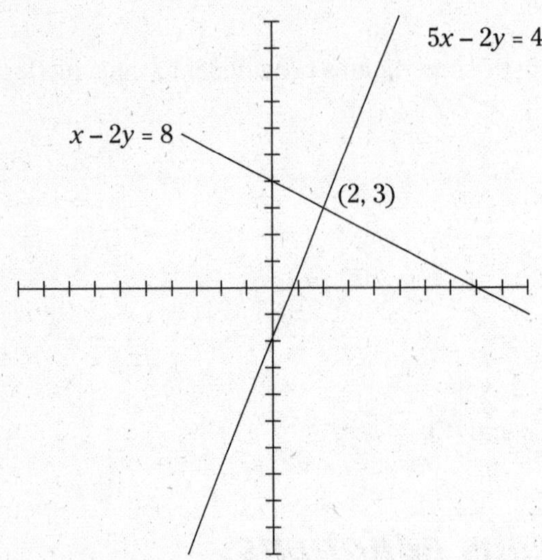

Method of substitution

One sure-fire way to solve simultaneous linear equations is with the method of substitution. Just follow these steps:

1. **Choose one equation and solve for one of its unknowns in terms of the other unknown.**
2. **Substitute the result from Step 1 into the other equation and solve for the unknown.**
3. **Plug the value for the first unknown into either equation and solve for the other unknown.**

$$\begin{aligned}5x-2y&=4\\x+2y&=8\end{aligned}$$

In this example, the second equation is the easier of the two to start with:

$$x=8-2y$$

Now, substitute $8-2y$ for x in the first equation and solve for y:

$$\begin{aligned}5(8-2y)-2y&=4\\40-10y-2y&=4\\-12y&=4-40\\-12y&=-36\\y&=3\end{aligned}$$

Finally, plug the value you just determined into either equation and solve for the other unknown:

$$\begin{aligned} x+2(3)&=8 \\ x+6&=8 \\ x&=8-6 \\ x&=2 \end{aligned}$$

Recognizing Patterns in Numerical Sequences

GRE sequence problems challenge you to identify the patterns in numerical sequences and then identify the next numbers in the sequence. To improve your ability to answer these questions correctly without wasting too much time, you should be able to identify various types of sequences, as described in the following sections.

Arithmetic

In an *arithmetic sequence*, each successive number is determined by adding or subtracting a fixed value from the previous number:

1, 5, 9, 13, 17, . . .

In this sequence, each number is 4 more than the previous number, so the next number is 21.

Identify all terms that can be in the following sequence:

15, 10.5, 6, 1.5, . . .

[A] –2.5

[B] –3

[C] –7

[D] –7.5

[E] 12

[F] –12

If you recognize that each subsequent number is 4.5 less than the previous number, solving this problem is just a matter of doing the math:

$$\begin{aligned} 1.5-4.5&=-3 \\ -3-4.5&=-7.5 \\ -7.5-4.5&=-12 \end{aligned}$$

The correct answers are **(B)**, **(D)**, and **(F)**.

Avoid careless mistakes by using the calculator instead of trying to crunch the numbers in your head.

Geometric

In a *geometric sequence,* each successive number is obtained by multiplying or dividing the previous number by a fixed value:

4, 8, 16, 32, 64, . . .

In this sequence, each number is double the previous number.

Fibonacci

In a *Fibonacci sequence*, each successive number is obtained by adding the two previous numbers:

3, 6, 9, 15, 24, 39, . . .

In this example, 9 = 6 + 3, 15 = 9 + 6, 24 = 15 + 9, and so on.

Not all sequence problems fit into these simple patterns. For example, they may combine addition and multiplication, like the following sequence:

4, 18, 60, 186, 564, . . .

In this sequence, each subsequent number is obtained by adding 2 to the previous number and then multiplying by 3.

You may also encounter a variation of the Fibonacci problem in which the question provides you with information about the sequence other than the starting numbers.

The sixth number in a sequence of numbers is 61, and each number after the first number in the sequence is equal to the number immediately preceding it plus 7. What is the second number in the sequence?

To answer a question like this, start by drawing spaces for the numbers, so you can better visualize the sequence. You know you have six numbers, the sixth of which is 61, so your sketch should look something like this:

____, ____, ____, ____, ____, 61

Now, working from right to left, subtract 7 from each number and you get the following:

26, 33, 40, 47, 54, 61

The second number in the sequence is 33, so that's your answer.

Sequential terms

In a *sequential term* question, the term is indicated with a letter, such as a, and counted with a subscript number, for example: $a_1, a_2, a_3, a_4, a_5, \ldots, a_n$.

You're given one of the values for a and an equation that describes the relationship between the sequential terms, such as this:

$a_1 = 10$

The 1 in a_1 means "the *first a*," and the statement tells you that the first a has a value of 10. Be sure not to confuse the subscript number with the value of that particular a.

Next is the equation:

$$a_{n+1} = a_n + 3$$

Though the value of n (the subscript of a) changes, it only has one value at a time in the equation. For example, if $n = 1$, then $n + 1 = 2$. The equation can thus be rewritten as this:

$$a_2 = a_1 + 3$$

or this:

$$a_3 = a_2 + 3$$

or even this:

"The next a = the current a plus 3."

In other words, if $a_1 = 10$, then $a_2 = 13$, $a_3 = 16$, and so forth. Your question is based on this pattern. For example, "What is the value of a_6?" Now that you understand the pattern, the question is easy to answer — just count 'em out:

$$a_1 = 10,\ a_2 = 13,\ a_3 = 16,\ a_4 = 19,\ a_5 = 22,\ a_6 = 25$$

Chapter 10

Shaping Up Your Geometry Skills

In This Chapter

- Getting straight with lines and angles
- Working with polygons
- Tackling a host of triangle and quadrilateral questions
- Conquering common circle questions
- Calculating the volume and surface area of solids

Geometry is all about the mathematics locked in lines, angles, triangles, rectangles, squares, circles, cubes, tubes, and more. This chapter introduces you to the many shapes you're likely to encounter on the GRE and the corresponding equations required for answering geometry questions. You also get some hands-on practice answering a few sample questions at the end.

Exploring Lines and Angles

The fundamental components of many geometric shapes are lines and angles, so before tackling shapes, wrap your brain around lines and angles.

Don't put blind trust in drawings that accompany questions. For example, an image may appear to contain a right angle, but if the right-angle box is missing and the question doesn't specify it as a right angle, you can't assume it is. In addition, images may not be drawn to scale, so when a question presents an image, look for numbers in the question or on the figure that specify dimensions. Two sides of a triangle, for example, may appear to be equal when one is actually slightly longer than the other. ***Remember:*** If the drawing actually has a label that says, "***Note:*** Figure not drawn to scale," then it's *way* off.

Lines

You've probably heard the term *straight line,* but in geometry, that phrase is a little redundant. All *lines* are straight. If a line curves, it's not a line — it's a curve. Also, unless a line is specifically referred to as a *line segment,* assume it goes on forever. If the line has one *endpoint* (point where the line starts) and the other end has an arrow indicating it goes on forever, it's a *ray.*

Parallel lines never cross and are represented by the symbol $||$. Perpendicular lines cross at right angles and are represented by the symbol $\perp$. A *perpendicular bisector* is a line that passes through the midpoint of a line segment and is perpendicular to it.

Angles

Angles are a big part of GRE geometry problems. An *angle* basically is the space between two rays that share an endpoint. Fortunately, understanding angles is easy after you memorize the different angle types and a few key concepts, as explained in this section.

Finding an angle is usually a matter of simple addition or subtraction. In addition to the rules in the following sections, these three rules apply to the angles on the GRE:

- You aren't going to see negative angles.
- You aren't going to see zero angles.
- You most likely aren't going to see any fractional angles. (For example, an angle won't measure $45\frac{1}{2}$ degrees or $32\frac{3}{4}$ degrees.) On the GRE, angles are whole numbers. If you're plugging in a number for an angle, plug in a whole number, such as 30, 45, or 90.

Right angle

Right angles are 90 degrees and are represented by perpendicular lines with a small box where the two lines meet.

ℓ_2

ℓ_2

Right angle

Watch out for lines that appear to be perpendicular but really aren't. An angle is a right angle *only* if (A) the description says, "This is a right angle," (B) you see the perpendicular symbol (⊥), or (C) you see the box in the angle (which is the most common). Otherwise, you can't assume the angle is 90 degrees.

$a°$ $b°$

Not necessarily a right angle

Acute angle

An *acute angle* is any angle greater than 0 degrees but less than 90 degrees.

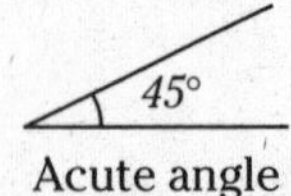

Acute angle

Acute means sharp, or perceptive, so an acute angle is sharp.

Obtuse angle

An *obtuse angle* is any angle greater than 90 degrees but less than 180 degrees.

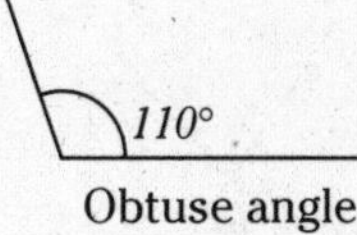

Obtuse angle

Angles around a point total 360 degrees — just as in a circle.

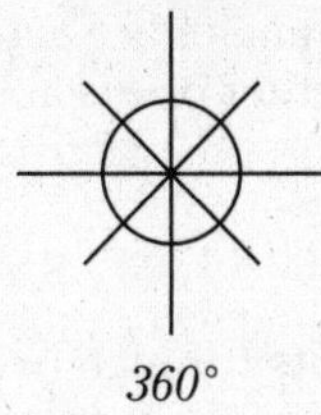

Complementary angles

Complementary angles together form a right angle: 90 degrees.

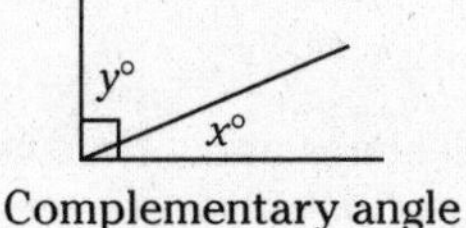

Complementary angle

Supplementary angles

Supplementary angles together form a straight line: 180 degrees.

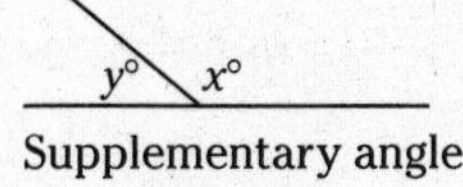

Supplementary angle

To avoid mixing the terms *supplementary* and *complementary,* just remember that *c* stands for both *corner* (the lines form a 90-degree corner angle) and *complementary;* and *s* stands for both *straight* and *supplementary.*

Vertical angles

Vertical angles are the angles opposite one another where two lines cross. Vertical angles have equal measures.

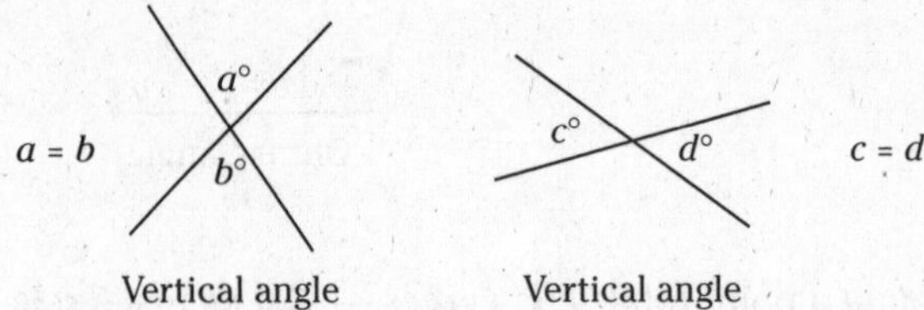

Vertical angle   Vertical angle

Just remember that vertical angles are across the *vertex* (the point where intersecting lines cross) from each other, whether one is above the other (vertical) or they're side by side (horizontal).

Transversal angles

A *transversal* is a line that cuts through two parallel lines. *Transversal angles* are the angles directly across from each other on the parallel lines and have the same measures.

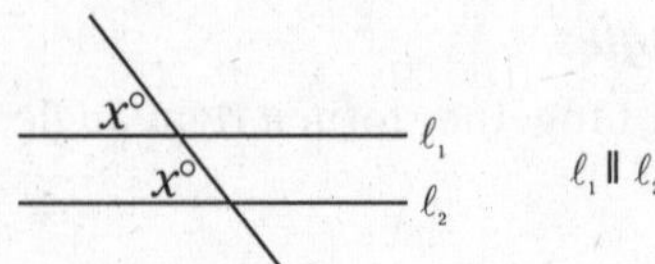

When you see two parallel lines and a transversal, number the angles. Start in the upper-right corner with 1 and go clockwise. For the second batch of angles, start in the upper-right corner with 5 and go clockwise:

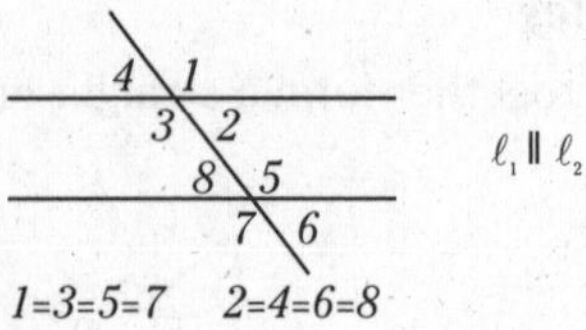

Note that all the odd-numbered angles are equal, as are all the even-numbered angles. Also, never assume the lines are parallel unless the question states that they are or the image indicates parallel lines as in the preceding figure; here, $\ell_1 \parallel \ell_2$ indicates that the two lines are parallel.

Be careful not to zigzag back and forth when numbering, like this:

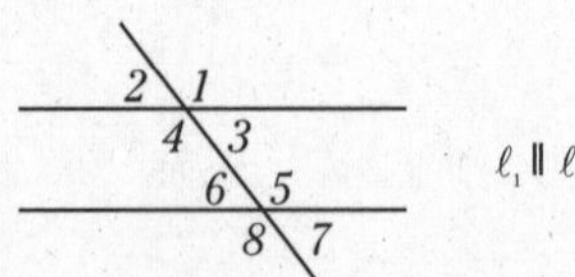

If you zig when you should've zagged, the fact that all even-numbered angles are equal to one another and all odd-numbered angles are equal to one another no longer holds true.

Recognizing the Many Sides of Polygons

A *polygon* is any closed shape consisting of line segments, which qualifies everything from a *triangle* (three sides) to a *dodecagon* (a dozen sides) and beyond as a polygon. The polygons you're most likely going to encounter on the GRE are triangles and *quadrilaterals* (four sides). Table 10-1 lists the names of a few others you may bump into.

Table 10-1 Polygons

Number of Sides	*Name*
5	Pentagon
6	Hexagon (think of *x* in six and *x* in hex)
7	Heptagon
8	Octagon
9	Nonagon
10	Decagon

Polygons that have all sides equal and all angles equal are considered to be *regular* or *equilateral polygons*. For example, an equilateral triangle is a regular triangle, and a square is a regular quadrilateral. Though *equilateral* usually refers to a triangle, it could actually define any polygon as having equal sides and angles, such as a square. Another term is *equiangular,* which defines a polygon with equal angles but different side lengths, such as a rectangle.

The GRE usually doesn't ask for the areas of any polygons with more than four sides. It may, however, ask you to find the *perimeter,* which is just the sum of the lengths of all the sides. The following explains what you do need to know about polygons for the GRE.

Determining total interior angle measure

Because you may be asked to find the total interior angle measure of a particular polygon, keep this formula in mind (where *n* stands for the number of sides):

$$(n-2)180$$

For example, the interior angles of the following polygons are

- **Triangle:** $(3-2)180 = 1 \times 180 = 180°$
- **Quadrilateral:** $(4-2)180 = 2 \times 180 = 360°$
- **Pentagon:** $(5-2)180 = 3 \times 180 = 540°$
- **Hexagon:** $(6-2)180 = 4 \times 180 = 720°$
- **Heptagon:** $(7-2)180 = 5 \times 180 = 900°$
- **Octagon:** $(8-2)180 = 6 \times 180 = 1{,}080°$
- **Nonagon:** $(9-2)180 = 7 \times 180 = 1{,}260°$
- **Decagon:** $(10-2)180 = 8 \times 180 = 1{,}440°$

Proportional multiplication is a great timesaving trick. Numbers are in proportion, and you can fiddle with them to make multiplication easier. Suppose you're going to multiply 5×180. Most people need to write down the problem and then work through it. But because the numbers are in proportion, you can double one and halve the other: Double 5 to make it 10. Halve 180 to make it 90. Now your problem is 10×90, which you can multiply in your head to get 900.

Try another one: 3×180. Double the first number: $3 \times 2 = 6$. Halve the second number: $\frac{180}{2} = 90$. Then multiply: $6 \times 90 = 540$.

Finding one interior angle

If you're asked to find the average measure of one angle in a polygon, use the following formula:

$$\frac{(n-2)180}{n}$$

Here, *n* stands for the number of sides (which is the same as the number of angles). So to find an interior angle of a pentagon:

$$\frac{(5-2)\times 180}{5} = \frac{3\times 180}{5} = \frac{540}{5} = 108°$$

Because all angles are equal in a regular polygon, the same formula applies to one angle in a regular polygon.

You can't solve for just one angle of an irregular polygon by using this formula. If the question doesn't specifically state that the polygon is regular or equilateral, then you can't assume it is.

Understanding Triangles from Top to Bottom

Although comprised of a mere three sides, the *triangle* is a key figure in geometry, especially on the GRE. Understand how triangles work, and you're well on your way to mastering other polygons. The following sections introduce you to the different types of triangles and explain how to do the math related to triangles.

Recognizing triangle types

Triangles come in three basic types: equilateral, isosceles, and right, as described in the following sections.

Equilateral triangle

An *equilateral triangle* has three equal sides and three equal angles. This can also be called an *equiangular triangle.*

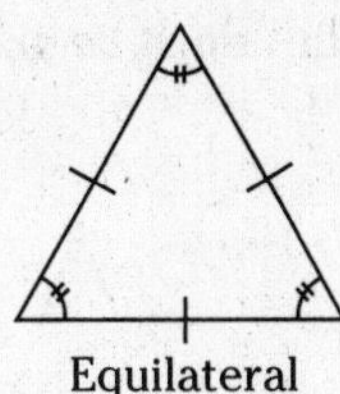

Equilateral

Isosceles triangle

An *isosceles triangle* has two equal sides and two equal angles. The angles opposite the equal sides are the two equal angles.

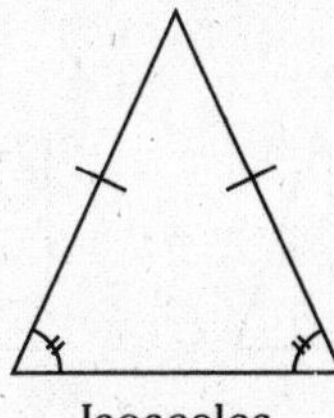

Isosceles

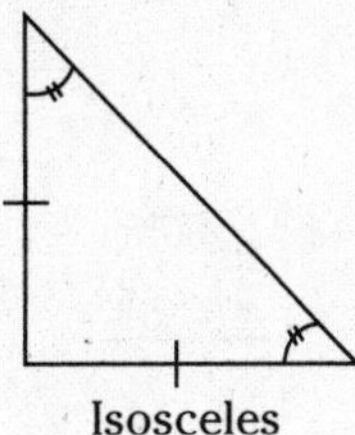

Isosceles

Right triangle

A *right* triangle has one 90-degree angle.

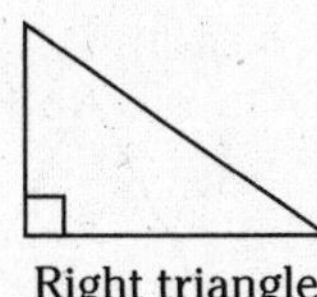

Right triangle

Noting key characteristics

Triangles have some notable characteristics that you may need to know to field some of the geometry questions on the test. The following points bring you up to speed:

- **The largest angle is opposite the longest side.** And, as you may surmise, the smallest angle is opposite the shortest side.

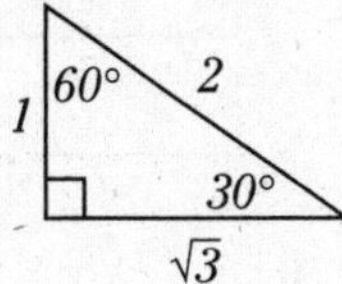

- **The sum of any two sides must be greater than the length of the remaining side.** This fact is often written as $a + b > c$ where a, b, and c are the sides of the triangle.

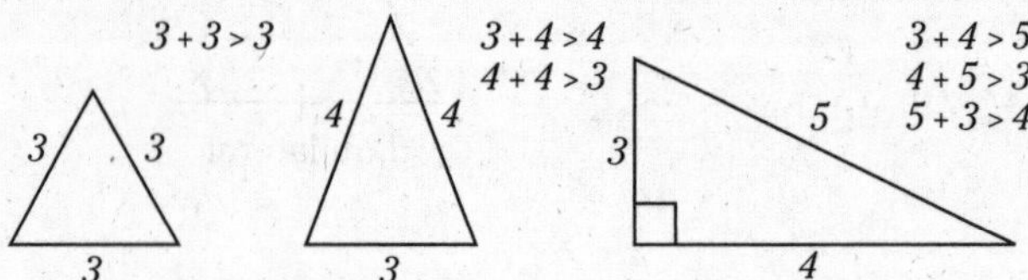

- **The sum of the interior angles is always 180 degrees.** Just because one triangle is bigger than another doesn't make the sum of its interior angles any larger. Every triangle's angles total 180 degrees.

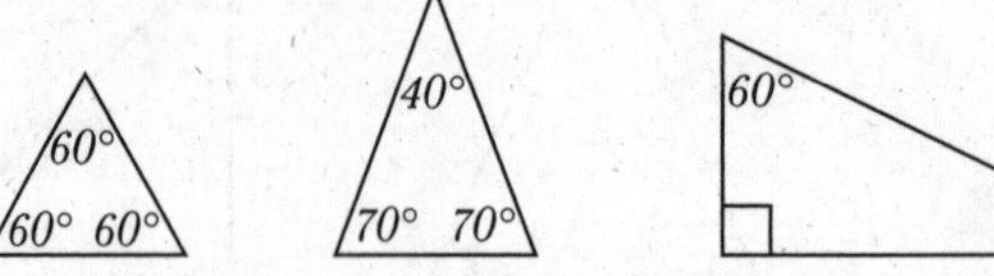

- **Any exterior angle is equal to the sum of the two remote interior angles.** When you think about this rule logically, it makes sense. The sum of supplementary angles is 180, and x (inside the triangle) and a (outside) are supplementary, so $x + a = 180$. The sum of the angles in a triangle is 180, and x, y, and z are inside the triangle, so $x + y + z = 180$. Substitution then gives you $x + a = x + y + z$. Then you subtract the x from both sides to get $a = y + z$.

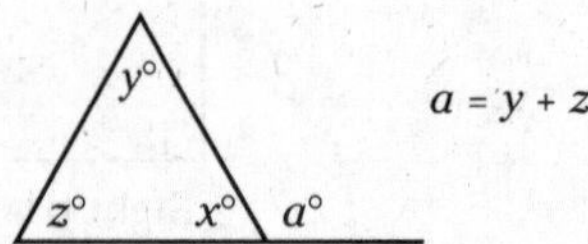

Working with similar triangles

Similar triangles have *congruent* (identical) angles and proportional sides. For example, if the heights of two similar triangles are in a ratio of 2:3, then the bases of those triangles are in a ratio of 2:3 as well.

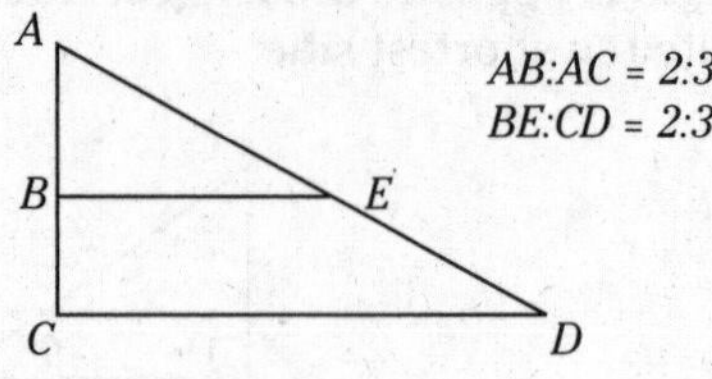

The ratio of the areas of similar triangles is equal to the square of the ratio of their sides. For example, if each side of triangle *BCD* is $\frac{1}{3}$ the length of each side of similar triangle *EFG*, then the area of triangle *BCD* is $\left(\frac{1}{3}\right)^2 = \frac{1}{9}$ the area of triangle *EFG*.

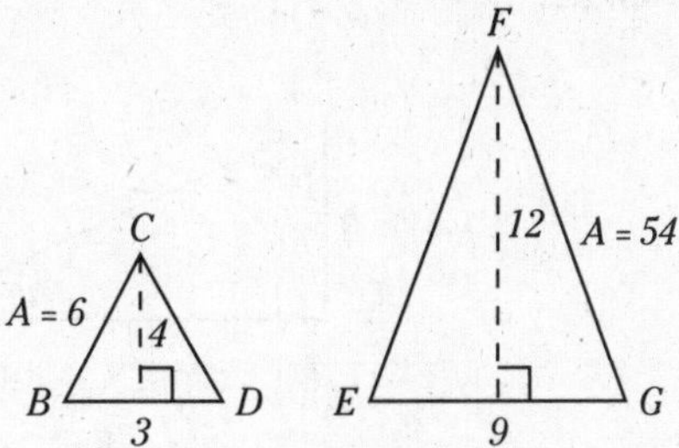

Two similar triangles have bases 5 and 25. Which of the following expresses the ratio of the areas of the two triangles?

Ⓐ 1:5

Ⓑ 1:15

Ⓒ 1:25

Ⓓ 2:15

Ⓔ It cannot be determined from the information given.

The ratio of the sides is $\frac{1}{5}$. The ratio of the areas is the square of the ratio of the sides: $\frac{1}{5} \times \frac{1}{5} = \frac{1}{25}$. Note that Choice (E) is a trap for the unwary. You can't figure out the exact area of either figure because you don't know the height. (The area of a triangle is $\frac{1}{2}bh$ or $\frac{1}{2}$*base* × *height*.) However, you aren't asked for an area, only for the ratio of the areas, which you can deduce from information in the question. *Correct answer:* Choice **(C)**.

Bonus: What do you suppose is the ratio of the volumes of two similar figures? Because volume is found in cubic units, the ratio of the volumes of two similar figures is the cube of the ratio of their sides. If Figure A has a base of 5 and similar Figure B has a base of 10, then the ratio of their volumes is 1:8 ($[1:2]^3$), which is $\frac{1}{2} \times \frac{1}{2} \times \frac{1}{2} = \frac{1}{8}$.

Don't assume that triangles are similar because they appear similar. If details in the question don't describe similar triangles, assume the triangles aren't similar.

Calculating a triangle's perimeter and area

You're likely to encounter at least one question on the test that asks for the perimeter or area of a triangle. The following sections can help you clear that hurdle.

Calculating perimeter

Perimeter is the distance around a triangle, so add up the lengths of the sides.

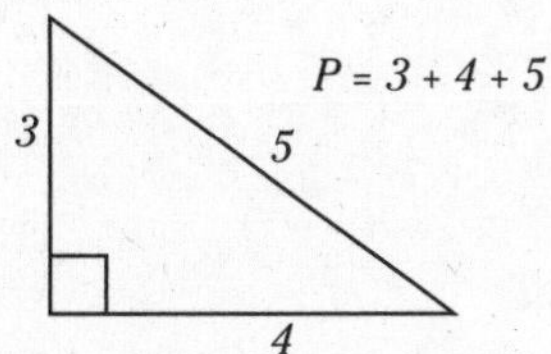

Calculating area

The area of a triangle is $\frac{1}{2}base \times height$.

The height is always a line perpendicular to the base. The height may be a side of the triangle, as in a right triangle.

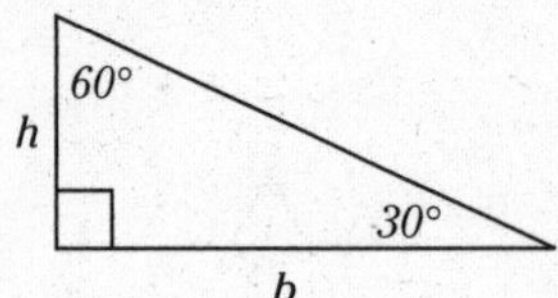

Then again, the height may be inside the triangle. A dashed line and a small 90-degree box often represent the height.

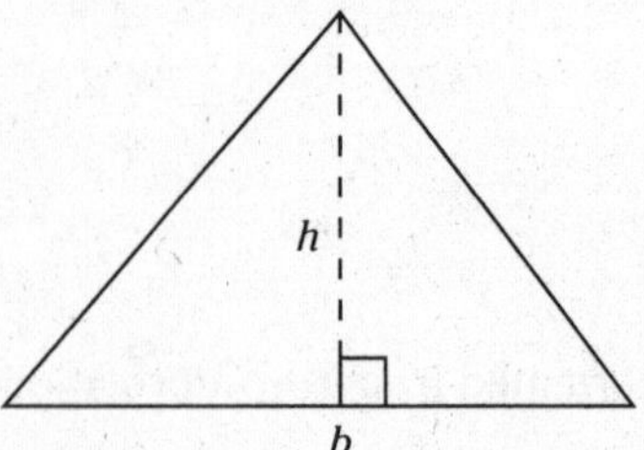

The height may even be outside the triangle. This fact is very confusing and is sometimes used to create trick questions. The good news is that you can always drop an altitude. That is, put your pencil on the tallest point of the triangle and draw an imaginary line (because the image will be on a computer screen on the actual GRE) straight from that point to the base or the extension of the base. The line you draw is the height, and it can be outside the triangle.

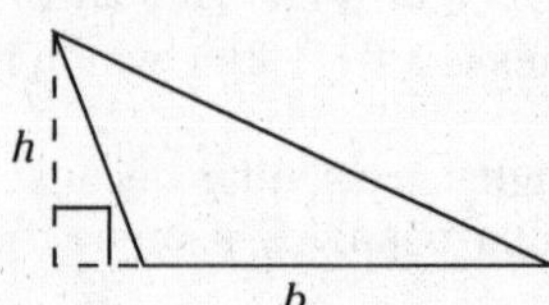

Understanding the Pythagorean theorem

The *Pythagorean theorem* (PT) states that the sum of the squares of the two sides of any right triangle is equal to the square of the hypotenuse. In any right triangle (and it has to be a right triangle), you can find the lengths of the sides with this formula:

$$a^2 + b^2 = c^2$$

Here, a and b are the sides of the triangle, and c is the hypotenuse. The *hypotenuse* is always opposite the 90-degree angle and is always the longest side of the triangle.

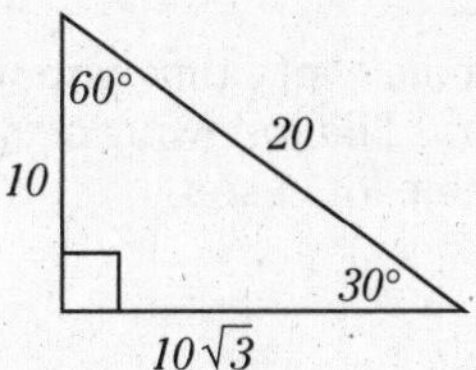

With PT, if you know the lengths of any two sides of a right triangle, you can find the length of the third side by plugging in the numbers and doing the math. For example, say you're asked for the length of the hypotenuse in this triangle:

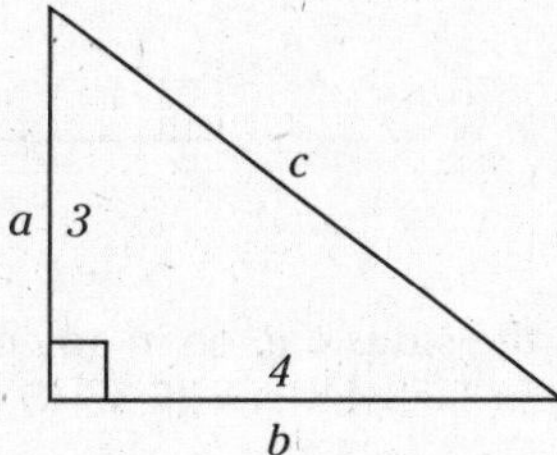

Here's what you do:

$$a^2 + b^2 = c^2$$
$$3^2 + 4^2 = c^2$$
$$9 + 16 = 25$$
$$c^2 = 25$$
$$c = 5$$

Here's an example in which you know the length of the hypotenuse and one of its sides:

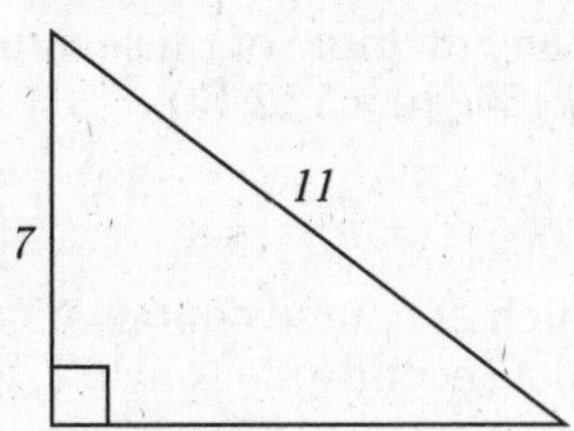

To find the unknown length of the third side, here's what you do:

$$a^2 + b^2 = c^2$$
$$7^2 + b^2 = 11^2$$
$$49 + b^2 = 121$$
$$b^2 = 121 - 49$$
$$b^2 = 72$$
$$b = 6\sqrt{2}$$

Identifying common Pythagorean ratios in right triangles

Doing the whole PT formula every time you want to find the third side length of a right triangle isn't always necessary. The following sections clue you in to four very common PT ratios that make your job a whole lot easier.

3:4:5

If one side of a right triangle is 3 and the other is 4, then the hypotenuse must be 5. Likewise, if the hypotenuse is 5 and the length of one side is 4, the other side must be 3.

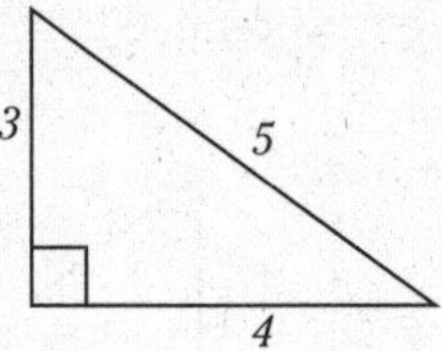

Because this is a ratio, the sides can be in any multiple of these numbers, such as 6:8:10 (2 × 3:4:5), 9:12:15 (3 × 3:4:5), or 27:36:45 (9 × 3:4:5).

5:12:13

If one side of a right triangle is 5 and another side is 12, then the hypotenuse must be 13. Likewise, if you know the hypotenuse is 13 and one of the sides is 5, then the other side must be 12.

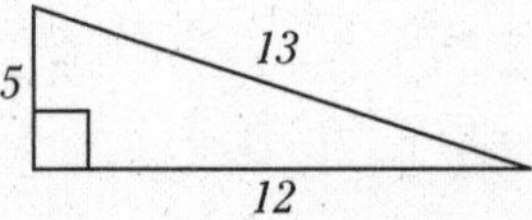

Because you're dealing with a ratio, the sides can be in any multiple of these numbers, such as 10:24:26 (2 × 5:12:13), 15:36:39 (3 × 5:12:13), or 50:120:130 (10 × 5:12:13).

$s{:}s{:}s\sqrt{2}$

This ratio is exclusively for isosceles right triangles (which of course contain 45-45-90 degree angles), and *s* stands for side. If one side is 2 and a second side is also 2, then the hypotenuse is $2\sqrt{2}$.

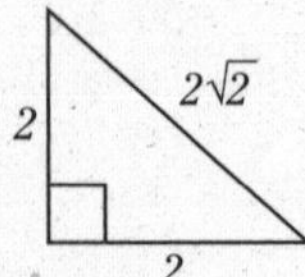

This formula is great to know for working with squares. If a question tells you that the side of a square is 5 and wants to know the diagonal of the square, you know immediately that the diagonal is $5\sqrt{2}$. Why? A square's diagonal cuts the square into two isosceles right triangles (*isosceles* because all sides of the square are equal; *right* because all angles in a square are right angles). What's the diagonal of a square of side 64? $64\sqrt{2}$. What's the diagonal of a square of side 12,984? $12{,}984\sqrt{2}$.

You can modify the formula to solve problems in which you're given the length of the hypotenuse of an isosceles right triangle and need to find the length of the other two sides:

$$\frac{s}{\sqrt{2}}:\frac{s}{\sqrt{2}}:s$$

The diagonal of a square is 5. What is the area of the square?

To determine the area, first you need to know the length of a side, so plug in the numbers:

$$\frac{5}{\sqrt{2}}:\frac{5}{\sqrt{2}}:5$$

The hypotenuse is 5, and the length of any side of the square is $\frac{5}{\sqrt{2}}$. The area of the square is simply $\frac{5}{\sqrt{2}}\times\frac{5}{\sqrt{2}}=\frac{25}{2}=12.5$.

$s:s\sqrt{3}:2s$

This is a special ratio for the sides of a 30:60:90 triangle, which has angles measuring 30, 60, and 90 degrees. *S* is the length of the short side (opposite the 30 degree angle), $s\sqrt{3}$ is the longer side, and 2*s* is the hypotenuse.

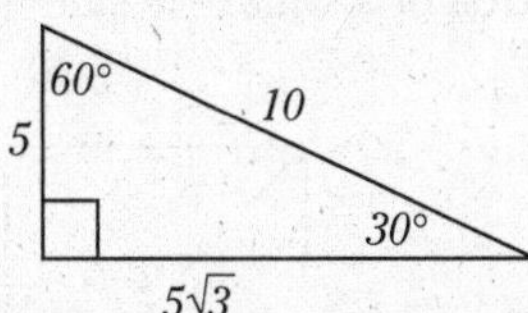

This type of triangle is a favorite of the test-makers. The important fact to keep in mind here is that the hypotenuse is twice the length of the short side (which must be opposite the 30 degree angle). If you encounter a word problem that says, "Given a 30:60:90 triangle of hypotenuse 20, find the area," or "Given a 30:60:90 triangle of hypotenuse 100, find the perimeter," you can do so because you can quickly find the lengths of the other sides.

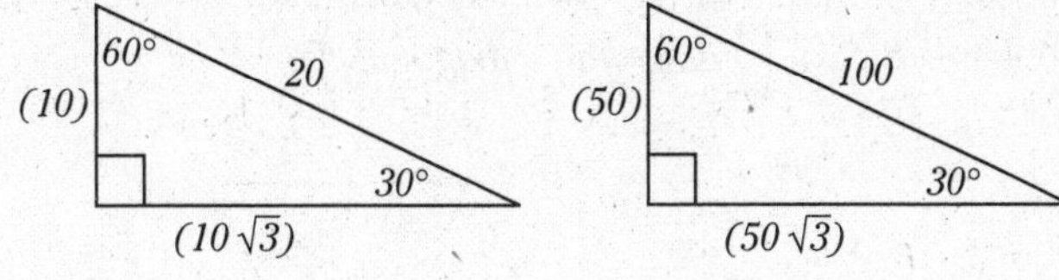

Knowing Quadrilaterals Inside and Out

After you master triangles, quadrilaterals are easy. Any four-sided figure is called a *quadrilateral.* The interior angles of any quadrilateral total 360 degrees, and you can cut any quadrilateral into two triangles, each of which has total interior angles of 180 degrees. The following sections present everything you need to know about quadrilaterals, including the names of the many types of quadrilaterals.

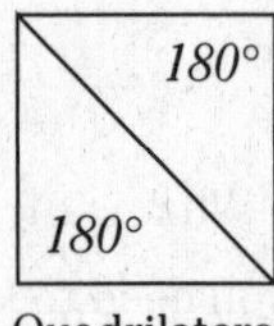

Quadrilateral

Recognizing a quadrilateral when you see one

Although all quadrilaterals have four sides, the sides can be arranged in numerous configurations to form squares, rectangles, and other types of quadrilaterals, as described in the following sections.

Square

The most famous quadrilateral is the *square* — a quadrilateral with four equal sides and four right angles. The area of a square is *side*^{2} (*base* × *height*), or $\frac{1}{2}$*diagonal*^{2}.

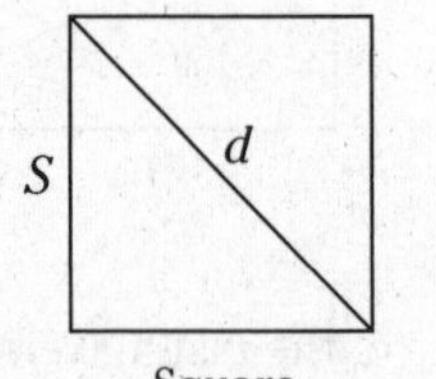

Square

Rhombus

A *rhombus* is a quadrilateral with four equal sides and four angles that aren't necessarily right angles. A rhombus often looks like a drunken square — tipsy and wobbly. The area of a rhombus is $\frac{1}{2}d_1d_2$ or $\left(\frac{1}{2}\textit{diagonal}_1 \times \textit{diagonal}_2\right)$.

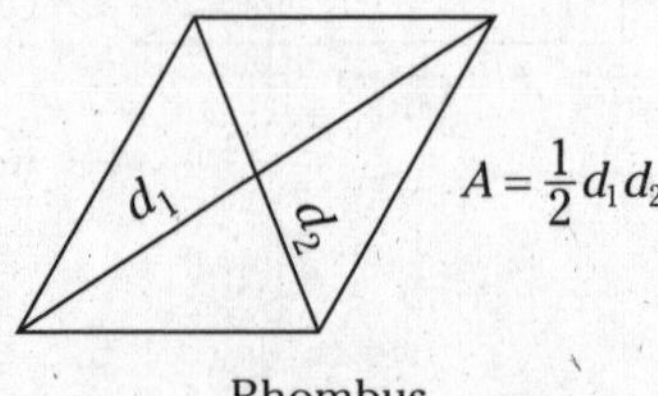

Rhombus

Any square is a rhombus, but not every rhombus is a square.

Rectangle

A *rectangle* is a quadrilateral with two opposite and equal pairs of sides and four right angles. The top and bottom sides are equal, and the right and left sides are equal. (*Rectangle* means right angle.) The area of a rectangle is *length* × *width* (which is the same as *base* × *height*).

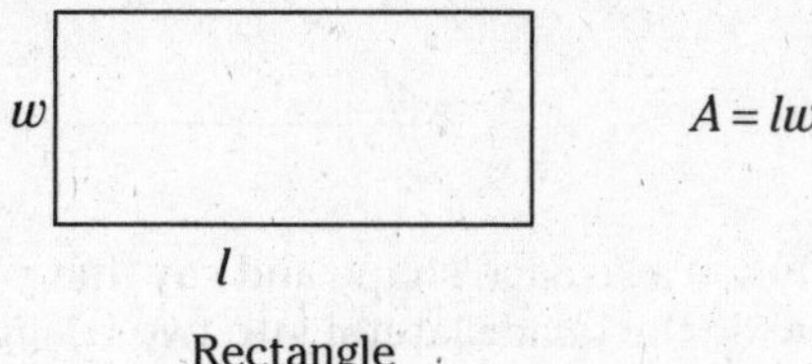

Rectangle

Parallelogram

A *parallelogram* is a quadrilateral with two opposite and equal pairs of sides. The top and bottom sides are equal, and the right and left sides are equal. Opposite angles are equal but not necessarily right (or 90 degrees). The area of a parallelogram is *base* × *height*. Remember that the height is the distance between the two bases, which are the parallel sides, and is always represented by a perpendicular line from the tallest point of the figure down to the base. Diagonals of a parallelogram bisect each other.

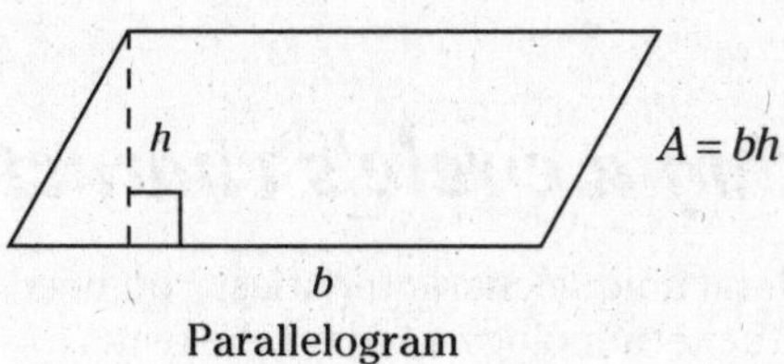

Parallelogram

All rectangles are parallelograms, but not all parallelograms are rectangles.

Trapezoid

A *trapezoid* is a quadrilateral with two parallel sides and two nonparallel sides. The area of a trapezoid is $\frac{1}{2}(base_1 + base_2) \times height$. It makes no difference which base you label *base 1* and which you label *base 2,* because you're adding them together anyway. Just be sure to add them *before* you multiply by $\frac{1}{2}$.

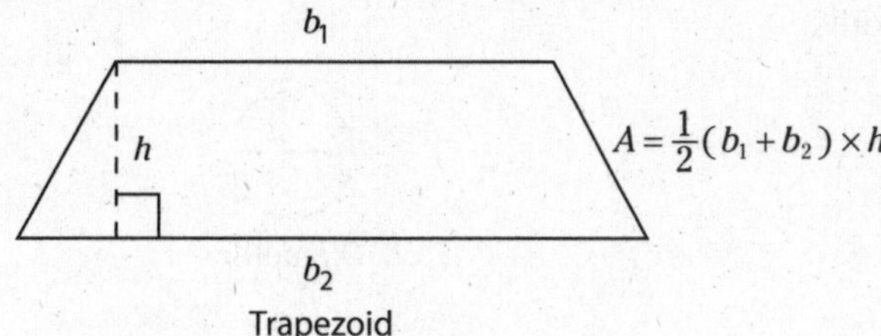

Trapezoid

Irregular quadrilaterals

Some quadrilaterals don't have nice, neat shapes or special names.

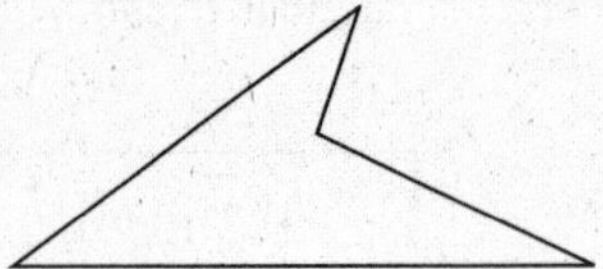

Don't immediately see a strange shape and say that you have no way to find its area. You may be able to divide the quadrilateral into two triangles and find the area of each triangle. You may also see a strange quadrilateral in a shaded-area problem; I tell you more about those problems in the next section.

Working with Circles

Determining a circle's *circumference* (distance around the circle) or area given only its *radius* (the distance from the center of the circle to its edge) is easy if you know the formulas and characteristics of the circle. The following sections cover the characteristics and the formulas you need to solve problems related to circles.

Recognizing a circle's characteristics

Circles have several unique characteristics. You need to know what these characteristics are to decipher the terminology used on the test.

- **Center:** The *center* is right in the middle of the circle. If a question references the circle by a capital letter, that's both the circle's center and its name.

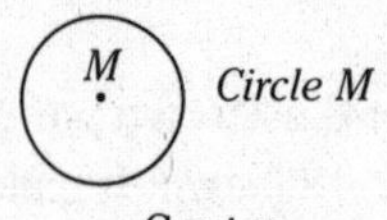

Center

- **Diameter:** *Diameter* is the length of a line between two points on opposite sides of the circle that passes through the center of the circle. The diameter is equal to two times the radius.

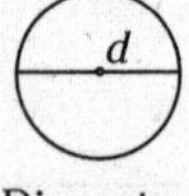

Diameter

- **Circumference:** *Circumference* is the distance around a circle, its perimeter.

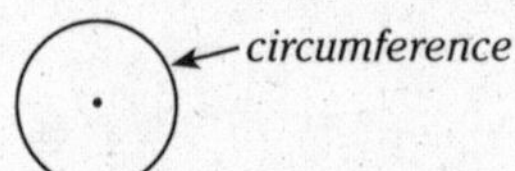

- π: Pronounced *pi,* π is the ratio of the circumference of a circle to the diameter of a circle. It equals approximately 3.14, but more often than not, circle-based questions have answer choices in terms of π, such as 2π rather than 6.28.
- **Radius:** *Radius* is the distance from the center of the circle to the edge of the circle. The radius of a circle is half the diameter.

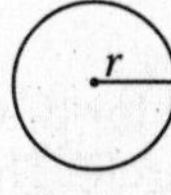

Radius

- **Tangent:** A *tangent* is a line outside a circle that touches the circle's perimeter at one point. A line drawn from the center of the circle to the point where the tangent touches the perimeter of the circle forms a right angle to the tangent.

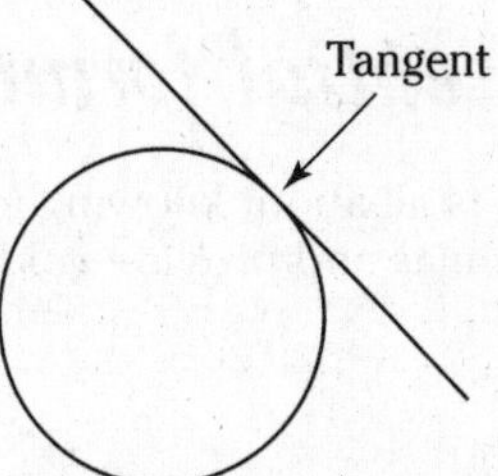

- **Chord:** A *chord* is a line that connects any two points on the perimeter of a circle. The longest chord in a circle is the diameter.

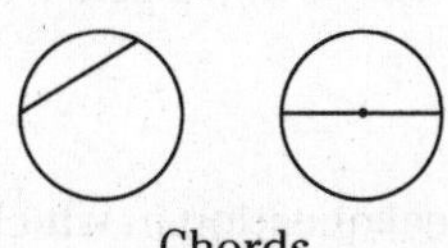
Chords

Choose from these answer choices for the two example questions that follow:

Ⓐ Quantity A is greater.

Ⓑ Quantity B is greater.

Ⓒ The two quantities are equal.

Ⓓ The relationship cannot be determined from the information given.

Quantity A	***Quantity B***
Area of a circle of radius 6	Area of a circle with a longest chord of 12

Many people choose Choice (D) for this question. Typically in QCs (Quantitative Comparisons) like this, the correct answer to a geometry question with no figure is Choice (D) because the answer *de*pends on how you draw the picture. However, a circle is frequently an exception. A circle is a circle is a circle; it rarely depends on how you draw it. The key here is to know that the *longest chord* is a fancy way of saying the *diameter.* Because the diameter is twice the radius, a circle of diameter (or longest chord) 12 has a radius of 6. Two circles with radii of 6 have the same area. (Don't waste even a nanosecond figuring out what that area actually is. It's irrelevant to comparing the quantities.) *Correct answer:* Choice **(C)**.

Quantity A	***Quantity B***
Area of a circle of radius 10	Area of a circle of chord 20

If you chose Choice (C), you fell for the trap. Remember that a chord is a straight line that connects any two points on a circle. The *longest* chord is the diameter, but Quantity B doesn't specify *longest* chord. If it were the longest chord, the two quantities would be equal, but if it's not the longest chord, then the diameter of the circle is greater than 20, making the radius greater than 10, which would make the value of Quantity B greater. In other words, the question doesn't provide enough information to make a determination. *Correct answer:* Choice **(D)**.

Mastering essential formulas

Solving circle problems is all about knowing formulas and how to use them. The following sections reveal the formulas and provide guidance on solving problems, complete with sample questions.

Circumference: $C = 2\pi r$

Circumference is a fancy word for perimeter — the distance around a circle. The formula is $C = 2\pi r$ (C is circumference, r is radius, and d is diameter). Because diameter is twice the radius, you may also use the equation $C = d\pi$.

For example, the circumference of a circle with a radius of 3 is

$$2 \times \pi \times 3 = 6\pi$$

You may encounter a wheel question in which you're asked how much distance a wheel covers, or how many times a wheel revolves. The key to solving this type of question is to know that one rotation of a wheel equals one circumference of that wheel. Though the answer choices are almost always in terms of π, once in a while you may have to multiply the answer by 3.14 instead.

A child's wagon has a wheel of radius 6 inches. If the wagon wheel travels 100 revolutions, approximately how many feet has the wagon rolled?

Ⓐ 325

Ⓑ 314

Ⓒ 255

Ⓓ 201

Ⓔ It cannot be determined from the information given.

The question gives the radius in inches, but the answer choices are all in feet, so the first order of business is to convert inches into feet: $6 \div 12 = 0.5$ feet. One revolution is equal to one circumference, so first find the circumference of the circle in feet:

$$C = 2\pi r$$
$$C = 2\pi \times 0.5$$
$$C = \pi$$

Then multiply by the number of revolutions:

$\pi \times 100 = 100\pi$ ft

Because π is approximately 3.14, multiply:

$3.14 \times 100 = 314$ ft

Choice (E) is definitely not the answer. If you have a radius, you can solve for nearly anything having to do with circles. *Correct answer:* Choice **(B).**

Area: $A = \pi r^2$

The area of a circle is πr^2, so if a circle has a radius of 4, you can find the area by doing the following:

$\pi \times 4^2 = 16\pi$

4 $A = 16\pi$

Angles inside a circle

By drawing two lines inside a circle from the center to two points on the circumference or a single point on the circumference to two points on the circumference, you form two types of angles inside the circle:

- A *central angle* has its vertex at the center of a circle and its endpoints on the circumference. The degree measure of a central angle is the same as the degree measure of its *intercepted arc* (the part of the circle's perimeter that falls between the two points where the central angle's lines touch the circle's perimeter).

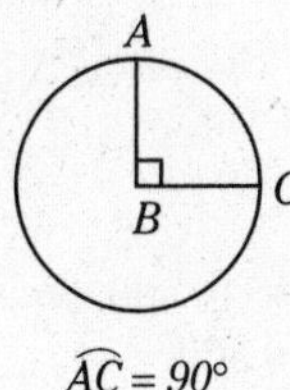

$\overset{\frown}{AC} = 90°$

- An *inscribed angle* has both its vertex and endpoints on the circumference. The degree measure of an inscribed angle is half the degree measure of its intercepted arc, as shown in the following figure. The intercepted arc is 80 degrees, and the inscribed angle is $80 \div 2 = 40$ degrees.

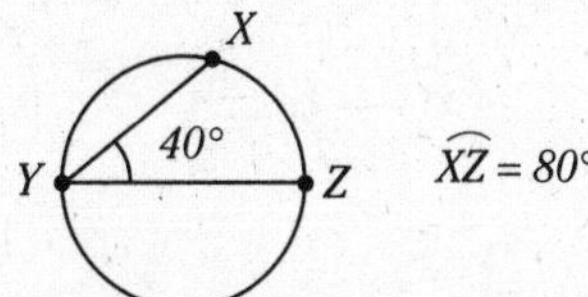

You may see a figure that looks like a dream catcher, with lines running every which way. Take the time to identify the endpoints of the angles and the vertex. You may be surprised at how easy the question suddenly becomes.

In this figure, find the sum of the degree measures of angles $a + b + c + d + e$.

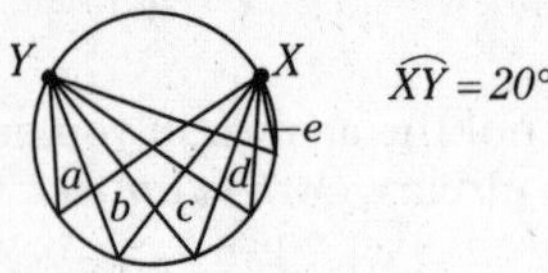

Note: Figure not drawn to scale.

Ⓐ 65

Ⓑ 60

Ⓒ 55

Ⓓ 50

Ⓔ 45

Each angle is an inscribed angle. That means the angle has half the degree measure of the central angle, or half the degree measure of its intercepted arc. If you look carefully at the endpoints of these angles, they're all the same: *XY*. Arc *XY* has a measure of 20 degrees. Therefore, each angle is 10 degrees, for a total of 50. *Correct answer:* Choice **(D).**

When a central angle and an inscribed angle have the same endpoints, the degree measure of the central angle is twice that of the inscribed angle.

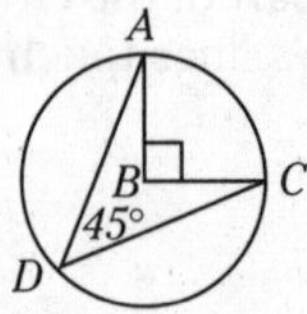

The degree measure of a circle is 360. Draw a cross in the middle of a circle, and you form four 90-degree angles: $4 \times 90 = 360$.

Arcs

An *arc* is a portion of the circumference of a circle. The degree measure of an arc is the same as its central angle and twice its inscribed angle.

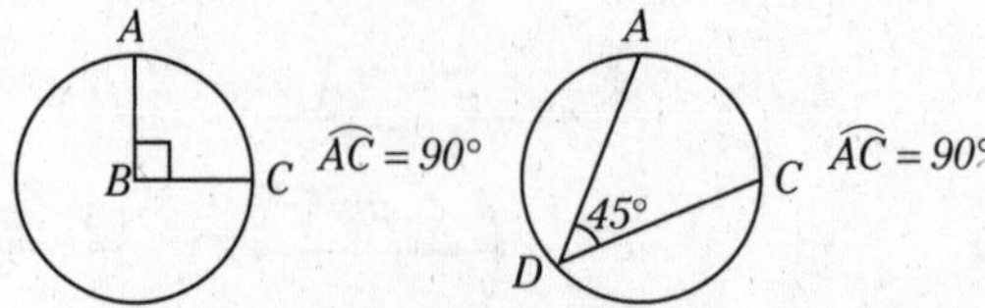

To find the length of an arc when you have its degree measure, follow these steps:

1. **Find the circumference of the entire circle.**
2. **Put the degree measure of the arc over 360 and then reduce the fraction.**
3. **Multiply the circumference by the fraction.**

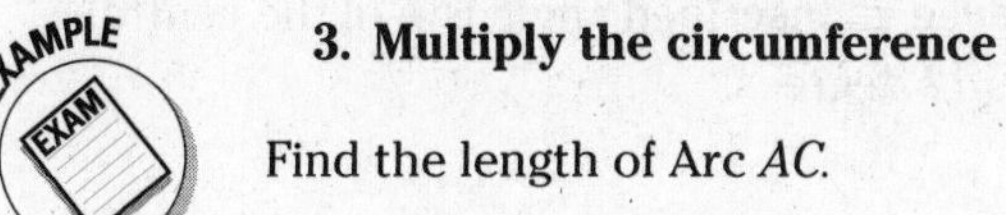

Find the length of Arc *AC*.

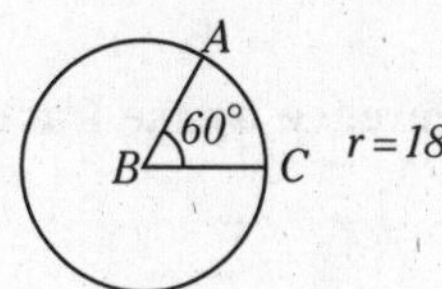

Ⓐ 36π

Ⓑ 27π

Ⓒ 18π

Ⓓ 12π

Ⓔ 6π

Take the steps one at a time:

1. **Find the circumference of the entire circle:**

   $C = 2\pi r = 2(18)\pi = 36\pi$

   Don't multiply π out; answer choices usually leave it in that form.

2. **Put the degree measure of the arc over 360.**

   The degree measure of the arc is the same as its central angle, 60 degrees:

   $$\frac{60}{360} = \frac{6}{36} = \frac{1}{6}$$

3. **Multiply the circumference by the fraction:**

   $$36\pi \times \frac{1}{6} = 6\pi$$

Correct answer: Choice **(E).**

Try another one. After you get the hang of arc problems, they're actually kind of fun.

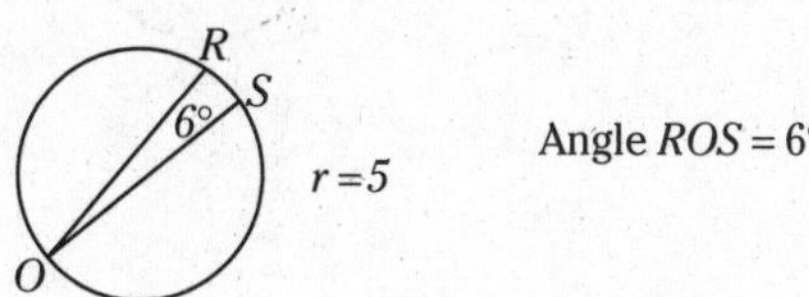

Find the length of Arc *RS* in this figure.

Ⓐ $\frac{1}{3}\pi$

Ⓑ π

Ⓒ 3π

Ⓓ 4π

Ⓔ 12

1. **Find the circumference of the entire circle:**

   $C = 2\pi r = 2(5)\pi = 10\pi$

2. **Put the degree measure of the arc over 360.**

   Here, the inscribed angle is 6 degrees. Because an inscribed angle is $\frac{1}{2}$ of the central angle and $\frac{1}{2}$ of its intercepted arc, the arc is 12 degrees:

   $$\frac{12}{360} = \frac{1}{30}$$

3. **Multiply the circumference by the fraction:**

   $$10\pi \times \frac{1}{30} = \frac{10}{30}\pi = \frac{1}{3}\pi$$

Correct answer: Choice **(A).**

Be very careful not to confuse the *degree measure* of the arc with the *length* of the arc. The length is always a portion of the circumference, always has a π in it, and is always in linear units. If you picked Choice (E) in this example, you found the degree measure of the arc rather than its length.

Sectors

A *sector* is a portion of the area of a circle. The degree measure of a sector is the same as its central angle and twice its inscribed angle.

To find the area of a sector, do the following:

1. **Find the area of the entire circle.**
2. **Put the degree measure of the sector over 360 and then reduce the fraction.**
3. **Multiply the area by the fraction.**

Finding the area of a sector is very similar to finding the length of an arc. The only difference is in the first step. Whereas an arc is a part of the *circumference* of a circle, a sector is a part of the *area* of a circle. With that in mind, try your hand at a few sample sector problems:

Find the area of Sector *ABC*.

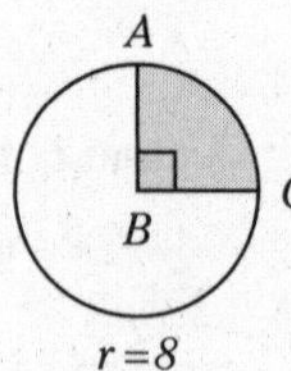

Ⓐ 64π

Ⓑ 36π

Ⓒ 16π

Ⓓ 12π

Ⓔ 6π

Use the three steps listed previously:

1. **Find the area of the entire circle.**

   $A = \pi r^2 = \pi \times 8^2 = 64\pi$

2. **Put the degree measure of the sector over 360 and then reduce the fraction.**

   The sector is 90 degrees, the same as its central angle:

   $$\frac{90}{360} = \frac{1}{4}$$

3. **Multiply the area by the fraction.**

   $$64\pi \times \frac{1}{4} = 16\pi$$

Correct answer: Choice **(C)**.

Find the area of Sector *XYZ* in this figure.

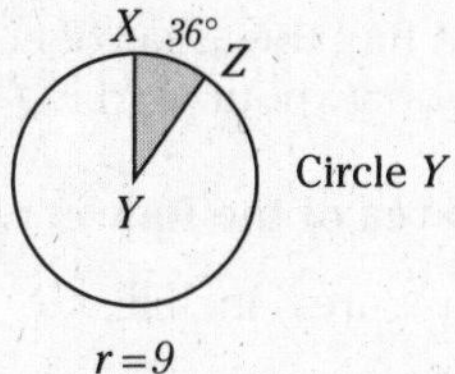

Ⓐ 9.7π

Ⓑ 8.1π

Ⓒ 7.2π

Ⓓ 6.3π

Ⓔ 6π

1. **Find the area of the entire circle.**

   $A = \pi r^2 = \pi \times 9^2 = 81\pi$

2. **Put the degree measure of the sector over 360 and then reduce the fraction.**

   A sector has the same degree measure as its intercepted arc:

   $$\frac{36}{360} = \frac{1}{10}$$

3. **Multiply the area by the fraction.**

   $$81\pi \times \frac{1}{10} = 8.1\pi$$

Correct answer: Choice **(B)**.

Tackling shaded-area problems

A shaded-area problem presents two shapes with one overlapping the other but not completely covering it. The part of the shape underneath what you can see is the shaded area. Your job is to calculate the total shaded area.

A circle of radius 4 inches is centered over an 8-inch square. Calculate the total shaded area.

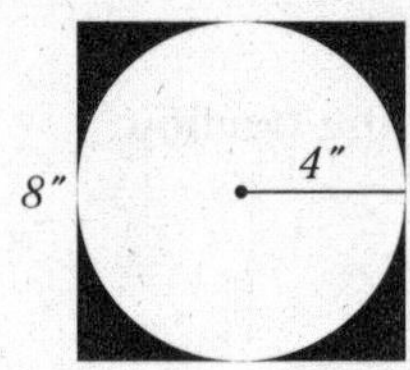

Shaded areas are often rather unusual shapes. Your first reaction may be that you can't possibly find the area of that shape. Generally, you're right, but you don't have to find the area directly. Instead just find the areas of each shape (the one overlapping and the one underneath) and don't worry about working the actual math.

1. **Calculate the total area of the figure, which is the area of the square.**

   All sides of the square are 8 inches, so:

   Area = $8 \times 8 = 64$

2. **Calculate the area of the circle:**

   Area = $\pi r^2 = \pi \times 4^2 = 16\pi$

3. **Subtract the area of the circle from the area of the square to determine the area of the shaded portion:**

   Area = $64 - 16\pi$

Going 3D with Volume and Surface Area

You can easily calculate volume and total surface area for any three-dimensional shape that you encounter on the GRE. Fortunately, the GRE features only two such shapes: the rectangular solid (which includes the cube) and the cylinder. In the following sections, I give you the formulas and guidance you need to do so.

Calculating volume

Volume is how much you can fit inside a three-dimensional object and is always expressed in cubic units. The following sections explain how to calculate the volume of a cube, rectangular solid, a cylinder, and any polygon.

Volume = (area of base) × height

If you can remember this formula (*volume = area of base × height*), and the formulas for the area of circle, rectangle, and square, you don't have to memorize additional formulas for cubes, rectangular solids, and cylinders. You simply calculate area as you normally do and then multiply by the object's height.

Cube = e^3

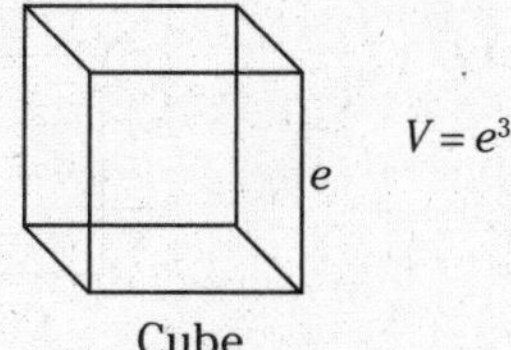

Cube

A *cube* is a three-dimensional square. Think of a die (one of a pair of dice). All of a cube's dimensions are the same, that is, *length* = *width* = *height.* In a cube, these dimensions are called *edges* and are represented by the letter *e.* The volume of a cube is thus *edge* × *edge* × *edge* = *edge*^{3} = e^3.

Rectangular solid = $l \times w \times h$

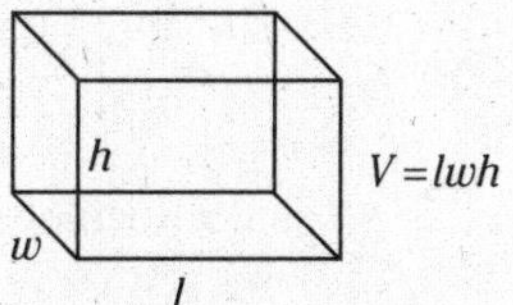

Rectangular solid

A rectangular solid is a box. The base of a box is a rectangle, which has an area of *length* × *width.* Multiply that by height to find volume: *Volume* = *(area of the base)* × *height,* or $V = l \times w \times h$.

Volume of a cylinder = $\pi r^2 \times h$

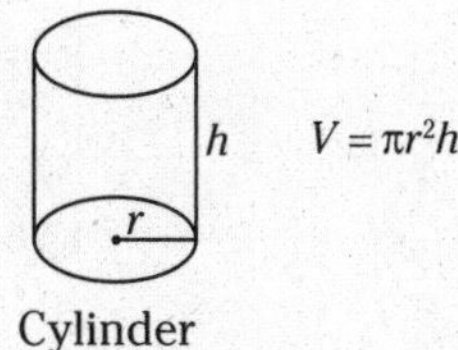

Cylinder

Think of a cylinder as a can of soup. The base of a cylinder is a circle. The area of a circle is πr^2. Multiply that by the height of the cylinder to get *(area of the base)* × *height* = $(\pi r^2) \times$ *height.* Note that the top and bottom of a cylinder are identical circles. If you know the radius of either the top base or the bottom base, you can find the area of the circle.

Calculating total surface area

Surface area is the measure of the exposed surface of an object — completely around it and its top and bottom. *Total surface area* (TSA), logically enough, is the sum of the areas of all the surfaces of the figure. The following sections provide formulas for calculating the surface area of several different solids.

Cube = $6e^2$

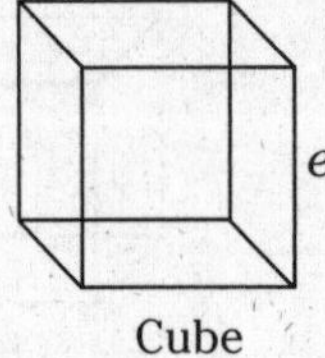

Cube

A cube has six identical faces, and each face is a square. The area of a square is *side*^{2}. Here, that's called *edge*^{2}. If one face is *edge*^{2}, then the total surface area is $6 \times$ *edge*^{2}, or $6e^2$.

Rectangular solid = $2(lw) + 2(wh) + 2(hl)$

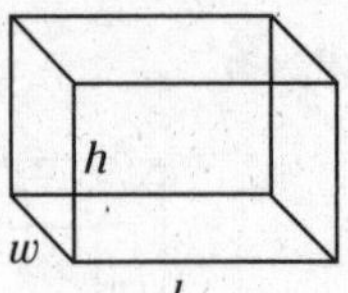

Rectangular solid

A rectangular solid is a box. You need to find the area of each of the six surfaces. The bottom and top each has the area of *(length × width)*. The area of the left side and right side each is equal to *(width × height)*. The front side and the back side each has the area of *(height × length)*. Together, they total $2(lw) + 2(wh) + 2(hl)$ or $2(lw + wh + hl)$.

Cylinder = Circumference × height + $2(\pi r^2)$

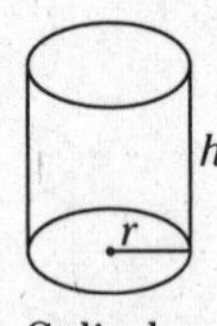

Cylinder

The TSA of a cylinder is definitely the most difficult TSA to figure out. Think of it as pulling the label off a can, flattening it out, finding its area, and then adding that to the area of the top and bottom lids.

The label is a rectangle. Its length is the circumference of the circle. Its height is the height of the object. And area of a rectangle is $l \times w$.

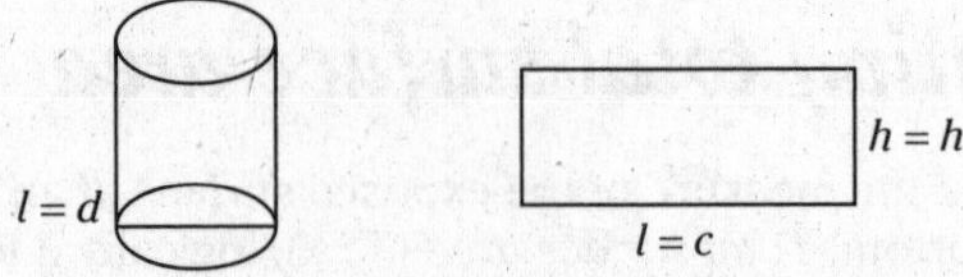

You also need to find the area of the top and bottom of the cylinder. Because both the top and bottom are circles, their TSA is $2(\pi r^2)$. Finally, add everything together:

area of label + 2(area top or bottom) = TSA

Chapter 11

Translating English into Math: Word Problem Strategies

In This Chapter

- Making sense of word problems
- Calculating distance, rate, time, averages, interest, probability, and more
- Grasping set theory while grappling with Venn diagrams
- Determining the order of items with permutations and combinations

Being able to do calculations in math is necessary for scoring well on the Math sections of the GRE, but number-crunching alone isn't enough. You also need to be able to translate a word problem from English into a mathematical expression.

Fortunately, the GRE uses several standard types of word problems, each of which you solve using one or more strategies. Recognize the type of problem you're dealing with and choose the right strategy, and you're well on your way to solving the problem.

This chapter introduces you to the various word problem types and reveals strategies for answering each type of question efficiently and accurately.

Working a Word Problem Step by Step

When you're eye-to-eye with a word problem, knowing where to start is often the most daunting challenge. The key is to begin with what you know and work toward what you don't know. You can solve almost all word problems by taking the following step-by-step approach:

1. **Read the entire problem carefully.**

   A question may provide three values and then ask for the total or the average. You may not know until the very end of the question what it's asking you to determine, so read the entire question.

2. **Jot down all the values and units you know.**

   When you see all the values, what you need to do to solve the problem often reveals itself. Values are the clues you need to solve the mystery.

3. **Identify the unknown variable — what the question is asking you to come up with.**

   The unknown variable, x, is whatever the question asks. Look for words such as *what is, how much, how many, how fast, at what price,* and so on.

4. **Construct the mathematical equation, plugging in all known values and the variable.**

   In most cases, the word problem is of a distinct type, and solving it requires the use of a special equation. The following sections bring you up to speed on the most common word problem types and their corresponding equations. With the equation, known values, and unknown variable in hand, you have everything you need to solve the problem.

5. **Solve the equation.**

   When you have everything in place, do the math.

6. **Plug in your choice to be sure.**

   Plug in the answer you chose and crunch the numbers to be sure it works, or at least use your common sense to gauge whether the answer seems reasonable.

Are We There Yet? Calculating Distance, Rate, and Time

You're probably going to encounter at least one question on the GRE that deals with distance, rate, and time. The question typically provides two of the three values and asks for the third value; for example, the question may specify the distance and rate and ask for the time. To solve these types of questions, create a DRT (distance, rate, time) chart and start filling in values.

Chapter 9 discusses how to balance algebraic equations, but another way to solve distance, rate, and time problems is to use the following mnemonic:

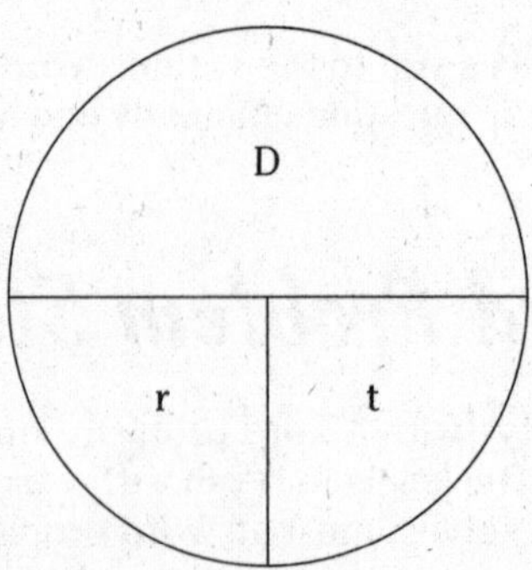

Cover up the letter for the value you don't have, and this little tool reveals the equation for determining that value:

- Cover the *D*, and you see that $D = rt$.
- Cover the *t*, and you see that $t = \frac{D}{r}$.
- Cover the *r* and you see that $r = \frac{D}{t}$.

Jennifer drives 40 miles an hour for two and a half hours. Her friend Ashley goes the same distance but drives at one and a half times Jennifer's speed. How many *minutes* longer does Jennifer drive than Ashley?

Don't start making intense formulas with x's and y's. Make a DRT chart instead. This chart lays out everything you know and what you need to know to answer the question:

Distance	**=**	***Rate***	×	***Time***

Start by writing down the values you know, including the units of measurement. When you fill in the 40 miles per hour and 2.5 hours for Jennifer, you can calculate that she went 100 miles. Think of it this way: If she goes 40 miles per hour for one hour, that's 40 miles. For a second hour, she goes another 40 miles. In a half-hour, she goes $\frac{1}{2}$ of 40, or 20 miles: $40 + 40 + 20 = 100$ miles.

Distance	**=**	***Rate***	×	***Time***
100 (Jennifer)		40 mph		2.5 hours

Because Ashley drives the same distance, fill in 100 under *distance* for her. She goes one and a half times as fast, so she's going $40 + 1.5(40) = 40 + 20 = 60$ miles per hour. You know Ashley's distance and rate, and you need to find the time.

Now this problem gets really easy. If Ashley drives at 60 miles per hour, she drives $\frac{60 \text{ m}/\cancel{\text{h}}}{60 \text{ min}/\cancel{\text{h}}} = 1$ mile per minute. Therefore, going 100 miles takes her 100 minutes. Because the question asks for your final answer in minutes, don't bother converting it to hours; leave it the way it is.

Distance	**=**	***Rate***	×	***Time***
100 (Ashley)		60 mph		100 minutes

Now all you need to do is convert Jennifer's 2.5-hour drive into minutes and subtract. One hour is 60 minutes. A second hour is another 60 minutes. A half-hour is 30 minutes. Add them together: $60 + 60 + 30 = 150$ minutes. If Jennifer drives for 150 minutes and Ashley drives for 100 minutes, Jennifer drives 50 minutes more than Ashley.

Distance	**=**	***Rate***	×	***Time***
100 (Jennifer)		40 mph		150 minutes
100 (Ashley)		60 mph		100 minutes

Be careful to note whether the people are traveling in the same direction or opposite directions. Suppose you're asked how far apart drivers are at the end of their trips. If Jordan travels 40 miles per hour east for 2 hours and Connor travels 60 miles per hour west for 3 hours, they're going in opposite directions. If they start from the same point at the same time, Jordan has gone 80 miles one way, and Connor has gone 180 miles in the opposite direction. They're actually 260 miles apart. The trap answer is 100, because careless people (not you!) simply subtract 80 from 180.

Figuring Averages

When it comes to averages, you can always do them the way your teacher taught you in the third grade: Add all the terms and then divide by the number of terms. First, add up all the terms:

$$5 + 11 + 17 + 23 + 29 = 85$$

Next, divide the total by the number of terms, which is 5:

$$\frac{85}{5} = 17$$

That's the surefire method. It works in every case, regardless of what the numbers look like.

The following sections reveal shortcuts for calculating averages and show you how to tackle problems that are variations on the averages theme: missing-term average problems and weighted averages.

Taking shortcuts: Finding averages of evenly spaced or consecutive terms

You can save time finding an average if the terms are consecutive or evenly spaced. With evenly spaced terms, you see an equal number of units between each pair of neighboring terms. After you make sure that the terms are evenly spaced, you can follow one of these rules to find the average:

- The average of a set containing an odd number of terms that are evenly spaced is equal to the middle term. For example, 2, 4, 6, 8, 10 has an average of 6.
- A set containing an even number of evenly spaced terms is equal to the average of the two middle terms. For example, 2, 4, 6, 8 has an average of $\frac{(4+6)}{2} = 5$.
- The average of a set of evenly spaced terms is $\frac{\text{first} + \text{last}}{2}$. For example, 2, 4, 6, 8, 10 has an average of $\frac{(2+10)}{2} = 6$.
- Conversely, with evenly spaced terms, the sum of the first and last terms is equal to twice the average of the terms.

These tricks are easy to love, but don't march down the aisle with them yet. These tips work only for evenly spaced terms. If you have just any old batch of numbers, such as 4, 21, 97, 98, and 199, you have to find the average of those numbers the old-fashioned way: adding them up and dividing by the number of terms.

Find the average of these numbers:

41, 50, 59, 68, 77, 86, 95

Don't reach for your pencil. Instead, look and see that the terms are all nine units apart. Because the set contains an odd number of terms that are evenly spaced, the average is equal to the middle term: 68.

Find the average of these numbers:

3, 10, 17, 24, 31, 38, 45, 52

First, double-check that they're evenly spaced. Here, the numbers are spaced by sevens. Next, look for the middle number . . . but wait! It doesn't exist. You can, of course, identify the two central terms, 24 and 31, and find the middle between them. That works, but what a pain. Suppose you have 38 numbers. Making a mistake as to which terms are the central ones is easy with this many numbers. If you're off just a little bit, you miss the question.

Instead, use the second rule: Just add the first and the last terms, which you can see at a glance, and divide that sum by 2. In this case, $3 + 52 = 55$, and $\frac{55}{2} = 27.5$.

Note: Double-check your answer by using your common sense. Perhaps you made a silly mistake and got 45 for your answer. A quick glance at the numbers tells you that 45 isn't in the middle and therefore can't be the average.

This tip on averaging the first and last terms works for *all* evenly spaced terms. It doesn't matter whether the series has a middle number, as in the first example, or no middle number, as in the second example. Go back to the first example:

32, 41, 50, 59, 68, 77, 86, 95, 104

Instead of finding the middle term, add the first and last terms and divide by 2, like this: $32 + 104 = 136$, and $\frac{136}{2} = 68$. Either way works.

Solving missing-term average problems

A missing-term average problem is one that gives you the average and all but one of the values and asks for that missing value.

A student takes seven exams. Her scores on the first six are 91, 89, 85, 92, 90, and 88. If her average on all *seven* exams is 90, what did she get on the seventh exam?

To solve a problem like this, you can use the algebraic method or the over-and-under method.

Algebraic method

To solve a missing-term average problem, use algebra to find the unknown, as explained in Chapter 9. Start with the average equation, plug in a variable for the unknown value, and then solve for that variable:

$$\text{Average} = \frac{\text{Sum}}{\#\text{Terms}}$$
$$90 = \frac{\text{Sum}}{7}$$

Because you don't know the seventh term, call it x. Add the first six terms to get 535 plus x and then solve for x.

$$90 = \frac{535 + x}{7}$$
$$630 = 535 + x$$
$$630 - 535 = x$$
$$95 = x$$

The seventh exam score was 95.

Over-and-under method

The over-and-under method for solving missing-term average problems is slightly more straightforward:

1. **List the values and then jot down how much each value is over or under the target average.**

   The example problem tells you that the student's first six scores are 91, 89, 85, 92, 90, and 88, and her average on all seven exams is 90. Find out how far each of the six scores is from 90. For example, 91 is 1 over 90, and 85 is 5 under 90. Do this for the rest of the scores, and here's what you get:

   Average* = *90

   91: +1

   89: –1

   85: –5

   92: +2

   90: 0

   88: –2

   You can toss the 90, because it's equal to the target average.

2. **Add the numbers showing the values over and under the target.**

   The +1 and –1 cancel each other out, and the +2 and –2 cancel each other out. You're left with –5.

3. **Use the sum from Step 2 to find out how far the last value needs to be over or under the target average.**

   The missing score needs to be +5 to make up for the –5. Therefore, the seventh test score must be 90 + 5 = 95.

The shortcut, over-and-under way is quick and easy, but don't forget to switch the sign on the sum of the over/under values. That is, if you decide that you're *minus five* points going into the final exam, you need to be *plus five* points on that last exam to come out even. If you subtract five points from the average instead of adding them, you'll probably arrive at one of the trap answers.

Try solving a missing-term average problem with the over-and-under method.

A student takes seven exams. She gets an 88 average on all of them. Her first six scores are 89, 98, 90, 82, 88, and 87. What does she get on the seventh exam?

Average* = *88

89: +1

98: +10

90: +2

82: –6

88: 0

87: –1

Toss the 88. Now add the numbers that show how far the numbers are from the target average. The +1 and –1 cancel. Then you have 10 + 2 = 12 and –6, for a total of +6. So this student is 6 points above what she needs for the ultimate outcome. She can afford to lose 6 points on the final exam, or to be six points below the average. That gives her an 82.

You may be given only five out of seven scores and asked for the average of the missing two terms. Take the same approach as when you have one missing number and then divide by 2, because you have two missing numbers.

Here's the algebraic way:

Average of seven exams: 85

Scores of the first five exams: 86, 79, 82, 85, 84

Find: The average score of each of the remaining exams

$$85 = \frac{(86+79+82+85+84)+x+x}{7}$$

$$85(7) = 416+2x$$

$$595 = 416+2x$$

$$179 = 2x$$

$$x = 89.5$$

And here's the over-and-under way to find the two missing numbers:

Average = 85

86: +1

79: –6

82: –3

85: 0

84: –1

Toss the 0. The +1 and –1 cancel each other out. You're left with –9 for two exams, or –4.5 per exam. If you're down four and a half points, you must gain those four and a half points on each of the two exams:

85 + 4.5 = 89.5

Working with weighted averages

A *weighted average* is one that takes into account statistical data, such as the number of students earning a score on a test or the number of employees earning a given salary. In a weighted average, some values count more than others.

To calculate a weighted average, multiply each value, such as a specific score or salary, by the number of occurrences of it, such as the number of students who got that score or the number of employees who earn that salary. Then, divide by the total occurrences, such as the total number of students or employees.

Find the average score for a student in a class of 15, given the following scores.

Number of Students	*Score*
5	120
10	90

To solve this problem, you can't simply add 120 and 90 and divide by 2 because the scores aren't evenly distributed among the students. Because 5 students got a 120, multiply $5 \times 120 = 600$. Do the same with the other score:

$$10 \times 90 = 900$$

Now, add them all up:

$$600 + 900 = 1{,}500$$

You now have the total number of points that all the students earned. To figure out the average score, divide by the total number of students ($5 + 10 = 15$):

$$\frac{1{,}500}{15} = 100$$

Calculating Simple Interest: I = Prt

Interest problems challenge you to calculate gains or losses on investments and the amount of interest paid on loans. To solve these problems, use this formula or some rendition of it: $I = Prt$.

I is interest, P is principal (the amount of money you start with), r is the interest rate, and t is time (always in years). An interest problem usually asks you how much interest someone earned on his or her investment, but the problem may ask how much interest someone paid on a loan.

Janet invested $1,000 at 5% annual interest for one year. How much interest did she earn?

This is the simplest type of problem. Plug in the numbers and do the math:

$$I = Prt$$
$$I = 1{,}000 \times 0.05 \times 1$$
$$I = \$50$$

The answer choices may try to trap you with variations on a decimal place, making the answers 5, 50, 500, and so on. You know that $5\% = \frac{5}{100} = 0.05$. Just be careful when multiplying and moving the decimal.

The GRE doesn't throw many curves on interest problems. You won't see something as technical as "calculate 5% annual interest compounded quarterly for 3 months."

You may encounter problems that provide the interest and ask for something else, such as the principal or rate. If you encounter a question like that, use the following memory device:

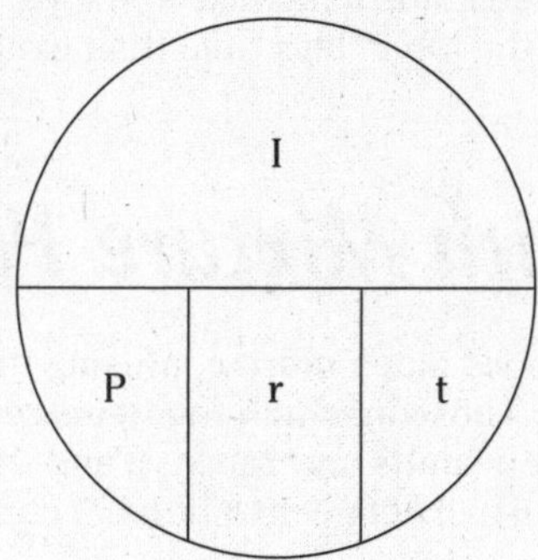

Cover up the letter for the value you don't have, and this little tool reveals the equation for determining that value. Cover the *I*, for example, and you see that $I = Prt$. Cover the *r*, and you see that $r = \frac{I}{Pt}$, and so on.

Working Out with Work Problems

Work problems typically tell you how long specific individuals would take to complete a task and then ask you how long they'd take to complete the task together, or some variation on that theme.

To solve work problems, the following formula comes in handy:

$$\frac{1}{Time_A} + \frac{1}{Time_B} + \frac{1}{Time_C} = \frac{1}{Time_{Total}}$$

where $Time_A$ is the time it takes the first person, $Time_B$ is the time it takes the second person, and so on, and $Time_{Total}$ is the total time it takes them working together. You may keep adding people to the left side of the equation as needed.

If Jonathan can paint a house in six days and David can paint a house in eight days, how many days does it take them to paint the house together?

To solve this problem, plug in the numbers and do the math:

$$\frac{1}{6} + \frac{1}{8} = \frac{1}{Time_{Total}}$$

$$\frac{4}{24} + \frac{3}{24} = \frac{1}{Time_{Total}}$$

$$\frac{7}{24} = \frac{1}{Time_{Total}}$$

$$\frac{24}{7} = Time_{Total}$$

$$3\frac{6}{14} = Time_{Total}$$

$$3\frac{3}{7} \text{ days}$$

It would take the two working together $R = 3\frac{3}{7}$ days to paint the house.

Double-check your answer by using your common sense. If you get an answer of 10, for example, you know you made a mistake somewhere because the two men working together should be able to do the job in less time than would either one working alone.

Mixing It Up with Mixture Problems

A mixture problem looks much more confusing than it really is. Plan to encounter two types of mixture problems: Those in which the items remain separate (when you mix peanuts and raisins, you still have peanuts and raisins), and those in which the two elements blend (these elements are usually concentrations of chemicals, like percents of salt in a mixture).

You can solve both types in the same general way, setting up tables that account for both the total mix and the component parts. Check out the separate mixture first.

Carolyn wants to mix 40 pounds of beads selling for 30 cents a pound with a quantity of sequins selling for 80 cents a pound. She wants to pay 40 cents per pound for the final mix. How many pounds of sequins should she use?

The hardest part for most test-takers is knowing where to begin. Stick to these steps to solve problems like this one:

1. **Make a chart and start with the bare essentials — the labels for all the data you have to work with.**

	Pounds	*Price*	*Total*
Beads			
Sequins			
Mixture			

2. **Fill in the values that the test gives you.**

   Here, beads are 40 pounds at 30 cents a pound. Sequins are 80 cents per pound. You want the mixture to cost 40 cents a pound.

	Pounds	*Price*	*Total*
Beads	40	$0.30	
Sequins		$0.80	
Mixture		$0.40	

3. **Use a variable to stand in for your unknown value.**

   You don't know how many pounds of sequins you have, so that's your variable, x. Now use a little logic to find the weight of the mixture. If you start with 40 pounds of beads and add this new unknown amount of sequins, x, you now have $40 + x$ pounds for the mixture.

	Pounds	*Price*	*Total*
Beads	40	$0.30	
Sequins	x	$0.80	
Mixture	$40 + x$	$0.40	

4. Multiply across the rows to fill in the total column.

	Pounds	*Price*	*Total*
Beads	40	$0.30	$12.00
Sequins	x	$0.80	0.80x$
Mixture	$40 + x$	$0.40	$0.40(40 + x)

5. Solve for *x*.

In the Total column, the total cost of beads plus sequins equals the total cost of the mixture, so the equation looks like this:

$$\$12.00 + \$0.80x = \$0.40(40 + x)$$

You know from the table that x is going to be in pounds, because it's in the Pounds column, so drop the dollar signs for simplicity and do the math:

$$\begin{aligned} 12.00 + 0.80x &= 0.40(40 + x) \\ 12.00 + 0.80x &= 16.00 + 0.40x \\ 0.40x &= 4.00 \\ x &= 10 \end{aligned}$$

In this case, you can drop the dollar signs *and* decimal points for simplicity, because the dollar amounts will cancel out on the two sides of the equation. The math then looks like this:

$$\begin{aligned} 1{,}200 + 80x &= 1{,}600 + 40x \\ 80x - 40x &= 1{,}600 - 1{,}200 \\ 40x &= 400 \\ x &= 10 \end{aligned}$$

Careful! Keep in mind what x stands for. It represents the number of pounds of sequins, which is what the question asks for.

Go back and double-check the answer by plugging this value into the equation. You already know that Carolyn spent $12 on beads. If she buys 10 pounds of sequins for 80 cents, she spends $8, for a total of $20. She spends that $20 on 50 pounds: 2,000 ÷ 50 = 40. Easy as that.

A mixture question based on a concentration of chemicals works the same way. The only difference is that the *total* column represents amounts of substances (5 liters of a 40 percent saline solution contains 2 liters of salt) rather than cost.

A chemistry student has one solution that's 25% acid and another that's 15% acid. Approximately how many liters of the 25% solution must be added to the 15% solution to make 10 liters of a solution that's 20% acid?

Ⓐ 2.5

Ⓑ 3.3

Ⓒ 5.0

Ⓓ 6.7

Ⓔ 7.5

To answer this question, first create your table with the data you have:

	Amount of Solution	% Solution	Amount Acid
25% solution	x	0.25	$0.25x$
15% solution	$10 - x$	0.15	$0.15(10 - x)$
20% solution	10	0.20	2

Now create your equation and do the math to solve for x. The total 15% salt solution plus the total 25% salt solution equals the total 20% salt solution, so your equation looks like this:

$$0.25x + 0.15(10 - x) = 2$$

Now do the math:

$$\begin{aligned} 0.25x + 0.15(10 - x) &= 2 \\ 0.25x + 1.5 - 0.15x &= 2 \\ 0.10x &= 0.5 \\ x &= 5 \end{aligned}$$

Sorting Out Sets and Groups

Set theory is a branch of mathematics that groups numbers, objects, or any items whatsoever into sets and describes the relationships between and among members of those sets. For example, you may group students by male and female and have members of each group form a subset for athletes. Of course, the math gets a little more involved than that, as the following sections reveal.

A *set* is a collection of numbers, values, or objects that are related in some way; a set's members are listed between curly braces, like this: {1, 3, 5, 7, 9}. An *empty set,* also referred to as a *null set,* is a set with nothing in it, and is noted as such by the symbol $\varnothing$: $\varnothing = \{\}$. If something is a member of a set, it's tagged with the $\in$ symbol, which stands for "is an element of." If it's tagged with $\notin$, it's not an element of the set. If the $\in$ is backwards, it means "contains as an element," so if $3 \in A$, then $A \ni 3$.

Set relationships: Dealing with unions, intersections, and subsets

Sometimes sets overlap. Some or all of the members of one set belong to another set, and vice versa. To describe specifically how the sets overlap, set theory uses a *u*-shaped symbol: ∪. The orientation of the symbol indicates a union, intersection, or subset relationship:

- **Union:** The union of two sets A and B, written as $A \cup B$, contains the members of both sets A and B. Suppose set $A = \{1, 2, 4, 6, 7, 9\}$ and $B = \{0, 2, 3, 5, 8, 10\}$. Then $A \cup B = \{0, 1, 2, 3, 4, 5, 6, 7, 8, 9, 10\}$.
- **Intersection:** The intersection of two sets A and B, written as $A \cap B$, contains only members belonging to both sets. If set $A = \{1, 2, 4, 6, 7, 10\}$ and $B = \{0, 2, 3, 5, 8, 10\}$, then $A \cap B = \{2, 10\}$.

- **Subset:** A subset, written as $B \subset A$, is a set within another set. All the members of the subset belong to both sets. If set $A = \{1, 2, 4, 6, 7, 10\}$ and $B = \{1, 7, 10\}$, then $B \subset A = \{1, 7, 10\}$.

Math provides visual aids, called Venn diagrams, for understanding set theory and the relationships between members of different sets. A *Venn diagram* consists of a rectangle representing an abstract universal set along with usually two to three circles representing sets within the universal set. In most cases, the rectangle is omitted to simplify the illustration. The circles overlap in different ways to show the relationships between members of the sets. If you encounter a set question on the test and have trouble visualizing how the members of two sets relate to one another, consider drawing a Venn diagram on your scratch paper.

The following diagrams show no overlap, $A \cup B$, $A \cap B$, and $B \subset A$:

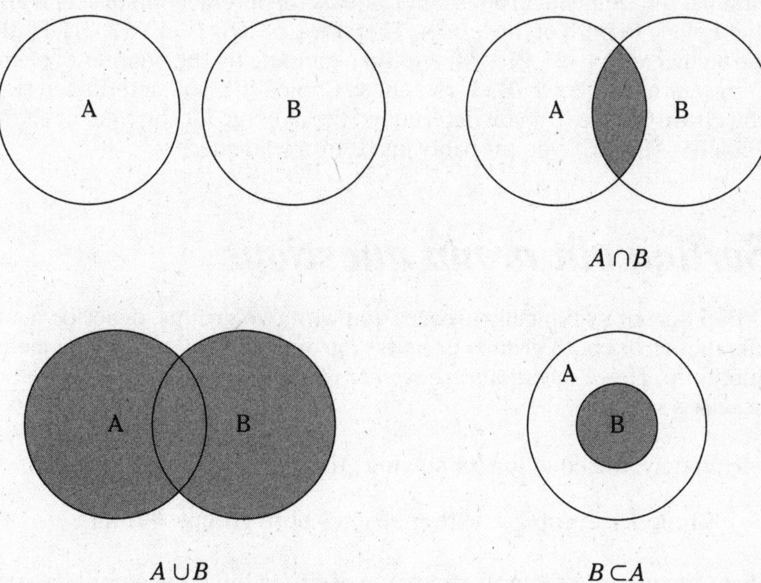

What are the elements of Set *C*?

$A = \{a, c, f, g, r\}$

$B = \{a, e, f, h, s, w\}$

$C = A \cup B$

Ⓐ $\{a, f\}$

Ⓑ $\varnothing$

Ⓒ $\{a, b, c, e, f, g, h, r, s, w\}$

Ⓓ $\{a, c, e, f, g, h, r, s, w\}$

Ⓔ $\{A, B\}$

Set *C* is *A* union *B*, or the combination of all members of *A* and *B* without any doubles. *Correct answer:* Choice **(D).** If you chose Choice (A), you mistook the union symbol for the intersection symbol.

Set questions may include other mathematical concepts, including *mean* (same as average) or absolute value, as in the following example.

What is the average of the elements in Set L?

$D = \{1, 3, 6, 12, 18, 21\}$

$F = \{2, 3, 5, 12, 21, 22\}$

$L = D \cap F$

Ⓐ 11

Ⓑ 12

Ⓒ 10

Ⓓ 10.5

Ⓔ 9.5

First list the elements in Set L. Set L equals the intersection of sets A and B, or the members that belong to both of those sets. Therefore, $L = D \cap F = \{3, 12, 21\}$. Find the average by adding the elements ($3 + 12 + 21 = 36$) and then dividing by the number of elements ($36 \div 3 = 12$). *Correct answer:* Choice **(B).** If you chose Choice (C), you determined the average for $D \cup F$. If you chose Choice (D), you determined the average for the total of all the values. If you chose Choices (A) or (E), you probably just took a wild guess.

Sorting out group questions

Group questions typically present you with two groups, describe a subgroup comprised of members from both groups or neither group, and ask how many members belong to that subgroup. These questions are similar to the set-relationships questions described in the previous section.

Fortunately, the equation for solving group problems is easy:

Group 1 + Group 2 + neither group – both groups = Total

Of 200 employees, 60 took advantage of educational benefits, 145 participated in the company retirement program, and 40 participated in both programs. How many employees took advantage of neither program?

This group problem is about as straightforward as you can get. Jot down the known values and the unknown variable so you know what you have to work with:

Group 1: 60

Group 2: 145

Both groups: 40

Neither group: x

Total: 200

Plug the numbers into the group formula and do the math:

$$60 + 145 + x - 40 = 200$$
$$165 + x = 200$$
$$x = 35$$

Solving Simple Probability Problems

Probability problems may seem a little intimidating at first. For example, a probability problem may ask your chances of drawing an ace, a king, and a queen from a deck of cards. Fortunately, three simple rules can help you solve nearly every probability problem tossed your way. In this section, I tell you how to find probability in general and how to find probabilities when multiple events occur.

A probability is always a number between 0 and 1. A probability of 0 means that an event definitely won't happen, and a probability of 1 means it definitely will happen. You can't have a negative probability, and you can't have a probability greater than 1, or 100 percent (absolute certainty).

Rule #1: Create a fraction

To find a probability, use this formula, which creates a fraction you can use to solve the problem:

$$P = \frac{\text{Number of possible desired outcomes}}{\text{Number of total possible outcomes}}$$

The denominator (the bottom part of the fraction) is usually the easier of the two parts to begin with. The denominator contains the total possible number of outcomes. For example, when you're flipping a coin, two possible outcomes exist: heads or tails; that gives you a denominator of 2. When you're tossing a die, six possible outcomes exist, giving you a denominator of 6. When you're pulling a card out of a deck, 52 possible outcomes exist (because a full deck has 52 cards), giving you a denominator of 52. The denominator is the whole shebang — everything that's possible.

The numerator shows the total possible number of the things you want. If you want to get heads when you toss a coin, exactly one side is heads, giving you a numerator of 1. The probability of tossing heads, therefore, is $\frac{1}{2}$ — one desired outcome over two possible outcomes. Suppose you want to get a 5 when you toss a die. A die has exactly one 5 on it, giving you a numerator of 1 and a denominator of 6. The probability of rolling a 5 is $\frac{1}{6}$.

What is the probability of drawing a jack out of a deck of playing cards? The deck has 52 cards (denominator) and four jacks (numerator), so the probability is $\frac{4}{52}$, which reduces to $\frac{1}{13}$. The probability of drawing the jack of hearts, however, is only $\frac{1}{52}$, because the deck contains only one jack in that suit.

A jar of marbles has 8 yellow marbles, 6 black marbles, and 12 white marbles. What is the probability of drawing out a black marble?

You have 6 black marbles and 26 marbles total. The number of black marbles goes in the numerator, and the total number of marbles goes in the denominator resulting in a probability of $\frac{6}{26}$, or $\frac{3}{13}$.

Rule #2: Multiply consecutive probabilities

A *consecutive probability* is the odds that a certain event will occur a specific number of times in a row; for example, if I flip a coin twice, the probability that it comes up heads both times. To solve a consecutive probability problem, find the probability of each event separately and then multiply them.

What's the probability that you'll get heads twice when you toss a coin twice? Find each probability separately and then multiply the two. The chance of tossing a coin the first time and getting heads is $\frac{1}{2}$. The chance of tossing a coin the second time and getting heads is $\frac{1}{2}$. Multiply those consecutive probabilities:

$$\frac{1}{2}\times\frac{1}{2}=\frac{1}{4}$$

The chances of getting two heads are one out of four. Note that the probability would be the same whether you toss one coin twice or toss two coins at the same time.

What's the probability of tossing a die twice and getting a 5 on the first toss and a 6 on the second toss? Treat each toss separately.

The probability of getting a 5 is $\frac{1}{6}$. The probability of getting a 6 is $\frac{1}{6}$. Multiply consecutive probabilities:

$$\frac{1}{6}\times\frac{1}{6}=\frac{1}{36}$$

Again, the probability is the same whether you toss one die twice or two dice at the same time.

Rule #3: Add either/or probabilities on a single event

An either/or probability on a single event is one in which either of two outcomes may occur; for example, the probability that you reach into a bag containing 10 blue, 10 red, and 10 green marbles and pull out a blue *or* a red marble. To solve an either/or probability problem, find the probability of each event separately and then add them together.

What's the probability of tossing a die once and getting either a 5 or a 6? Either outcome has a one in six chance of occurring:

$$\frac{1}{6}+\frac{1}{6}=\frac{2}{6}=\frac{1}{3}$$

The probability of rolling either a 5 or a 6 on a single die roll is $\frac{1}{3}$. Note that if you roll two separate dice, the probability would be different, but the GRE won't ask you to make this calculation.

Surveying Different Counting Methods

Counting certainly sounds easy enough, but when you're counting the number of ways that several objects or events can be arranged, selected, or combined, counting becomes much more complex. The following sections explain some tricks to help you count these objects or events quickly and easily.

Putting the counting principle to work

According to the *counting principle,* if an event has *m* possible outcomes and another independent event has *n* possible outcomes, then the total possible outcomes of both events occurring together is *mn*.

Suppose you have five shirts, two pairs of pants, and two jackets. How many different outfits can you put together? To answer this question, apply the counting principle:

1. **Make a space for each item that can change.**

   In this case, you have three spaces: one for shirts, one for pants, and one for jackets.

2. **In each space, jot down the number of options.**

   You now have something like this:

Shirts	***Pants***	***Jackets***
5	2	2

3. **Multiply the numbers.**

   $5 \times 2 \times 2 = 20$ different outfits

Use the same technique to calculate the possible combinations you have when rolling two six-sided dice. Each die has 6 possible outcomes, so the total number of different ways the numbers on the dice can be combined are $6 \times 6 = 36$.

When order matters: Permutations

A *permutation* is a change in the arrangement of a given number of items or events. If the order in which items are arranged or in which events occur matters, you're looking at a permutation problem. One of the simplest examples looks at the possible number of ways the three letters A, B, and C can be arranged (the possible number of permutations). The answer is six:

ABC	BAC	CAB
ACB	BCA	CBA

Based on the counting principle discussed in the previous section, you can figure this out without having to write out all the possible combinations. The first event (or letter in this case) has three possible outcomes (A, B, or C), the second event has two possible outcomes (the remaining two letters), and the third event has only one possible outcome (the last remaining letter):

1st Letter	***2nd Letter***	***3rd Letter***
3	2	1

$3 \times 2 \times 1 = 6$

Whenever a question asks for the possible number of ways a certain number of objects may be arranged or events may occur, you may use the following formula:

$(n)(n-1)(n-2)(n-3)\ldots$

In which n represents the total number of items or events.

Mathematics uses the *factorial* as a convenient way to represent the product of integers up to and including a specific integer, so 3!, which stands for " factorial," is $3 \times 2 \times 1 = 6$. Factorials play a key role in calculating possible permutations and combinations.

0! breaks the rule. $0! = 1$.

You can solve simple permutation problems using *n!* where *n* represents the number of objects to arrange or the order of events.

Toby, Jill, Ashley, and Mark are racing their bicycles. How many different ways can they finish the race?

Because four people are in the race, the different orders in which the four may finish is $4! = 4 \times 3 \times 2 \times 1 = 24$.

Permutation problems become more involved when you're working with a subset of the entire number of objects or events, such as determining the possible number of ways three people out of 20 can finish a race first, second, and third or the total number of 4-digit sequences on a key pad that has 8 digits. To solve this type of permutation problem, use the following formula:

$$P_r^n = \frac{n!}{(n-r)!}$$

where *P* is the number of permutations you're trying to determine, *n* is the total number of objects or events, and *r* is the subset of objects or events you're working with at one time.

Ten high school soccer teams are competing for a berth in the upcoming tournament. How many possible ways can the top three teams be ranked from first to third?

Because order matters, this is a permutation problem. In this example, you have ten total teams, but you're working with a subset of only three of those teams, so $n = 10$ and $r = 3$. Plug in the numbers and do the math:

$$P_3^{10} = \frac{10!}{(10-3)!} = \frac{10!}{7!}$$

The numbers will always be simple enough to easily multiply. You can make it easier by reducing the fraction to its simplest terms first and then multiplying the remaining factors in the factorial:

$$P_3^{10} = \frac{10 \times 9 \times 8 \times \cancel{7!}}{\cancel{7!}}$$

$$P_5^{20} = 720$$

Be careful when reducing the fraction. The fraction $\frac{10!}{7!}$ doesn't equal $1\frac{3!}{7!}$, although that may be one of the trap answer choices. However, it does reduce:

$$\frac{10!}{7!} = \frac{10 \times 9 \times 8 \times \cancel{7!}}{\cancel{7!}} = 10 \times 9 \times 8 = 720$$

When order doesn't matter: Combinations

A *combination* is a subset of objects or events in which order doesn't matter; for example, choosing four pieces of fruit from a selection of 20 different types. If a question asks about choosing a number of items and the order in which items are arranged or events occur doesn't matter, you're looking at a combination problem.

REMEMBER

To solve a combination problem, use the following formula:

$$C_r^n = \frac{n!}{r!(n-r)!}$$

where C is the number of combinations you're trying to determine, n is the number of objects or events, and r is the number of objects or events you're choosing.

From a group of ten colleagues, Sally must choose three to serve on a committee. How many possible combinations does she have to choose from?

Because the order doesn't matter, this is a combination problem, so proceed as follows:

$$C_{10}^{3} = \frac{10!}{3!(10-3)!}$$

$$\begin{aligned}\frac{10!}{3!(10-3)!} &= \frac{(10)\left({}^{3}\cancel{9}\right)\left({}^{4}\cancel{8}\right)\cancel{(7!)}}{\left({}^{1}\cancel{3}\right)\left({}^{1}\cancel{2}\right)(1)\cancel{(7!)}} \\ &= 120\end{aligned}$$

Using counting methods to solve probability problems

Counting methods can be relevant to probability questions if you need to calculate the number of desired outcomes (top of the probability fraction) or the number of total possible outcomes (bottom of the probability fraction). For example, to calculate the odds of flipping a coin four times and getting four tails, use the counting method. With each flip, you have a one in two chance of it landing tails. You have four independent events (the four coin tosses), so multiply the odds of each event:

$$\frac{1}{2} \times \frac{1}{2} \times \frac{1}{2} \times \frac{1}{2} = \frac{1}{16}$$

Now suppose you want to figure your odds of winning the lottery when you purchase a ticket. You pick two numbers out of 100. What are your odds that your two numbers will match the two winning lottery numbers?

Here, you're choosing 2 out of 100 and the order doesn't matter, so first use the combinations formula to determine the total possible two-number combinations:

$$\begin{aligned}C_{200}^{2} &= \frac{200!}{2!(200-2)!} \\ &= \frac{200!}{2!(198)!} \\ &= \frac{(200)(199)\cancel{(198!)}}{2!\cancel{(198)}} \\ &= \frac{(200)(199)}{2} \\ &= \frac{(100)(199)}{1} \\ &= 19{,}900\end{aligned}$$

You have only one ticket, so your chances of winning are one out of that number, which is that number's reciprocal:

$$\frac{1}{19{,}900}$$

Chapter 12

Interpreting Data and Graphs

In This Chapter

- Crunching numbers with basic statistics
- Picking details out of tables
- Making sense of graphs

Regardless of your subject area of choice in grad school, you need a general understanding of a few concepts in statistics and the ability to make sense of data presented in tables and on graphs. The folks who developed the GRE are well aware of this fact, so they include several questions in the Math sections of the exam to test your skills in data analysis.

This chapter gets you up to speed on the basics of understanding graphs and different kinds of data. In this chapter, you wrap your brain around the concepts of median, mode, range, mean, and standard deviation; figure out how to read tables and answer questions about the data they contain; and sharpen your ability to extract and analyze data from graphs.

Brushing Up on Basic Stats

The mere mention of statistics makes some people's brains swirl, but most statistic questions on the GRE are fairly basic. If you can master a few basic concepts, you can solve any statistics problem on the GRE. In this section, I cover the concepts of median, mode, range, mean, and standard deviation you need to know.

The only trap you're likely to see in the statistics questions is in the wording of the answer choices. The questions themselves are quite straightforward, but the answer choices may trick you if you tend to mix up the terms. For example, one answer choice to a *median* question may in fact be the *mean* (the average). One answer choice to a *range* question may be the *mode.* To keep from falling for this trap, be sure to note the word in the question that tells you what you're looking for — median, mode, range, mean, or standard deviation.

Defining the median

The *median* is the middle number when all the terms are arranged in order. Think of the median strip in the middle of a road. Be sure to arrange the numbers in order (increasing or decreasing, it makes no difference) before you find the median.

Find the median of –3, 18, –4, $\frac{1}{2}$, 11.

Ⓐ –3

Ⓑ 18

Ⓒ –4

Ⓓ $\frac{1}{2}$

Ⓔ 11

Put the numbers in order: –4, –3, $\frac{1}{2}$, 11, 18. The one in the middle, $\frac{1}{2}$, is the median. Finding the median is as simple as that. *Correct answer:* Choice **(D).**

If the list has an even number of terms, put them in order and find the middle two. Then find the average of those two terms.

Find the median of 5, 0, –3, –5, 1, 2, 8, 6.

Ⓐ 0

Ⓑ 1

Ⓒ 1.5

Ⓓ 2

Ⓔ 5

Put the numbers in order: –5, –3, 0, 1, 2, 5, 6, 8. The middle two terms are 1 and 2, and their average is $\frac{1+2}{2} = \frac{3}{2} = 1.5$. That's it. *Correct answer:* Choice **(C).**

Don't confuse median (middle) with mean. A *mean* is simply the average, as explained later in the section "Finding the mean."

Understanding mode

The *mode* is the most frequent number. Think *mode* = *more* = *most.* Put the numbers in order again, and the one that shows up the most often is the mode.

Find the mode of 11, 18, 29, 17, 18, –4, 0, 19, 0, 11, 18.

Ⓐ 11

Ⓑ 17

Ⓒ 18

Ⓓ 19

Ⓔ 29

The list of terms contains three 18s but no more than two of any other number. *Correct answer:* Choice **(C).**

If the list has two or more numbers that appear the most, then the list has more than one mode, and you count each one.

Find the modes of 6, 7, 8, 8, 8, 9, 10, 10, 11, 11, 11, 12, 15. Choose more than one answer choice if necessary.

A 6

B 8

C 10

D 11

E 12

F 15

The list of terms contains three 8s and three 11s, so it has two modes. *Correct answers:* Choices **(B)** and **(D)**.

If the list has an even number of values, calculate the median by averaging the two middle numbers. If the list has two modes, count them both.

Establishing the range

The *range* is the distance from the largest to the smallest. In other words, take the largest term and subtract the smallest term. Your answer is the range.

Find the range of the numbers 11, 18, 29, 17, 18, –4, 0, 19, 0, 11, 18.

Ⓐ 33

Ⓑ 29

Ⓒ 19

Ⓓ 0

Ⓔ –4

To find the range, subtract the smallest number from the largest: 29 – (–4) = 29 + 4 = 33. *Correct answer:* Choice **(A)**.

Finding the mean

Mean is another word for average. To calculate the mean, sum up all the values and divide by the number of values.

Suppose you have a data set consisting of the numbers 1, 6, 8, 10, 12, and 17. To calculate the mean, do the following:

1. **Sum up all the values.**

   $1 + 6 + 8 + 10 + 12 + 17 = 54$

2. **Divide this sum by the number of values.**

   $\frac{54}{6} = 9$

   And the mean is 9.

Calculating the standard deviation

Standard deviation is the average distance from the mean for a set of numbers. Outside the GRE, standard deviation can be very complicated, but for the purpose of the GRE, a general understanding is sufficient. Fortunately, on the GRE, you calculate the standard deviation only on a simple set of data, which makes the calculations much easier and simpler.

Begin with the same data set used in the preceding section: 1, 6, 8, 10, 12, and 17.

1. **Find the average.**

   $$\frac{1+6+8+10+12+17}{6}=\frac{54}{6}=9$$

2. **Find the distance of each value from the mean.**

   This distance is always positive.

   In this example, the first value, 1, has a distance of 8 from the mean (9 – 1 = 8). The second value, 6, has a distance of 3 (9 – 6 = 3). The third value, 8, has a distance of 1; 10 has a distance of 1; 12 has a distance of 3; and 17 has a distance of 8.

   The actual method of calculating standard deviation is much more complicated than this, with a slightly different result. However, this method is fine for any standard deviation question you may encounter on the GRE. The test will never ask you to name a standard deviation, but it may ask you which set of data has a greater or lesser standard deviation. If it does, this method is perfect to use.

3. **To find the standard deviation, take the average of these distances.**

   $$\frac{8+3+1+1+3+8}{6}=\frac{24}{6}=4$$

   And the standard deviation for this set of data is 4.

Analyzing Data in Tables

Tables display data in rows and columns to make it more easily accessible. You've probably used tables without even knowing it, such as when you look in the TV listings to find programs to watch or look at a scoreboard. On the GRE, however, tables do more than merely help you find pieces of data; they often contain details for analyzing that data.

A table is different from a graph. A *graph,* which I discuss in greater detail later in this chapter, is a drawing that shows the relationship between the data and how the data changes. A *table,* discussed in this section, organizes the data into a matrix.

To handle the table questions that you're likely to encounter on the test, you need an eye for detail and a knack for drawing information from the data. In other words, the GRE challenges you to determine the significance of the data that's in the table. Take the following approach to answering any question that contains a table:

1. **Cover the question and answer choices.**
2. **Read and understand the title, column headings, and units of measure in order to get the gist of the data presented.**
3. **Carefully read the question and understand *exactly* what it's asking.**

4. **Return to the table and collect only the data necessary to answer the question.**
5. **Determine your answer to the question before looking at the answer choices.**
6. **Compare the answer choices to your answer to find the best match.**

Distribution of Video Rentals by Category for 2010 and 2011

Category	*2010*	*2011*
Action	15.2%	13.7%
Comedy	18.9%	19.1%
Drama	7.4%	10.5%
Family	22.0%	19.2%
Foreign	4.8%	7.2%
Independent	5.6%	9.3%
Romance	8.1%	5.2%
Sci-Fi	5.3%	4.0%
Thriller	12.7%	11.8%
Total	100.0%	100.0%
Total video rentals	3,225	4,189

Based on the information in the table, which of the following three statements is true? Select all that are true.

Ⓐ In each of the years 2010 and 2011, video rentals in the Action, Drama, and Thriller categories accounted for more than 35% of all video rentals.

Ⓑ The total number of Sci-Fi rentals increased from 2010 to 2011.

Ⓒ From 2010 to 2011, the total number of video rentals increased by more than 25%.

For Choice (A), add the percentages in the Action, Drama, and Thriller categories for each year: $15.2 + 7.4 + 12.7 = 35.3\%$ and $13.7 + 10.5 + 11.8 = 36\%$, so Choice (A) is true. For Choice (B), multiply the Sci-Fi percentage by the total number of video rentals for each year and compare the numbers: $0.053 \times 3{,}225 = 171$ for 2010 and $0.04 \times 4{,}189 = 168$ for 2011, so Choice (B) is false — the number of Sci-Fi rentals actually decreased slightly. For Choice (C), subtract 2010's total video rentals from 2011's total video rentals to determine how many more videos were rented in 2011, and then divide by 2010's total video rentals $[(4{,}189 - 3{,}225) \div 3{,}225] \times 100\% = 29\%$ (the percentage change formula from Chapter 8), so Choice (C) is true. The correct answers are Choices **(A)** and **(C)**.

Analyzing Data in Graphs

You'll likely see a few graphs on the GRE, each of which is followed by one or more questions. You need to first figure out the question that is being asked and then be able to extract the essential data from the graph and crunch some numbers to answer each question. To accomplish this effectively and efficiently, you need to know how to make sense of data presented on different types of graphs.

The following sections reveal the most common graph types you're likely to encounter, provide you with some practice questions to test your graph-reading ability, and reveal a quicker method for estimating graph totals.

The graphs are always drawn to scale, so you can rely on them as accurate visual representations of the data.

Reading different graph types

To make sense of data presented in a graph, familiarize yourself with the different graph types, as described in the following sections.

Line graphs

Line graphs consist of two or three axes with data points connected by a line, sort of like a connect-the-dots exercise. How data points are plotted on the graph depends on the graph type:

- **Two axes:** A typical line graph consists of an *x*- (horizontal) and *y*- (vertical) axis, each of which represents a different unit of measure. For example, the *x*-axis may represent years, while the *y*-axis represents profits in millions of dollars. In this example, each data point represents the profit for a specific year, and connecting the dots forms a line (hence the name *line* graph).

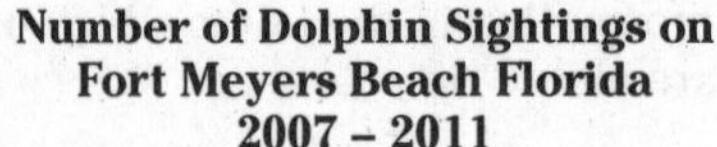

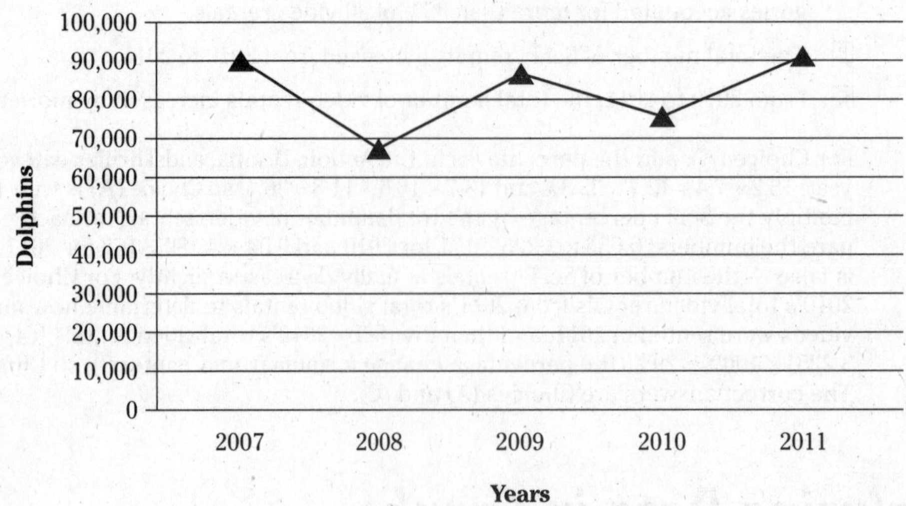

- **Three axes:** A graph with three axes contains a second *y*-axis on the right. As in this example, the left axis represents the minutes per day spent exercising, whereas the right axis represents the pounds lost per month. You read the points on a three-axes graph the same way you do on a two-axes graph, but make sure to look at the correct *y*-axis, depending on what the question asks you to determine. Here's an example of a three-axes line graph.

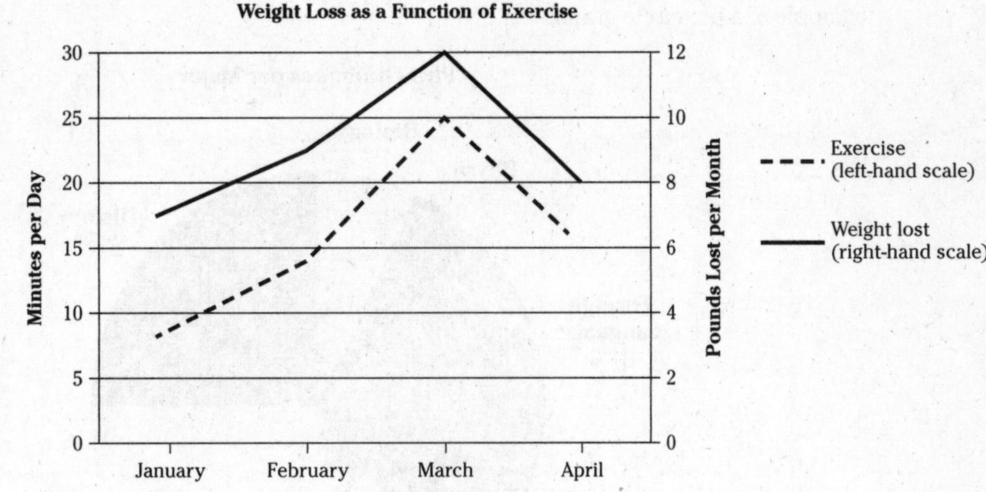

Bar graphs

A *bar graph* has vertical or horizontal bars that may represent actual numbers or percentages. Although they look significantly different from line graphs, bar graphs are very similar. The only difference is that instead of a point, the top or right side of the bar, depending on the bar's orientation (vertical or horizontal), represents the data point. See the following example.

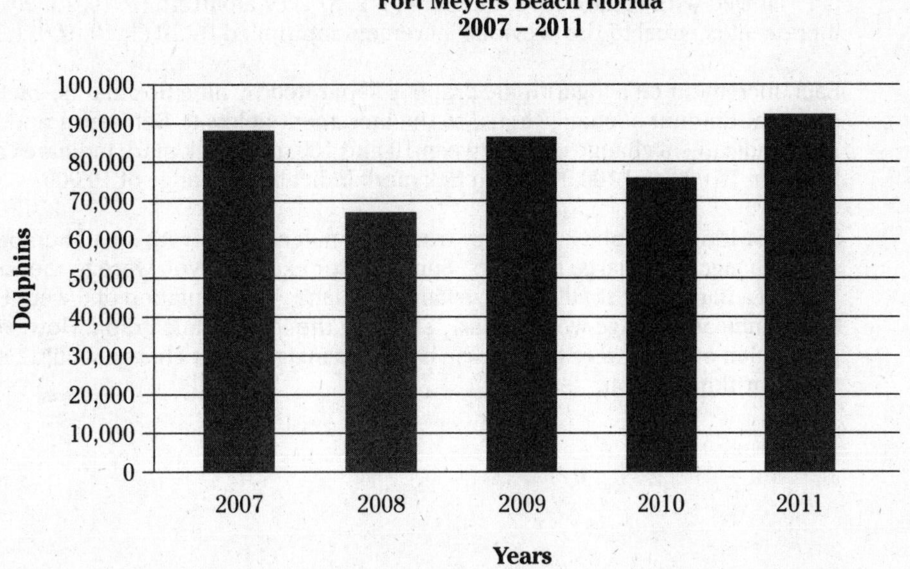

Circle or pie graphs

Each *circle* or *pie graph* represents 100 percent or 360 degrees, while slices of the pie represent percentages or degrees of that whole. To read a circle graph, first make a mental note of what the whole pie represents, so you know what each slice of the pie represents. For example, below a circle graph, you may be told that in 2001, 5,000 students graduated with PhDs. Because the graph shows a 25% segment on the circle graph is labeled "History," you know that the number of PhDs in history is 25% or $\frac{1}{4}$ of 5,000, or $5{,}000 \div 4 = 1{,}250$. Check out this example of a pie circle graph.

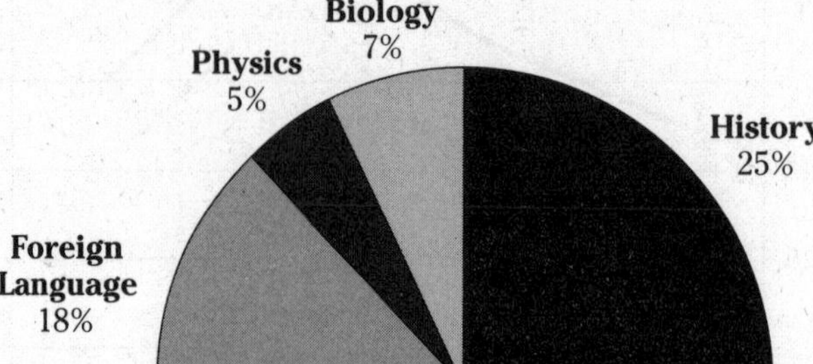

Logarithmic graphs

A *logarithmic graph* is a graph with an axis scale that changes by multiples of 10. The axis isn't labeled with consecutive numbers (1, 2, 3, 4) or a pattern (5, 10, 15, 20), instead, each increment is equal to the previous increment multiplied by 10 (1, 10, 100, 1,000, and so on).

Each increment on a logarithmic graph is separated by nine tick marks, each of which indicates the amount of change equal to the increment below it. Between 1 and 10, each tick mark indicates a change of 1. Between 10 and 100, each tick mark indicates a change of 10. Between 10,000 and 100,000, each tick mark indicates a change of 10,000.

The logarithmic graph is useful for tracking small changes with small numbers but ignoring small changes with large numbers. Suppose, for example, you were to measure the populations of a handful of small Pacific islands. If Island A's population of 6 were to increase by 2, this significant change would clearly show on the logarithmic graph. However, if Island D's population of 2,134 were to increase by 2, this insignificant change would be obscured in the logarithmic graph.

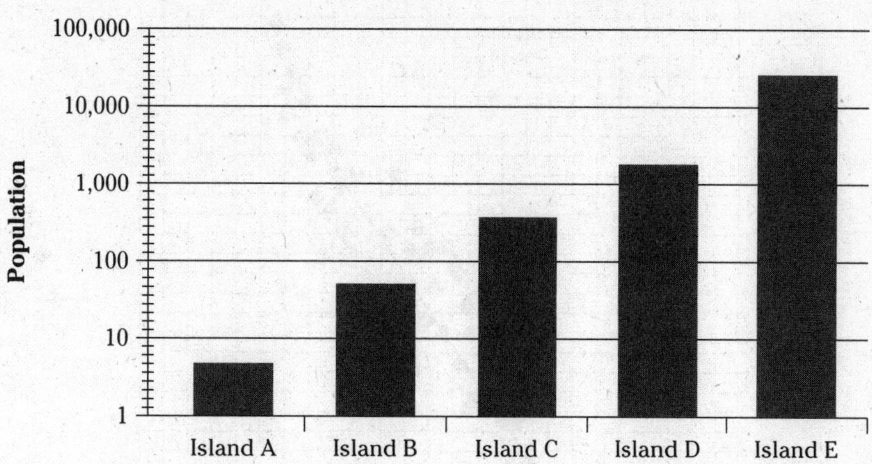

The graph on the GRE may not have the data labels like this graph does (inside the gray bars), but the GRE may ask you whether Island D has more than three times the population of Island C. Just looking at the bars, the initial answer appears to be no. However, with a grasp of how the logarithmic graph works, you know that the first tick mark after 1,000 indicates 2,000, so the answer is yes.

Scatter plots

Scatter plots are useful for spotting trends and making predictions. They're similar to line graphs in that they use horizontal and vertical axes to display the values of the points plotted on them. With a scatter plot, however, instead of connecting the dots, you may draw a line through the data to predict where the future data points are likely to fall.

The following two terms are important in interpreting scatter plots:

- **Best-fit line:** The line that passes as closely as possible through the middle of the scattered points.
- **Correlation:** Correlation specifies the direction of the best-fit line and how closely the two variables correspond:
    - **Positive correlation:** The best-fit line has a positive slope; that is, the line rises from left to right.
    - **Negative correlation:** The best-fit line has a negative slope; that is, the line runs downhill from left to right.
    - **No correlation:** If the points are scattered all over the graph like buckshot, or if the best-fit line is horizontal or forms a U or upside-down U, the variables have no correlation to one another.
    - **Strong or weak correlation:** The closer the points are to the best-fit line, the stronger the correlation. The farther they are from the line, the weaker the correlation.

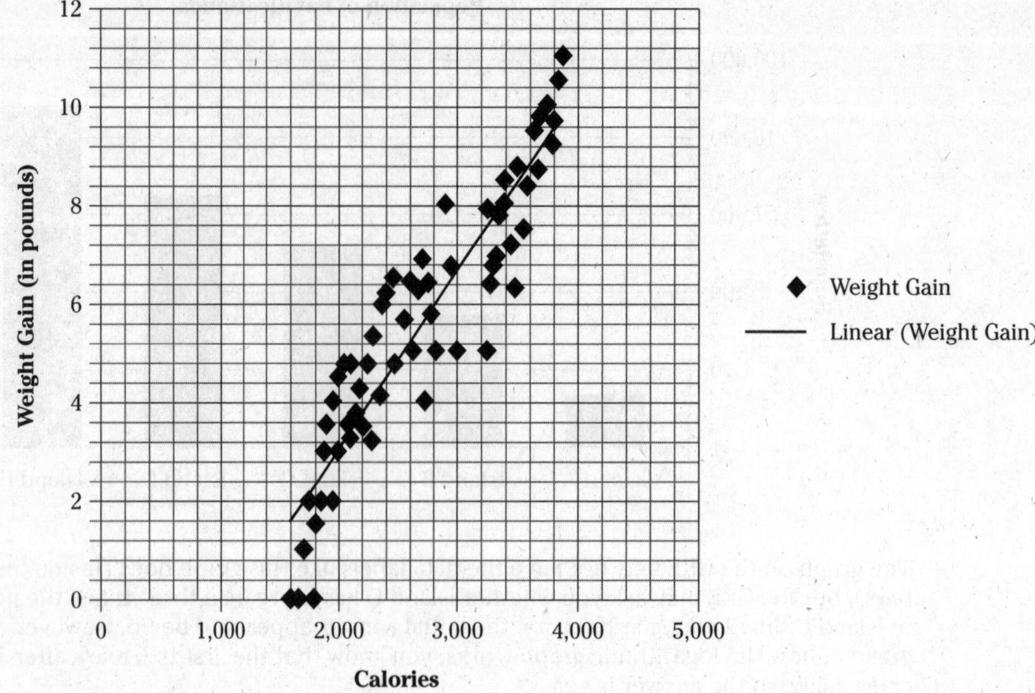

Based on the data in this scatter plot, about how many calories would need to be consumed to result in a 12-pound gain?

Ⓐ 3,000

Ⓑ 3,500

Ⓒ 4,000

Ⓓ 4,500

Ⓔ 5,000

Lay a pencil on top of the best-fit line to see where it intersects the graph at 12 pounds, follow the nearest vertical line down, and you have your answer. Extending the best-fit line to the top of the graph intersects the 12-pound line at about 4,500, which is the answer. *Correct answer:* Choice **(D)**.

Answering questions with two graphs

Some graph questions on the GRE contain two graphs, each of which is usually a different type. To answer a question, you may need to extract data from one or both graphs.

Here's an example.

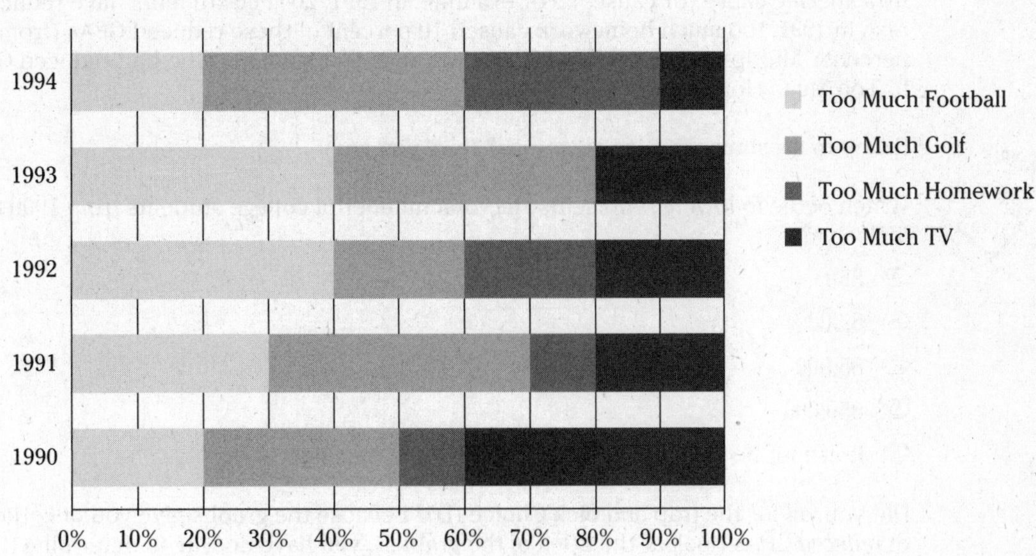

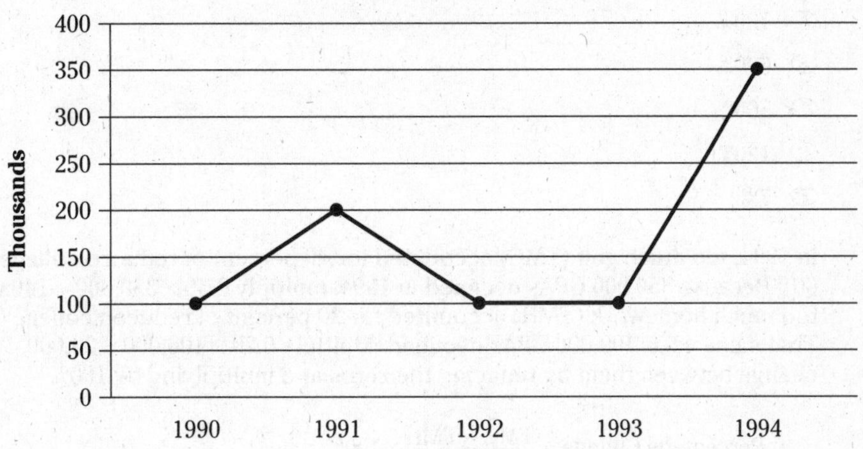

The two graphs here must be read in conjunction. The first graph is a bar graph that ranges from 0 to 100 percent. For this specific graph, calculate the impact of a cause of reduced GPAs by calculating the range of the cause. For example, in 1990, the Too Much Golf category (as a cause of reduced GPAs) began at 20 and rose to 50, a difference of 30 percent. If you say that Too Much Golf rose 50 percent, you're falling for a trap. In 1993, the Too Much TV category rose from 80 to 100, meaning TV caused 20 percent of reduced GPAs.

The second graph gives you the actual number of reduced GPAs in thousands. Be sure to look at the labels of the axes. For example, in 1990, the GPAs of 100,000 participants, not 100, in the study went down.

Now, use the graphs together to find out the number of students whose GPAs were reduced by a specific cause (or causes). For example, in 1991, 200,000 students have reduced GPAs. Also in 1991, too much homework caused 10 percent of these reduced GPAs (from 70 to 80 percent). Multiply 10% or 0.10 × 200,000 to get 20,000 students who had reduced GPAs due to Too Much Homework.

Ready to try some practice questions? Here you go:

Which of the following represents the total number of college students from 1990 to 1994 inclusive?

Ⓐ 850

Ⓑ 8,500

Ⓒ 85,000

Ⓓ 850,000

Ⓔ It cannot be determined from the information given.

Did you fall for the trap and pick Choice (D)? Because the graphs give you only the number of *reduced* GPAs (look at the titles of the graphs), you have no way to determine the total number of college students. *Correct answer:* Choice **(E)**.

The number of GPAs in 1994 that declined due to too much golf was what percent greater than the number of GPAs in 1992 that declined due to too much homework?

Ⓐ 700%

Ⓑ 600%

Ⓒ 500%

Ⓓ 120%

Ⓔ 7%

In 1994, too much golf (TMG) accounted for 40 percent of reduced college GPAs (from 20 to 60). Because 350,000 GPAs declined in 1994, multiply 0.40 × 350,000 = 140,000 TMG. In 1992, too much homework (TMH) accounted for 20 percent of reduced college GPAs (60 to 80). That same year, 100,000 GPAs declined. Multiply 0.20 × 100,000 = 20,000. Find the percent change between them by reducing the zeros and multiplying by 100%:

$$\text{Percentage Change} = \frac{\text{TMG} - \text{TMH}}{\text{TMH}} \times 100\%$$

$$\text{Percentage Change} = \frac{140{,}000 - 20{,}000}{20{,}000} \times 100\%$$

$$\text{Percentage Change} = \frac{14\cancel{0{,}000} - 2\cancel{0{,}000}}{2\cancel{0{,}000}} \times 100\%$$

$$= \frac{12}{2} \times 100\%$$

$$= 600\%$$

Correct answer: Choice **(B)**.

Estimating graph totals quickly

When choosing from five answer choices that are far apart, consider rounding as you perform your calculations, especially if you're working with really big numbers. Here's an example:

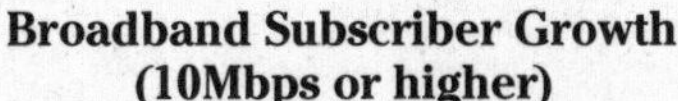

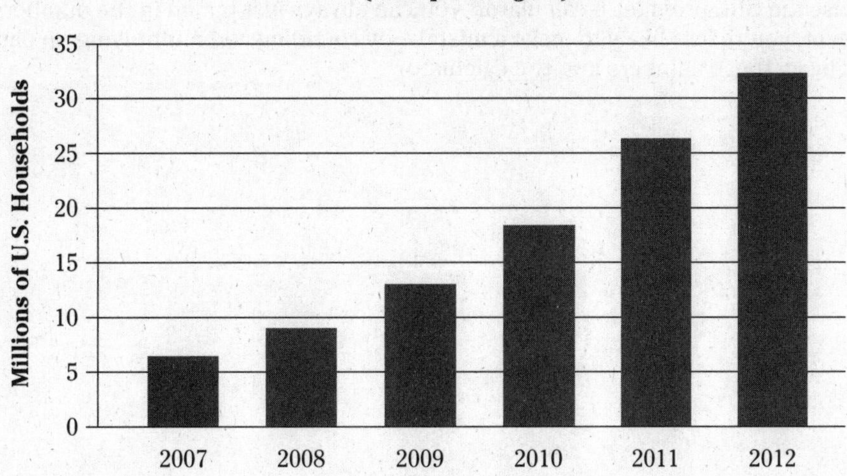

If the average cost of broadband was \$43 per month in 2010, which of the following is closest to the gross earnings for U.S. broadband companies in 2010?

Ⓐ 111,000,000

Ⓑ 946,000,000

Ⓒ 11,000,000,000

Ⓓ 94,600,000,000

Ⓔ 946,000,000,000

To estimate the gross earnings for U.S. broadband companies in 2010, you have to multiply the monthly 2010 amount of \$43 by the number of 2010 households with broadband, approximately 18 million as shown on the graph, and multiply by 12 to account for the 12 months of the year.

Now you're looking at something like this:

$$(43)(18)(10^6)(12)$$

Look at the answer choices: they're far apart. To ease the math task, you can round the numbers to the nearest tens place:

$$(40)(20)(10^6)(10)$$

Because you rounded two numbers down, and one number up, you know your answer is slightly shy of the actual answer. Multiply everything out for:

$$8{,}000 \times 10^6 = 8{,}000{,}000{,}000$$

You don't actually need to multiply $8{,}000 \times 10^6$, as long as you know that raising 10 to the sixth power gives you 1 with 6 zeros after it (a million), so six zeros plus the three zeros after the 8 gives you 8,000,000,000. (By the way, 10^9 gives you 1 with nine zeros after it, which is one billion.)

Because you rounded more numbers down than up, look for an answer that's slightly higher than your result. The 11,000,000,000 answer is the closest answer choice. *Correct answer:* Choice **(C)**.

Because the GRE provides a calculator, you can always just punch in the numbers. However, you're less likely to make a mistake by rounding and multiplying on paper than by entering all these numbers into the calculator.

Chapter 13

Comparing Quantities: They Report, You Decide Which Is Greater

In This Chapter

- Memorizing the elusive QC answer choices
- Knowing how to approach a QC problem
- Spotting and avoiding common traps
- Putting it all together so you can work smarter, not harder

Almost one-third of the GRE math questions are Quantitative Comparisons (QC) with plenty of traps to trip you: QCs demand careful thought and insight to recognize and sidestep common traps; otherwise, you may stumble into some heavy duty and unnecessary math.

A QC question lists Quantity A and Quantity B. The quantities can be numbers, variables, equations, words, figures, and so on. Your job is to compare Quantity A to Quantity B and then determine whether one is greater than the other, they're equal, or the relationship can't be determined. The good news: This chapter gives you the lowdown on QC questions and how to solve them and also points out how to steer clear of common pitfalls.

The Answer Choices Are Always the Same: Memorize Them Now

With QC questions comprising about a third of each Math section, they consume a good chunk of your time allotment. To conserve time, memorize the QC answer choices prior to test day. Whatever the problem, the answer choices for QCs are always the same:

Ⓐ Quantity A is greater.

Ⓑ Quantity B is greater.

Ⓒ The two quantities are equal.

Ⓓ The relationship cannot be determined from the information given.

Because the QC answer choices are always the same, memorizing them conserves precious time and energy during the test. As long as you know the choices, you don't need to read and think about them each time.

Consider paraphrasing the answer choices to make them easier to memorize and save even more time:

Ⓐ A is more.

Ⓑ B is more.

Ⓒ They're the same.

Ⓓ Need more information.

As Easy as π: Approaching QC Questions

The hardest part of answering a QC question is knowing where to begin. You can save considerable time and frustration by following this simple, three-step approach:

1. **Solve for Quantity A.**

   Solve may mean solving an equation, talking through a word problem, or simply looking at what's there. Here are some examples of what you may see in Quantity A:

   Quantity A

   x^2

   40% of 340

   The number of miles hiked by Ken, who hikes at 3 mph for $6\frac{1}{2}$ hours

2. **Solve for Quantity B.**

   Again, *solve* can mean solving an equation, talking through a word problem, or just looking at the quantity, as you can see in the following examples:

   Quantity B

   x^3

   340% of 40

   18

3. **Compare the two quantities.**

   Sounds simple enough, right? But just wait until you see some of the cunning traps the GRE-developers build into the QCs.

Gotchas and Other Groaners: Tips, Traps, and Tricks

QC questions have so many tricks and traps that I provide a separate section for each one, with a few examples to illustrate how easily you can fall for the traps.

Keep in mind that the following sections feature tips, not rules. A *tip* is a pointer that works most of the time, but not always — like a general rule. Never shut off your own brain in favor of a tip. The purpose of most tips is to make your job easier. Tips can help you avoid traps, but you can't follow them blindly. You still have to use your judgment.

Remembering that equal appearances can be deceiving

If Quantity A and Quantity B appear to be equal at first glance, don't fall for it — a trap is almost always involved. Check out the following examples:

Quantity A	***Quantity B***
π	3.14

Your gut reaction may be to choose Choice (C) because both quantities are equal. After all, wasn't it drilled into your head in school that π equals 3.14? (If you've been out of school for quite a while, you may be very pleased with yourself for remembering the numerical value of π. Put the self-congratulations on hold; you've just fallen for a trap.) The value of π is only *approximately* 3.14. For convenience, your teachers and math books rounded π to two decimal places: 3.14. However, π is actually larger than that and continues as a nonrepeating, nonterminating decimal: 3.141592 . . . making π greater than 3.14 and Choice (A) the right choice. *Correct answer:* Choice **(A).**

Quantity A	***Quantity B***
$.0062 \times 3600$	$6200 \times .3600$

You probably checked that the number of digits and decimal places are the same and chose Choice (C). But the answer is Choice (B). When you do the multiplication, Quantity A equals 22.32, and Quantity B equals 2,232. *Big* difference. The moral of the story? If your first reaction is that the problem is a no-brainer — that the answer is obviously, clearly, undoubtedly Choice (C) — then you're hovering over a trap, so do the math to be sure. *Correct answer:* Choice **(B).**

Keeping an eye out for scale

If a figure in a QC problem isn't drawn to scale, the answer is often Choice (D). How can you tell? Some figures may contain the guidance "***Note:*** Figure not drawn to scale" below the picture, but don't rely on the test-makers to offer this guidance. Instead, use your skills to gather information, such as line lengths or angle measurements, that enable you to answer the question. If those details are missing, you often can't determine the relationship between the quantities and must choose Choice (D). Also, avoid the temptation to eyeball figures to arrive at your answer. If you don't have a clue about how to gather the necessary information, use eyeballing only as a last resort.

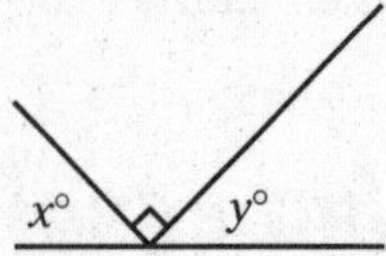

Note: Figure not drawn to scale.

Quantity A	***Quantity B***
x	y

Sure, x and y each *appear* to be 45 degrees, but because the figure isn't drawn to scale, you can't use it to estimate. You can't look at the figure and deduce that x and y are equal. Yes, x and y add up to 90 degrees. That's because angles along a straight line add up to 180 degrees, and you already have a right angle (the tiny box): $180 - 90 = 90$. But you *don't* know how much of the 90 is x and how much is y. Are they 45 and 45? 60 and 30? The figure isn't to scale, so any of those values may be correct. Because you don't have enough information to compare the quantities, go with Choice (D). *Correct answer:* Choice **(D).**

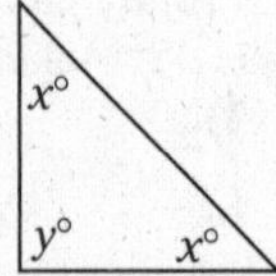

Note: Figure not drawn to scale.

Quantity A	***Quantity B***
$2x$	y

This QC question is an example of a classic Choice (D) answer. Yes, the figure *appears* to be an isosceles right triangle. You know that the two x's are equal and that the angles in a triangle add up to 180 degrees. But no one said that Angle y is 90 degrees. It certainly *looks* like 90 degrees, but without having 90° specified or the tiny box that marks a 90-degree angle, you can't be sure. ***Remember:*** Nothing is obvious; you can't use the figure if it's not drawn to scale. Because anything is possible, choose Choice (D). *Correct answer:* Choice **(D).**

"Not drawn to scale" problems are rare, but they definitely do appear.

Avoiding distraction from a pretty picture

The GRE may provide pictures (figures) to assist you in visualizing what the question is asking, but they may also use these pictures as traps. These drawings are never to scale. The GRE is challenging your grasp of the concept, not your ability to eyeball the lines and angles.

Two types of drawings are always to scale: the data graph or table and the coordinate grid (with x and y axes). (More on these drawings in Chapters 12 and 9, respectively.) Other than that, if the GRE doesn't tell you the shape is a square, you can't assume the angles are 90 degrees or the sides are equal.

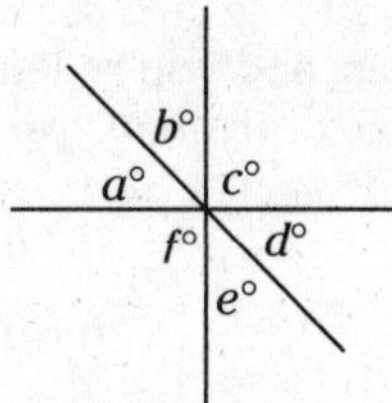

Quantity A	Quantity B
$a + b$	$d + e$

Angle a is a vertical angle to Angle d, meaning they're opposite and of equal measure. Angle b is a vertical angle to Angle e, meaning they're opposite and of equal measure. These are true regardless of whether the drawing is to scale. Because each part of Quantity A is equal to its counterpart in Quantity B, both quantities are equal. *Correct answer:* Choice **(C).**

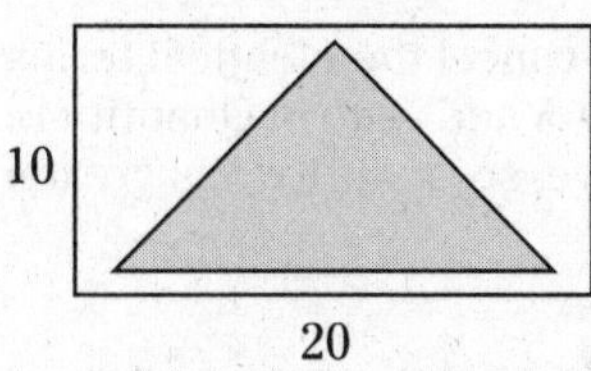

Quantity A	Quantity B
The area of the triangle	100

Fight the temptation to choose Choice (D) automatically just because you don't have numbers for the lengths of the sides of the triangle. Though not drawn to scale, you can still estimate what you need to answer the question and compare the quantities.

The formula for the area of a triangle is $\frac{1}{2}$ *base* × *height*. What's the base? You don't know, but you *do* know that it's less than the base of the rectangle because the sides of the triangle don't extend all the way to the sides of the rectangle. Just call it *less than 20*. What's the height? You don't know that either, but you do know that it's less than 10 because the top and bottom of the triangle don't touch the top and bottom of the rectangle. Call it *less than 10*. Multiply *less than 10* × *less than 20* to get *less than 200*. Half of *less than 200* is *less than 100*. Because *less than 100* is smaller than 100, choose Choice (B). *Correct answer:* Choice **(B).**

Canceling out identical quantities

Canceling quantities that are identical is like clearing the decks or simplifying the picture so you can more easily compare the two quantities. After all, a QC problem is like a balance: If something is the same on one side as on the other, it doesn't affect the balance, so you can ignore it. Be careful that you cancel only *identical* terms though. For example, you can't use –5 to cancel 5.

Quantity A	Quantity B
$x^2 - 21$	$x^2 - 35$

Cancel the x^2 in both quantities, and you're left with –21 and –35. Remember that a *negative* 21 is greater than a *negative* 35. *Correct answer:* Choice **(A).**

$a < 0$

$b < 0$

Quantity A	Quantity B
$(a+b)^2$	$(a-b)^2$

You can't cancel out a and b on both sides and say that the quantities are equal. The expression $a + b$ is *not* the same as $(a - b)^2$. You should memorize these two expressions (covered in detail in Chapter 9):

$$(a + b)^2 = a^2 + 2ab + b^2 \qquad (a - b)^2 = a^2 - 2ab + b^2$$

After foiling, you can cancel the identical terms a^2 and b^2 from both quantities. You're left with $+2ab$ in Quantity A and $-2ab$ in Quantity B. You know that because a and b are both negative, ab is positive, so Quantity A is greater. *Correct answer:* Choice **(A).**

Weighing the quantities

Pretend the QC problem is a balance when comparing each part of Quantity A to its counterpart in Quantity B. If both parts of Quantity A are greater, or heavier, than both parts of Quantity B, Quantity A is greater.

Quantity A	Quantity B
$\frac{17}{21} + \frac{47}{80}$	$\frac{19}{81} + \frac{23}{97}$

Don't even *think* about reaching for your pencil to work this problem through. Compare each part of Quantity A to its counterpart in Quantity B. Which is greater: $\frac{17}{21}$ or $\frac{19}{81}$? Reason that 17 is more than half of 21, whereas 19 is much less than half of 81. The same is true for the second pair of numbers. You know that 47 is more than half of 80; in contrast, 23 is less than half of 97. Because both parts of Quantity A are greater than both parts of Quantity B, Choice (A) is the answer. No muss, no fuss. *Correct answer:* Choice **(A).**

The point of the question is to recognize and use the test-makers' hidden tricks so you can work smarter, not revert to a basic arithmetic, pull-out-your-pencil-type problem. Once in a while, you have to do the math, but not often.

Plugging in the Sacred Six

Here's the best tip you're likely to get outside a racetrack: Whenever you have variables, plug in the Sacred Six: 1, 2, 0, –1, –2, and $\frac{1}{2}$, specifically in that order. These numbers cover most of the contingencies: positive, negative, zero, odd, even, fraction, and 1, which has special properties. Memorize these numbers and throw them into a problem whenever possible. ***Note:*** This tip works even if an equation contains more than one variable.

Quantity A	*Quantity B*
x^2	x^4

The trap answer is Choice (B). At first glance, a number to the fourth power seems greater than the same number squared. (Two x's in one problem always have the same value at one time, even in Quantities A and B. That is, if x is 5 in Quantity A, it's also 5 in Quantity B. Always. No exceptions.)

Unfortunately, obvious answers are usually wrong answers. Play the "what if" game: What if $x = 1$? Then the two quantities are alike, and Choice (C) prevails. What if $x = 2$? Then Quantity A = 4 and Quantity B = 16, and the answer is Choice (B). Therefore, the answer can be Choices (C) or (B), depending on what you plug in. Using the Sacred Six removes any doubt that the answer is Choice (D). *Correct answer:* Choice **(D).**

You don't always have to go through all the Sacred Six numbers. As soon as you find two numbers that give you two different answers, you can stop. If plugging in $\frac{1}{2}$ and 2 gives you the same answer, go on to 1, 0, –1, and –2. You'll be pleasantly surprised, however, to find out how often $\frac{1}{2}$ and 2 alone get the job done.

When the failsafe Sacred Six fail

The Sacred Six method isn't 100 percent failsafe. You can plug in all the Sacred Six and still fall for a QC trap, but it's highly unlikely. Here's an example:

Quantity A	*Quantity B*
$x \neq 0$	
$\frac{1}{x}$	3

Try the Sacred Six, and each time Quantity B is greater. However, x isn't limited to these: the Six are only a starting point. By now you have a better grasp of the question, and can immediately try a number for x that will make Quantity A greater, such as 0.1. If x were 0.1, then Quantity A would be 10 and greater than Quantity B, making Choice **(D)** the correct answer.

Remember: Shortcuts such as the Sacred Six are helpful, but no rule or method works every single time. The Sacred Six is an excellent starting point, bu`t the GRE uses creative ways to challenge your critical-thinking abilities beyond these shortcuts.

Quantity A		***Quantity B***
	$x \neq 0$	
$\frac{1}{x}$		$\frac{x}{1}$

Again, Choice (B) is the trap answer. Most people think that Quantity A comes out to be a fraction of less than 1. It may, or it may not. If x were less than 1, then Quantity A would be greater than 1.

Play the "what if" game again. What if $x = \frac{1}{2}$? Then Quantity A is greater. What if $x = 2$? Then Quantity B is greater. Because you can make either Quantity A or B greater, choose Choice (D). *Correct answer:* Choice **(D).**

On the real exam, you'd stop here, but for now, plug in a few more numbers to see what else may happen. You can't plug in 0 because the problem tells you that x isn't equal to 0 (division by 0 is undefined). What if $x = -1$? Then Quantity A is –1 and Quantity B is –1; they're equal. What if $x = -2$? Then Quantity A = $\frac{1}{2}$ and Quantity B = –2; now Quantity A is bigger. You've seen all the possibilities at this point: Quantity A can be bigger, Quantity B can be bigger, or the two quantities can be the same.

Throwing down a hundred

If a question deals with dollars or percentages, plug in 100 to make it an easier number. Any way to make the question easier is good.

Quantity A		***Quantity B***
	A book bag costs x dollars.	
Cost of the book bag on sale at 60% off		\$0.6x

If you make x \$100, you can easily determine that 60% of 100 is 60; subtract 100 – 60, and you get 40. In Quantity B, 0.6(100) = 60. The answer is Choice (B). This type of problem is easy to miss because of carelessness. Many people choose Choice (C) automatically. (Of course, if you read the earlier "Remembering that equal appearances can be deceiving" section, you know that *if the quantities appear equal, you're probably looking at a trap.*) To improve your QC-problem-solving success, slow down, plug in 100, and do the math. *Correct answer:* Choice **(B).**

Quantity A	***Quantity B***
One year's interest on x dollars at 6% annual interest	\$12

Gotcha! I tossed in this one to remind you that this chapter features *tips,* not rules, and you should never sacrifice common sense in favor of a tip. Sure, if you plug in 100 for x dollars, you know that the interest is \$6 and Choice (B) is the answer. But what if x = \$1,000,000? Then Quantity A is significantly larger. Although plugging in 100 often works, it won't always work (like any shortcut, it's not infallible), which is why you approach these questions critically. *Correct answer:* Choice **(D).**

Inserting variety when working with multiple variables

Some questions may provide you with multiple variables, such as the following:

$a > b > c$ or $x < y < z$

In questions such as these, plug in consecutive terms first and then nonconsecutive terms. If you need to plug in numbers for two or three variables, first plug in the numbers all in a row: 1, 2, and 3. Then try plugging in numbers that aren't in a row: 1, 5, and 7. Sometimes the spacing between the numbers makes a difference.

Quantity A		Quantity B
	$a<b<c$	
$\frac{a+c}{2}$		b

The normal response is to plug in consecutive numbers: 1, 2, and 3. If you do that, Quantity A is 1 + 3, or 4, divided by 2 = 2. In Quantity B, b is 2. The quantities are equal — a bright red warning flag. Remember that equal-looking quantities are often a trap, so double-check your work.

Plug in numbers that are farther apart: 2, 5, and 200. Now Quantity A is 2 + 200 = 202, divided by 2 = 101. In Quantity B, b is 5. Now the answer is Choice (A). If the answer changes based on which values you plug in for the variables, choose Choice (D). *Correct answer:* Choice **(D).**

Quantity A		Quantity B
$y+z$	$x>y>z$	x

The immediate trap answer is Choice (C), but because x, y, and z can be anything, the right answer is Choice (D). If you plug in 3, 2, and 1, $y + z = 2 + 1 = 3$. Because $x = 3$, the quantities are equal. But when you plug in very different numbers, 100, 2, and 1, now, $y + z = 2 + 1 = 3$. But $x = 100$; Quantity B is larger. The answer changes depending on what you plug in, making Choice (D) the correct answer. *Correct answer:* Choice **(D).**

Deciding On Your Own: Quantitative Comparison Practice Questions

Here are some more QC practice questions in case you need a little extra work with these types of problems.

1. $4 < x < 5$

Quantity A	***Quantity B***
x^3	125

Ⓐ Quantity A is greater.

Ⓑ Quantity B is greater.

Ⓒ The two quantities are equal.

Ⓓ The relationship cannot be determined from the information given.

If x is less than 5, then x^3 must be less than 125. *Correct answer:* Choice **(B).**

2.

Quantity A	***Quantity B***
5^{-8}	25^{-4}

Ⓐ Quantity A is greater.

Ⓑ Quantity B is greater.

Ⓒ The two quantities are equal.

Ⓓ The relationship cannot be determined from the information given.

Remember that 25^{-4} can also be expressed as $(25)^{-4}$, which becomes $(5^2)^{-4}$ and then 5^{-8}. *Correct answer:* Choice **(C).**

3. x and y are integers

Quantity A	***Quantity B***
The average of x and y	The sum of x and y

Ⓐ Quantity A is greater.

Ⓑ Quantity B is greater.

Ⓒ The two quantities are equal.

Ⓓ The relationship cannot be determined from the information given.

If x and y are positive integers, the correct answer would be Choice (A). If they're negative, then the correct answer would be Choice (B). If they're equal to zero, which is an integer, the correct answer would be Choice (C). Because you don't know, the relationship can't be determined. *Correct answer:* Choice **(D).**

4. The lengths of two sides of a certain triangle are 12 and 20.

Quantity A	***Quantity B***
The longest possible length of the third side of the triangle	32

Ⓐ Quantity A is greater.

Ⓑ Quantity B is greater.

Ⓒ The two quantities are equal.

Ⓓ The relationship cannot be determined from the information given.

Because the length of the third side of any triangle must be less than the sum of the lengths of the other two sides, the third side of this triangle must be less than 32. *Correct answer:* Choice **(B).**

5. $x > 0$

Quantity A	***Quantity B***
x^2	0.5

Ⓐ Quantity A is greater.

Ⓑ Quantity B is greater.

Ⓒ The two quantities are equal.

Ⓓ The relationship cannot be determined from the information given.

If x is an integer, then any value squared would be more than 0.5. However, because x could be a decimal, such as 0.2, x^2 would equal 0.04. Because you can't assume that x is an integer, you can't tell which value is higher. *Correct answer:* Choice **(D).**

6. A circle has a radius of 1.

Quantity A	***Quantity B***
The circumference of the circle	6.28

Ⓐ Quantity A is greater.

Ⓑ Quantity B is greater.

Ⓒ The two quantities are equal.

Ⓓ The relationship cannot be determined from the information given.

The circumference of a circle is $2\pi r$, making the circumference of this circle 2π. If π were equal to 3.14, then the answer would be Choice (C). However, the value of π is slightly higher, closer to 3.1416. You don't have to know the exact value of π, but you do have to know that 3.14 is the value rounded down. *Correct answer:* Choice **(A).**

7. One of the angles of an isosceles triangle is 80°.

Quantity A	***Quantity B***
The measure of one of the other two angles of the triangle	50°

Ⓐ Quantity A is greater.

Ⓑ Quantity B is greater.

Ⓒ The two quantities are equal.

Ⓓ The relationship cannot be determined from the information given.

If one of the angles is 80 degrees, then the other two angles could each be 50 degrees for a total angle measure of 180 degrees and a correct answer of Choice (C). However, the other two angles could also be 80 degrees and 20 degrees, bringing the angle total to 180 degrees for a correct answer of Choice (D). You don't know which one is the case, so you can't tell which quantity is greater. *Correct answer:* Choice **(D).**

8. At a certain factory, machines A and B have a maximum production capacity of p and q parts, respectively, where $p < q < 100$.

Quantity A	***Quantity B***
The number of days required for machine A, working at maximum capacity, to fill an order of 1,000 parts	The number of days required for machine B, working at maximum capacity, to fill an order of 1,000 parts

Ⓐ Quantity A is greater.

Ⓑ Quantity B is greater.

Ⓒ The two quantities are equal.

Ⓓ The relationship cannot be determined from the information given.

It's easy to get lost in the description, picking numbers and trying math. Actually, after you get past the verbiage, this question is very simple. Pretend machine A produces 1 part per day and machine B produces 99 parts per day. Thus, machine A would take longer to produce 1,000 parts. *Correct answer:* Choice **(A).**

Part IV

Penning Powerful Analytical Essays

"I finished my essay early, so I wrote essays on all the other questions, and then I had some time, so I wrote a few more essays on some spooky stuff I've been thinking about."

In this part . . .

The GRE begins with the Analytical Writing section, which is comprised of two essay-writing tasks. Each essay lasts 30 minutes, which means you write for 60 minutes before even beginning the questions. The two essay assignments are Analyze an Issue and Analyze an Argument.

This part helps you prepare for the Analytical Writing section of the GRE by giving you a sneak peek at what the essay evaluators look for. You basically need to be able to read and understand an issue statement, pick apart an argument, clearly state your position in writing, and then support your position with solid information. Also, your essay must be clear, well organized, and mostly error free.

Knowing what the evaluators are looking for and having a clear idea of how to structure each essay are the keys to success. The first chapter in this part guides you in writing a solid essay in the 30-minute timeframe for each task. The second chapter presents three sample essays — good, fair, and poor — for each essay-writing task, along with evaluator comments for each essay, to better equip you to meet the essay-writing requirements.

Chapter 14

Writing Analytical Essays on Issues and Arguments

In This Chapter

- Understanding the two types of essays on the GRE
- Meeting the minimum essay requirements
- Knowing how to score well with evaluators
- Writing sound Issue and Argument Analysis essays, paragraph by paragraph

The GRE doesn't exactly ease you into the test-taking process. It begins with two challenging essays: *Analyze an Issue* and *Analyze an Argument.* These essays are 30 minutes each, for a total of 60 minutes of intense writing before you even encounter any of the other test questions. As you prepare for the essay-writing portion, remember the following goals:

- Complete each essay in 30 minutes or less.
- Write well-organized, insightful essays clearly stating and fully supporting your position.
- Avoid grammatical and spelling errors and typos.
- Conserve your energy for the rest of the test.

Thirty minutes for each essay should be sufficient — especially if you've practiced writing the essays. The more essay-writing practice you do, the more comfortable you become with your organization and ability to write within the time constraints on test day. Take a trial run-through with the Issue and Argument essays, using the topics presented in Chapter 15 and the methods outlined in this chapter. Then you can check your work against the sample essays in Chapter 15.

In this chapter, I explain what evaluators look for in a quality essay and how they ultimately score your essay. I then guide you through the process of writing each essay paragraph by paragraph.

The computer program used for writing the GRE essays is just like the Notepad program on most personal computers. It has a cut-and-paste feature for moving stuff around and an undo feature for reversing changes, and that's it — no spell checker, grammar checker, or automated anything, so the burden of proofreading falls squarely on your shoulders.

A Half Dozen Is Good: How the Essays Are Scored

Before you can score well on the essay, you need to have a basic grasp of how the GRE essay section is graded. Two evaluators grade each essay, assigning a score of 0 to 6 for each — the higher the score, the better. Your final score for each essay is the average of the two scores. If the two evaluators arrive at wildly different scores (off by more than a couple points), which is uncommon, then your essay goes to a third evaluator, and your score is the average of the three evaluators' scores. You get one score for each essay, and your writing score is the average of the two essay scores.

The following sections break down how the essays are scored and provide some tips you can use to get a better score.

What the essay scores really mean

After waiting for weeks to receive your GRE essay scores, you're sure going to want to know what your scores mean. Following are the descriptions evaluators associate with each essay score as they grade your essays:

- **Outstanding (6):** The essay demonstrates the ability to develop a position on an issue, identify strengths and weaknesses of an argument, support personal views and insights, and write with clarity and focus.
- **Strong (5):** The essay demonstrates a generally thoughtful analysis of the issue or argument and presents a clear and convincing analysis of the argument or presentation of the issue. Presentation is logical and main points are well supported. The essay may have minor errors in grammar and spelling but demonstrates control of the language, good diction (word choice), and variety of sentence structure.
- **Adequate (4):** The essay demonstrates overall competence in adequately analyzing the argument or presenting the issue, organizing and supporting the thoughts, and expressing them clearly. It may not flow smoothly due to lack of effective transitions, and it may contain some errors, but it demonstrates sufficient control of the language.
- **Limited (3):** Competent but flawed, the essay misses the main point or ideas in the argument or presents the issue poorly, lacks order, offers little or no support for the ideas presented, and contains occasional glaring errors or lots of minor errors in grammar, diction, and mechanics.
- **Seriously flawed (2):** The essay completely misses the point, presents the author's point of view with no or irrelevant support, is poorly organized, and is riddled with errors in grammar, diction, mechanics, and sentence construction.
- **Fundamentally deficient (1):** The essay demonstrates little or no evidence of the ability to understand the issue, analyze the argument, or develop a well-organized presentation of ideas. In addition, the essay contains extensive errors in grammar, diction, mechanics, and sentence structure.
- **No essay (0):** This one is self-explanatory: If no essay is submitted or the essay doesn't address the comment, the score is a 0.

Your goal is to score a perfect 6 on each essay, especially if your test score or GPA are borderline.

Some graduate schools weigh your performance on the Analytical Writing section differently from others. Some schools place little importance on it; others consider it critical. Additionally, graduate programs within the same school often prioritize the essay section quite differently. Before you allocate a lot or a little time to preparing for this section of the GRE, you may want to contact the admissions offices of your target schools and find out how important this section is to them. Then again, you may just be determined to do your best no matter what.

Key methods to scoring well

Essay writing (and scoring) is subjective to some degree. There's no right or wrong answer, and every essay is slightly different based on the essayist's perspective, knowledge, experience, writing style, and so on. Evaluators, however, have clear criteria for assessing the quality of an essay. To perform well, be sure to do the following:

- **Take a clear stand.** Although arguing both sides of an issue or discussing strengths and weaknesses is good, you must — *must* — make your opinion or conclusion clear. Don't expect the evaluators to infer your position. You can acknowledge the merits of both sides of an issue, but make sure you clearly declare *your* position.
- **Get to the point.** The evaluator will always look for your point in the first two lines of each paragraph, so don't try to be clever and write an essay with a surprise ending. State clearly and unequivocally in the first paragraph of each essay where you stand on the issue or what you think of the argument you're about to analyze.
- **Back up your point with specific examples.** Anyone can state a position, but you must defend your position with specific examples. For example, if you describe why mass-produced goods are both higher quality and less expensive, include a case study, such as how your $40 manufactured Casio wristwatch outperforms your uncle's $7,000 handmade Patek Philippe. You don't have to be right, but you do need to provide solid support for whatever you claim.

  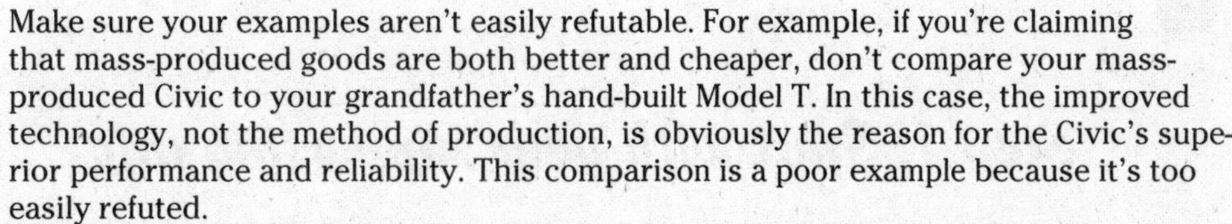

  Make sure your examples aren't easily refutable. For example, if you're claiming that mass-produced goods are both better and cheaper, don't compare your mass-produced Civic to your grandfather's hand-built Model T. In this case, the improved technology, not the method of production, is obviously the reason for the Civic's superior performance and reliability. This comparison is a poor example because it's too easily refuted.
- **Stay on topic.** After stating your position (in the first paragraph), make sure every succeeding paragraph supports that position instead of wandering off topic. If the issue is about low commodity prices versus quality of workmanship, for example, and you're discussing factory output, don't go off topic and start talking about offshore labor — as I once saw a student do on that very subject. Each paragraph should have a sentence (preferably at the end) that ties the paragraph directly to your position statement.
- **Avoid fluff.** Though longer essays typically earn higher scores, the higher scores are due to the fact that the essay provides sufficient support, not because it rambles on and on. Your essay won't be judged solely on word count.
- **Maintain a professional tone.** The essay section isn't for creative writing. It's more like business writing, so avoid off-color language, slang, and inappropriate humor. Creativity, done well, will be rewarded, but be appropriate.

Writing the Issue Essay

In the Analyze an Issue task, the GRE gives you an issue statement and asks you to introduce and then support your position on that issue. The format is like this:

> *Directions:* Write an essay in response to the following statement in which you discuss the extent that you agree or disagree with the statement. Explain your reasoning in a clear, well-organized essay that supports your position. Consider both sides of the issue when developing your response.
>
> "Today's cheap, mass-produced goods lack the precision and quality of yesterday's hand-built, carefully crafted products."

Where do you begin? What do they want? Only 29 minutes left! Getting started is the hardest part and staying focused is the most important. By having a game plan and structure in place, you're better equipped to do both. The following sections provide details for the plan and structure I recommend.

1. **Identify relevant information you already know about the issue.**
2. **Take a position that's in line with the supporting data you have.**
3. **Write your introductory paragraph clearly stating your position.**
4. **Use your best supporting detail to write your second paragraph.**
5. **Write paragraphs three and four to cover two more cases that support your position.**
6. **Write a concluding paragraph that reiterates the position statement from your introduction.**

Your essay doesn't have to be flawless. The evaluators know that you're writing a rough draft under time constraints, so they're ready to forgive the occasional typo and misplaced modifier. Still, they will notice large or repeated errors, so be careful and spend a minute or two editing your essay.

Step 1: Start with your supporting info

Your first inclination may be to state your position on the issue and then try to come up with data to support it. This strategy is certainly acceptable if you already have a well-informed position on the issue. Otherwise, you're usually better off starting with the supporting details and basing your position on those details. You don't want to waste time stating a position you can't possibly defend.

Before taking a position, use your scratch paper to write down five supporting details related to the issue statement. Along with each supporting detail, write down which side of the issue you think it supports. For an essay on handmade versus mass-produced goods, such a list may look something like this:

- Your mass-produced Casio wristwatch versus your uncle's handmade Patek Philippe — favors cheap manufacturing.
- An off-the-rack suit versus a tailored suit — favors handmade quality.
- Your HP computer versus your friend's custom-built PC from catalog-ordered parts — can go either way.

- The $100 One-Laptop-Per-Child initiative — favors cheap manufacturing as sometimes the only option, but issue topic is on product quality, not product availability.
- Your Honda Civic versus your grandpa's Ford Model T — favors cheap manufacturing, but this example can easily be refuted.

Don't worry if your examples aren't perfect — you're racing the clock, so just throw some down. You need only three examples, so writing down five gives you room to discard a couple.

Your examples can be taken from personal or professional experiences, readings, or other general background knowledge that you possess: What have you seen, done, or heard about that formed your opinion? You may find that your examples support the opposite of your initial response, and you want to discover this before writing the introduction.

Step 2: Take a position that's in line with the supporting data

From your examples, formulate the position you want to take. I know, this may seem like you're working backwards, but you want to take the position that you know you're able to support best. This essay isn't a personal statement; it's a test of your ability to compose a clear, coherent essay. In this case, your best examples favor cheap manufacturing over handmade quality. So run with that, even if you personally disagree. If necessary, adjust your personal position for the essay. Your goal isn't self-expression, and you're not making a commitment. You're trying to score a perfect 6.

The examples you write in Step 1 provide a good sense of where your essay will go. Now that your examples are down on paper and your thoughts are gathered, you're ready to write your introduction.

Step 3: Write the introduction

The third step focuses on writing the essay's introduction. The first paragraph of your essay (the introduction) must demonstrate your understanding of the issue and clearly state your position. Structure the paragraph as follows:

- **First sentence:** Introduce the issue and state your position.
- **Second sentence:** Acknowledge the presence of both sides of the issue and that you, in fact, anticipate and address objections to your point of view while crushing them under the weight of your brilliant logic and reasoning.
- **Remaining sentences:** Prepare the reader for your supporting details.

Refer to this bulleted list as you read the following example to see how I apply this structure.

> The broad assertion that all mass-produced goods are inferior to hand-crafted products is clearly overreaching, and I disagree with the statement. Certainly, in some instances hand-crafted products are superior, but more often mass production yields more precise, higher-quality products. Considering the type of product and the context of its use is crucial in determining which manufacturing process is best. A couple real-world examples demonstrate why this is so.

As you write your introductory paragraph, adhere to the following guidelines:

- **State your position clearly and succinctly.** The evaluators favor a concise writing style. If you can clearly state your point with fewer words, do it. That said, be thorough when making your point.
- **Convey confidence.** You're stating a position and supporting it with relevant examples. You know you're right, so act like it.
- **Stay on topic.** Digressing and expanding your scope to support your position is tempting, but keep your discussion within scope of the issue topic. For example, mass production may lower the product cost for mass-market availability, but that's not what the issue is about.
- **Reference key terms.** The topic is about mass production, quality, and precision; use those terms whenever possible. Doing so signals that you're responding directly to the prompt.

Step 4: Use your best supporting detail for the second paragraph

The next step involves writing the second paragraph. Pick your best example and use it to write a single paragraph that supports your position. Structure the paragraph as follows:

- **First sentence:** Present your best supporting detail or example and mention that it supports your position as stated in the introduction.
- **Next several sentences:** Describe your example in greater detail.
- **Next sentence or two:** Show how your example supports your position as stated in the introduction.
- **Last sentence:** State unequivocally that the example you just presented clearly supports your position or refutes the counter-argument.

Make sure one sentence (preferably the last sentence) of each paragraph connects back to your introduction and the issue topic. This assures the evaluator that you're on track and your thoughts are organized. Check out the following example and compare it to the previous list to see how I structured this second paragraph.

> The wristwatch is an example of a product that is better when mass-produced. My Casio watch was mass-produced with probably 10,000 other identical units. I purchased this watch five years ago, and it has consistently worked perfectly, with the occasional interruption for a battery replacement. The quality is fine, and the precision couldn't be better. Contrast this with my uncle's Patek Philippe, which was handmade with maybe a dozen others. Due to the motion-generated winding feature, his watch stops working when he doesn't wear it for more than two days! Clearly, this is neither precise timekeeping nor quality of utility. At any given moment, the Casio will always show the correct time, while the Patek's accuracy is a coin toss. The claim that mass-produced products lack the precision and quality of handmade goods, in this commonly-occurring context, is clearly wrong.

Your examples don't need to be 100 percent correct. They serve to demonstrate how your powers of observation and insight support your point. The evaluators understand that you can't research anything while writing the essay. However, don't manufacture examples out of thin air, because they're likely to sound phony.

A clever writing style, such as describing the Patek's accuracy as "a coin toss," is encouraged. Again, though, be appropriate.

Step 5: Write paragraphs three and four

The third and fourth paragraphs of your essay are similar to the second paragraph. Each paragraph should present a single supporting example from your notes, show how the example supports your position, and reference back to the introduction. Refer to the previous section for how to construct a strong paragraph.

> However, some products are better as handmade items than as mass-produced commodities, such as gentlemen's suits. For example, I wore an off-the-rack two-piece suit to my high-school graduation. The jacket was slightly large, but the next size smaller jacket was too small. The workmanship was mediocre, with loose threads and a misplaced stitch. It wasn't cheap, but it was mass-produced, and thus had neither quality nor precision. Contrast this with the handmade, professionally tailored suit that I bought last year. The precise fit is flawless and the quality unparalleled. Though the claim that mass-produced products lack the quality and precision of handmade goods is true in this example, the claim still cannot be applied to all products.
>
> Furthermore, some products can feature high or low quality and precision regardless of whether they are mass-produced or handmade. Computers are a good example of this. My mass-produced HP computer demonstrates both precision and quality, while the eMachines computer I bought in 2001 lacked the quality to last more than 18 months. On the other hand, my friend hand-built a computer from parts ordered in a catalog, and his computer works with extremely high quality and precision. I have heard stories, however, of hand-built computers that didn't fare as well. Therefore, the general claim that mass-produced products lack the quality and precision of handmade goods is clearly flawed, because in this case, the method of computer production has no bearing on the outcome.

Step 6: Write the conclusion

Think of paragraph five (the conclusion) as the closing bracket of your essay, with the introduction being the beginning. Your conclusion should mirror your introduction while leaving the evaluator with a sense of closure. Structure your concluding paragraph as follows:

- **First sentence:** Restate your position or once again refute the issue statement presented on the test.
- **Middle sentence or two:** Remind the reader of the supporting details and/or examples you presented and the logical conclusion those details and examples support.
- **Final sentence:** Summarize why you agree or disagree with the issue statement presented on the test, leaving the evaluator with a sense of closure.

As you read the following example, refer to the preceding list and see how I structured this conclusion.

> To sum up, one cannot correctly claim that all mass-produced products are inferior to handmade goods. The examples describing the wristwatch, the gentlemen's suit, and the personal computer clearly demonstrate that the claim may or may not be true, depending on the context and product. A blanket statement that may or may not be true is an invalid statement, so I disagree with this statement.

Tying everything together with smooth transitions

As you write, work toward transitioning smoothly from one paragraph to the next. Strong transitions connect the points you're making, especially when your examples take different sides of the issue. Transitions contribute greatly to the organization and coherence of your essay. Here are a few examples of commonly used transitions:

- Closely related to this idea is . . .
- Conversely . . .
- On the other hand . . .
- However . . .
- In contrast . . .
- Similarly . . .

Besides transitions, a more subtle technique for tying everything together and staying on point is to repeat key terms throughout the essay. Identify key terms in the issue statement. For example, in the following issue statement, you may identify the following as key terms: *cheap, mass-produced, precision, quality, hand-built.*

> "Today's **cheap, mass-produced** goods lack the **precision** and **quality** of yesterday's **hand-built,** carefully crafted products."

Here's the sample paragraph again, bolding the repetition of key terms drawn directly from the issue statement:

> The wristwatch is an example of a product that is better when **mass-produced.** My Casio watch was **mass-produced** with probably 10,000 other identical units. I purchased this watch five years ago, and it has consistently worked perfectly, with the occasional interruption for a battery replacement. The **quality** is fine, and the **precision** couldn't be better. Contrast this with my uncle's Patek Philippe, which was **handmade** with maybe a dozen others. Due to the motion-generated winding feature, his watch stops working when he doesn't wear it for more than two days! Clearly, this is neither **precise** timekeeping nor **quality** of utility. At any given moment, the Casio will always show the correct time, while the Patek's accuracy is a coin toss. The claim that **mass-produced** products lack the **precision** and **quality** of **handmade** goods, in this commonly-occurring context, is clearly wrong.

Analyzing an Argument in Six Paragraphs

The second essay is called Analyze an Argument. The test provides a paragraph that states a position and provides several reasons in support of it. Your job is to analyze the argument and its reasoning and evidence and describe why the argument is either faulty or sound. Check out the following example:

> *Directions:* Write a response to the following argument that analyzes its stated or implied assumptions, reveals how the argument's position depends on the assumptions, and explains the effect of any flawed assumptions on the argument's validity.
>
> "Many considerations point to the conclusion that Flint's restaurant should be changed from a youth-oriented, family-style restaurant to a Western-style saloon serving alcoholic beverages and featuring country bands. First, few families live in the area surrounding

> the restaurant; most have gone farther out into the suburbs. Second, Flint owns and operates two other saloons that have liquor licenses, making him experienced in the field. And finally, alcohol has a higher profit margin than food."

The clock's ticking, so you need to work fast, but you also need to spend time analyzing the argument before you start writing. By having a plan of attack and a structure in place, you're better equipped to produce an outstanding essay in the allotted time. The following sections provide steps to writing a good argument.

1. **Identify the position stated in the argument.**
2. **List the reasons given to support the stated position.**
3. **Identify any flawed assumptions behind each reason.**
4. **Write your introductory paragraph demonstrating your understanding of the position stated in the argument and whether you think the evidence provided supports that position.**
5. **Write three paragraphs each of which refutes a faulty assumption/conclusion presented in the argument or, if you agree with the stated position, provides additional evidence to support it.**
6. **Write a concluding paragraph that recaps your essay and reinforces why the argument is or isn't valid.**

Unlike the Analyze an Issue essay, which is based on your opinion, the Analyze an Argument essay isn't based on your opinion on a subject. For example, in this argument, a personal preference of family restaurants to saloons shouldn't affect this essay.

Step 1: Identify the stated position

The argument on the GRE test is so brief that finding the position statement is a snap. The position statement is almost always in the first sentence. In the example from the previous section, the position is this:

> ". . . Flint's restaurant should be changed from a youth-oriented, family-style restaurant to a Western-style saloon serving alcoholic beverages and featuring country bands."

Identifying the position stated in the argument is a crucial first step because you need to show how each reason presented in support of that position succeeds or fails to do so.

Step 2: List the reasons given to support the stated position

Every argument includes a list of facts to support the position. In the example we're following, the facts are easy to pick out, because they're identified by number:

- **First:** Few families live in the area surrounding the restaurant; most have gone farther out into the suburbs.
- **Second:** Flint owns and operates two other saloons that have liquor licenses, making him experienced in the field.
- **Third:** Alcohol has a higher profit margin than food.

Step 3: Analyze the assumption and conclusion based on the facts

As you begin to write your essay, look for the author's flawed assumption(s) — anything the author claims or implies without providing sufficient evidence to back it up. (See Chapter 6 for more about assumptions.) For example, stating that "alcohol has a higher profit margin than food" doesn't necessarily mean it's more profitable.

You can argue assumptions, but you can't argue facts. In this example, you can argue that selling alcohol in this area may not be more profitable because few residents in the area drink or because the loss of revenue from food sales will more than offset the increased profit from alcohol sales, but you can't argue the fact that alcohol has a higher profit margin than food. The argument analysis consists of providing new evidence that refutes each flawed assumption.

You can either support or refute the argument, but refuting is typically much easier. The arguments presented on the GRE are so brief that they can't possibly provide enough evidence to support a particular position. This enables you to easily poke holes in the argument and the reasons given to support the stated position.

On your scratch paper, jot down about five assumptions and new facts that support or refute those assumptions. Write down only keywords — save your prose for the essay. The following list is an example of what someone may come up with to refute the argument presented earlier (you can make your notes less precise):

- **Faulty assumption:** Families won't make the drive from the distant suburbs.

  New fact: Though they don't live nearby, families may drive to the area for other reasons, such as shopping or recreation.

- **Faulty assumption:** Because Flint's other two saloons are successful, this new saloon will also be successful.

  New fact: Several factors may contribute to the success of the two saloons that aren't present in the restaurant's location, such as the proximity of a popular sports arena or theater.

- **Faulty assumption:** Flint's experience with saloons will make this newly converted saloon a success.

  New fact: Other factors affect success, including what else is in the area. There could be five other saloons across the street from this restaurant, but no other family restaurants within five miles.

- **Faulty assumption:** A liquor license that brings success to one locale will bring success to another.

  New fact: Regions are different. What works in Dallas won't work in Salt Lake City.

- **Faulty Assumption:** Alcohol's higher profit margin will lead to higher overall profits, because the level of sales will be the same.

  New Fact: Though alcohol has a higher profit margin than food, the sales volume could be less. Selling 200 dinners at a profit margin of 40 percent is more profitable than selling one case of beer at a profit margin of 80 percent.

If you think the argument is valid, list the reasons given in support of the argument followed by new facts that support those reasons. However, even if you believe the argument is fundamentally sound and you support it, you should still be able to show the GRE evaluator that you can recognize claims in the argument that others may find questionable.

You don't have to use all five points in your essay. Whittle down your list to the best three — while writing the essay, you may discover that a couple points aren't valid. With only 30 minutes, having three well-developed points is very good, and far better than having five sketchy ideas.

Be sure to never refute a fact — just refute an assumption. You can't refute that alcohol has a higher profit margin, because that's a fact and is, therefore, irrefutable. Instead, accept the fact as true, and think of something else that would affect the outcome, such as sales volume. Refuting facts leads to point reductions on your essay.

Step 4: Write the introduction

The first paragraph of your Analyze an Argument essay (the introduction) must demonstrate your understanding of the argument and whether you think the argument is valid or invalid. Structure the paragraph as follows:

- **First sentence:** Briefly state the argument you're analyzing and whether it's sound.
- **Second sentence:** Acknowledge the reasons in the argument and indicate whether the presence of faulty assumptions or the reasons provided offer solid evidence in support of the argument's main point.
- **Remaining sentences:** Touch upon the points you're going to bring up in subsequent paragraphs.

As you read the following example introduction paragraph, refer to the preceding list and see how I apply this structure.

> The author provides a compelling, though flawed, argument for Flint to convert his restaurant to a saloon. Although converting the restaurant to a saloon may indeed be a wise course of action, the assumptions used to support the argument lack sufficient supporting evidence, and are, therefore, flawed. A lot of information is missing that would validate or weaken the assumptions. These unknown facts are very important to the validity of the argument, and Flint would be unwise to risk his business without knowing these facts.

Step 5: Write paragraphs two, three, and four

Your second, third, and fourth paragraphs each cover one of the argument's reasons or faulty assumptions and present a new fact or reason to support or refute it. Start with your strongest point first, and structure each paragraph as follows:

- **First sentence or two:** Present one of the argument's reasons/assumptions in your own words.
- **Next sentence:** Transition into the new fact you have to support or refute this particular reason/assumption.
- **Remaining sentences:** Provide additional details to support your new fact.
- **Last sentence:** Summarize how your new fact supports or refutes the argument's reason/assumption.

Read my example second, third, and fourth paragraphs in this section and compare them to the previous list to see how I use this structure.

As you compose the body of your essay, follow these guidelines:

- Spell out exactly why each reason is valid or why each assumption is invalid. Don't expect the evaluators to draw conclusions from your description — make it clear.
- Cover only one reason or assumption per paragraph.
- Use transition words at the beginning of each subsequent paragraph to move from one paragraph to the next. For more about transitions, see the section "Tying everything together with smooth transitions" earlier in this chapter.

Following is a sample second paragraph that conforms to the recommended structure.

> First of all, the author states that most families live too far away, which may be true. However, the author assumes that because they live so far away, they'll never be in the area. This may not be the case, because families may take a day trip into town and want to stop somewhere to eat. The author doesn't mention whether the restaurant is near a children's museum or a shopping mall that caters to families. The restaurant could be near plenty of family-based traffic, even though the suburbs are far away from the restaurant.

Note the transition words at the beginning of each of the following paragraphs (paragraphs three and four from the same essay) that help smooth the movement from one paragraph to the next.

> Furthermore, the author attributes the success of Flint's two saloons to the liquor license and asserts that the same will bring success to his restaurant. The author assumes that the conditions are the same at both locations. What works at one location, however, will not necessarily work at another. For example, the saloons could be in Dallas, where saloons can thrive, and the restaurant could be in Salt Lake City, with a much smaller drinking population.
>
> In addition, the author mentions the higher profit margin of alcohol as key to increased profits. The author assumes, however, that sales will be the same. No information is provided to suggest liquor sales will be comparable to food sales. Although profit margin is key to profits, sales volume is also important. A 20 percent profit from $500,000 in sales is worth more than a 50 percent profit from $100,000 in sales. The level of future alcohol sales is not known, so Flint would be ill advised to throw away his existing food sales for a throw-of-the-dice level of alcohol sales, regardless of the profit margin.

Don't fall into your own trap. If you argue that the writer's assumption is based on personal logic and unsupported by facts, be sure that your refutation isn't based on personal logic and unsupported by facts. The last thing you want to do is point out the author's weakness and then make the evaluator chuckle as he marks you down for having the exact same weakness.

Step 6: Draft the conclusion

The last step to writing the Analyze an Argument essay is to compose paragraph five (the conclusion). The conclusion is the closing bracket of your essay, with the introduction being the opening bracket. Your conclusion should mirror your introduction while leaving the evaluator with a sense of closure. Structure your concluding paragraph as follows:

- **First sentence:** Acknowledge the argument's main point and generally explain why you think it has or hasn't been adequately proven.
- **Next sentence or two:** Remind the reader of the reasons or assumptions that you think support or question the main point of the argument.
- **Closing:** The closing need not be a separate sentence, but it should complete your essay, leaving the evaluator with a sense of closure.

Look at my example conclusion and how I utilize the preceding list to draft the sentences.

> Though the author provides a strong argument for converting Flint's restaurant to a saloon, the argument relies on several assumptions that are based on uncertain facts. These assumptions are discussed above, and Flint should verify the key facts, also discussed above, before making a decision.

Chapter 15

Practicing Analytical Writing and Sample Essays

In This Chapter

- Creating a realistic setting for writing your sample essays
- Composing an Analyze an Issue essay
- Composing an Analyze an Argument essay

Knowing how to write an essay and actually writing one on the day of the test are two entirely different things. In this chapter, you have an opportunity to put into practice everything I cover in Chapter 14 and write essays that are likely to earn high scores.

In this chapter, I provide two essay questions — one Analyze an Issue and one Analyze an Argument — complete with the directions similar to those you'll see on the actual GRE. You have 30 minutes to write each essay. Following each essay question, I provide sample essays (one good, one sort of good, and one poor) along with evaluator comments, so you can gauge how well you feel you did, comparatively speaking, and have a clearer idea of what evaluators look for.

Practicing the essays is crucial to writing well under pressure, finishing in the allotted time, and avoiding writer's block that can sap your energy. Write both essays — the Analyze an Issue and the Analyze an Argument essays — giving yourself 30 minutes each, so you have a good feel for what each type of essay entails. After you're done writing, read through the sample essays and evaluator comments so you know what separates an outstanding essay from a poor one.

Setting the Stage for a Realistic Experience

To make your practice session more like what you'll experience on test day, set the stage by doing the following:

- **Write your essay on a computer rather than by hand.** Typing on a computer more effectively simulates the actual test-taking experience. You're more likely to make typos and other careless errors when you type compared to writing by hand.
- **Turn off your word processor's spelling and grammar checking features.** The word processor you'll use during the actual test doesn't correct or even check for grammar and spelling errors or typos. You can turn these features back on after writing your essay to identify any errors. (If you have a Windows PC, using Notepad is similar to the program the GRE uses.)

- **Set your timer for 30 minutes per essay, but if time runs out, go ahead and finish the essay anyway.** You still have to practice writing the end of the essay, and the practice will help you write faster next time. Also, keep track of the extra time you needed, so you know how much faster you need to work on test day.

Don't skip ahead and read the essays or evaluations before writing your own essay. Doing so gives you an unfair advantage and an unrealistic experience. Read the directions followed by the issue or argument and then immediately write your essay. If you're not very impressed with your own essay after reading the samples and commentary, you may rewrite your essay for additional practice. Unfortunately, you don't get a second chance on the actual GRE.

Writing an Analyze an Issue Essay: Some Samples

Directions: Write an essay in response to the following statement in which you discuss the extent to which you agree or disagree with the statement. Explain your reasoning in a clear, well-organized essay that supports your position. Consider both sides of the issue when developing your response.

> "Because society is always changing, laws should always change to reflect the times as well. In addition, laws should be open to interpretation based on the facts of each individual circumstance."

In the following sections are three sample essays based on this Issue topic, presented from best (with a score of 6) to worst (with a score of 2). Following each sample essay are evaluator comments that explain reasons for the score.

Sample essay — score 6 (outstanding)

My French grandmother was fond of saying, "Plus ça change, plus c'est la même chose," which roughly means that the more something seems to change, the more it actually remains the same. This saying is appropriate when considering the laws of our nation. By changing or updating laws and statutes, by being flexible in their interpretation, we fundamentally remain the same: We continue to be fair and just, as the creators of the laws intended. In law, considering the spirit of the law is often necessary before creating the letter of the law.

A prime example of the need for flexibility is the Three Strikes Law in California. This law is paraphrased as "Three strikes, you're out!" by police officials and other law-enforcement personnel who have supported it whole-heartedly. The law states that a person who previously has been convicted of two crimes will be sent to prison for life when convicted of a third crime. Newspapers are fond of reporting stories of a transient who receives a life sentence for stealing a candy bar from a gas station, or a young man who goes to prison for life for smoking a marijuana joint in public. Although one may argue there are, in fact, incorrigible criminals, ones who will continue to commit crime after crime despite all legal deterrents, common sense would dictate that spending twenty, thirty, or even fifty years in prison is not a suitable punishment for stealing a 59-cent bag of chips.

Some laws have never changed, yet they are rarely enforced. Every time a new law goes into effect, news reporters present human-interest stories about unusual laws that have officially never been repealed. There is the example of "It's illegal to walk on the sidewalks of Philadelphia carrying goldfish," or "It is a crime to sing to your horses in the hearing of others." Every state and every county has a number of these laws that newspapers and television stations trot out occasionally for the amusement of the audiences on slow news days. Ridding our legal system of such pointless laws would be another helpful outcome of a flexible approach to the law.

And what should we make of the so-called "Blue Laws," laws that attempt to mandate morality? In certain counties, it's illegal to sell or purchase alcoholic beverages on Sunday. In the county in Indiana where I grew up, it was against the law to dance on Sundays. Of course, no one ever enforced that statute; it was simply a curiosity. The question is raised, therefore, do we need to enact new laws, rescind the old ones, or practice a policy of benign neglect, simply not enforcing those laws we consider unnecessary? And if we neglect certain laws, who gets to choose which laws are enforced and which are ignored? By being more flexible in the passage and creation of the laws, we are able to avoid this dilemma.

Many years ago, England had two court systems: The courts of law (which is why lawyers are called "attorneys at law") and the courts of equity. The courts of equity attempted to "make known the King's conscience," showing mercy and treating cases equitably even when such treatment was against the law. Both courts were merged years ago but leave a legacy of flexibility and moral justice in their interpretation of the law. A legal system that cannot change with the times *will* not survive, and a legal system that will not treat cases fairly and justly *should* not survive.

Evaluator comments on the score 6 essay

This essay presents an excellent answer to the question. The writer uses interesting, intriguing comments (such as the opening with the grandmother's French saying); strong, evocative vocabulary (such as "incorrigible" and "trot out"); and a good variety of sentence structures. (The use of the occasional question was particularly effective.)

The writer's opinion is clear from the start and is supported by well-reasoned and thoroughly developed examples. The three examples are separated, yet they flow together well via the use of good transitions. The ending is perhaps a bit dramatic, but leaves no doubt as to the author's opinion.

Sample essay — score 4 (adequate)

Laws must change when Society changes. This is true for all types of laws, the major laws and the minor laws. This is true for all types of Societies, the so called First World, and the so-called Third World. This is true for all types of situations, from the serious to the silly to the macabre.

An example of when a law must change is the death penalty. Many years ago, condemned prisoners were executed routinely. Such executions became major events, almost parties, with the public making an excursion to watch the hanging. The irony, of course, is that the huge crowds at the execution attracted additional criminals who then committed more crimes (theft, pickpocketing, assault) and perpetated the cycle. Today, while there are less executions, they have become media events. We don't attend the executions in person, but we live through them vicariously, watching them on tv. When Timothy McVeigh, the Oklahoma City bomber, was given a lethal injection, the tv stations carried a minute-by-minute report. The amount of money and time and energy that was put into this could have been better spent elsewhere.

A second reason laws must be flexible is in time of war or social upheaval. Take, for example, the 1960's. The United States had a sea change during that decade. Many more things were acceptable socially then than had ever been before, and the laws had to change to reflect that fact. The possession of certain drugs became much less serious than it had been before. People weren't sentenced to twenty years for *using* drugs, just for *pushing* them. Today even more liberal attitudes towards drugs enable people to use them legally, as in the case of glaucoma or AIDS patients who smoke pot.

Traffic laws are a less serious, but still good, example of when laws should change. The speed limit in downtown New York must obviously be less than that in the outskirts of Podunk, Idaho (my apologies to the Podunkians!). Many people in Wyoming and other sparsely-populated Western states fought against having a federally-mandated speed limit of 55 on the freeways, argueing that in their areas, 65 or even 75 would be more logical. This is an example of the need for a change to meet the needs of a local community or Society. The same is true for the age at which youngsters can get a license, as they are more mature earlier now than before.

In conclusion, laws are not static because people are not static. We change from decade to decade, and from locale to locale. While it is important to adhere to the Declaration of Independence's statement that "all men are created equal," and thus should have equal rights, not all times are created equal, and thus should not have equal laws.

Evaluator comments on the score 4 essay

This is a generally acceptable response. The writer presents an unequivocal answer to the question and uses some good vocabulary ("macabre," "vicariously"). In addition, the length is good, with three well-organized examples.

However, the examples are out of scope. The money, time, and energy spent watching McVeigh's execution isn't relevant to changing laws. It's not clear why wars and social upheavals mandate a change in laws, or during which times whether the laws or the enforcement changed. And the speed limit differences in differently populated areas aren't shown to have changed; they are shown to be different.

The essay has additional weaknesses that prevent it from receiving a higher score, such as instances of inappropriate humor ("my apologies to the Podunkians!"). Although minor grammatical flaws are acceptable, "less executions" isn't one of them.

Sample essay — score 2 (seriously flawed)

"Because Society is always changing, laws should always change to reflect the times as well." This is a very true statement. Nothing ever remains exacly the same, and things change all the time. Isn't it logical to think that the laws should change as people and other situations change? My example the American society. We are much more ethnical diverse than we were a generation or two ago, and our laws have guaranteed this diversity. Old laws said that, for example, African-American people were not allowed in certain clubs or given certain jobs and this of course was wrong. Now there are laws to show how Society has changed and accepted this variety of people. Maybe someday there will be laws needed to protect White people who can't get jobs neither.

"In addition, laws should be open to interpretation based on the facts of each individual circumstance." This also is true. What about car accidents? If a person has an honest accident and hits and kills someone because he just lost control, that's a lot different than if he has been drunk and lost control that way and killed someone. It's not fair to send someone to prison for life because he had one horrible minute, but maybe it is fair to send someone to prison for life because he made the choice to drink and drive, the wrong choice.

In conclusion, I agree totally with both parts of the statement above. People need to realize that our Society changes and because laws are meant to protect Society, those laws must also change, too.

Evaluator comments on the score 2 essay

The writer presents a clear response to the question, both at the beginning and the end of the essay. The writer, however, simply repeats the issue and makes a general statement of agreement.

Although a few examples are given to support the writer's opinion, the organization of the essay isn't developed well. The writer makes the comment that, "Now there are laws to show how Society has changed. . . ." The quality of the essay would be improved were the writer to add more examples and explain each example more fully. The closing statement in the second paragraph appears to introduce a new topic, which isn't fully covered.

Poor spelling ("exacly") and grammar ("much more ethnical diverse") hurt the response as well. Although the writer's opinion is still understandable, these errors contribute to the low score.

Writing an Analyze an Argument Essay: Some Samples

Directions: Write a response to the following argument that analyzes its stated or implied assumptions, reveals how the argument's position depends on the assumptions, and explains the effect of any flawed assumptions on the argument's validity.

The following appeared in an in-house memo sent from a marketing director to the editorial department of a television news station.

> "Our research shows that when the news director comes on screen at the end of the newscast to present his perspective on an issue, many viewers switch stations or turn off the television entirely. Besides losing viewers, which lowers our ability to charge top dollar for advertising spots, we are wasting extra time that we could be filling with more ads. In addition, people tell us that they feel editorials are best read in the newspaper, not heard on television. Therefore, we recommend stopping all editorials at the ends of newscasts."

In the following sections are three sample essays written in response to this Argument, presented from best (with a score of 6) to worst (with a score of 2). Following each sample essay are evaluator comments that explain reasons for the score.

Sample essay — score 6 (outstanding)

The marketing director concludes that the news station should stop all editorials because viewership decreases when the news director presents his perspective on an issue at the end of the newscast. The memo argues that when people don't watch the end of the newscast, the station loses advertising revenue.

The conclusion is based on a number of questionable assumptions. First, the director recommends that the station stop all editorials at the end of newscasts because people are turning off what is currently offered. By proposing that the station eliminate *all* editorials, the memo assumes that viewers would not watch any kind of editorial. It could be that viewers simply don't like the news director or are turned off by the "perspective on an issue" format.

Second, the director claims that the time devoted to the current editorial could be sold to advertisers. He assumes, then, that people who turn off the television or switch stations when the news director comes on will not do so when an advertisement comes on in the editorial's place. If viewers stop watching the station when they know the news is over, they will probably do the same when commercials come on instead of the editorial. When advertisers find out that people are not watching their commercials, they will pay the station less.

Third, the director notes that people tell the station's marketing team that editorials are best read in the newspaper, not heard on television. As with any survey, this finding assumes that the people who are saying these things are representative of the larger population. In other words, the marketing department assumes that these "people" are representative of the station's viewers. The memo is vague about the identity of these people. Perhaps they are not viewers at all and, therefore, cannot be used to represent the television viewing audience. The director also fails to mention how numerous these people are and does not include any information about how many people may have expressed the opposite opinion to the marketing team. An analogous situation: Just because some people support a political candidate does not mean that others don't prefer somebody else. In addition, the people who said that editorials are best read in the newspaper could have been people who are more oriented towards reading and writing. There is a good chance that these people wrote letters to the station. If station employees had called viewers during the newscast, they may have received many responses claiming that editorials are better to watch on TV than read.

Finally, that director bases his argument on making money for the news station. This proposal assumes that the purpose of a news station is to make money. The editorials may not generate as much advertising revenue as other television presentations would, but the editorials are better to include if one assumes that the purpose of a news station is to inform viewers and stimulate their thinking.

To improve the argument, the news director needs to address the above issues. He needs evidence that shows that viewers would turn off any kind of editorial at the end of the newscast. He also needs to demonstrate that viewers would watch advertisements after the presentation of news. He should also clarify how the marketing team received the comments about editorials in newspapers. Ideally, the director should show that such comments were generated by a scientific survey of people who actually watch the news station. The director should also articulate that the primary aim of the news station is to attract viewers and generate revenue.

Evaluator comments on the score 6 essay

This very strong response presents a coherent, well-organized, direct analysis that introduces and fully develops the various points. It identifies four central issues that weaken or even undermine the argument, and it supports each point with evidence before summarizing in a brief conclusion. The language, grammar, spelling, and general writing skills also contribute to the excellence of this essay.

Sample essay — score 4 (adequate)

This editorial is relatively well-reasoned, although flawed in some aspects. The primary weakness, in my opinion, is found at the beginning, where the memo states, "Our research has shown. . . ." without specifying what that research is. Did someone poll viewers who regularly watched the show? Did someone send out a questionaire which was returned only by a small percentage of people, some of whom did not regularly watch the news? How were the questions phrased by the researcher (as we all know, a question can easily beg the answer, be skewed so as to direct the response in the direction the questioner wants it to go). A good editorial will state the basis for the conclusions it makes.

The argument has inspecificity. Nowhere does the editorial say why the viewers switch stations. Maybe they don't like that particular news director. The station can experiment by having the editorials read by others on the staff, by reporters, or even by the public at large. There are some stations where I live that do that, have local people at the end of the newscasts tell their opinions. Many of my friends, at least, tune in to watch what their peers have to say.

Is the purpose of the last few minutes of a newscast to sell ads? Maybe, if there were no editorial, there would be an extra two minutes of news reporting, not of advertisements. There are already so many ads in a newscast as it is; more would possibly alienate the viewers even more than the editorial does. Also, I believe there is an FCC mandate as to how many minutes per hour or half hour can be commercials, at least in prime time. If the station didn't have the editorial, but ran commericials, they may acceed this limit.

Evaluator comments on the score 4 essay

This response is adequate. The organization is acceptable, although it would be improved by the use of transitional phrases. The writer appears to have a basic understanding of the argument but doesn't fully develop his comments except in a personal vein.

The writer seems to come close to nailing the points, but doesn't quite do so. The start of the second paragraph says, "Nowhere does the editorial say why the viewers switch stations." That the research, not the editorial, indicates viewers switch stations notwithstanding, I was expecting the writer to hit the nail on the head with "We don't know why viewers switch stations, so we can't attribute it to the editorial." Instead, the author speculates as to why viewers switch, proposes an evaluation of the news director and editorial, then follows up with a digression about his own local news stations. While these points might be relevant in an editorial meeting, they neither support nor weaken the argument.

Finally, the lack of a coherent conclusion shifts this paper from a possible 5 to a 4.

Sample essay — score 2 (seriously flawed)

The reasoning in this arguement is not well-reasoned. The writer didn't convince me of their point at all. He doesn't talk about the possibility of moving the editorial, maybe putting the perspective at the beginning of the newscast, when people are probly more interested than at the end when they've already heard everything they tuned in for. He doesn't say anything about maybe having the editorials paid for by an advertisement. He doesn't cover the possibility of the fact that the government considers some editorials public service anouncements. He doesn't go into enough detail to make a good case on anything.

If I was the memo-writer, I would also talk about how the editorials maybe appeal to a more educated, higher-class (to use a politically incorrect term) audience, one that maybe spends more money on the products. Like some sitcoms appeals to a different audience (some to older viewers or white viewers, some to younger more hip maybe black viewers) the newscast can appeal to more educated viewers with the editorials.

Evaluator comments on the score 2 essay

This essay is seriously hurt by the lack of organization. Ideas are introduced but not fully developed before new ideas are added. No one argument or theme is developed. There are too many errors in grammar (pronoun agreement, saying "The writer" and "their" and "If I was") and spelling ("arguement," "probly," "anouncements"), and the essay demonstrates a lack of variety in its sentence structure.

The writer shows little ability to analyze the argument and gives no support for the points made. Instead, the writer presents a personal opinion, giving his own views rather than analyzing and evaluating the points made by the author of the memo.

Part V

Taking Full-Length Practice GREs: It's All You

"Remember, there are 4 types of questions on the GRE: verbal, math, essay, and 'How would you like to drive big rigs for a living?'"

In this part . . .

Now that you've brushed up on the basics and practiced your skills, the next step in preparing for the GRE is to take and review the practice tests.

This part has three complete practice exams carefully constructed to be as similar as possible to what you'll encounter on the actual GRE. If you purchased the Premier edition of this book, the included CD has two additional exams that not only provide more practice but also simulate the computerized GRE test-taking experience.

Approach these practice tests as seriously as you would approach the actual GRE on test day. Take them under normal test conditions in a quiet room with a timer. Have blank scratch paper on hand to jot down notes and crunch numbers, and feel free to use a simple (not scientific) calculator — the computerized version of the GRE supplies you with an on-screen calculator.

After you've gone through these practice exams, be sure to read through the answers and explanations to strengthen any weak areas and reinforce your understanding of the reasoning behind the answers. Even if you picked the right answer choice for a given question, the explanation may provide additional shortcuts or insight.

Chapter 16

Practice Exam 1

You're now ready to take a practice GRE. Like the actual, computer-based GRE, the following exam consists of two 30-minute essays, two 30-minute Verbal Reasoning sections (20 questions each), and two 35-minute Quantitative Reasoning sections (20 questions each). The actual GRE may also include an extra Verbal or Quantitative Reasoning section, which doesn't count toward your score, but this practice exam has nothing like that.

Take this practice test under normal exam conditions and approach it as you would the real GRE:

- **Work when you won't be interrupted.**
- **Use scratch paper that's free of any prepared notes.** On the actual GRE, you receive blank scratch paper before your test begins.
- **Answer as many questions as time allows.** Consider answering all the easier questions within each section first and then going back to answer the remaining, harder questions. Because you're not penalized for guessing, go ahead and guess on the remaining questions before time expires.
- **Set a timer for each section.** If you have time left at the end, you may go back and review answers (within the section), move on and finish your test early, or kick back and relax until time expires.
- **Don't leave your desk while the clock is running on any section.**
- **Take a one-minute break after each section and the optional ten-minute break after the first Verbal section.**
- **Type the essays.** Because you type the essays on the actual GRE, typing them now is good practice. Don't use software, such as Microsoft Word, with automatic spell-checker or other formatting features. Instead, use a simple text editor, such as Notepad, with copy and paste but no other features. The GRE essay-writing field features undo, redo, copy, and paste functionality but nothing else.

After completing this entire practice test, go to Chapter 17 to check your answers with the answer key and go through the answer explanations to *all* the questions, not just the ones you miss. The answer explanations provide a plethora of valuable insight — material that provides a good review of everything you went over in the previous chapters. Reviewing answer explanations to all the questions also ensures that you understand the reason why any answers you guessed correctly are correct.

Chances are good that you'll be taking the computerized GRE, which doesn't have answer choices marked with A, B, C, D, E, and F. Instead, you'll see clickable ovals and check boxes, fill-in-the-blank text boxes, and click-a-sentence options (in some Reading Comprehension questions). I formatted the questions and answer choices to make them appear as similar as possible to what you'll see on the computer-based test, but I had to retain the A, B, C, D, E, F choices for marking your answers.

Answer Sheet

Section 1: Verbal Reasoning

1. Ⓐ Ⓑ Ⓒ Ⓓ Ⓔ
2. Ⓐ Ⓑ Ⓒ Ⓓ Ⓔ
3. Ⓐ Ⓑ Ⓒ Ⓓ Ⓔ Ⓕ
4. Ⓐ Ⓑ Ⓒ Ⓓ Ⓔ Ⓕ
5. Ⓐ Ⓑ Ⓒ Ⓓ Ⓔ Ⓕ
6. Ⓐ Ⓑ Ⓒ Ⓓ Ⓔ Ⓕ Ⓖ Ⓗ Ⓘ
7. Ⓐ Ⓑ Ⓒ Ⓓ Ⓔ Ⓕ Ⓖ Ⓗ Ⓘ
8. Ⓐ Ⓑ Ⓒ Ⓓ Ⓔ Ⓕ Ⓖ Ⓗ Ⓘ
9. Ⓐ Ⓑ Ⓒ Ⓓ Ⓔ
10. Ⓐ Ⓑ Ⓒ Ⓓ Ⓔ
11. [A] [B] [C]
12. Ⓐ Ⓑ Ⓒ Ⓓ Ⓔ
13. Ⓐ Ⓑ Ⓒ Ⓓ Ⓔ
14. Ⓐ Ⓑ Ⓒ Ⓓ Ⓔ
15. [A] [B] [C] [D] [E] [F]
16. [A] [B] [C] [D] [E] [F]
17. [A] [B] [C] [D] [E] [F]
18. [A] [B] [C] [D] [E] [F]
19. [A] [B] [C] [D] [E] [F]
20. Ⓐ Ⓑ Ⓒ Ⓓ Ⓔ

Section 2: Quantitative Reasoning

1. Ⓐ Ⓑ Ⓒ Ⓓ
2. Ⓐ Ⓑ Ⓒ Ⓓ
3. Ⓐ Ⓑ Ⓒ Ⓓ
4. Ⓐ Ⓑ Ⓒ Ⓓ
5. Ⓐ Ⓑ Ⓒ Ⓓ Ⓔ
6. Ⓐ Ⓑ Ⓒ Ⓓ Ⓔ
7. Ⓐ Ⓑ Ⓒ Ⓓ
8. $ [,]
9. Ⓐ Ⓑ Ⓒ Ⓓ Ⓔ
10. [A] [B] [C] [D]
11. Ⓐ Ⓑ Ⓒ Ⓓ Ⓔ
12. [A] [B] [C] [D]
13. Ⓐ Ⓑ Ⓒ Ⓓ Ⓔ
14. Ⓐ Ⓑ Ⓒ Ⓓ Ⓔ
15. [:]
16. Ⓐ Ⓑ Ⓒ Ⓓ Ⓔ
17. Ⓐ Ⓑ Ⓒ Ⓓ Ⓔ
18. [ ]
19. [A] [B] [C] [D] [E] [F]
20. Ⓐ Ⓑ Ⓒ Ⓓ Ⓔ

Section 3: Verbal Reasoning

1. Ⓐ Ⓑ Ⓒ Ⓓ Ⓔ
2. Ⓐ Ⓑ Ⓒ Ⓓ Ⓔ
3. Ⓐ Ⓑ Ⓒ Ⓓ Ⓔ Ⓕ
4. Ⓐ Ⓑ Ⓒ Ⓓ Ⓔ Ⓕ
5. Ⓐ Ⓑ Ⓒ Ⓓ Ⓔ Ⓕ
6. Ⓐ Ⓑ Ⓒ Ⓓ Ⓔ Ⓕ Ⓖ Ⓗ Ⓘ
7. Ⓐ Ⓑ Ⓒ Ⓓ Ⓔ Ⓕ Ⓖ Ⓗ Ⓘ
8. Ⓐ Ⓑ Ⓒ Ⓓ Ⓔ Ⓕ Ⓖ Ⓗ Ⓘ
9. Ⓐ Ⓑ Ⓒ Ⓓ Ⓔ
10. [A] [B] [C]
11. Ⓐ Ⓑ Ⓒ Ⓓ Ⓔ
12. Ⓐ Ⓑ Ⓒ Ⓓ Ⓔ
13. Ⓐ Ⓑ Ⓒ Ⓓ Ⓔ
14. Ⓐ Ⓑ Ⓒ Ⓓ Ⓔ
15. Ⓐ Ⓑ Ⓒ Ⓓ Ⓔ
16. [A] [B] [C] [D] [E] [F]
17. [A] [B] [C] [D] [E] [F]
18. [A] [B] [C] [D] [E] [F]
19. [A] [B] [C] [D] [E] [F]
20. [A] [B] [C] [D] [E] [F]

Section 4: Quantitative Reasoning

1. Ⓐ Ⓑ Ⓒ Ⓓ
2. Ⓐ Ⓑ Ⓒ Ⓓ
3. Ⓐ Ⓑ Ⓒ Ⓓ
4. Ⓐ Ⓑ Ⓒ Ⓓ
5. Ⓐ Ⓑ Ⓒ Ⓓ
6. Ⓐ Ⓑ Ⓒ Ⓓ
7. Ⓐ Ⓑ Ⓒ Ⓓ
8. Ⓐ Ⓑ Ⓒ Ⓓ
9. Ⓐ Ⓑ Ⓒ Ⓓ Ⓔ
10. Ⓐ Ⓑ Ⓒ Ⓓ Ⓔ
11. Ⓐ Ⓑ Ⓒ Ⓓ Ⓔ
12. $ [,]
13. Ⓐ Ⓑ Ⓒ Ⓓ Ⓔ
14. Ⓐ Ⓑ Ⓒ Ⓓ Ⓔ
15. Ⓐ Ⓑ Ⓒ Ⓓ Ⓔ
16. [A] [B] [C] [D] [E] [F]
17. Ⓐ Ⓑ Ⓒ Ⓓ Ⓔ
18. Ⓐ Ⓑ Ⓒ Ⓓ Ⓔ
19. Ⓐ Ⓑ Ⓒ Ⓓ Ⓔ
20. [A] [B] [C]

Analytical Writing 1: Analyze an Issue

Time: 30 minutes

Directions: Present and explain your view on the following issue. Although there is no one right or wrong response, be sure to consider various points of view as you explain the reasons behind your own perspective. Support your position with reasons and examples from your own reading, personal or professional experience, and observations.

"The right to bear arms is not the direct cause of the level of violence in a country."

Express the extent to which you agree or disagree with the preceding statement and explain the reasoning behind your position. In support of your position, think of ways in which the statement may or may not be true and how these considerations influence your position.

Analytical Writing 2: Analyze an Argument

Time: 30 minutes

Directions: Critique the following argument. Identify evidence that will strengthen or weaken the argument, point out assumptions underlying the argument, and offer counterexamples to the argument.

The following appeared in a memo sent by an outside efficiency expert hired by a firm to evaluate employee performance.

> "In the six months that I have been watching the employees, their productivity has increased by over 12 percent. Therefore, my recommendation is that the employees either be watched by, or think that they are watched by, an outside evaluator at all times from this point on."

Discuss the merits of the preceding argument. Analyze the evidence used as well as the general reasoning. Present points that would strengthen the argument or make it more compelling.

Section 1

Verbal Reasoning

Time: 30 minutes for 20 questions

Directions: Choose the best answer to each question. Blacken the corresponding oval(s) on the answer sheet.

Directions: For Questions 1–8, choose the one entry best suited for each blank from its corresponding column of choices.

1. With countries around the world struggling to finance their current obligations, most world leaders are _____ to pledge additional money to fund international initiatives.

Ⓐ eager
Ⓑ apt
Ⓒ deleterious
Ⓓ reticent
Ⓔ judicious

2. Thousands of feet below the ocean's surface at depths that even light cannot penetrate is a world of creatures that _____ human imagination.

Ⓐ elude
Ⓑ adapt
Ⓒ defy
Ⓓ explore
Ⓔ renounce

3. Although Mary was (i)_____ in the way she dressed, her housekeeping was (ii)_____.

Blank (i)	*Blank (ii)*
Ⓐ creative	Ⓓ atrocious
Ⓑ drab	Ⓔ bilious
Ⓒ impeccable	Ⓕ sincere

4. Feeling a greater sense of (i)_____, baby boomers tend to be (ii)_____.

Blank (i)	*Blank (ii)*
Ⓐ history	Ⓓ apprehensive
Ⓑ independence	Ⓔ reserved
Ⓒ approbation	Ⓕ adventuresome

5. The Presidio of San Francisco is an architectural (i)_____, exhibiting numerous (ii)_____ styles, including the small Funston Avenue cottage with a large mansard roof.

Blank (i)	*Blank (ii)*
Ⓐ anomaly	Ⓓ eclectic
Ⓑ specification	Ⓔ similar
Ⓒ prototype	Ⓕ standard

Go on to next page

6. Though 5 feet in length and resembling the (i)_____ cottonmouth, the Northern Water Snake is relatively (ii)_____. Despite this fact, even in areas uninhabited by cottonmouths, the Northern Water Snake is commonly killed based on (iii)_____ fears.

Blank (i)	*Blank (ii)*	*Blank (iii)*
Ⓐ venomous	Ⓓ small	Ⓖ irrational
Ⓑ slimy	Ⓔ innocuous	Ⓗ reasonable
Ⓒ tempestuous	Ⓕ dangerous	Ⓘ justifiable

7. Theodore "Teddy" Roosevelt once said, "Speak softly and carry a big stick," but his actions (i)_____ his words. He was actually one of the most (ii)_____ heroes of the Spanish-American War and was known for being quite (iii)_____.

Blank (i)	*Blank (ii)*	*Blank (iii)*
Ⓐ confirmed	Ⓓ conspicuous	Ⓖ gentle
Ⓑ belied	Ⓔ unobtrusive	Ⓗ complex
Ⓒ reinforced	Ⓕ modest	Ⓘ boisterous

8. In an attempt to (i)_____ other members of the school board, the school board president made numerous (ii)_____ that mitigated some of the more (iii)_____ issues.

Blank (i)	*Blank (ii)*	*Blank (iii)*
Ⓐ provoke	Ⓓ considerations	Ⓖ contentious
Ⓑ appease	Ⓔ concessions	Ⓗ agreeable
Ⓒ inspire	Ⓕ accusations	Ⓘ seditious

Go on to next page

Directions: Each of the following passages is followed by questions pertaining to the passage. Read the passage and answer the questions based on information stated or implied in that passage. For each question, select one answer choice unless instructed otherwise.

The Canyon Pintado Historic District in northwest Colorado was occupied by numerous prehistoric peoples for as long as 11,000 years, including the Fremont culture that left behind rock-art sites. Fremont rock art has recurring motifs that link it to other cultures in that time period. Strange humanlike figures with broad shoulders, no legs, and horned headdresses are similar to the Barrier Canyon style of southwestern Utah. Figures with shields or shieldlike bodies are like Fremont figures from the San Rafael region of Southern Utah.

Some figures have large, trapezoidal-shaped bodies, sticklike legs, trapezoidal heads, and in many cases, are adorned with necklaces. Another motif of the Fremont culture is the mountain sheep, with graceful curvilinear horns. Designs such as concentric circles, snakelike lines, hands, corn plants, and rows of dots are also often found in Fremont art. A unique figure in Douglas Creek is Kokopelli, the humpbacked flute player of Anasazi mythology. His presence indicates some kind of tie with the more advanced culture of the Four Corners area.

9. The author mentions the connection to the culture of the Four Corners area to

Ⓐ Challenge the claim that the Fremont culture was the most advanced of its time.

Ⓑ Refute the assertion that Fremont rock art merely copied art from other cultures.

Ⓒ Suggest that the mimicking of art from other cultures may indicate contact between the cultures.

Ⓓ Prove the relationship between art and the level of civilization.

Ⓔ Ridicule the suggestion that there is a connection between artistic images and warfare success.

10. In which sentence of the passage does the author identify what links Fremont rock art to other cultures in the same time period?

Ⓐ The first sentence ("The Canyon Pintado . . . sites.")

Ⓑ The second sentence ("Fremont rock . . . period.")

Ⓒ The third sentence ("Strange humanlike . . . Utah.")

Ⓓ The fourth sentence ("Figures . . . Utah.")

Ⓔ The last sentence ("His presence . . . area.")

The war that many people commonly refer to as the Civil War has had many appellations throughout history. While the war was being fought, the South labeled it the "War Between the States." Sundry Southerners used the term "The Second American Revolutionary War," emphasizing their belief that they were attempting to secede from what they considered a tyrannical federal government.

One primary etiology of the Civil War may have been the 1820 Missouri Compromise. The compromise admitted Missouri into the Union as a slave state, while accepting Maine as a free state. The compromise also banned slavery in all western territories. However, it wasn't until 1860 when Abraham Lincoln, who was known to be against slavery, was elected president that South Carolina withdrew from the Union. At that time, the president was James Buchanan, who did not fight against the secession. By 1860, six more states had withdrawn, banding together to form the Confederate States of America, which eventually was comprised of 11 states. Their president was Jefferson Davis; the Confederacy's capital, which originally was Montgomery, Alabama, moved to Richmond, Virginia.

The first battle of the Civil War was fought at Bull Run in Virginia. Schoolchildren today are still told how the local people treated the battle as if it were a social event, taking picnic baskets and sitting on top of the hill to watch the fighting. The Federal troops lost the battle and had to retreat. Later, there was a Second Battle of Bull Run, which the Union lost as well.

Go on to next page

General Ulysses S. Grant, later president of the United States, gained fame as a great Civil War strategist. When he captured Vicksburg, Mississippi, he made it possible for the Union to control all the Mississippi River, a critical point given that goods were often shipped along that river. The Union, therefore, was able to prevent materials from reaching the Confederate troops, a situation which many historians considered essential to the quick termination of the war. Grant had the honor of receiving the surrender of the South from General Robert Lee at Appomattox Courthouse, near Richmond, Virginia, on April 9, 1865. It was only five days later that President Lincoln was assassinated.

The Civil War was the first war to have photographers, leaving to posterity the real evidence of the battles. This war also was more industrialized than many other wars, employing railroads, iron ships, and submarines.

For the following question, consider each answer choice separately and select all answer choices that are correct.

11. All of the following were discussed in the passage:

    [A] The causes of the Civil War

    [B] The South after the Civil War

    [C] Great generals of the Civil War

12. The author would best strengthen his point in the first paragraph by doing which of the following?

    Ⓐ Supplying alternate names that the Northerners called the Civil War

    Ⓑ Explaining the ambiguity of the term "Civil" War

    Ⓒ Listing reasons the South wanted to secede from the Union

    Ⓓ Discussing the actions the North had taken that the South considered tyrannical

    Ⓔ Refuting the common misconception that slavery issues caused the Civil War

13. By stating, "It was only five days later that President Lincoln was assassinated," the author implies that

    Ⓐ Southern troops fighting the war had made their way to the capital seeking revenge on Lincoln.

    Ⓑ The president was improperly protected because the guards believed that when the war had ended, there was little threat to Lincoln.

    Ⓒ The course of history, especially the reconstruction of the country and rehabilitation of the former slaves, would have been greatly altered had Lincoln lived to serve out his term.

    Ⓓ There may have been a connection between the end of the war and the assassination.

    Ⓔ The former Confederate government wanted a chance to place its people in positions of power.

14. Which of the following statements would most logically follow the last sentence of the passage?

    Ⓐ The photographs proved that the Civil War was the bloodiest war ever fought on American soil.

    Ⓑ The new technology, especially submarines, gave the North an advantage in the war that the less industrialized South did not possess.

    Ⓒ Many of the photographs are kept in the Smithsonian Museum in Washington, D.C.

    Ⓓ People not fighting directly in the war were, for the first time, able to comprehend the reality of the war.

    Ⓔ The railroad technology developed during this time led eventually to the expansion of the West.

Go on to next page

Directions: Each of the following sentences has a blank indicating that a word or phrase is omitted. Choose the two answer choices that best complete the sentence and result in two sentences most alike in meaning.

15. Although the governor was frugal in managing the state's budget, he could be quite _____ when making personal purchase decisions.

 A extravagant
 B impulsive
 C generous
 D profligate
 E enigmatic
 F erroneous

16. The defense attorney presented a host of exculpatory evidence in an attempt to _____ her client.

 A incriminate
 B exonerate
 C castigate
 D legitimize
 E forgive
 F vindicate

17. Given the complexity of the issue, the audience was pleasantly surprised to hear the committee deliver such a _____ summary of the solution.

 A succinct
 B discursive
 C laconic
 D historic
 E sardonic
 F euphemistic

18. Like many writers and artists, Virginia Woolf, though very prolific, struggled with her own _____ moods.

 A ebullient
 B effusive
 C spasmodic
 D saturnine
 E sinister
 F melancholy

19. The mayor's _____ remarks insulted so many politicians in both parties that city councilmembers began demanding his resignation.

 A enthusiastic
 B acerbic
 C encouraging
 D reassuring
 E sardonic
 F confident

Directions: The following passage is followed by a question pertaining to the passage. Read the passage and answer the question based on information stated or implied in the passage. Select only one answer.

This passage is an excerpt from A History of Modern Latin America: 1800 to the Present *by Teresa A. Meade (Wiley-Blackwell).*

Latin America is a vast, geographically and culturally diverse region stretching from the southern border of the United States to Puerto Toro at the tip of Chile, the southernmost town of the planet. Encompassing over 8 million square miles, the 20 countries that make up Latin America are home to an estimated 550 million people who converse in at least five European-based languages and six or more main indigenous languages, plus African Creole and hundreds of smaller language groups.

20. According to this passage, the boundaries of Latin America are

 Ⓐ United States and Mexico
 Ⓑ United States and the southern tip of Chile
 Ⓒ Canada and Chile
 Ⓓ Puerto Toro and Chile
 Ⓔ Mexico and Guatemala

Section 2

Quantitative Reasoning

Time: 35 minutes for 20 questions

Notes:

- All numbers used in this exam are real numbers.
- All figures lie in a plane.
- Angle measures are positive; points and angles are in the position shown.

Directions: For Questions 1–4, choose from the following answer choices:

Ⓐ Quantity A is greater.

Ⓑ Quantity B is greater.

Ⓒ The two quantities are equal.

Ⓓ The relationship cannot be determined from the information given.

1. a is an integer greater than zero

Quantity A	Quantity B
$\left(\frac{1}{2a}\right)^2$	$\frac{1}{2a^2}$

2. $0 > a > b > c$

Quantity A	Quantity B
$a - c$	$a + b$

3.

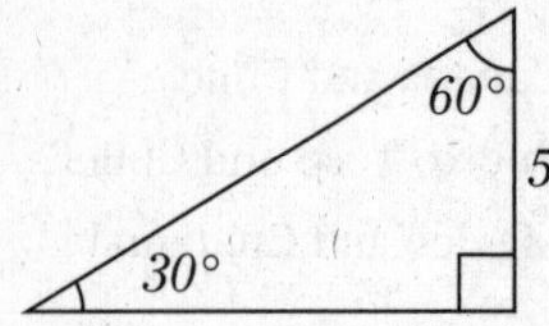

Quantity A	Quantity B
Area of the triangle	$25\sqrt{3}$

4. $16a + 5b = 37$; $3b - 8a = -21$

Quantity A	Quantity B
$a + b$	2

5. Square *RSTU* has a perimeter of 48. If A, B, C, and D are the midpoints of their respective sides, what is the perimeter of Square *ABCD?*

Ⓐ 32

Ⓑ $24\sqrt{2}$

Ⓒ 24

Ⓓ $12\sqrt{3}$

Ⓔ $12\sqrt{2}$

6. Gigi and Neville, working together at the same rate, can mow the estate's lawn in 12 hours. Working alone, what fraction of the lawn can Gigi mow in three hours?

Ⓐ $\frac{1}{24}$

Ⓑ $\frac{1}{12}$

Ⓒ $\frac{1}{8}$

Ⓓ $\frac{1}{4}$

Ⓔ $\frac{1}{3}$

Go on to next page

The answer choices for Question 7 are

Ⓐ *Quantity A is greater.*

Ⓑ *Quantity B is greater.*

Ⓒ *The two quantities are equal.*

Ⓓ *The relationship cannot be determined from the information given.*

7.

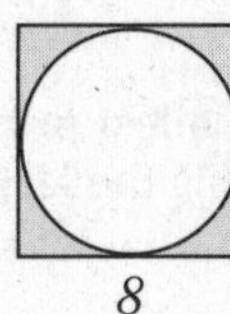

Quantity A	**Quantity B**
Number of square units in the shaded portion of the square	20

Use the following graphs to answer Questions 8–10.

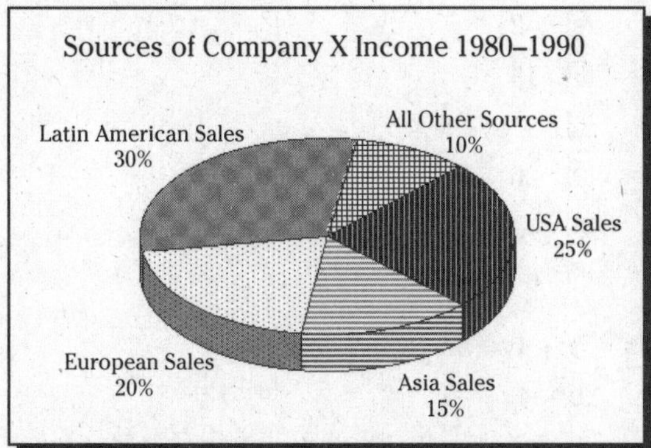

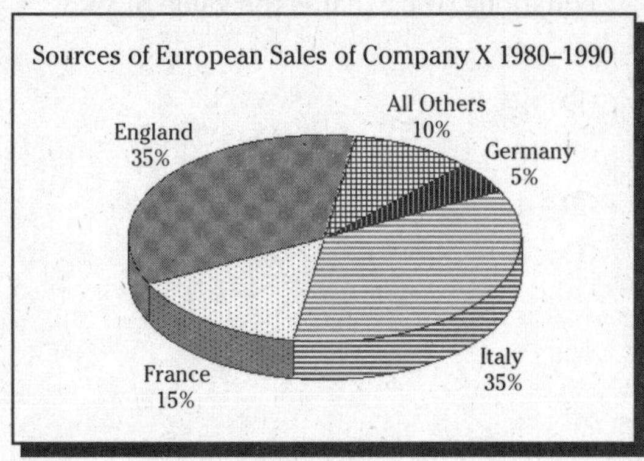

8. If Company X received \$50,000 in Latin American Sales from 1980 through 1990, how much money did it receive from sales to France?

Give your answer to the nearest thousand.

\$ [,]

9. From the information given, the 1985 sales to England were what percent of the sales to Europe?

Ⓐ 100

Ⓑ 50

Ⓒ 35

Ⓓ 25

Ⓔ It cannot be determined.

For the following question, choose exactly two answer choices.

10. From the information given, sales to France accounted for which of the following in European sales?

[A] Half as much as sales to Italy and Germany combined

[B] Exactly 20% of total European sales less than to either Italy or England

[C] 20% of total European sales less than England and 10% of total European sales more than Germany

[D] More than half as much as sales to Italy

11. If $x \neq -1$ or 0 and $y = \frac{1}{x}$, then $\frac{1}{(x+1)} + \frac{1}{(y+1)} =$

Ⓐ 1

Ⓑ 3

Ⓒ x

Ⓓ $x + 1$

Ⓔ $\frac{(x+1)}{(x+2)}$

Go on to next page

For the following question, choose exactly two answer choices.

12. If $5(x + 2)^2 - 125 = 0$, then x =

[A] 3

[B] –3

[C] –7

[D] 25

13. If ten plums cost a cents and six apples cost b cents, what is the cost of two plums and two apples in terms of a and b?

Ⓐ $\frac{3a+5b}{15}$

Ⓑ $3a + 5b$

Ⓒ $15ab$

Ⓓ $5a+\frac{3b}{15}$

Ⓔ $\frac{1}{15ab}$

14. If $x \neq 4$, solve for $\frac{\sqrt{x}+2}{\sqrt{x}-2}$.

Ⓐ –1

Ⓑ $\frac{x+4}{x-4}$

Ⓒ $-\sqrt{x}-1$

Ⓓ $\sqrt{x}+4$

Ⓔ $\frac{x+4\sqrt{x}+4}{x-4}$

15. Each of two right circular cylinders has a height of 10. Cylinder A has a circumference of 10. Cylinder B has a circumference of 20. What's the ratio (in its simplest terms) of the volume of Cylinder A to the volume of Cylinder B?

[:]

16. A plane flies from Los Angeles to New York at 600 miles per hour and returns along the same route at 400 miles per hour. What is the average (arithmetic mean) flying speed for the entire route?

Ⓐ 460 mph

Ⓑ 480 mph

Ⓒ 500 mph

Ⓓ 540 mph

Ⓔ It cannot be determined from the information given.

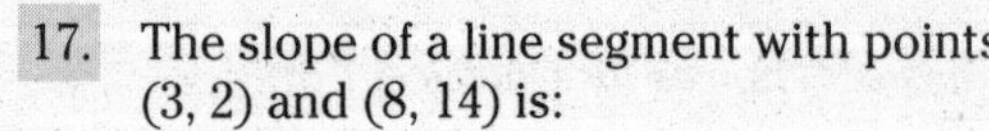

17. The slope of a line segment with points (3, 2) and (8, 14) is:

Ⓐ $\frac{5}{12}$

Ⓑ 1.5

Ⓒ $1\frac{5}{6}$

Ⓓ 2.4

Ⓔ 4.2

18. If a is the smallest prime number greater than 7 and b is the largest prime number less than 19, then ab =

[ ]

For the following question, choose all answer choices that apply.

19. $|x| > 17$

Which of the following integers makes the preceding equation true?

[A] –21

[B] 15

[C] –15

[D] 20

[E] –32

[F] 6

20. $7x + 4y = 53$

$9x - 4y = -5$

If x and y make the preceding system of equations true, what is the value of $x \times y$?

Ⓐ –69

Ⓑ –24

Ⓒ 16

Ⓓ –16

Ⓔ 24

DO NOT TURN THE PAGE UNTIL TOLD TO DO SO. DO NOT RETURN TO A PREVIOUS TEST.

Section 3

Verbal Reasoning

Time: 30 minutes for 20 questions

Directions: Choose the best answer to each question. Blacken the corresponding oval(s) on the answer sheet.

Directions: For Questions 1–8, choose the one entry best suited for each blank from its corresponding column of choices.

1. Marcella approached her latest project with such _____ that her boss not only took her off probation but also gave her a raise.

Ⓐ zeal
Ⓑ turpitude
Ⓒ guile
Ⓓ apathy
Ⓔ certainty

2. The mayor's tendency toward being _____ was well known, so her recent outburst was no surprise.

Ⓐ inchoate
Ⓑ demented
Ⓒ incorrigible
Ⓓ irascible
Ⓔ pedantic

3. Given his predecessor's (i)_____ reputation, the new manager decided to (ii)_____ her leadership style rather than change it.

Blank (i)	*Blank (ii)*
Ⓐ lackadaisical	Ⓓ emulate
Ⓑ stellar	Ⓔ obviate
Ⓒ enigmatic	Ⓕ preclude

4. The speaker was extremely (ii)_____, bringing the audience to a peaceful (ii)_____.

Blank (i)	*Blank (ii)*
Ⓐ fastidious	Ⓓ lucidity
Ⓑ unassuming	Ⓔ interest
Ⓒ soporific	Ⓕ torpor

5. One of the possum's primary (i)_____ maneuvers is to (ii)_____ death until a potential predator loses interest.

Blank (i)	*Blank (ii)*
Ⓐ aggressive	Ⓓ play
Ⓑ defensive	Ⓔ subjugate
Ⓒ avoidance	Ⓕ feign

Go on to next page

6. The instructions were so (i)_____ that the possibility anyone could (ii)_____ them was completely (iii)_____.

Blank (i)	*Blank (ii)*	*Blank (iii)*
Ⓐ implicit	Ⓓ misconstrue	Ⓖ inconceivable
Ⓑ explicit	Ⓔ comprehend	Ⓗ understandable
Ⓒ sincere	Ⓕ mistake	Ⓘ laughable

7. The crowd's exuberance was (i)_____. Soon after they dispersed, a riot (ii)_____, and even some of the most (iii)_____ of the group brandished weapons.

Blank (i)	*Blank (ii)*	*Blank (iii)*
Ⓐ ephemeral	Ⓓ endured	Ⓖ docile
Ⓑ enduring	Ⓔ dissipated	Ⓗ eager
Ⓒ passive	Ⓕ ensued	Ⓘ pugnacious

8. Unable to arrive at a (i)_____, attorneys for the two parties engaged in (ii)_____ to resolve the (iii)_____.

Blank (i)	*Blank (ii)*	*Blank (iii)*
Ⓐ variance	Ⓓ provocation	Ⓖ dispute
Ⓑ disparity	Ⓔ arbitration	Ⓗ agreement
Ⓒ consensus	Ⓕ amelioration	Ⓘ concurrence

Go on to next page

Directions: Each of the following passages is followed by questions pertaining to the passage. Read the passage and answer the questions based on information stated or implied in that passage. For each question, select one answer choice unless instructed otherwise.

The following passage was taken from Alternative Energy For Dummies *by Rik DeGunther (Wiley).*

Humans have evolved in step with sophistication of their energy consumption. Human populations, quality of life, and life expectancy have increased as energy sources have become more sophisticated.

Think about it: Early man couldn't even light a fire. Many froze in the winter, with only wooly mammoth skins to keep them warm, and the quality of life was not much different than that of animals. Once fire was discovered and humans were able to create flames at will, humanity began a gradual but consistent climb from savagery to what it is today. Upon the advent of fire, humans could warm themselves and cook their food. This began the consistent push toward bigger and better cultural and material gains, and it led to healthier, happier lives.

Throughout time, the human population remained steady for the first 1,500 years and then began a steep, consistent climb. The increase is due largely to the availability of versatile, convenient energy. As controlled, or useable, energy became more prevalent, the population expansion accelerated.

9. According to the passage, which of the following contributed most significantly to human population growth?

   Ⓐ The invention of fire

   Ⓑ The push toward bigger and better cultural and material gains

   Ⓒ Availability of energy

   Ⓓ The availability of convenient, useable energy

   Ⓔ The advent of civilization

For the following question, consider each answer choice separately and select all answer choices that are correct.

10. Which of the following can reasonably be inferred from the passage?

   [A] Increased sources of energy helped to fuel population growth.

   [B] Increases in quality of life are directly related to the availability of convenient energy.

   [C] Population growth fueled the availability of convenient energy sources.

11. Based on this passage, one could logically conclude which of the following?

   Ⓐ Without fire, people would freeze to death.

   Ⓑ The human ability to harness various sources of energy has improved the quality of life.

   Ⓒ The human population is likely to shrink as oil becomes less plentiful.

   Ⓓ Civilization could not possibly exist without the human ability to harness energy.

   Ⓔ Controlling population growth is largely a matter of reducing energy use.

Studies have shown that certain components of the immune system behave abnormally in people with chronic fatigue syndrome. Chemicals called interleukin-2 and gamma interferon, which the body produces during its battle against cancer and infectious agents, may not be made in normal amounts. There is evidence that a low-grade battle is being waged by the immune system of CFS patients, given the slight increase in the number of white cells that usually accumulate in the blood when people are fighting off an infection. Natural killer cells, though, that also help the body in this battle are found in slightly reduced numbers. It's important to note that clinical depression has the identical small reduction in natural killer cell activity. In addition, some depressed patients produce higher amounts of antibodies to certain viruses. There may be more of a connection between depression, the immune system, and chronic fatigue syndrome than is realized even now, which introduces the somewhat controversial aspect of the syndrome — its neuropsychological features.

Go on to next page

12. Which of the following does the author mention to support his theory that the immune system may be affected by chronic fatigue syndrome?

Ⓐ Clinical depression may be more physical than psychological.

Ⓑ Interleukin-2 and gamma interferon are not produced in normal amounts.

Ⓒ Antibody levels are higher in depressed people than in nondepressed people.

Ⓓ White-cell levels in people with neuropsychological problems tend to decrease.

Ⓔ Natural killer cells reduce the number of white blood cells.

13. According to the passage, when the body battles cancer, it

Ⓐ Produces chemicals such as gamma interferon

Ⓑ Turns against its own immune system

Ⓒ Stimulates the condition known as clinical depression

Ⓓ Reduces the number of antibodies available to battle viruses

Ⓔ Develops abnormal lesions around the area of the cancer

The following excerpt was taken from GMAT For Dummies, *5th Edition, by Scott Hatch, JD, and Lisa Hatch, MA (Wiley).*

For millennia, the circulation of music in human societies has been as free as the circulation of air and water; it just comes naturally. Indeed, one of the ways that a society constitutes itself as a society is by freely sharing its words, music, and art. Only in the past century or so has music been placed in a tight envelope of property rights and strictly monitored for unauthorized flows. In the past decade, the proliferation of personal computers, Internet access, and digital technologies has fueled two conflicting forces: the democratization of creativity and the demand for stronger copyright protections.

While the public continues to have nominal fair use rights to copyrighted music, in practice the legal and technological controls over music have grown tighter. At the same time, creators at the fringes of mass culture, especially some hip-hop and remix artists, remain contemptuous of such controls and routinely appropriate whatever sounds they want to create interesting music.

Copyright protection is a critically important tool for artists in earning a livelihood from their creativity. But as many singers, composers, and musicians have discovered, the benefits of copyright law in the contemporary marketplace tend to accrue to the recording industry, not to the struggling garage band. As alternative distribution and marketing outlets have arisen, the recording industry has sought to ban, delay, or control as many of them as possible. After all, technological innovations that provide faster, cheaper distribution of music are likely to disrupt the industry's fixed investments and entrenched ways of doing business. New technologies allow newcomers to enter the market and compete, sometimes on superior terms. New technologies enable new types of audiences to emerge that may or may not be compatible with existing marketing strategies.

No wonder the recording industry has scrambled to develop new technological locks and broader copyright protections; they strengthen its control of music distribution. If metering devices could turn barroom singalongs into a market, the music industry would likely declare this form of unauthorized musical performance to be copyright infringement.

14. Which of the following most accurately states the main idea of the passage?

Ⓐ Only with the development of technology in the past century has music begun to freely circulate in society.

Ⓑ The recording industry is trying to develop an ever-tighter hold on the distribution of music, which used to circulate freely.

Ⓒ Copyright protection is an important tool for composers and musicians who earn their living from their music.

Ⓓ Technology allows new distribution methods that threaten to undermine the marketing strategies of music companies.

Ⓔ If music is no longer allowed to flow freely through the society, then the identity of the society itself will be lost.

Go on to next page

15. According to the passage, new technology has resulted (or will result) in each of the following, *except:*

Ⓐ New locks on music distribution

Ⓑ Newcomers competing in the music market

Ⓒ Better music

Ⓓ Democratization of creativity

Ⓔ Faster, cheaper distribution of music

Directions: Each of the following sentences has a blank indicating that a word or phrase is omitted. Choose the two answer choices that best complete the sentence and result in two sentences most alike in meaning.

16. Because dog owners failed to adhere to the rules, the municipality issued _____ requiring owners to carry a permit when walking their dogs in the park.

[A] a regulation

[B] an ordinance

[C] a prognostication

[D] a restraining order

[E] a tenet

[F] a verdict

17. The dancer's movements were so smooth and fluid that she _____ grace and elegance.

[A] undermined

[B] embodied

[C] synthesized

[D] extirpated

[E] epitomized

[F] dissipated

18. Although the governor was well aware of his role as a civil servant, he demanded a certain level of _____ in making decisions.

[A] dependence

[B] supremacy

[C] independence

[D] solvency

[E] neutrality

[F] autonomy

19. Although the judge delivered the harshest verdict possible, he showed _____ during the sentencing hearing.

[A] clemency

[B] austerity

[C] stringency

[D] affluence

[E] magnanimity

[F] leniency

20. Stereotyping is one of many ways in which society _____ those individuals who suffer from mental illness.

[A] chastise

[B] disaffect

[C] denigrate

[D] emulate

[E] stigmatize

[F] characterize

STOP DO NOT TURN THE PAGE UNTIL TOLD TO DO SO. DO NOT RETURN TO A PREVIOUS TEST.

Section 4

Quantitative Reasoning

Time: 35 minutes for 20 questions

Notes:

- All numbers used in this exam are real numbers.
- All figures lie in a plane.
- Angle measures are positive; points and angles are in the position shown.

Directions: For Questions 1–8, choose from the following answer choices:

Ⓐ *Quantity A is greater.*

Ⓑ *Quantity B is greater.*

Ⓒ *The two quantities are equal.*

Ⓓ *The relationship cannot be determined from the information given.*

1.

Quantity A	***Quantity B***
Area of a rectangle of perimeter 20	Area of a triangle of perimeter 20

2. $a \neq 0, 1$

Quantity A	***Quantity B***
a^2	1

3. $3a + 5b = 12$; $3b + 5a = 28$

Quantity A	***Quantity B***
$3(a+b)$	15

4. A right circular cylinder of volume 200π cubic units has a height of 8.

Quantity A	***Quantity B***
Circumference of the base	10

5.

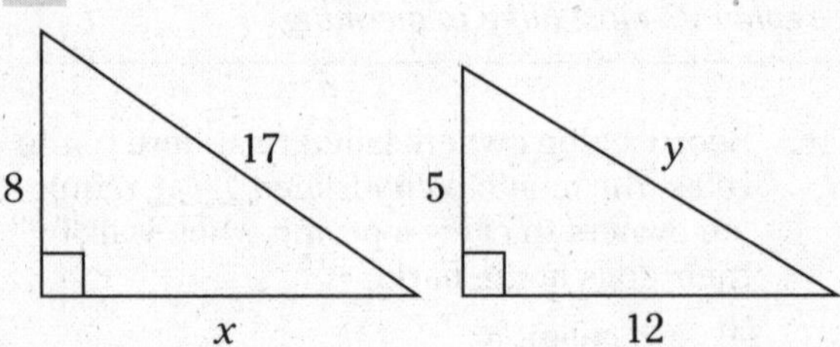

Quantity A	***Quantity B***
x	y

6. $10 < \sqrt{x} < 14$

Quantity A	***Quantity B***
144	x

7. Rolling two six-sided dice

Quantity A	***Quantity B***
Odds of rolling a total of 6	Odds of rolling a total of 9

8. Sixteen ounces of lemonade mix makes two gallons of lemonade. (One gallon = four quarts.)

Quantity A	***Quantity B***
Amount of mix needed to make three quarts of lemonade	Six ounces of mix

Go on to next page

9. Bob traveled 40 percent of the distance of his trip alone, went another 20 miles with Anthony, and then finished the last half of the trip alone. How many miles was the trip?

Ⓐ 240

Ⓑ 200

Ⓒ 160

Ⓓ 100

Ⓔ 50

Questions 10 and 11 refer to the following graphs.

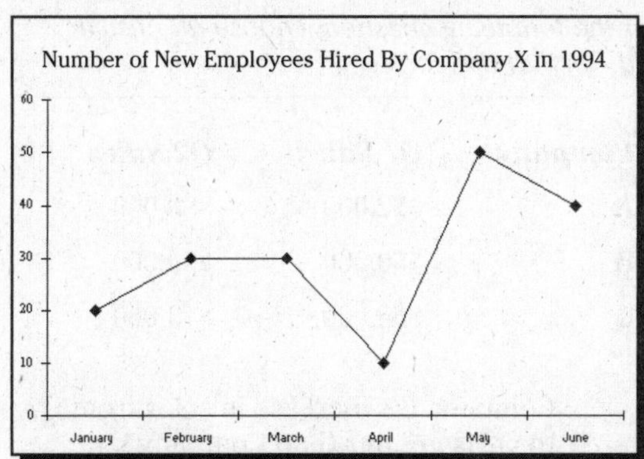

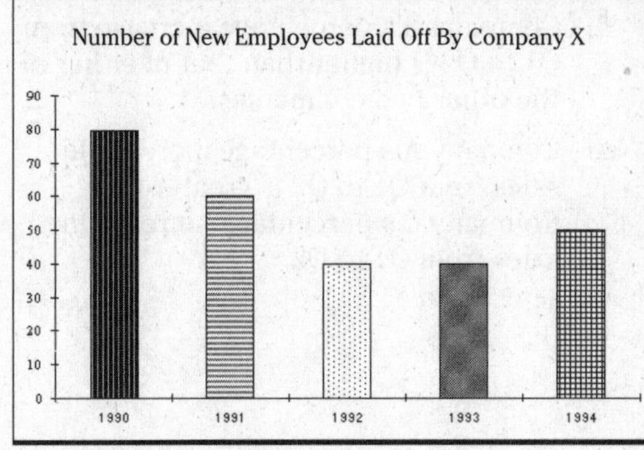

10. If new employees hired in May 1994 were $\frac{1}{5}$ of the total employees, new employees laid off in 1994 would be what percent of the total employees in the company?

Ⓐ 60

Ⓑ 50

Ⓒ $33\frac{1}{3}$

Ⓓ 24

Ⓔ 20

11. In 1995, the increase in the percentage of new employees laid off over that of the previous year was the same as the increase in the percentage of new employees hired between January and February of 1994. How many new employees were laid off in 1995?

Ⓐ 10

Ⓑ 20

Ⓒ 50

Ⓓ 60

Ⓔ 75

12. Now in his second year at the firm, Carlos is earning an annual salary of $37,450. At the beginning of the year, he received a 7% raise. What was Carlos's starting salary?

Give your answer to the nearest thousand.

$ [,]

13. Jerry drives 30 miles an hour for two and a half hours. Susan goes the same distance but drives 40 miles per hour. How many hours does Susan drive?

Ⓐ 37.5

Ⓑ $1\frac{7}{8}$

Ⓒ 2

Ⓓ $1\frac{5}{8}$

Ⓔ 2.5

14. Out of a class of 25 students, the teacher must choose 5 to represent the class in the school's spelling bee. Assuming the teacher chooses randomly, how many different combinations of students could possibly represent the class?

Ⓐ 5

Ⓑ $\frac{25!}{(25-5)!}$

Ⓒ $\frac{25!}{5!}$

Ⓓ $\frac{25!}{5!20!}$

Ⓔ 1

Go on to next page

15. Of 175 employees, 30 took advantage of prepaid legal services, 165 participated in the company retirement program, and 25 participated in both programs. How many employees did not participate in either program?

Ⓐ 5

Ⓑ 10

Ⓒ 25

Ⓓ 30

Ⓔ There is not enough information to answer this question.

For the following question, choose all answer choices that are correct.

16. Common factors of 18 and 48 are

[A] 9

[B] 3

[C] 4

[D] 6

[E] 1

[F] 0

17. –5, 0, 5, –5, 0, 5, –5, 0, 5

In this repeating sequence, what is the sum of the 250th and 251st terms?

Ⓐ 5

Ⓑ 10

Ⓒ –5

Ⓓ 0

Ⓔ –10

18. How many ounces of 40% salt solution must be added to 75 ounces of 10% salt solution to make a 35% salt solution?

Ⓐ 75

Ⓑ 375

Ⓒ 150

Ⓓ 187.5

Ⓔ 125

19. If $\frac{(x+5)}{(x-7)} = y$, what is the value of x in terms of y?

Ⓐ $7y - 5$

Ⓑ $xy - 7y - 5$

Ⓒ $\frac{(7y-5)}{(1-y)}$

Ⓓ $\frac{-(7y+5)}{(1-y)}$

Ⓔ $y - 5 + 7$

For the following question, choose all answer choices that are correct.

Company	***Q1 Sales***	***Q2 Sales***
A	$72,000	$80,000
B	$50,000	$59,000
C	$65,000	$73,000

20. [A] Company B's increase in sales from Q1 to Q2 is greater than Company C's increase in sales from Q1 to Q2.

[B] Company B's percentage increase from Q1 to Q2 is higher than that of either of the other two companies.

[C] Company A's percentage increase in sales from Q1 to Q2 is greater than Company C's percentage increase in sales from Q1 to Q2.

STOP DO NOT TURN THE PAGE UNTIL TOLD TO DO SO.
DO NOT RETURN TO A PREVIOUS TEST.

Chapter 17

Practice Exam 1: Answers and Explanations

After taking the Practice Exam 1 in Chapter 16, use this chapter to check your answers and see how you did. Carefully review the explanations because doing so can help you understand why you missed the questions you did and also give you a better understanding of the thought process that helped you select the correct answers. If you're in a hurry, flip to the end of the chapter for an abbreviated answer key.

Analytical Writing Sections

Give your essays to someone to read and evaluate for you. Refer that helpful person to Chapters 14 and 15 for scoring guidelines.

Section 1: Verbal Reasoning

1. **D.** ***Reticent*** means reluctant. Given the statement that many countries around the world are struggling financially, it makes sense that leaders would be reluctant to pledge money to help others. If you chose Choice (A), *eager,* you fell for a common trap — an answer choice with the opposite meaning of the correct answer. Choice (B), ***apt***, means leaning toward — somewhere between eager and reticent. Choice (C), ***deleterious***, means harmful, which obviously doesn't make sense, and Choice (E), ***judicious***, means using good judgment, which also doesn't make much sense.
2. **C.** ***Defy*** means to challenge, which matches the first part of the sentence that implies a dark, mysterious world with creatures that *challenge* human imagination. Choice (A), ***elude***, means to avoid, but a creature wouldn't avoid imagination. Choice (B), *adapt,* doesn't fit due to meaning and usage — for the choice to remain in the running, it would have to be "adapt to," and even that makes little sense. Choice (D), *explore,* fits in the sentence but doesn't match the meaning. Choice (E), ***renounce***, means to give up something or disown it — a meaning that doesn't fit in this context.
3. **C, D.** ***Impeccable*** means perfect, flawless, and ***atrocious*** means exceptionally bad. The sentence begins with the word *although,* which clues you in that the two correct answers have opposite meanings. Choice (C), *impeccable,* and Choice (D), *atrocious,* are the only two answer choices opposite in meaning. Mary could be *creative* in the way that she dressed, but there's no word choice for the second blank that is opposite of creative. She could also be ***drab***, which means dull, but again there's no opposing word choice for Blank (ii). ***Bilious*** means angry or irritable, and ***sincere*** means open or genuine.
4. **B, F.** One meaning of ***independence*** is freedom from control, which would tend to make someone more *adventuresome* than ***apprehensive*** (anxious, fearful) or ***reserved*** (withholding one's opinion). *History* obviously doesn't fit well with any of the choices in the second column.

Approbation (approval) sort of fits; *approbation* would tend to make someone more confident, but *independence* suggests both confidence and an ability to stand on one's own two feet, making it the better choice.

5. **A, D.** ***Anomaly*** means non-standard, and ***eclectic*** means pieced together from several sources. The word *numerous* makes *eclectic* the best choice for the second column, and because of that, *anomaly* is the better choice for the first column. You can rule out Choice (B), *specification,* because a building or collection of buildings cannot be a specification. You can also rule out Choice (C), ***prototype*** (model), because the sentence implies that the Presidio is an existing architectural structure in San Francisco. Choices (E) and (F), *similar* and *standard,* don't work, because the last part of the sentence points out a building style (cottage) that has a mansard roof not normally used in cottages.

6. **A, E, G.** ***Venomous*** means poisonous, ***innocuous*** means harmless, and ***irrational*** means not logical or based on facts. The first word of the first sentence is *though,* providing a clue that the two blanks in that sentence require *antonyms* (words opposite in meaning). The only words in the first two columns that are nearly opposite in meaning are *venomous* and *innocuous.* ***Tempestuous*** means agitated, like a storm or tempest. If you chose *venomous* and *dangerous,* you fell for the trap of choosing words similar in meaning. You can also rule out *slimy* for the first blank, because none of the choices in the second column is opposite in meaning. In the second column, you can rule out *small* and *dangerous,* because neither is opposite in meaning to any of the choices in the first column. The second sentence starts with the word *despite,* indicating that the fact stated in the first part of the sentence is going to receive a response that's not in line with that fact. So regardless that the Northern Water Snake is harmless, some people often kill it based on ***irrational*** fears, or fears not supported by the fact. Because the water snake is harmless, such fears could not be *reasonable* or *justifiable* (supported by fact).

7. **B, D, I.** The key word in the first sentence is *but,* indicating that the missing word is going to undercut everything before *but.* This rules out Choice (A), ***confirmed***, and Choice (C), ***reinforced***, both of which convey a sense of support. The only choice left in the first column is Choice (B), ***belied*** (contradicted). In the second sentence, the word *actually* clues you in that the next two missing words are contrary to speaking softly. In the second column, you can rule out ***unobtrusive*** and ***modest***, because both convey a sense of trying not to be noticed; so ***conspicuous*** (easily noticeable), is the word you want. In the third column, *gentle* isn't the word you're looking for, and *complex* doesn't fit either. The only remaining choice is ***boisterous*** (rowdy, unruly).

8. **B, E, G.** If you read the sentence without filling in any words, it conveys a sense that the school board president is trying to negotiate something that everyone on the school board can live with. Using your own words to complete the sentence, you may fill in the blanks with *please, compromises,* and *touchy.* Then, all you need to do is to identify the word in each column that's closest to the word you came up with: *please* ≈ ***appease***, *compromises* ≈ ***concessions***, and *touchy* ≈ ***contentious***. For the first blank, *provoke* isn't typically what school board presidents set out to do. *Inspire* may make a good second choice, but it doesn't fit with the rest of the sentence, which deals more with issues than ideas. For the second blank, *accusations* would work if the school board president wanted to provoke, but because she's trying to appease, it's the opposite of what you need here. *Considerations* would make a good second choice, but concessions fits better with appeasement. For the third blank the issues must be something the members disagree about, so you can instantly rule out *agreeable.* You can also rule out ***seditious*** (rebellious), because it's way too strong for this context.

9. **C.** First, use the verbs to help eliminate wrong answers. Passages are rarely negative and don't *ridicule* anything (Choice [E]). This very factual passage doesn't *refute* (deny or disprove) anything, which eliminates Choice (B). A strong word like *prove* (Choice [D]) is rarely correct. (And how much can be proven in two paragraphs, anyway?) Just by examining the verbs, you can narrow your answers to two, giving you a 50/50 shot at the right one.

   Although Choice (A) is tempting, the author never makes the claim that the Fremont culture was the most advanced, so how can that claim be challenged? Choice (C) fits: Recurring motifs between cultures may indicate connections between those cultures.

On the GRE, you can return to a question within the section if time remains. If you're down to two answer choices, pick one for now and write the question number down on your scratch paper. If time remains when you get to the end of the section, go back to that question. If time is running out, you've already answered the question and don't have to worry about rushing back.

10. **B.** The word *links* in the question almost gives away the answer. "Fremont rock art has recurring motifs that *link* it to other cultures in that time period."

11. **A, C.** These "choose all" questions are tough, because you can't just eliminate wrong choices; you also need to confirm right choices. You may need to go back to the passage again and again and again to find support for each correct answer choice and to make sure any answer choices you believe are wrong really are.

12. **A.** The key to this question is to identify the purpose of the first paragraph. The main idea of the first paragraph was to discuss the names given to the Civil War. The material listed names that the South called the war, but didn't mention any names used by the North. Supplying names used by the North would strengthen the point.

13. **D.** When something is implied, it's stated indirectly, meaning that the author may not be making a very strong point. Choose a wishy-washy, "possibly" or "maybe" style of answer. The other choices go too far. Nothing was said about Southern troops going to the capital, about the protection of Lincoln (or threats made against him), or about a conspiracy by the Confederate government. Choice (C) is a logical answer, and it may be true, but the statement in the passage doesn't imply it.

Just because a statement is true, doesn't mean it's a correct answer. Something in the passage must support the answer.

14. **B.** The theme of the paragraph is the new technology. The rest of the paragraph would probably discuss the impact of that technology on the war. Choices (A), (C), and (D), dealing with photography, are too specific. Choice (E) may be true but probably isn't the point of the passage. Industrialization in general and its effect on the war are the important parts, not the photography or railroads per se.

15. **A, D.** ***Extravagant*** means excessive or unrestrained, the opposite of *frugal* (spending sparingly, in this case). Choice (D), ***profligate***, means wasteful. Choice (B), ***impulsive*** (without caution), would be a good third choice, but it conveys more of a sense of being reckless rather than excessive. Choice (C), *generous,* doesn't work in the context of making purchase decisions. Neither of the last two answer choices is a good fit, either: ***Enigmatic*** means mysterious, and ***erroneous*** means incorrect.

16. **B, F.** To answer this question correctly, you need to know what ***exculpatory*** means. If you've heard the Latin expression *mea culpa* or "my fault," you can figure it out: *Culpa* means fault and *ex-* means not, so *exculpa* would mean not one's fault. The two choices that fit are Choice (B), ***exonerate*** (to clear from blame), and Choice (F), ***vindicate*** (to prove right).

    You can also answer this question, or at least improve your chances of answering correctly, by the process of elimination: Rule out Choice (A), ***incriminate*** (prove guilty), and Choice (C), ***castigate*** (scold), because a defense attorney is unlikely to do either of these to a client. You can also rule out Choice (D), ***legitimize*** (to make something legal or acceptable), because that's not really something a lawyer does to a client, nor would a lawyer use evidence to *forgive* a client.

17. **A, C.** The key word in this question is *surprised,* telling you that the parts before and after that word are opposite or nearly opposite. Because the issue is referred to as complex, expect something simple at the end. ***Succinct*** means brief and to the point, which is contrary to complex, and ***laconic*** is another word for succinct or concise. ***Discursive*** means lengthy. *Historic* doesn't fit. ***Sardonic*** is scornful. ***Euphemistic*** means indirect or understated.

18. **D, F.** ***Saturnine*** means ***melancholy*** or sad. The word *though* is a clue that what's before *though* and what's after are very different, so if Virginia Woolf was very ***prolific*** (productive), what kind of moods would she be struggling with to make her less productive?

Choices (A) and (B), ***ebullient*** and ***effusive***, both convey a sense of enthusiasm, so cross those off the list. ***Spasmodic*** means sporadic, which doesn't really fit. ***Sinister*** conveys a sense of evil.

19. **B, E.** ***Acerbic*** means harsh, and ***sardonic*** means scornful or with disdain. If the mayor's remarks insulted people, the remarks must have been negative in some way, which enables you to rule out *enthusiastic, encouraging,* and *reassuring. Confident* remarks can be negative or positive, so rule that one out, too.

20. **B.** The first sentence states that Latin America is the region between the southern border of the United States to Puerto Toro at the tip of Chile, which implies the southernmost point in Chile. Choices (A) and (E) are obviously wrong — Choice (A) because no land exists between Mexico and the United States, and Choice (E) because the passage says nothing about Guatemala. You could make a case for Choice (C), Canada and Chile, but the passage is more precise, specifying the southern border of the United States as the northern boundary.

Section 2: Quantitative Reasoning

1. **B.** Plug in numbers. Suppose $a = 1$. Then Quantity A is $\frac{1}{2}\times 1=\frac{1}{2}$, and then $\left(\frac{1}{2}\right)^2=\frac{1}{4}$. Quantity B requires you to square the 1 first, which is simply 1, and then multiply by $\frac{1}{2}$ to get $\frac{1}{2}$. So far, Quantity B is bigger. Try a different number. Suppose $a = 2$. Then Quantity A is half of 2, which is 1. You know that $1^2 = 1$. Quantity B is half of 4 (because $2^2 = 4$) and guess what — Quantity B is still greater. No matter what you plug in, Quantity B is larger.

With the type of problem in Question 1, always plug in more than one number. Otherwise, you never know whether the answer depends on what you plug in. Do you remember the Sacred Six you need to plug in for variables? They are 1, 2, 0, –1, –2, and $\frac{1}{2}$. Usually, just plugging in 1 and 2 gets the job done. (Turn back to Chapter 13 for more info.)

2. **A.** Remember the tip from Chapter 13: Cancel quantities that are identical. Slash off the a in both quantities so that you're left with $-c$ and $+b$. Because c is negative, a negative c is a double negative, which is actually a positive. In Quantity B, b remains negative (because a positive times a negative is negative). Because any positive is greater than any negative, Quantity A is larger.

Did you look at all the variables and choose Choice (D), thinking the answer depended on what you plugged in? That's a very good first reaction, but be sure to do the actual plugging in with numbers that fit the inequality, such as –1, –2, and –3. Be careful not to get messed up and put –3, –2, –1. With negatives, everything is backward: –1 is greater than –2.

Quantity A is $-1 - (-3) = -1 + 3 = 2$. Quantity B is $-1 + (-2) = -3$.

3. **B.** If you chose Choice (D), you fell for the trap. You probably looked at the question, saw that only one side was given, and figured you didn't have enough info to answer the question. Wrong. You should've reminded yourself of this tip: When a figure is given, the answer is rarely Choice (D). (This is the flip of the tip that when a QC geometry problem gives words but no pictures, the answer is usually Choice [D].)

Do you remember your common right triangles? Chapter 10 covers these. A 30:60:90 triangle has a side ratio of $side : side\sqrt{3} : 2side$. The side opposite the 30-degree angle is the shortest side — the 5 in this case. The side opposite the 60-degree angle is the next shortest side, the "$side\sqrt{3}$" side. With this question, that's $5\sqrt{3}$. Although you don't need to know this fact to find the area of the triangle, the *hypotenuse* (the side opposite the 90-degree angle) is the longest side — the "2*side*" side. Here, it's 10.

The area of a triangle is $\frac{1}{2}$*base* × *height*. The base is $5\sqrt{3}$; the height is 5. Therefore, the area is $\frac{1}{2} \times 5\sqrt{3} \times 5 = \frac{25}{2}\sqrt{3}$. Don't bother finding the exact number — it's certainly less than $25\sqrt{3}$. If you chose Choice (C), you did *all* that work and, because you forgot the very last step, fell for a different trap: forgetting to divide the *base* × *height* by 2.

How can you prevent making a careless mistake like forgetting to multiply by $\frac{1}{2}$ in this problem? Simple. Immediately write down the formula for the problem on the scratch paper. Writing the formula may seem amateurish or like extra work, but it only takes a second and can prevent careless errors. When you see the formula, you can more easily plug in the numbers and work it through.

4. **C.** It's amazing how many QC questions that require you to actually do the work and solve the problem turn out to have Choice (C) answers. We're not saying that you should choose Choice (C) as soon as you start shoving the pencil around, but the more calculations a question requires, the more often the answer seems to be Choice (C). (That's the flip of the tip in Chapter 13 that if the quantities appear to be equal at first glance, without doing any work, a trap is probably lurking.) Here, set up the equations vertically:

   $16a + 5b = 37$

   $-8a + 3b = -21$

   You want to either add or subtract to get the same *numerical coefficient* (the number that goes in front of the variable) for the *a* and the *b*. When you add the equations here, you get $8a + 8b = 16$. (Notice how I moved the *a* to the front of the second equation to make the variables add up neatly?) Divide both sides by 8 to get $a + b = 2$.

5. **B.** The four sides of a square are equal, such that one side of Square *RSTU* is 12. If the points are midpoints, each one divides the large square's sides into two parts, with each part consisting of 6 units. Connecting these midpoints gives you four isosceles right triangles (*RAD, SAB, TCB,* and *UDC*). The ratios of the sides of an isosceles right triangle are *side* : *side* : *side*$\sqrt{2}$. That means the hypotenuse of Triangle *RAD,* for example, is $6\sqrt{2}$. These hypotenuses are the sides of Square *ABCD.* Add the four sides to get $24\sqrt{2}$, Choice (B).

   If you chose Choice (A), you said that four "root 2s" equaled 8 and added 24 + 8 = 32. You can't add square roots like that.

6. **C.** The key to this problem is knowing that Gigi and Neville work at the same rate. If they finish the lawn in 12 hours, each did $\frac{1}{2}$ of the job in 12 hours. Therefore, Gigi working alone would've taken 24 hours to finish the lawn. Because 3 hours is $\frac{1}{8}$ of 24 hours, she could've done $\frac{1}{8}$ of the job in that time.

7. **B.** Think of a shaded area as a leftover: It's what's left over after you've subtracted the unshaded area from the figure as a whole. Because Quantity A tells you that the figure is a square, you find its area by multiplying *side* × *side:* 8 × 8 = 64. The diameter of the circle is the same as the length of the square, 8. The radius of a circle is half the diameter, or 4. The area of a circle is $\pi radius^2$, or 16π. Find the shaded area by subtracting $64 - 16\pi$.

   Don't bother figuring out how much 16π is. You know that π is slightly larger than 3.14, but don't even make it that complicated. Just say that π is bigger than 3. Multiply 16 × 3 to get 48. Subtract 64 – 48 to get 16. The actual area will be even smaller than that because you'll be subtracting some number larger than 48 (whatever you get when you multiply 3.14 × 16, which I'm not about to do, and neither should you). Because 16 is smaller than 20, and the *real* answer is even smaller than 16, Quantity B is bigger.

   If you can't recall how to find the remaining area of a shape that's partially occluded by another shape, flip to Chapter 10, where I provide a simple, three-step approach.

8. **\$5,000.** Latin American sales account for 30 percent of total income. The equation is thus \$50,000 = $0.3x$. Divide both sides through by 0.3 to get x (total income) = \$166,667. European sales were 20 percent of total income, or \$166,667 × 0.20 = \$33,333. Sales to France were 15 percent of that figure: 0.15 × \$33,333 = \$5000.

   Feel free to estimate, especially because the answer is rounded to the nearest thousand. Say that \$50,000 is slightly less than a third of the total, making the total slightly more than \$150,000. Call it \$160,000. Then European sales are 20 percent, or a fifth of that, which is \$32,000. Then French sales are 15 percent of that. Fifteen percent of \$30,000 is \$4,500, so 15 percent of \$32,000 is greater than \$4,500 and less than \$5,000. The closest thousand is \$5,000.

   The dollar sign is already there, to the left of the answer box, so you don't need to enter the \$ symbol in the box. In fact, in the computer-based GRE, you can't enter the dollar sign in the answer box — you can enter only numbers, a decimal point, and a negative sign. Also, the comma in 5,000 appears automatically.

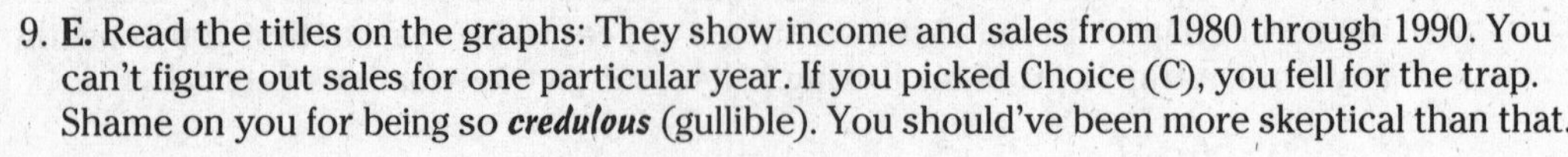

9. **E.** Read the titles on the graphs: They show income and sales from 1980 through 1990. You can't figure out sales for one particular year. If you picked Choice (C), you fell for the trap. Shame on you for being so ***credulous*** (gullible). You should've been more skeptical than that.

   If something looks too good to be true, it's probably a trap.

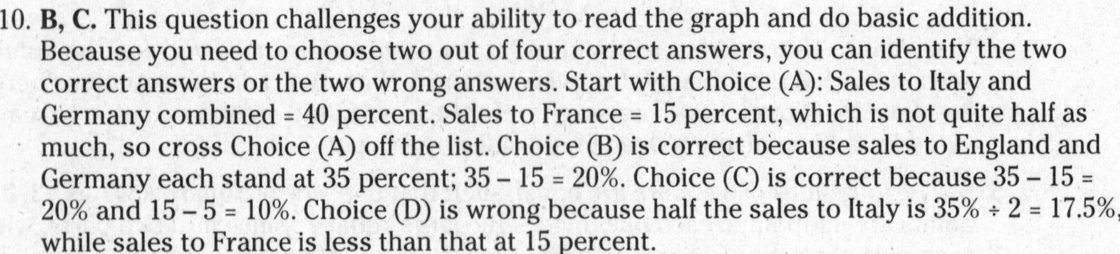

10. **B, C.** This question challenges your ability to read the graph and do basic addition. Because you need to choose two out of four correct answers, you can identify the two correct answers or the two wrong answers. Start with Choice (A): Sales to Italy and Germany combined = 40 percent. Sales to France = 15 percent, which is not quite half as much, so cross Choice (A) off the list. Choice (B) is correct because sales to England and Germany each stand at 35 percent; 35 – 15 = 20%. Choice (C) is correct because 35 – 15 = 20% and 15 – 5 = 10%. Choice (D) is wrong because half the sales to Italy is 35% ÷ 2 = 17.5%, while sales to France is less than that at 15 percent.

11. **A.** Because the first equation provides a value for y in terms of x, start by substituting the value for y in terms of x into the second equation:

$$\frac{1}{(x+1)}+\frac{1}{\left(\frac{1}{x}+1\right)}$$

   Simplify the second fraction, multiplying it by $\frac{x}{x}$:

$$\frac{1}{\left(\frac{1}{x}+1\right)}\times\frac{x}{x}=\frac{x}{\left(\frac{x}{x}+1x\right)}=\frac{x}{(1+x)}=\frac{x}{(x+1)}$$

   Now rewrite the original equation using the new value and solve it:

$$\frac{1}{(x+1)}+\frac{x}{(x+1)}=\frac{(x+1)}{(x+1)}=1$$

12. **A, C.** Simplify and solve:

$$5(x+2)^2-125=0$$
$$5(x+2)^2=125$$
$$(x+2)^2=25$$
$$x+2=\pm 5$$
$$x+2=5\Rightarrow x=5-2=3$$
$$x+2=-5\Rightarrow x=-7$$

13. **A.** If ten plums cost a cents, then each plum costs $\frac{1}{10}a$, and two plums cost $\frac{2}{10}a = \frac{1}{5}a$. If six apples cost b cents, then each apple costs $\frac{1}{6}b$ cents, and two apples cost $\frac{2}{6}b = \frac{1}{3}b$ cents.

Now use 15 as a common denominator for 5 and 3. Convert: $\frac{1}{5}a = \frac{3}{15}a$, and $\frac{1}{3}b = \frac{5}{15}b$. Now, add the two:

$$\frac{3}{15}a = \frac{3a}{15}$$

$$\frac{5}{15}b = \frac{5b}{15}$$

$$\frac{3a}{15} + \frac{5b}{15} = \frac{3a+5b}{15}$$

Though plugging in numbers may be useful at times, this can be a pitfall when the answer choices are in terms of letters, such as Question 13. Say you declare ten plums cost \$1, making the plums \$0.10 each, and six apples cost \$0.30, making the apples \$0.05 each. Two plums and two apples total \$0.30. This, however, doesn't match any of the answer choices. You need to keep the a and b in your equation, because that's the only way to produce an answer that matches one of the choices.

14. **E.** Unlike the previous question, work through this one by *plugging in numbers.* Choose a number with an easy square root. Make $x = 9$ (because $\sqrt{9} = 3$). Now, solve the question:

$$\frac{\sqrt{9}+2}{\sqrt{9}-2} = \frac{3+2}{3-2} = \frac{5}{1} = 5$$

Keep in mind that 5 is the answer to the problem. It isn't the value of x. Jot down the 5 to remind yourself that the answer you want is 5. Better yet, make a chart to the side, simply writing down $x = 9$ and *answer* = 5. Now go through each answer choice and see which one comes out to be 5. Only Choice (E) works:

$$\frac{9+4\sqrt{9}+4}{9-4} = \frac{9+(4\times3)+4}{5} = \frac{9+12+4}{5} = \frac{25}{5} = 5$$

Be very, very careful not to put 3 in for x in the problem. Remember $x = 9$ — the square root of x equals 3.

You can also solve this problem with an algebraic approach: Simplify the denominator by multiplying each side through by $\left(\sqrt{x}+2\right)$:

$$\frac{\sqrt{x}+2}{\sqrt{x}-2} \times \frac{\sqrt{x}+2}{\sqrt{x}+2}$$

The numerator is $\left(\sqrt{x}+2\right)\left(\sqrt{x}+2\right)$. Use FOIL (First, Outer, Inner, Last) to multiply these terms: $\sqrt{x} \times \sqrt{x} = x$. Then $\sqrt{x} \times 2 = 2\sqrt{x}$. Next, $2 \times \sqrt{x} = 2\sqrt{x}$. Finally, $-2 \times 2 = -4$. Add: $x + 4\sqrt{x} + 4$. The denominator is $\left(\sqrt{x}-2\right)\left(\sqrt{x}+2\right)$. Use FOIL again to multiply these terms: $\sqrt{x} \times \sqrt{x} = x$. Then $\sqrt{x} \times 2 = 2\sqrt{x}$. Next, $\sqrt{x} \times -2 = -2\sqrt{x}$. Finally, $2 \times 2 = 4$.

The $2\sqrt{x}$ and $-2\sqrt{x}$ cancel each other out, leaving you with $x - 4$. Combine the numerator and denominator, and you get your answer:

$$\frac{x+4\sqrt{x}+4}{x-4}$$

REMEMBER

Flip to Chapter 9 for more on basic FOIL problems and be sure to memorize the following:

$(a + b)(a + b) = a^2 + 2ab + b^2$

$(a + b)(a - b) = a^2 - b^2$

15. **1:4.** The volume of any right circular cylinder (and every cylinder that you calculate for on the GRE is a *right circular* cylinder) is $\pi r^2 h$. (More on this in Chapter 10.) To find the volume of any cylinder, you need its height and radius. You have the heights of Cylinders A and B, but not the radii.

    The circumference of any circle (or any cylinder) is $2\pi r$. Cylinder A has a circumference of 10, so to find the radius, back-solve using the circumference formula: $10 = 2\pi r$. Solve for r to find Cylinder A's radius of $\frac{5}{\pi}$. Do the same thing with Cylinder B to find its radius of $\frac{10}{\pi}$.

    Now that you have the radii of the two cylinders, calculate their volumes. Plug the height and radius of each into the formula $\pi r^2 h$. With a height of 10 and a radius of $\frac{5}{\pi}$, Cylinder A has a volume of $\frac{250}{\pi}$. Cylinder B, with a height of 10 and a radius of $\frac{10}{\pi}$, has a volume of $\frac{1{,}000}{\pi}$. The ratio, at this point, is $\frac{250}{\pi}:\frac{1{,}000}{\pi}$.

    Multiply both sides by π to get rid of the denominators, for a new ratio of 250:1,000. Reduce this to 1:4 for your answer.

    A ratio is like a fraction — you can multiply or divide both sides by the same thing without changing its value. For example, 2:5 is equivalent to 4:10.

    The GRE doesn't provide the formulas needed to solve the type of problem in Question 15, so be sure to memorize the geometry formulas from Chapter 10.

16. **B.** To find the average speed of a trip, place the total distance over the total time (as discussed in Chapter 11). You don't have the actual distance, but anything you pick will work, because the answer is in the form of a fraction that you reduce.

    Pick a number for the distance. To simplify the math, use the lowest common multiple of the two speeds, 600 and 400, which is 1,200.

    If the plane flew to New York, a distance of 1,200 miles at 400 mph, it flew for three hours. If it flew back at 600 mph, it covered the 1,200 miles in two hours. Now you have the total distance and total time, which is 2,400 miles over 5 hours. Set it up as a fraction

    $\frac{2{,}400 \text{ mi}}{5 \text{ h}}$ and reduce to $\frac{480 \text{ mi}}{1 \text{ h}}$, or 480 mph.

17. **D.** The formula for calculating slope is rise over run or $\frac{y_2 - y_1}{x_2 - x_1}$, so plug in the numbers and do the math:

    $$\frac{14-2}{8-3} = 2\frac{2}{5} = 2.4$$

    If you chose Choice (A), you probably did run over rise, like so:

    $$\frac{8-3}{14-2} = \frac{5}{12}$$

    If you chose Choice (C), you probably got mixed up and did something like this:

    $$\frac{14-3}{8-2} = \frac{11}{6} = 1\frac{5}{6}$$

    If you chose Choices (B) or (E), I don't have any idea how you came up with those answers.

18. **187.** To answer this question, first jot down the prime numbers from 3 to 19:

    3, 5, 7, 11, 13, 17, 19

    Of those numbers, choose the smallest prime number greater than 7, which is 11, and the largest prime number less than 19, which is 17. Now, do the math: 11 × 17 = 187.

19. **A, D, E.** Because you're looking at the absolute value of x, the easiest way to answer this question is to ignore the negative signs in the answer choices, because the absolute value of a number is always its positive value. Drop the negative signs, and you immediately see that 21, 20, and 32 are all greater than 17.

20. **E.** With a system of equations problem, you may add the equations and then solve for either of the variables: x or y. In this case, you can quickly see that if you add the equations, the $4y$ and $-4y$ cancel each other out, leaving $16x = 48$, so $x = 3$. Plug 3 into either equation to find y: $9(3) - 4y = -5$, which simplifies to $27 - 4y = -5$. Subtract 27 from both sides, and you get $-4y = -32$, so $y = 8$. So $x \times y$, being 3×8, is 24.

Section 3: Verbal Reasoning

1. **A.** ***Zeal*** is an enthusiasm to do something. You can immediately rule out ***turpitude*** (immorality) and ***apathy*** (disinterest, the opposite of *zeal*). ***Guile*** means cunning, which sort of fits but would work better in a sentence about someone being cunning. ***Certainty*** (confidence) sort of fits, too, but *zeal* is still the better choice.

2. **D.** ***Irascible*** means irritable, cantankerous. Because the mayor's irritability was well known, outbursts were probably to be expected. ***Inchoate*** (undeveloped, as in an idea or plan) doesn't fit, nor does ***pedantic*** (overly focused on details and rules). ***Demented*** (wild, irrational) sort of fits, but an outburst isn't necessarily irrational, nor would a demented individual likely be mayor. ***Incorrigible*** means hopeless, which the mayor may well be, but nothing in the sentence suggests that.

3. **B, D.** ***Stellar*** means excellent and ***emulate*** means to imitate. The second part of the sentence includes the key phrase *rather than change it,* meaning the new manager thought of the leadership style as something positive, so you know the two words are both going to be positive. This rules out ***lackadaisical*** (apathetic, careless) in the first column and ***obviate*** (remove) and ***preclude*** (prevent, exclude) from the second column. ***Enigmatic***, in the first column, means mysterious or difficult to understand, which really doesn't fit in the first blank, either.

4. **C, F.** You're looking for two words that match. If the speaker was ***soporific*** (sleep inducing), the audience would lull into a ***torpor*** (state of sleepiness). ***Fastidious*** (finicky or picky) and ***lucidity*** (clarity or lack of confusion) would be a reasonable match, because a fastidious speaker is likely to be lucid, but *soporific* and *torpor* are a better match. In the first column, ***unassuming*** means humble, which has no suitable match from the second column. And *interest* doesn't match *peaceful.*

5. **B, F.** If you fill in the blanks with your own words before looking at the answer choices, you may come up with something like, "One of the possum's primary *defense* maneuvers is to *fake* death until a potential predator loses interest." This makes picking the right choice from the first column a snap, because *aggressive* and *avoidance* obviously don't fit. The second column is a little more challenging. If you selected Choice (D), *play,* you probably misread *death* as *dead.* Animals may play dead, but they don't play death, except maybe at Halloween. ***Subjugate*** means to overcome, and that doesn't quite fit, either.

6. **B, D, G.** "The instructions were so ***explicit*** (clear) that the possibility anyone could ***misconstrue*** (misunderstand) them was completely ***inconceivable*** (unable to believe)." You have to look at the answers to figure this out, because the sentence could go one way or another. By filling in your own words, you may come up with, "The instructions were so *baffling* that the possibility anyone could *comprehend* them was completely *unbelievable.*" or "The instructions were so *clear* that the possibility anyone could *misunderstand* them was completely *unbelievable.*" Because the first column has no word comparable to *baffling,* you have to go with the second sentence and find words in the answer choices that match up with your own words. For the first blank, *sincere* obviously doesn't work, and instructions aren't ***implicit*** (understood without being communicated), because if they were, people wouldn't need them. In the second column, you can rule out ***comprehend*** (to understand), because the instructions are so clear. Also, scratch *mistake* off the list, because it leaves you wondering "mistake them from what?" In the last column, rule out *understandable,* which is pretty close to the opposite of what's needed here, and rule out ***laughable*** (ridiculous), because it goes a little too far.

7. **A, F, G.** "The crowd's exuberance was *ephemeral.* Soon after they dispersed, a riot *ensued,* and even some of the most *docile* of the group brandished weapons." The easiest way to answer this question is to start by filling in words from the end. The phrase, *even the most ____ of the group brandished weapons* begs for a word like *passive* (peaceful). With that word filled in, you know that the riot started instead of ended, and if that happened, the ***exuberance*** (enthusiasm or good spirits) probably ended, too. You may come up with something like, "The crowd's exuberance was *short-lived.* Soon after they dispersed, a riot *began,* and even some of the most *passive* of the group brandished weapons."

   Then, you just have to find the word in each column that matches the words you inserted. ***Ephemeral*** means short-lived, ***ensued*** means began, and ***docile*** means passive.

   As for the other choices, rule out *passive* from the first blank, because it clashes with exuberance and rule out *enduring,* because if the crowd's exuberance was enduring, a riot wouldn't have broken out. For the second blank, cross off ***endured*** (continued) and ***dissipated*** (faded), because it would have had to start before it could do either of those. For the third blank, cross *eager* and ***pugnacious*** (aggressive) off the list, because it wouldn't be a surprise if they brandished weapons.

8. **C, E, G.** "Unable to arrive at a ***consensus*** (agreement), attorneys for the two parties engaged in ***arbitration*** (negotiation) to resolve the *dispute* (disagreement)." Without looking at the answers, fill in the blanks with your own words, and you're likely to get something like, "Unable to arrive at a *deal,* attorneys for the two parties engaged in *discussions* to resolve the *issues.*" Scan the columns for the possible answers, and the correct ones should jump out at you, but if you don't know what some of the words mean, they may throw you off. In the first column, ***variance*** and ***disparity*** mean a discrepancy or difference, not something you arrive at. In the second column, ***provocation*** is a threat of some sort, while ***amelioration*** is an enhancement, neither of which two attorneys would engage in to resolve anything. In the third column, *agreement* is something positive not needing to be resolved, and ***concurrence*** is agreement, so it doesn't work either.

9. **D.** The answer is in the final two sentences: "The increase is due largely to the availability of versatile, convenient energy. As controlled, or useable, energy became more prevalent, the population expansion accelerated."

10. **A, B.** The passage links the availability of convenient energy to population growth and an improved quality of life for human beings. It doesn't support the idea that population growth contributed to the availability of convenient energy, although the two trends may appear to be concurrent.

11. **B.** "The human ability to harness various sources of energy has improved the quality of life." Choice (A) describes only one possible effect that may be caused by an inability to start a fire; I'm sure people living along the equator wouldn't have this problem. Choice (C) is speculative and not supported by any evidence in the passage. Choice (D) is hypothetical, based on the assumption that a necessary component of civilization is an ability to harness different sources of energy. Choice (E) is an example of faulty reasoning; just because increased energy availability is linked to population growth does not mean that reducing energy usage would decrease population growth.

12. **B.** The first two sentences of the passage tell you that ". . . certain components of the immune system behave abnormally in people with chronic fatigue syndrome" and ". . . interleukin-2 and gamma interferon . . . may not be made in normal amounts." This one is a simple detail or fact question.

   Choice (C) is a trap answer. The author does in fact say that antibody levels are higher in depressed people; however, he doesn't make that statement to support the theory that the immune system may be affected by chronic fatigue syndrome. Just because a statement is true doesn't mean that it's the correct answer. Always be sure to address what a question is asking.

Questions usually go in order through the passage — especially science passages (which require you to find specific facts rather than make inferences). For the first question to a passage, go back to the first sentence or two to support your answer.

13. **A.** This is a very simple detail or fact question. The passage tells you that the body produces chemicals such as interleukin-2 and gamma interferon during its battle against cancer.

As you've probably noticed by now, the questions on science passages are often easier than the questions on other types of passages. Even if the science passages themselves are boring or difficult to understand, the questions relating to them are usually quite straightforward. Frequently, you just need to skim for a specific fact or detail.

14. **B.** Choices (C) and (D) each focus on sub-themes in the passage but not the main idea. Copyright protection and technology are specific subjects covered in the passage, but they aren't the main idea, which is that the music industry is trying to control distribution of music. You can eliminate Choice (A) because it's not supported by any part of the passage. The passage clearly states that music has circulated freely in society for millennia. Choice (E) is wrong because it goes beyond what's stated in the passage. The author may well imply that without the free flow of music, society will lose its identity, but this isn't the passage's main idea.

15. **C.** Examine the text and eliminate the answers you find there. The one that remains is your correct answer. In connection with technology, the passage mentions Choice (A), new locks on music distribution; Choice (B), newcomers competing in the market; Choice (D), democratization of creativity; and Choice (E), faster, cheaper distribution of music. The author certainly doesn't mention better music.

16. **A, B.** *Regulation* and ***ordinance*** refer to rules. None of the other choices come close to being correct answers. A ***prognostication*** is a prediction. A *restraining order* is an injunction or command to stay clear of someone or some place. A ***tenet*** is a principle or belief. A *verdict* is a formal decision, typically issued by a judge or jury.

17. **B, E.** "The dancer's movements were so smooth and fluid that she ***epitomized*** or ***embodied*** (represented) grace and elegance." None of the other choices fit: ***Undermined*** means weakened, ***synthesized*** means combined, ***extirpated*** means demolished, and ***dissipated*** means dispersed.

18. **C, F.** ***Independence*** means being able to act without having to consult others. ***Autonomy*** is along the same lines, meaning freedom to act on your own. ***Supremacy*** is a bit too strong, meaning something like all powerful. Choice (A), ***dependence***, is the opposite of *autonomy*. ***Solvency*** means worthy of credit. ***Neutrality*** is the quality of being objective or impartial, which would be a possibility if the sentence was about negotiating agreements.

19. **A, F.** The sentence starts with *although,* so you know the first and second halves of the sentence are going to be nearly opposite. If the judge delivered a harsh verdict, you can expect the judge to lighten up at the end. ***Clemency*** means mercy, compassion. ***Leniency*** is also mercy or compassion. ***Austerity*** and ***stringency*** are nearly the opposite, conveying a sense of toughness and being strict. ***Affluence*** means wealth and ***magnanimity*** means generosity, neither of which quite fit.

20. **C, E.** ***Denigrate*** is to put someone down or treat as lacking in value. ***Stigmatize*** is to mark someone as disgraceful. ***Chastise*** means to reprimand or punish. ***Disaffect*** means to alienate, which may be a good second choice if it had a suitable match. ***Emulate*** means to try to be like someone, so that obviously doesn't work. *Characterize* is sort of like stigmatize without the negative connotation that would make it a good match.

Section 4: Quantitative Reasoning

1. **D.** The areas depend on how the figures are drawn. A rectangle of perimeter 20 can have, for example, sides of 1 and 9 and 1 and 9, making the area 9. Or it can have sides of 6 and 4 and 6 and 4, making the area 24. (The area of a rectangle is *length* × *width*.) A triangle of perimeter 20 can have sides of 5.5 and 5.5 with a base of 9, giving it a small area, or sides of 6 and 6 with a base of 7, giving it a large area. Insufficient information is available to compare the quantities.

2. **D.** If a is a whole number, such as 2, then Quantity A is bigger. If a is a fraction, such as $\frac{1}{2}$, then $\left(\frac{1}{2}\right)^2 = \frac{1}{4}$ and Quantity B is bigger. Because you don't know what a is, the answer is Choice (D).

Remember the Sacred Six numbers for plugging in from Chapter 13? These numbers are 1, 2, 0, –1, –2, and $\frac{1}{2}$. You don't need to plug in all the numbers to find that Choice (D) is the answer.

3. **C.** Line the equations up vertically and either add or subtract them to get the same *numerical coefficients* (the numbers before the variables). In this case, you add.

$$\begin{array}{l} 3a + 5b = 12 \\ \underline{5a + 3b = 28} \\ 8a + 8b = 40 \end{array}$$

Now divide both sides of the equation by 8 to get $a + b = 5$. So $3(a + b)$, or $3(5)$, = 15.

4. **A.** The volume of any 3D figure on the GRE is *area of the base* × *height*. Because the base of a cylinder is a circle, the volume of a cylinder is $\pi r^2 \times$ *height*. Divide the volume, 200π, by the height, 8, to find that the area of the base is 25π. Because the base is a circle of area = πr^2, the radius is 5. But don't choose Choice (B); you're not finished yet.

Circumference of a circle is $2\pi r$, which here is 10π. If you chose Choice (C), you fell for the trap. You forgot π, which is a common mistake. The circumference of 10π is actually 10 × approximately 3.14, which is more than 10 (don't bother to figure it out exactly).

5. **A.** Both are right triangles, so you can solve this one using Pythagorean's theorem: The square of the hypotenuse is equal to the sum of the squares of the other two sides. If you recall your common right triangles from Chapter 10, this is a snap to solve. Quantity A has the 8, 15, 17 triple; whereas Quantity B has the 5, 12, 13 triple. Because 15 is more than 13, that's the end of story. You could also solve this question by doing the math:

$$\begin{aligned} 8^2 + x^2 &= 17^2 \\ 64 + x^2 &= 289 \\ x^2 &= 289 - 64 = 225 \\ x &= \sqrt{225} = 15 \end{aligned}$$

$$\begin{aligned} y^2 &= 5^2 + 12^2 \\ y^2 &= 25 + 144 = 169 \\ y &= \sqrt{169} \\ y &= 13 \end{aligned}$$

6. **D.** If $\sqrt{x}$ is between 10 and 14, x must be a number between $10^2 = 100$ and $14^2 = 196$. Quantity A, 144, is also between 100 and 196, but without knowing the exact value of x, you don't have enough information to determine whether x is more or less than 144.

7. **A.** Write down the possible combinations for rolling each number, and you instantly see that the odds of rolling a total of 6 are greater:

   You can roll a 6 five different ways: 1 + 5, 2 + 4, 3 + 3, 5 + 1, and 4 + 2.

   You can roll a 9 four different ways: 3 + 6, 4 + 5, 5 + 4, and 6 + 3.

   Chapter 11 explains that probability is the number of events you want divided by the number of events possible. With 36 possible outcomes for this roll of the dice, the probability of a total of 6 is $\frac{5}{36}$ and the probability of a total of 9 is $\frac{4}{36}$. Don't bother reducing the $\frac{4}{36}$, because the fractions are easier to compare if they have the same denominator.

8. **C.** The GRE always gives you the units of conversion, except for units of time. Because a gallon is four quarts, two gallons are eight quarts. If 16 ounces of mix make 8 quarts, then each quart requires 16 ÷ 8 = 2 ounces of mix. To make three quarts, you'd need 3 × 2 = 6 ounces of mix, so Quantities A and B are equal.

9. **B.** If Bob traveled the last half of his trip alone, then the 40 percent and the 20 miles are the first half, or 50 percent. Because 50% – 40% = 10%, 20 miles = 10%. Thinking in terms of fractions may be easier: 10% = $\frac{1}{10}$. If $\frac{1}{10}$ of *something* is 20, that *something* is 200. (Arithmetically: $\frac{1}{10}x = 20$. Multiply both sides by 10 to get $x = 200$.) This problem is based more on reasoning than arithmetic.

10. **E.** This relatively simple problem takes two steps. The top graph shows that 50 new employees were hired in May; therefore, $50 = \frac{1}{5}$ *Total*; solve for *Total* = (50)(5) = 250 Employees. Next, the bottom graph shows that 50 employees were laid off in 1994; therefore, $\frac{50 \text{ laid off}}{250 \text{ total}} = \frac{1}{5} = 20\%$.

    Did you see the shortcut in this problem? The 50 in the top graph is the same as the 50 in the bottom graph. Therefore, whatever percent you have for the top graph is the same as the percent for the bottom graph. You don't need to go through all that work.

11. **E.** First, figure out the percent increase in new hires between January and February. Twenty new employees were hired in January and 30 were hired in February. To find a percent increase or decrease, you use the formula: *number increase or decrease divided by original whole* (the number you began with). Here, that's $\frac{10}{20} = \frac{1}{2} = 50\%$.

    According to the bottom graph, the number of employees laid off in 1994 was 50. The number laid off in 1995 was 50 percent greater. Fifty percent of 50 is $\frac{1}{2} \times 50 = 25$. Add 50 + 25 = 75.

    Did you fall for Choice (D)? The increase in new hires between January and February was ten, but that doesn't mean that the number of layoffs in 1995 was ten higher than the number in 1994. You must figure the *percentage*.

12. **$35,000.** Because Carlos received a 7 percent raise, he's now earning 107 percent of what he was earning initially (what he was earning was 100 percent of his pay; if you add 7 percent, you get 107 percent). He's earning $37,450 now, so 107 percent of what he was earning is equal to $37,450. And 107 percent = 1.07, so the equation looks like this: $1.07x$ = $37,450. To isolate the *x*, divide both sides by 1.07 and you get $35,000.

    With the on-screen calculator available in the Math sections of the GRE, clicking Transfer Display will throw whatever's in the calculator display window into the answer box.

13. **B.** First determine the distance Jerry drove: 30 × 2.5 = 75 miles. Because Susan drove the same distance, she drove 75 miles, too. Knowing this, and that Susan drove 40 miles per hour, you now have everything you need to solve the problem:

$$40x = 75$$

$$x = \frac{\overset{15}{\cancel{75}}}{\underset{8}{\cancel{40}}}$$

$$x = 1\frac{7}{8}$$

14. **D.** This is a combination problem in which order doesn't matter, because to "choose 5" means students A, B, C, D, E are the same as students E, D, C, B, A (or any other mixture of these 5) so use the following formula to solve it:

$$C_n^r = \frac{n!}{r!(n-r)!}$$

where *C* is the number of combinations you're trying to determine, *n* is the total number of objects or events (25 in this case), and *r* is the number of objects or events you're choosing at one time (5 in this case). You don't actually have to do the math — just set it up:

$$C_{25}^5 = \frac{25!}{5!(25-5)!} = \frac{25!}{5!20!}$$

If you chose one of the other answers, you probably either didn't know the equation or you tried to simplify the fraction. Remember that simplifying fractions that contain factorials is tricky; for example, $\frac{25!}{5!}$ doesn't equal $\frac{5}{1}$. It actually equals 129,260,083,694,424,883,200,000. However, you may cancel identical terms in the numerator and denominator. Here's an example in which 7! is cancelled out:

$$\frac{9!}{7!2!} = \frac{9\times8\times7!}{7!2!} = \frac{9\times8\times1}{1\times2!} = \frac{72}{2} = 36$$

15. **A.** To solve this problem, you need to remember the following equation:

Group 1 + Group 2 + Neither Group – Both Groups = Total

Plug in the numbers and do the math:

$$30 + 165 + x - 25 = 175$$
$$x = 175 - 30 - 165 + 25$$
$$x = 5$$

16. **B, D, E.** You could find all the common factors of 18 and 48, but instead, just try each answer choice. Choice (A), 9, doesn't work, because the closest you can get to 48 is $5 \times 9 = 45$, and another 9 puts you over into 54. Choice **(B)**, 3, works for 18: $3 \times 3 \times 2 = 18$. It also works for 48, because $2 \times 24 = 48$ and $3 \times 8 = 24$. You can rule out Choice (C), 4, because the closest you can get to 18 using 4 is $4 \times 4 = 16$, and another 4 gives you 20. Choice **(D)**, 6, works for 18, because $3 \times 6 = 18$. It also works for 48, because you already saw that $2 \times 3 \times 8 = 48$. Choice **(E)**, 1, is a gimme because 1 is a factor of all integers.

17. **C.** The sequence has three terms (–5, 0, and 5), and every third term is 5. Divide 250 by 3 to get 83 with a remainder of 1. That means that the 249th number is 5 (because 249 divides evenly by 3), the 250th number is –5, and the 251st number is 0. Add –5 + 0 = –5.

In this particular problem, you're adding two consecutive terms in the series, so you're adding –5 + 5, –5 + 0, or 0 + 5, so there's no possible way you can end up with 10 or –10. You can eliminate Choices (B) and (E).

The people who devise the GRE put questions like Question 17 on the test to get you to waste your time. You could've counted on your fingers up to the 250th term, but who has that sort of time? Find the closest number that divides by 3 and then work from there.

18. **B.** Start with what you know and work toward what you don't know. You know you have 75 ounces of a 10 percent salt solution, and you're adding x ounces of a 40 percent salt solution, so $(75 \times 0.10) + 0.40x =$ what? Your final solution will consist of 75 ounces plus x ounces, and it'll have a 35 percent salt concentration:

$$\begin{aligned}(75\times 0.10)+0.40x = 0.35(75+x) &= 26.25+0.35x\\ 7.5+0.4x &= 26.25+0.35x\\ 0.4x-0.35x &= 26.25-7.5\\ 0.05x &= 18.75\\ x &= 375\end{aligned}$$

19. **D.** Multiply both sides by $(x - 7)$ and you get $x + 5 = xy - 7y$. Subtract 5 from both sides, and you get $x = xy - 7y - 5$. Now, subtract xy from both sides to get $x - xy = -7y - 5$. You can factor the left side of the equation to get $x - xy = x(1 - y)$. Finally, divide both sides of the equation by $(1 - y)$, and you have your answer:

$$\frac{(-7y-5)}{(1-y)} = \frac{-(7y+5)}{(1-y)}$$

If you chose Choice (C), you fell for a trap. In the numerator, both $7y$ and 5 must be negative; in Choice (C), the $7y$ is positive.

20. **A, B.** If you quickly scan the answer choices, you can see that they're all comparisons of either total sales or percentage increases, so you may as well figure out all the numbers before closely examining each choice:

- Company A's increase in sales is \$80,000 – \$72,000 = \$8,000, representing a percentage increase of $\frac{\$8,000}{\$72,000} = 0.11 = 11\%$.
- Company B's increase in sales is \$59,000 – \$50,000 = \$9,000, representing a percentage increase of $\frac{\$9,000}{\$50,000} = 0.18 = 18\%$.
- Company C's increase in sales is \$73,000 – \$65,000 = \$8,000, representing a percentage increase of $\frac{\$8,000}{\$65,000} = 0.12 = 12\%$.

Answer Key for Practice Exam 1

Section 1: Verbal Reasoning	Section 2: Quantitative Reasoning	Section 3: Verbal Reasoning	Section 4: Quantitative Reasoning
1. **D**	1. **B**	1. **A**	1. **D**
2. **C**	2. **A**	2. **D**	2. **D**
3. **C, D**	3. **B**	3. **B, D**	3. **C**
4. **B, F**	4. **C**	4. **C, F**	4. **A**
5. **A, D**	5. **B**	5. **B, F**	5. **A**
6. **A, E, G**	6. **C**	6. **B, D, G**	6. **D**
7. **B, D, I**	7. **B**	7. **A, F, G**	7. **A**
8. **B, E, G**	8. **$5,000**	8. **C, E, G**	8. **C**
9. **C**	9. **E**	9. **D**	9. **B**
10. **B**	10. **B, C**	10. **A, B**	10. **E**
11. **A, C**	11. **A**	11. **B**	11. **E**
12. **A**	12. **A, C**	12. **B**	12. **$35,000**
13. **D**	13. **A**	13. **A**	13. **B**
14. **B**	14. **E**	14. **B**	14. **D**
15. **A, D**	15. **1:4**	15. **C**	15. **A**
16. **B, F**	16. **B**	16. **A, B**	16. **B, D, E**
17. **A, C**	17. **D**	17. **B, E**	17. **C**
18. **D, F**	18. **187**	18. **C, F**	18. **B**
19. **B, E**	19. **A, D, E**	19. **A, F**	19. **D**
20. **B**	20. **E**	20. **C, E**	20. **A, B**

Chapter 18

Practice Exam 2

Like the actual, computer-based GRE, the following exam consists of two 30-minute essays, two 30-minute Verbal Reasoning sections (20 questions each), and two 35-minute Quantitative Reasoning sections (20 questions each). The actual GRE may also include an extra Verbal or Quantitative Reasoning section, which doesn't count toward your score, but this practice exam has nothing like that.

Take this practice test under normal exam conditions and approach it as you would the real GRE:

- **Work when you won't be interrupted.**
- **Use scratch paper that's free of any prepared notes.** On the actual GRE, you receive blank scratch paper before your test begins.
- **Answer as many questions as time allows.** Consider answering all the easier questions within each section first and then going back to answer the remaining, harder questions. Because you're not penalized for guessing, go ahead and guess on the remaining questions before time expires.
- **Set a timer for each section.** If you have time left at the end, you may go back and review answers (within the section), move on and finish your test early, or kick back and relax until time expires.
- **Don't leave your desk while the clock is running on any section.**
- **Take a one-minute break after each section and the optional ten-minute break after the first Verbal section.**
- **Type the essays.** Because you type the essays on the actual GRE, typing them now is good practice. Don't use software, such as Microsoft Word, with automatic spell-checker or other formatting features. Instead, use a simple text editor, such as Notepad, with copy and paste but no other features. The GRE essay-writing field features undo, redo, copy, and paste functionality but nothing else.

After completing this entire practice test, go to Chapter 19 to check your answers with the answer key and go through the answer explanations to *all* the questions, not just the ones you miss. The answer explanations provide valuable insight — material that provides a good review of everything you went over in the previous chapters. Reviewing answer explanations to all the questions also ensures that you understand the reason why any answers you guessed correctly are correct.

I formatted the questions and answer choices to make them appear as similar as possible to what you'll see on the computer-based test, but I had to retain the A, B, C, D, E, F choices for marking your answers.

Answer Sheet

Section 1: Verbal Reasoning

1. Ⓐ Ⓑ Ⓒ Ⓓ Ⓔ
2. Ⓐ Ⓑ Ⓒ Ⓓ Ⓔ
3. Ⓐ Ⓑ Ⓒ Ⓓ Ⓔ Ⓕ
4. Ⓐ Ⓑ Ⓒ Ⓓ Ⓔ Ⓕ
5. Ⓐ Ⓑ Ⓒ Ⓓ Ⓔ Ⓕ
6. Ⓐ Ⓑ Ⓒ Ⓓ Ⓔ Ⓕ Ⓖ Ⓗ Ⓘ
7. Ⓐ Ⓑ Ⓒ Ⓓ Ⓔ Ⓕ Ⓖ Ⓗ Ⓘ
8. Ⓐ Ⓑ Ⓒ Ⓓ Ⓔ
9. Ⓐ Ⓑ Ⓒ Ⓓ Ⓔ
10. [A] [B] [C]
11. Ⓐ Ⓑ Ⓒ Ⓓ Ⓔ
12. Ⓐ Ⓑ Ⓒ Ⓓ Ⓔ
13. Ⓐ Ⓑ Ⓒ Ⓓ Ⓔ
14. Ⓐ Ⓑ Ⓒ Ⓓ Ⓔ
15. [A] [B] [C] [D] [E] [F]
16. [A] [B] [C] [D] [E] [F]
17. [A] [B] [C] [D] [E] [F]
18. [A] [B] [C] [D] [E] [F]
19. [A] [B] [C] [D] [E] [F]
20. Ⓐ Ⓑ Ⓒ Ⓓ Ⓔ

Section 2: Quantitative Reasoning

1. Ⓐ Ⓑ Ⓒ Ⓓ
2. Ⓐ Ⓑ Ⓒ Ⓓ
3. Ⓐ Ⓑ Ⓒ Ⓓ
4. Ⓐ Ⓑ Ⓒ Ⓓ
5. Ⓐ Ⓑ Ⓒ Ⓓ
6. Ⓐ Ⓑ Ⓒ Ⓓ
7. Ⓐ Ⓑ Ⓒ Ⓓ
8. Ⓐ Ⓑ Ⓒ Ⓓ
9. Ⓐ Ⓑ Ⓒ Ⓓ Ⓔ
10. Ⓐ Ⓑ Ⓒ Ⓓ Ⓔ
11. [A] [B] [C] [D] [E] [F]
12. [ ]
13. [ ]
14. Ⓐ Ⓑ Ⓒ Ⓓ Ⓔ
15. Ⓐ Ⓑ Ⓒ Ⓓ Ⓔ
16. Ⓐ Ⓑ Ⓒ Ⓓ Ⓔ
17. Ⓐ Ⓑ Ⓒ Ⓓ Ⓔ
18. Ⓐ Ⓑ Ⓒ Ⓓ Ⓔ
19. Ⓐ Ⓑ Ⓒ Ⓓ Ⓔ
20. [ ]

Section 3: Verbal Reasoning

1. Ⓐ Ⓑ Ⓒ Ⓓ Ⓔ
2. Ⓐ Ⓑ Ⓒ Ⓓ Ⓔ
3. Ⓐ Ⓑ Ⓒ Ⓓ Ⓔ Ⓕ
4. Ⓐ Ⓑ Ⓒ Ⓓ Ⓔ Ⓕ
5. Ⓐ Ⓑ Ⓒ Ⓓ Ⓔ Ⓕ
6. Ⓐ Ⓑ Ⓒ Ⓓ Ⓔ Ⓕ Ⓖ Ⓗ Ⓘ
7. Ⓐ Ⓑ Ⓒ Ⓓ Ⓔ Ⓕ Ⓖ Ⓗ Ⓘ
8. [A] [B] [C]
9. Ⓐ Ⓑ Ⓒ Ⓓ Ⓔ
10. Ⓐ Ⓑ Ⓒ Ⓓ Ⓔ
11. Ⓐ Ⓑ Ⓒ Ⓓ Ⓔ
12. Ⓐ Ⓑ Ⓒ Ⓓ Ⓔ
13. Ⓐ Ⓑ Ⓒ Ⓓ Ⓔ
14. [A] [B] [C]
15. [A] [B] [C] [D] [E] [F]
16. [A] [B] [C] [D] [E] [F]
17. [A] [B] [C] [D] [E] [F]
18. [A] [B] [C] [D] [E] [F]
19. [A] [B] [C] [D] [E] [F]
20. Ⓐ Ⓑ Ⓒ Ⓓ Ⓔ

Section 4: Quantitative Reasoning

1. Ⓐ Ⓑ Ⓒ Ⓓ
2. Ⓐ Ⓑ Ⓒ Ⓓ
3. Ⓐ Ⓑ Ⓒ Ⓓ
4. Ⓐ Ⓑ Ⓒ Ⓓ
5. Ⓐ Ⓑ Ⓒ Ⓓ
6. Ⓐ Ⓑ Ⓒ Ⓓ
7. Ⓐ Ⓑ Ⓒ Ⓓ
8. Ⓐ Ⓑ Ⓒ Ⓓ Ⓔ
9. [A] [B] [C] [D] [E] [F]
10. Ⓐ Ⓑ Ⓒ Ⓓ Ⓔ
11. [ ]
12. [ ]
13. Ⓐ Ⓑ Ⓒ Ⓓ Ⓔ
14. Ⓐ Ⓑ Ⓒ Ⓓ Ⓔ
15. Ⓐ Ⓑ Ⓒ Ⓓ Ⓔ
16. Ⓐ Ⓑ Ⓒ Ⓓ Ⓔ
17. Ⓐ Ⓑ Ⓒ Ⓓ Ⓔ
18. [A] [B] [C] [D] [E] [F]
19. Ⓐ Ⓑ Ⓒ Ⓓ Ⓔ
20. Ⓐ Ⓑ Ⓒ Ⓓ Ⓔ

Analytical Writing 1: Analyze an Issue

Time: 30 minutes

Directions: Present and explain your view on the following issue. Although there is no one right or wrong response, be sure to consider various points of view as you explain the reasons behind your own perspective. Support your position with reasons and examples from your own reading, personal or professional experience, and observations.

> "Equal opportunity means parity in pay. Everyone should not earn the same amount of money, but it's ridiculous to see an athlete earning tens of millions of dollars in a single year while the average household income is slightly more than $50,000."

Express the extent to which you agree or disagree with the preceding statement and explain the reasoning behind your position. In support of your position, think of ways in which the statement may or may not be true and how these considerations influence your position.

Analytical Writing 2: Analyze an Argument

Time: 30 minutes

Directions: Critique the following argument. Identify evidence that strengthens or weakens the argument, point out assumptions underlying the argument, and offer counterexamples to the argument.

> "More and more cities and towns are installing red light cameras to catch red light runners in the act. In 2008 alone, red light running accounted for 762 fatal crashes in the United States and 137,000 injuries. A study conducted by the Federal Highway Administration attributed a 25 percent reduction in T-bone accidents at intersections to the installation of red light cameras. Because people fail to voluntarily honor the law, these traffic cameras are essential in enforcing these laws and protecting public safety."

Discuss the merits of the preceding argument. Analyze the evidence used as well as the general reasoning. Present points that would strengthen the argument or challenge it.

Section 1

Verbal Reasoning

Time: 30 minutes for 20 questions

Directions: Choose the best answer to each question. Blacken the corresponding oval(s) on the answer sheet.

Directions: For Questions 1–7, choose the one entry best suited for each blank from its corresponding column of choices.

1. During the funeral service, mourners sang a _____.

Ⓐ tune
Ⓑ dirge
Ⓒ melody
Ⓓ song
Ⓔ chant

2. During the meeting, Gwendolyn became upset and launched into _____ about how unfair it was to cut pay as living expenses increased.

Ⓐ a speech
Ⓑ a discussion
Ⓒ a homily
Ⓓ an argument
Ⓔ a tirade

3. Although the (i)_____ system typically can detect only five different tastes, individuals with a more (ii)_____ palate are capable of distinguishing subtle differences in even the most similar foods.

Blank (i)	*Blank (ii)*
Ⓐ gustatory	Ⓓ discrete
Ⓑ lymphatic	Ⓔ discerning
Ⓒ digestive	Ⓕ distended

4. The latest tsunami (i)_____ the small seaside resort. Fortunately, no lives were lost, and the loss of property served as a (ii)_____ for a much needed renovation.

Blank (i)	*Blank (ii)*
Ⓐ inundated	Ⓓ symbol
Ⓑ dissembled	Ⓔ mendicant
Ⓒ drowned	Ⓕ catalyst

5. The castle walls were (i)_____ to attack. After several unsuccessful assaults, the enemy's enthusiasm began to (ii)_____, and the troops dispersed.

Blank (i)	*Blank (ii)*
Ⓐ amenable	Ⓓ flag
Ⓑ impeccable	Ⓔ rally
Ⓒ impervious	Ⓕ flee

Go on to next page

6. Aware of the (i)_____ national debt, congress passed legislation to impose a strict (ii)_____ program to (iii)_____ spending.

Blank (i)	Blank (ii)	Blank (iii)
Ⓐ pervasive	Ⓓ austerity	Ⓖ curtail
Ⓑ shrinking	Ⓔ spending	Ⓗ attenuate
Ⓒ burgeoning	Ⓕ defense	Ⓘ desiccate

7. The (i)_____ between the man's demeanor and his account of what he was doing at the time of the crime made police officers suspicious, but with so much of the evidence (ii)_____, their case against him was (iii)_____ at best.

Blank (i)	Blank (ii)	Blank (iii)
Ⓐ correlation	Ⓓ corroborated	Ⓖ compelling
Ⓑ discrepancy	Ⓔ vetted	Ⓗ tenuous
Ⓒ relationship	Ⓕ unsubstantiated	Ⓘ conclusive

Go on to next page

Directions: Each of the following passages is followed by questions pertaining to the passage. Read the passage and answer the questions based on information stated or implied in that passage. For each question, select one answer choice unless instructed otherwise.

In a poll conducted by Washington Post-ABC News, 70 percent of Americans support the use of passenger profiling to determine which passengers are most closely scrutinized at airports. They believe that the cost savings and added convenience for a large majority of passengers is worth the questionable practice of singling out a minority of passengers for closer scrutiny. In addition, passengers feel that pat downs and full body scans are highly invasive.

When most Americans discuss profiling, they are referring to profiling based on race, nationality, religion, and gender, which many people consider a civil rights violation. However, most experts agree that profiling in this way is inefficient and ineffective. They recommend profiling by behavior and intelligence, using no-fly and watch lists, personal data, travel histories, and so forth to identify potential threats.

Civil liberty organizations claim that this solution is no better and perhaps worse in terms of violating civil liberties, because it gives government agencies license to collect sensitive information on any and all citizens. They believe that the only fair solution is to inspect all passengers and luggage.

When it comes to airport security, ultimately we face a choice. Either we protect civil liberties and accept the cost and inconvenience of inspecting all passengers and luggage, or we relinquish our civil liberties or the civil liberties of certain groups or individuals to reduce costs and streamline baggage and checkpoint inspections.

8. According to experts, which of the following is most effective in ensuring airline security?

   Ⓐ Profiling passengers based on race, nationality, religion, and gender

   Ⓑ Inspecting all passengers and their luggage

   Ⓒ Profiling by behavior and intelligence

   Ⓓ Interviewing all passengers before boarding

   Ⓔ Streamlining baggage and checkpoint inspections

9. Which of the following, if true, most effectively undermines the argument that the only choice we have is between security and civil liberties?

   Ⓐ Bomb-sniffing dogs are more effective and less intrusive at detecting explosives than human inspectors or expensive devices.

   Ⓑ A combination of profiling and targeted interviews has proven most effective and efficient.

   Ⓒ Precertification as a safe flyer significantly improves efficiency at checkpoints.

   Ⓓ Checked baggage is more likely than carry-on luggage to contain explosives.

   Ⓔ No security measures are 100 percent effective.

The following passage is an excerpt from Causes of War *by Jack S. Levy and William R. Thompson (Wiley-Blackwell).*

It is hard to imagine what life would have been like in the late twentieth century in the absence of World War I and World War II, which had such profound effects on the global system and on domestic societies. The same can be said for the Cold War. For nearly a half century it shaped both international and domestic politics and cultures, not only in the United States and the Soviet Union, but also in Western Europe and the Third World (Weart, 1989). The development of new states in the contemporary era continues to be influenced by warfare and preparations for war. With the proliferation of nuclear weapons, and with the threat of the acquisition of nuclear weapons by terrorist groups and "rogue states," new threats to the security of even the most powerful states in the system have emerged. The proliferation of civil wars and conflicts involving "non-state" actors has changed life throughout the developing world. A better understanding of the causes of war is a necessary first step if we are to have any hope of reducing the occurrence of war and perhaps mitigating its severity and consequences.

Go on to next page

For the following question, consider each answer choice separately and select all answer choices that are correct.

10. According to the passage, which of the following are effects of war and preparations for war?

    A Reshaping of international and domestic politics and cultures

    B The proliferation of civil wars and conflicts

    C Development of new states

For Questions 11–13, select only one answer choice.

11. One could reasonably infer from this passage that the greatest security threat is which of the following?

    Ⓐ Proliferation of civil wars

    Ⓑ Terrorists

    Ⓒ Rogue states

    Ⓓ The Cold War

    Ⓔ Proliferation of nuclear weapons

The following passage is an excerpt from UnMarketing: Stop Marketing. Start Engaging. *by Scott Stratten (Wiley).*

To successfully UnMarket your business, your goal should be to get to the point where you are a recognized expert in your field. You can choose to be recognized for a certain discipline, whether it is time management or sales or marketing in general. You can also aim to be recognized as an expert to a specific industry. What you have to realize is that there is an important difference between somebody who is selling something and somebody who is an expert. This is one of the problems when you use advertising or direct mail for your marketing — if your potential customer does not have an immediate need for your product or service, then you are potentially turning them off and losing them for the future. When you position yourself as an expert with useful information for people, your marketplace will always have a need for that information. You have successfully pulled people into your funnel, you have their attention, and now you need to do something great for them.

12. Which of the following sentences most clearly describes the goal of UnMarketing?

    Ⓐ Sentence 2: "You can choose . . . in general."

    Ⓑ Sentence 4: "What you have to . . . an expert."

    Ⓒ Sentence 5: "This is . . . the future."

    Ⓓ Sentence 6: "When you position . . . that information."

    Ⓔ Sentence 7: "You have successfully . . . for them."

13. Which of the following is the most important difference between marketing and UnMarketing as explained in the passage?

    Ⓐ Advertising versus direct mail

    Ⓑ Salesperson versus expert

    Ⓒ Time management versus marketing

    Ⓓ Expert in a field versus expert in a discipline

    Ⓔ Salesperson versus marketing maven

With the passage of a universal healthcare bill, the government not only has the right but also the responsibility to regulate what people eat. Face it, the fact that the United States spends 50 percent more per capita for healthcare than most European countries is because people in the United States consume far more junk food. If taxpayers are footing the bill for healthcare, then the government is responsible for controlling healthcare costs, and the most effective way to do that is to crack down on the junk food industry.

Go on to next page

14. Which of the following, if true, most effectively challenges the argument that the government has the responsibility to regulate what people eat?

Ⓐ Countries in Europe do not impose such regulations on their food producers.

Ⓑ Labeling foods enables people to regulate their own consumption.

Ⓒ In the United States, prices of health services, including prescription medications, hospital stays, and doctor visits, on average, are more than 50 percent higher than the prices of comparable services in European countries.

Ⓓ The healthcare bill does not mandate dietary restrictions.

Ⓔ Some food items considered junk food actually contain some healthy ingredients.

Directions: Each of the following sentences has a blank indicating that a word or phrase is omitted. Choose the two answer choices that best complete the sentence and result in two sentences most alike in meaning.

15. With nothing to lose and the coach's _____ approval, the teammates decided to abandon the game plan and just have some fun.

A ambiguous

B tacit

C cautious

D implicit

E enthusiastic

F salubrious

16. Few could believe that Kazuki was an accomplished sumo wrestler because he was generally so _____ when eating out.

A hedonistic

B self-indulgent

C epicurean

D courteous

E abstemious

F ascetic

17. The actual incident had been nothing out of the ordinary, but when Mark told it with his penchant for _____, the audience was captivated.

A sarcasm

B allegory

C embellishment

D hyperbole

E ennui

F overemphasis

18. Nobody understood why the puppy was so _____; others in the same litter seemed to have a much gentler disposition.

A pugnacious

B lackadaisical

C quiescent

D truculent

E irascible

F soporific

19. Mary's offer to help plan the party struck everyone as _____, because in her characteristic fashion, she seemed to be up to something.

A sincere

B disingenuous

C duplicitous

D unpretentious

E hypocritical

F authentic

Go on to next page

Directions: The following passage is followed by a question pertaining to the passage. Read the passage and answer the question based on information stated or implied in the passage. Select only one answer.

This passage is an excerpt from Environment and Society: A Critical Introduction *by Paul Robbins, John Hintz, and Sarah Moore (Wiley-Blackwell).*

News headlines from forests, fields, rivers, and oceans suggest we are in a world of trouble. Fresh water is increasingly scarce around the globe, owing not only to heavy water use but also widespread pollution; there is not a single drop of water in the Colorado River in the United States or the Rhone River in France that is not managed through complex dams and distribution systems, or affected by city and industrial waste along their paths to the sea. Agricultural soils are depleted from years of intensive cropping and from ongoing application of fertilizers and pesticides in the search for ever-sustained increases of food and fiber; in North India, after decades of increasing population, yields of wheat and rice have hit a plateau. Global temperatures are on the rise and, with this increase, whole ecosystems are at risk. Species of plants and animals are vanishing from the earth, never to return. Perhaps most profoundly, the world's oceans — upon which these global systems rest — show signs of impending collapse. The accumulation of these acute problems led observers to conclude that the environment may be irreversibly lost or that we may have reached "the end of nature."

20. Which of the following best summarizes the main point of this passage?

Ⓐ Due to heavy water use, pollution, and agriculture that is becoming more and more reliant on chemical fertilizers and pesticides, fresh water is becoming increasingly scarce.

Ⓑ Environmental warning signs increasingly highlight the deleterious effects of overpopulation on the planet.

Ⓒ Global warming is putting entire ecosystems at risk.

Ⓓ If the oceans collapse, the environment will be irreversibly lost.

Ⓔ Environmental warning signs indicate that the global environment is suffering potentially irreversible damage.

STOP DO NOT TURN THE PAGE UNTIL TOLD TO DO SO. DO NOT RETURN TO A PREVIOUS TEST.

Section 2

Quantitative Reasoning

Time: 35 minutes for 20 questions

Notes:

- All numbers used in this exam are real numbers.
- All figures lie in a plane.
- Angle measures are positive; points and angles are in the position shown.

Directions: For Questions 1–8, choose from the following answer choices:

Ⓐ *Quantity A is greater.*

Ⓑ *Quantity B is greater.*

Ⓒ *The two quantities are equal.*

Ⓓ *The relationship cannot be determined from the information given.*

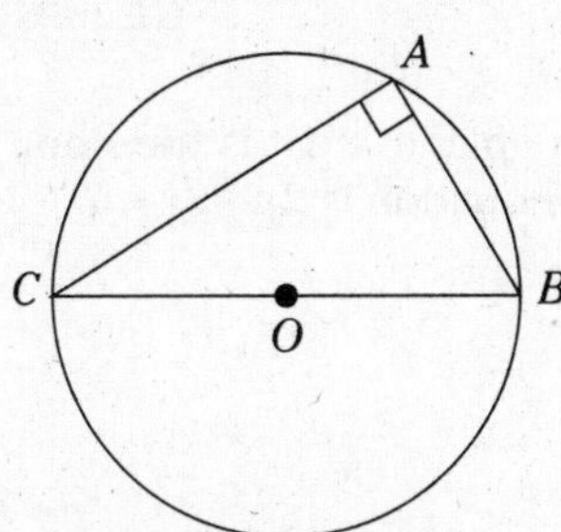

1. The radius of the circle is 1, and $AB = 1$.

Quantity A	***Quantity B***
The area of triangle ABC	$\frac{\sqrt{3}}{2}$

2. The average (arithmetic mean) of ten test scores is 120, and the average of 20 additional test scores is 90.

Quantity A	***Quantity B***
The weighted average of these scores	105

3. $10 < n < 15$ and $d = 20$

Quantity A	***Quantity B***
$\frac{n}{d}$	0.72

4. A certain recipe requires $\frac{4}{3}$ cups of lentils and makes six servings.

Quantity A	***Quantity B***
The amount of lentils required for the same recipe to make 15 servings	3 cups

Go on to next page

5.

F 9 G

5

E 11 H

Quantity A	Quantity B
The area of rectangular region *ABCD*	The area of trapezoidal region *EFGH*

6.

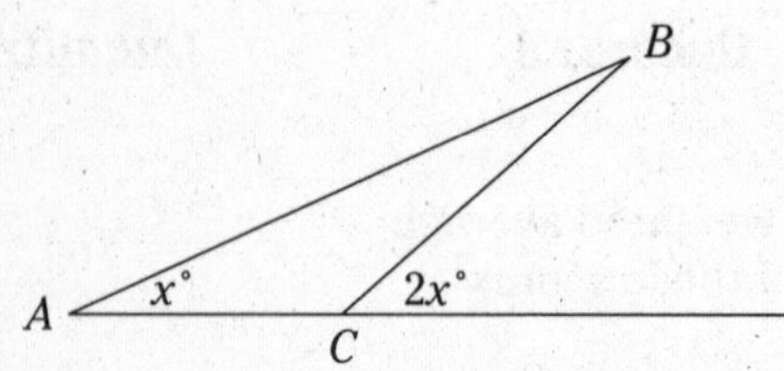

Quantity A	Quantity B
Line segment *AC*	Line segment *BC*

7. $x^2 - x - 6 = 0$

Quantity A	Quantity B
The sum of the roots of the equation	–1

8. Set *S* contains the numbers 3, 4, 5, 6, 7, and 8.

Quantity A	Quantity B
The range of set *S*	The median of set *S*

9. What is the units digit of $219{,}473 \times 162{,}597$?

Ⓐ 1

Ⓑ 2

Ⓒ 3

Ⓓ 4

Ⓔ 5

10. In the *xy* plane, what is the slope of the line whose equation is $2x + 3y = 5$?

Ⓐ 1

Ⓑ $\frac{3}{2}$

Ⓒ $-\frac{3}{2}$

Ⓓ $\frac{2}{3}$

Ⓔ $-\frac{2}{3}$

11. Bill is budgeting the expenditure of a new car based on his gross income from last year. If his gross income from last year was $50,000 and Bill wants to spend between 15% and 30% on a new car, which of the following could be the cost of the new car?

Indicate all possible costs of the new car.

[A] $8,000

[B] $10,000

[C] $12,000

[D] $14,000

[E] $16,000

[F] $18,000

Go on to next page

12. If the sporting center has 2 baseballs for every 9 baseball gloves, and 3 baseball bats for every 5 baseballs, what is the lowest number of sporting items that could be in the sporting center?

13. If the average of x, y, and z is 5, what is the average of $4x + y$, $2y - x$, and $3z + 27$?

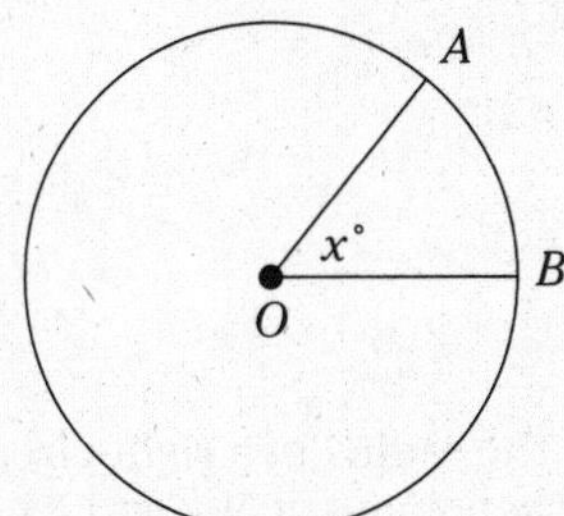

14. The circle shown has the center O and a radius of 8. If $x = 45$, what is the length of minor arc AB?

Ⓐ $\frac{\pi}{2}$

Ⓑ π

Ⓒ $\frac{3\pi}{2}$

Ⓓ 2π

Ⓔ $\frac{5\pi}{2}$

Questions 15–17 are based on the following data.

Score Distribution of 1,412,393 Examinees from Sept. 2007 to Aug. 2010

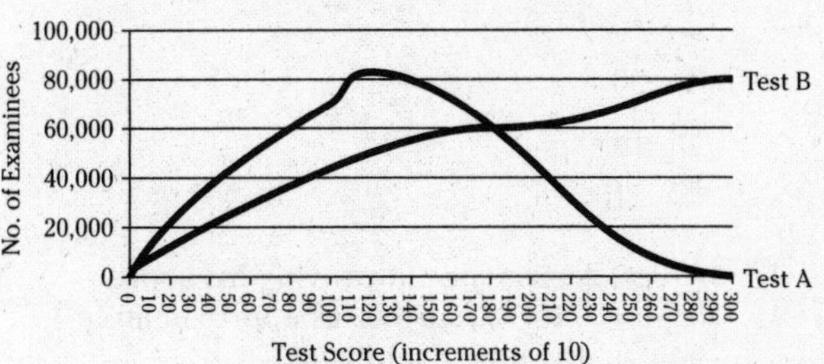

Note: Chart is drawn to scale.

Percentile Ranking Based on Score

Score	Test A	Test B
0	0	0
10	0	1
20	1	1
30	2	2
40	4	3
50	7	4
60	12	6
70	17	7
80	22	9
90	27	11
100	33	13
110	38	16
120	44	18
130	50	21
140	55	24
150	61	28
160	66	32
170	71	35
180	77	40
190	81	44
200	85	48
210	89	53
220	91	58
230	94	63
240	96	67
250	97	72
260	98	76
270	99	81
280	99	86
290	99	90
300	99	94

15. Approximately what ratio of examinees taking Test B scored a perfect 300?

Ⓐ 1 out of 100

Ⓑ 1 out of 90

Ⓒ 1 out of 50

Ⓓ 1 out of 20

Ⓔ 1 out of 10

Go on to next page

16. If a Test A examinee is among a group of 40,000 examinees with the same score, what could be the examinee's score?

Ⓐ 20

Ⓑ 40

Ⓒ 90

Ⓓ 180

Ⓔ 210

17. A Test A examinee improving his score from 100 to 120 surpasses approximately how many other examinees?

Ⓐ 40,000

Ⓑ 80,000

Ⓒ 155,000

Ⓓ 240,000

Ⓔ 300,000

18. The radius *r* of a circle increases by 50%. In terms of *r*, what is the area of the circle with the increased radius?

Ⓐ $\frac{3\pi r^2}{2}$

Ⓑ $2\pi r^2$

Ⓒ $\frac{4\pi r^2}{3}$

Ⓓ $3\pi r^2$

Ⓔ $\frac{9\pi r^2}{4}$

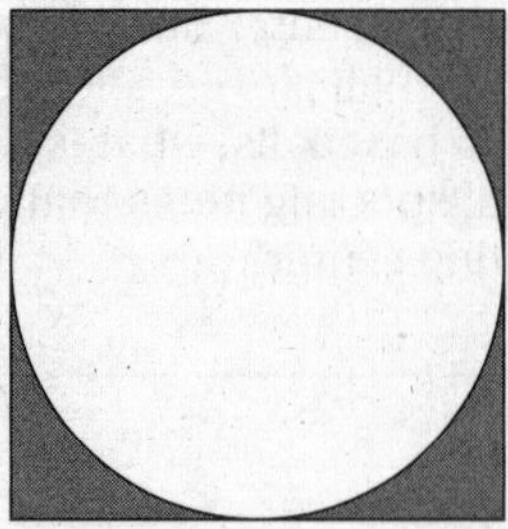

The circle is inscribed within the square of area 36.

19. In the preceding drawing, what fraction of the square is occupied by the circle?

Ⓐ $\frac{\pi}{2}$

Ⓑ $\frac{\pi}{3}$

Ⓒ $\frac{\pi}{4}$

Ⓓ $\frac{1}{3}$

Ⓔ $\frac{1}{6}$

20. What is the radius of a right circular cylinder with a volume of 50π and a height of 2?

STOP DO NOT TURN THE PAGE UNTIL TOLD TO DO SO. DO NOT RETURN TO A PREVIOUS TEST.

Section 3

Verbal Reasoning

Time: 30 minutes for 20 questions

Directions: Choose the best answer to each question. Blacken the corresponding oval(s) on the answer sheet.

Directions: For Questions 1–7, choose the one entry best suited for each blank from its corresponding column of choices.

1. The *Oxford English Dictionary* consists of 20 _____, is 21,728 pages long, and weighs in at about 143 pounds.

Ⓐ novellas
Ⓑ tomes
Ⓒ manuscripts
Ⓓ publications
Ⓔ titles

2. The neighbors were so incredibly _____, that within six weeks, the couple decided to move somewhere more remote.

Ⓐ accomodating
Ⓑ ambivalent
Ⓒ sincere
Ⓓ banal
Ⓔ officious

3. More than 50 percent of online shoppers abandon their shopping carts simply because they've changed their minds, proving just how (i)_____ they can be. Many online merchants have observed shoppers' (ii)_____ for failing to complete their transactions.

Blank (i)	***Blank (ii)***
Ⓐ capricious	Ⓓ inkling
Ⓑ predictable	Ⓔ penchant
Ⓒ fatuous	Ⓕ passion

4. Because his salary and benefits were (i)_____ with the time and effort he expected to invest in the project, Jerry decided not to (ii)_____ over the deadlines.

Blank (i)	***Blank (ii)***
Ⓐ discordant	Ⓓ quibble
Ⓑ pursuant	Ⓔ acquiesce
Ⓒ commensurate	Ⓕ concede

Go on to next page

5. By the time the speaker approached the microphone, the impatient audience was (i)_____. Everything he said in an attempt to silence the rabble only seemed to (ii)_____ the situation.

Blank (i)	*Blank (ii)*
Ⓐ intractable	Ⓓ precipitate
Ⓑ imperturbable	Ⓔ exonerate
Ⓒ indolent	Ⓕ exacerbate

6. With the accidental addition of the (i)_____, the mixture became very (ii)_____. Knowing that student safety (iii)_____ all other concerns, the teacher ushered her students out of the lab.

Blank (i)	*Blank (ii)*	*Blank (iii)*
Ⓐ neutralizer	Ⓓ volatile	Ⓖ superseded
Ⓑ chemical	Ⓔ acidic	Ⓗ preceded
Ⓒ catalyst	Ⓕ piquant	Ⓘ negated

7. When asked whether the antique vase was in (i)_____ condition, its owner (ii)_____ that it certainly was. When the buyer received it, however, she discovered that she had been (iii)_____.

Blank (i)	*Blank (ii)*	*Blank (iii)*
Ⓐ pristine	Ⓓ corroborated	Ⓖ sidetracked
Ⓑ primordial	Ⓔ proved	Ⓗ duped
Ⓒ rudimentary	Ⓕ averred	Ⓘ ostracized

Go on to next page

Directions: Each of the following passages is followed by questions pertaining to the passage. Read the passage and answer the questions based on information stated or implied in that passage. For each question, select one answer choice unless instructed otherwise.

The following passage is an excerpt from Carnegie *by Peter Krass (Wiley).*

Great Britain had taken an early lead in the Industrial Revolution. The isles, with rich coal-fields to provide fuel for steam engines, many natural waterways for cheap transportation, and a booming international trade with its colonies, was ideally suited for a transformation from an agricultural-based economy to a manufacturing-based economy, from a handicraft system to a factory system. As country folk, in search for steady jobs, migrated to the cities in increasing numbers, the transition proved painful because already poor living conditions in urban centers were exacerbated by a population explosion. Contributing to this unprecedented growth were the Irish, who, seeking work, arrived in waves. Thus, employers had such a large labor pool to select from that they were able to dictate low wages and long hours, further suppressing the working poor. Disillusioned and embittered, the working class formed both trade and political unions to exert pressure, and activism increased dramatically.

For the following question, consider each answer choice separately and select all answer choices that are correct.

8. Which of the following is specifically cited as contributing to Great Britain's ability to take an early lead in the Industrial Revolution?

   A Trade unions

   B International trade

   C Abundance of coal

For Questions 9–12, select only one answer choice.

9. Which one of the following sentences most clearly explains why wages were so low?

   Ⓐ Sentence 2: "The isles . . . factory system."

   Ⓑ Sentence 3: "As country folk . . . population explosion."

   Ⓒ Sentence 4: "Contributing . . . arrived in waves."

   Ⓓ Sentence 5: "Thus, employers . . . working poor."

   Ⓔ Sentence 6: "Disillusioned and embittered . . . increased dramatically."

Go on to next page

10. Which of the following would make the most accurate title for this passage?

Ⓐ Great Britain's Industrial Revolution: From Boom to Bust

Ⓑ Exploitation of the Poor during Great Britain's Industrial Revolution

Ⓒ The Birth of Unions in the Industrial Revolution

Ⓓ Britain's Industrial Revolution from the Eyes of the Poor

Ⓔ Great Britain's Industrial Revolution: Natural Resources, Migration, and Unions

The current trend to hold teachers accountable for the failures of our school systems and students is nothing more than a blame game that makes teachers the scapegoats. Even with the passage of No Child Left Behind, which was intended to make our schools and teachers more accountable, students in the U.S. continue to underperform students in other countries in math and science. If we are to get serious about education in the United States, we need to hold everyone accountable, not only schools and teachers, but also students, parents, and society at large. As long as sports, celebrity worship, television, video games, and consumerism are higher on our list of priorities than education, academic performance will continue to decline.

11. Which of the following, if true, most effectively undermines the argument that holding teachers accountable is not a solution to improving student academic performance?

Ⓐ A study conducted at one school found that students of some of the teachers showed significant improvement year after year while students of other teachers at the same school did not.

Ⓑ Socio-economic differences among students contribute significantly to student performance.

Ⓒ Studies show a direct link between school funding and student performance.

Ⓓ With the passage of No Child Left Behind, students of teachers who teach to the test perform significantly better on standardized tests.

Ⓔ The decline in SAT scores from 1975 to 1990 can be attributed to the fact that more lower-ranking students now take the test.

Many argue that at the root of the most serious threats to human existence is overpopulation. Putting the blame solely on overpopulation, however, is oversimplified. You also need to account for consumption. For example, Americans constitute 5 percent of the world's population but consume 24 percent of its energy. While more than half of the world's population lives on 25 gallons of water per day, the average American uses 159 gallons daily. In addition, 56 percent of the available farmland is used for beef production. That overconsumption is a far bigger problem than overpopulation is obvious.

12. Which of the following is most effective in countering the argument that overconsumption is a bigger problem than overpopulation?

Ⓐ The world population doubles every 40 years.

Ⓑ Consumption rates are on the rise in developing countries.

Ⓒ Population growth offsets any savings in resources from improved efficiency as well as gains in per-capita consumption reduction.

Ⓓ As average incomes rise, per capita consumption also increases.

Ⓔ One-third of the population living in South Asia and sub-Saharan Africa account for only 3.2 percent of consumer spending.

Go on to next page

This passage is an excerpt from Film Theory: An Introduction *by Robert Stam (Wiley-Blackwell).*

There are many possible ways to describe the history of film theory. It can be a triumphant parade of "great men and women": Munsterberg, Eisenstein, Arnheim, Dulac, Bazin, Mulvey. It can be a history of orienting metaphors: "cine-eye," "film language," "window on the world," camera-pen," "film language," "film mirror," "film dream." It can be a story of the impact of philosophy on theory: Kant and Munsterberg, Mounier and Bazin, Bergson and Deleuze. It can be a history of cinema's *rapprochement* with (or rejection of) other arts: film as painting, film as music, film as theater (or anti-theater). It can be a sequence of paradigmatic shifts in theoretical/interpretive grids and discursive styles — formalism, semiology, psychoanalysis, feminism, cognitivism, queer theory, postcolonial theory — each with its talismanic keywords, tacit assumptions, and characteristic jargon.

For Question 13, select only one answer choice.

13. In the context of this passage, which of the following is the best synonym for the word *rapprochement*?

Ⓐ relationship

Ⓑ reconciliation

Ⓒ disapproval

Ⓓ agreement

Ⓔ harmony

For the following question, consider each answer choice separately and select all answer choices that are correct.

14. Which of the following does the author list as possible ways to describe the history of film theory?

[A] History of psychoanalysis

[B] History of film language

[C] Triumphant parade of great men and women

Directions: Each of the following sentences has a blank indicating that a word or phrase is omitted. Choose the two answer choices that best complete the sentence and result in two sentences most alike in meaning.

15. Among her peers, Amanda was known as the life of the party, but during the graduation ceremony, her antics made her appear _____.

[A] courteous

[B] loutish

[C] decorous

[D] capricious

[E] boorish

[F] contentious

16. The manager's plans were so _____ that nobody on his staff could figure out exactly what they were supposed to be doing.

[A] straightforward

[B] desultory

[C] methodical

[D] convoluted

[E] proscribed

[F] tortuous

17. While citizens were demanding strong leadership, the _____ candidates continued to pander to the polls.

[A] pusillanimous

[B] impudent

[C] audacious

[D] sanctimonious

[E] craven

[F] intransigent

Go on to next page

18. Although parents are often reluctant to _____ their children, they know it is their duty to do so.

A sanction

B admonish

C vilify

D disparage

E castigate

F congratulate

19. The department of transportation offered the _____ couple double the market value of their home, but they continued to refuse to move out.

A obdurate

B recalcitrant

C implacable

D assiduous

E subversive

F fundamentalist

Directions: The following passage is followed by a question pertaining to the passage. Read the passage and answer the question based on information stated or implied in the passage. Select only one answer.

This passage is an excerpt from Art in Theory: 1900–2000: An Anthology of Changing Ideas *edited by Charles Harrison and Dr. Paul J. Wood (Wiley-Blackwell).*

In Naturalist theories the effect of the work of art was supposed to be traceable back into the world. That it had its origin in that world — or some direct experience of it — was the guarantee of the work's authenticity. In forms of theory subject to the gravitational pull of Symbolism, on the other hand, the effects of art were signs of the authenticity of an inner life; they were understood, that is to say, as originating in the mind or soul of the artist. There were some clear implications of this position. With the abandonment of naturalistic correspondence as a criterion, a premium was placed on the strength and authenticity of individual responses and feelings. A requirement of vividness of expression tended to supplant the traditional requirement of accuracy of description.

20. Which of the following comparisons is the main focus of this passage?

Ⓐ Art versus nature

Ⓑ Description versus expression

Ⓒ Mind versus soul

Ⓓ Theory versus reality

Ⓔ Authenticity versus vividness

STOP DO NOT TURN THE PAGE UNTIL TOLD TO DO SO. DO NOT RETURN TO A PREVIOUS TEST.

Section 4
Quantitative Reasoning

Time: 35 minutes for 20 questions

Notes:

- All numbers used in this exam are real numbers.
- All figures lie in a plane.
- Angle measures are positive; points and angles are in the position shown.

Directions: For Questions 1–7, choose from the following answer choices:

Ⓐ *Quantity A is greater.*

Ⓑ *Quantity B is greater.*

Ⓒ *The two quantities are equal.*

Ⓓ *The relationship cannot be determined from the information given.*

1. A furniture dealer sold two sofas for $400 each, for a 25% profit on one and a 20% loss on the other.

Quantity A	***Quantity B***
The dealer's net gain	The dealer's net loss

2. n is a positive integer between 200 and 500

Quantity A	***Quantity B***
The number of possible values of n with a units digit of 5	31

3. $ab < 0$

Quantity A	***Quantity B***
$\lvert a + b \rvert$	$\lvert a \rvert + \lvert b \rvert$

4. $\frac{a}{b} = \frac{2}{3}$

Quantity A	***Quantity B***
a	b

Questions 5 and 6 are based on the following information:

Square *ABCD* is in the *xy*-coordinate plane, and each side of the square is parallel to either the *x*-axis or the *y*-axis. Points *A* and *C* have coordinates (–2, –1) and (3, 4), respectively.

5.

Quantity A	***Quantity B***
The area of square *ABCD*	24

Go on to next page

6.

Quantity A	***Quantity B***
The distance between points *A* and *C*	$5\sqrt{2}$

7. $n > 0$

Quantity A	***Quantity B***
n	$\frac{1}{n}$

8. A car travels at a constant rate of 20 meters per second. How many kilometers does it travel in 10 minutes? (1 kilometer = 1,000 meters.)

Ⓐ 5
Ⓑ 12
Ⓒ 15
Ⓓ 20
Ⓔ 25

9. If $(x - 5)^2 = 900$, what are the two possible values for x?

Indicate two such numbers.

[A] 10
[B] –10
[C] –25
[D] 30
[E] 35
[F] 40

10. A circular pool of radius r feet is surrounded by a circular sidewalk of width $\frac{r}{2}$ feet. In terms of r, what is the area of the sidewalk?

Ⓐ $2\pi r^2$
Ⓑ $\frac{5\pi r^2}{4}$
Ⓒ $\frac{9\pi r^2}{4}$
Ⓓ πr^2
Ⓔ $\frac{\pi r^2}{2}$

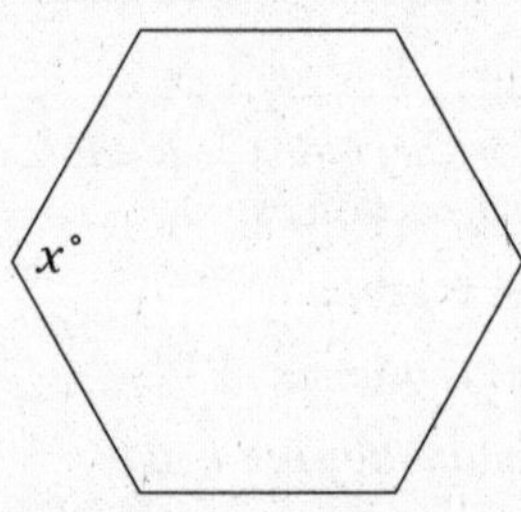

11. The preceding figure shows a regular hexagon. What is the value of x?

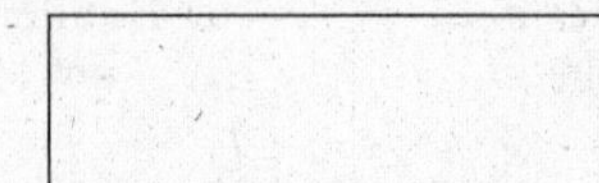

12. If n divided by 35 has a remainder of 3, what is the remainder when n is divided by 7?

13. If the length of a rectangle were increased by 20% and the width were decreased by 20%, what is the ratio of the original area to the new area?

Ⓐ 4:3
Ⓑ 5:4
Ⓒ 10:9
Ⓓ 15:13
Ⓔ 25:24

Go on to next page

Questions 14–16 are based on the following data.

Education pays

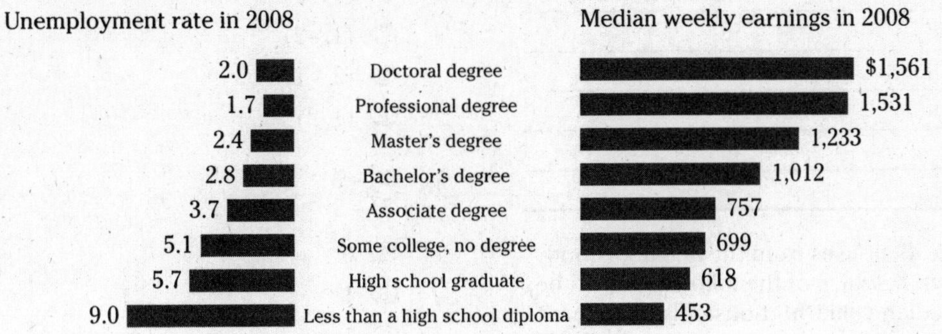

Unemployment rate in 2008		Median weekly earnings in 2008
2.0	Doctoral degree	$1,561
1.7	Professional degree	1,531
2.4	Master's degree	1,233
2.8	Bachelor's degree	1,012
3.7	Associate degree	757
5.1	Some college, no degree	699
5.7	High school graduate	618
9.0	Less than a high school diploma	453

Source: Bureau of Labor Statistics. Current Population Survey

14. Approximately what were the median monthly earnings of someone with a Bachelor's degree in 2008?

Ⓐ $1,012
Ⓑ $1,233
Ⓒ $4,050
Ⓓ $4,350
Ⓔ $4,750

15. In 2008, if there were 10,000 Doctoral-degree holders and 200,000 Master's-degree holders, what was the ratio of unemployed Doctoral-degree holders to unemployed Master's-degree holders?

Ⓐ 1:20
Ⓑ 1:24
Ⓒ 1:48
Ⓓ 1:50
Ⓔ 1:200

16. If an Associate-degree holder earning 20% less than the median for that degree went on to get a Bachelor's degree and earn 25% more than the median for that degree, which of the following is closest to the change in the degree holder's annual income?

Ⓐ $28,200
Ⓑ $30,500
Ⓒ $31,500
Ⓓ $34,300
Ⓔ $49,500

17. What is the area of an equilateral triangle with a base of 6?

Ⓐ $6\sqrt{3}$
Ⓑ $9\sqrt{3}$
Ⓒ $12\sqrt{3}$
Ⓓ $15\sqrt{3}$
Ⓔ $18\sqrt{3}$

House Values of a Neighborhood in Town X

Value Range (In Thousands of Dollars)	*Number of Houses*
Under $100	6
$100–$149	14
$150–$199	12
$200–$250	10
Over $250	7

18. For the 49 houses from the neighborhood in Town X, which of the following could be the median value, in thousands of dollars?

Indicate all such values.

Ⓐ $148

Ⓑ $162

Ⓒ $170

Ⓓ $195

Ⓔ $210

Ⓕ $225

19. Two lines represented by the equations $y = x + 3$ and $y = 2x + 5$ intersect at point *P*. What are the coordinates of *P*?

Ⓐ (–2, 1)

Ⓑ (–1, 2)

Ⓒ (1, –2)

Ⓓ (2, –1)

Ⓔ (1, 2)

20. $\frac{5^{10} - 5^8}{5^9 - 5^7} =$

Ⓐ 0

Ⓑ 1

Ⓒ 5

Ⓓ 25

Ⓔ 125

STOP DO NOT TURN THE PAGE UNTIL TOLD TO DO SO. DO NOT RETURN TO A PREVIOUS TEST.

Chapter 19

Practice Exam 2: Answers and Explanations

Analytical Writing Sections

Give your essays to someone to read and evaluate for you. Refer that helpful person to Chapters 14 and 15 for scoring guidelines.

Section 1: Verbal Reasoning

1. **B.** A ***dirge*** is a funeral hymn. All the other choices refer to songs but are less descriptive of the type of song you'd hear at a funeral.
2. **E.** A ***tirade*** is a long, violent speech, something a person may deliver in the midst of perceived injustice. *Speech* and *discussion* are too neutral to be correct. *Homily* is more like a sermon you hear at a church service, and although Gwendolyn's speech may have triggered an argument, nobody launches into an argument.
3. **A, E.** The ***gustatory*** system is responsible for the sense of taste, and a more ***discerning*** (perceptive) palate is able to distinguish subtle differences. The ***lymphatic*** system fights infection, while the ***digestive*** system breaks down food. For the second blank, ***discrete*** (distinct) doesn't work, and ***distended*** (swollen) isn't even in the ballpark.
4. **A, F.** A ***tsunami*** is a wave that would ***inundate*** (flood) the resort, causing a loss of property that would act as a ***catalyst*** (stimulus) for any renovation. Choice (C), *drowned,* fits the meaning but isn't the proper word. Because the resort isn't a living thing, it can't drown. ***Dissembled*** (concealed) isn't even close. Although a loss of property could be a *symbol* for something, it's not a very good symbol for much needed renovation. A loss of property could result in many ***mendicants*** (vagrants), but the word just doesn't make sense in context.
5. **C, D.** Castle walls that are ***impervious*** to attack cannot be penetrated, and after several attempts to break through the walls, an enemy's energy and enthusiasm would begin to ***flag*** (weaken). Walls cannot be ***amenable*** (agreeable). The walls may be ***impeccable*** (flawless), but because they frustrated the enemy's attempts to get inside, *impervious* is a better choice. As for the other choices for the second blank, the enemy's enthusiasm wouldn't ***rally*** (become stronger) as a result of failure, nor would it ***flee*** (run away), although the enemy certainly would.
6. **C, D, G.** Aware of the ***burgeoning*** (growing) debt, congress would impose an ***austerity*** (disciplined) program to ***curtail*** (reduce) spending. For the first blank, ***pervasive*** (widespread) would be a good second choice, but *shrinking* is the opposite of what's needed here. For the second blank, ***spending*** would be a decent second choice, but not quite strong enough and a little redundant because it's used at the end of the sentence. *Defense* definitely doesn't fit. For the third blank, ***attenuate*** may be okay, but it means something more like to decrease in strength. ***Desiccate*** (dehydrate) doesn't make the cut, either.

7. **B, F, H.** A ***discrepancy*** (difference) between a person's demeanor and statement would make officers suspicious; a ***correlation*** or ***relationship***, both meaning connected, would not. The word *but* provides a clue that although the officers were suspicious, they couldn't do much, so you know that their evidence would be ***unsubstantiated*** (without support), not ***corroborated*** (confirmed) or ***vetted*** (examined closely). This means their case would be ***tenuous*** (shaky) at best, not ***compelling*** (convincing) or ***conclusive*** (certain).

8. **C.** The second paragraph, third sentence states that experts recommend profiling by behavior and intelligence.

9. **A.** If true, Choice (A) describes a solution that improves security without compromising civil liberties. Choice (B) may be true, but the passage cites profiling as a violation of civil liberties. Choice (C) also may be true, but precertification requires a background check, which some people may consider a violation of civil liberties. Choices (D) and (E) fail to address the question.

10. **A, C.** The third sentence states that the Cold War shaped international and domestic politics and cultures, and the fourth sentence states that war has influenced the development of new states. Choice (B) is wrong, because sentence six presents civil wars and conflicts as causes, not effects of war.

11. **E.** Terrorists and rogue states are mentioned only in respect to the possibility of them acquiring nuclear weapons, while nuclear proliferation is singled out as a threat in itself. According to the passage, the Cold War has ended, although nobody seems to have let the Russians know, and the proliferation of civil wars is mentioned not as a threat but only as an agent of change in the developing world.

12. **D.** The sixth sentence describes the goal stated in the first sentence — to position yourself as an expert with useful information, so the marketplace will always need what you have to offer.

13. **B.** The fourth sentence answers this question: ". . . [T]here is an important difference between somebody who is selling something and somebody who is an expert." Most of the choices are differences mentioned in the passage but are not *the* difference between marketing and UnMarketing.

14. **C.** If the prices of health services are more than 50 percent higher in the United States, then this accounts for the fact that the United States spends more than 50 percent as much per capita on healthcare than most European countries, undermining the argument that poor diet is responsible for the difference.

15. **B, D.** ***Tacit*** and ***implicit*** both indicate that the coach approved without having to say so. Perhaps during practice the coach had expressed a desire that the team play with more heart and throw caution to the wind. Choices (C), *cautious,* and (E), *enthusiastic,* both are fitting words to describe approval but neither has a suitable match in the list. ***Ambiguous*** (unclear) and ***salubrious*** (healthy) obviously don't fit.

16. **E, F.** As a sumo wrestler, Kazuki would need to be fairly robust so people may be surprised to see him so ***abstemious*** (moderate) or ***ascetic*** (prone to self-denial) when he was eating. Choice (D), *courteous,* doesn't fit, and the other three choices all mean the opposite of moderate.

17. **C, D.** ***Embellishment*** and ***hyperbole*** both mean exaggeration and carry the positive connotation that the exaggeration is meant to make something better or more interesting. Choice (F), ***overemphasis***, also means exaggeration, but in a negative way. None of the remaining choices even come close: ***sarcasm*** (irony), ***allegory*** (parable), and ***ennui*** (boredom).

18. **A, D.** ***Pugnacious*** means aggressive and ***truculent*** means defiantly aggressive. ***Irascible*** (irritable) is nearly a match, but the two correct choices are better. Choices (B) and (C), ***lackadaisical*** (easy-going) and ***quiescent*** (calm) are nearly identical in meaning, but they don't fit the sentence; because the other puppies in the litter were gentle, this one would stand out as being the opposite. If the puppy were ***soporific***, it would tend to calm those around it.

19. **B, C.** If Mary seemed to be up to something (in a bad way), then her offer to help would come across as ***disingenuous*** (think genuine with a dis in front of it) or ***duplicitous*** (think dupli as two or two-faced). Choices (A), ***sincere***, and (F), ***authentic***, are nearly the opposite of what's needed here, both meaning genuine or real. ***Hypocritical*** is close but has more to do with pretending to hold a certain belief.

20. **E.** The passage identifies several features of the global environment that are sending out warning signs. All the other choices focus on each warning sign and aren't broad enough to be summaries of this passage.

Section 2: Quantitative Reasoning

1. **C.** To get the area of triangle *ABC*, you need the base and the height. Because the radius of the circle is 1, side *CB* is 2. You already know $AB = 1$, making the right triangle a 30-60-90 triangle. Because the side ratio of this triangle is 1, 2, $\sqrt{3}$, the base is 1 and the height is $\sqrt{3}$. And $\frac{1}{2} base \times height = \frac{base \times height}{2}$ is the area of a triangle, making Quantity A equal to Quantity B.

2. **B.** To get the weighted average, add the product of 10 and 120 to the product of 20 and 90. Divide by the total number of test scores (30), and the weighted average is 100.

3. **D.** If you assumed the highest possible value of n is 14, making $\frac{n}{d} = \frac{14}{20} = 0.7$, then you fell for the trap and chose Choice (B). However, because n isn't necessarily an integer, it could be equal to 14.999, which is greater than 0.72 when placed over 20. Because n could also be 11, $\frac{n}{d}$ could be either less than or greater than 0.72.

4. **A.** If $\frac{4}{3}$ cups of lentils are required to make six servings, and $(2)(6)+\frac{1}{2}(6)=15$ servings, the amount of lentils required to make 15 servings is

$$(2)\left(\frac{4}{3}\right)+\frac{1}{{}_{1}2}\left(\frac{{}^{2}\!\not{4}}{3}\right)=\frac{8}{3}+\frac{2}{3}=\frac{10}{3}$$

Because $\frac{10}{3}$ is more than 3, Choice **(A)** is the correct answer.

5. **C.** Remember how to find the area of a trapezoid? Average the two bases and multiply by the height. Because the bases are 9 and 11, the average is 10. Multiplying by the height gives you 50, which is the same as the area of the rectangle.

6. **C.** Call the interior angles of the triangle *A, B,* and *C,* according to the labels on the drawing. Because the angle supplementary to angle *C* is $2x$, angle C equals $180 - 2x$. The three angles of any triangle total 180, making angle *B* equal to 180 minus the other two angles, or $180 - x - (180 - 2x)$, which can also be written as $180 - x - 180 + 2x$. The 180s cancel, and $-x + 2x$ becomes x. Now you know two of the angles are equal, making the triangle isosceles and segments *AC* and *BC* equal.

7. **A.** The equation $x^2 - x - 6 = 0$ becomes $(x - 3)(x + 2) = 0$, making the roots of the equation 3 and –2. (The roots are the two values for x, either of which makes the statement true.) The sum of these two numbers total 1, making Quantity A greater than Quantity B. If you thought the roots are –3 and 2 and chose Choice (C), then you fell for the trap by thinking that – 3 and + 2 in the equation are the roots.

8. **B.** The *median* is the middle number, but if you have two middle numbers, you average them. The two middle numbers are 5 and 6, which averages to 5.5. The *range* is the distance between the lowest and highest values. The range of this set, being 8 – 3, is 5.

9. **A.** The units digit of any product depends on the units digits of the two numbers being multiplied. To find the units digit of 219,473 × 162,597, just use the units digits of the two numbers: 3 and 7. Then, $3 \times 7 = 21$, so the units digit of 219,473 × 162,597 is 1.

10. **E.** To find the slope of the line, convert the equation to the slope-intercept formula, which is $y = mx + b$. Solve for y, and m is the slope.

11. **A, B, C,** and **D.** These four answer choices are correct because 15 to 30 percent of $50,000 is $7,500 to $15,000. In this type of question, you select *all* of the correct answer choices.

12. **61.** Set the ratios up as baseballs:gloves = 2:9 and baseballs:bats = 5:3. Because baseballs are in both ratios, once as 2 and once as 5, the actual number of baseballs has to be a multiple of both 2 and 5. The question asks for the *lowest* number, so the lowest multiple of 2 and 5 is 10. If the ratio of baseballs to gloves is 2:9, and there are 10 baseballs, there must be 45 gloves (multiply both sides of the ratio by 5). Also, if the ratio of baseballs to bats is 5:3, and there are 10 baseballs, there must be 6 bats (multiply both sides of the ratio by 2). Add these up for the number of sporting items: 10 baseballs + 45 gloves + 6 bats = 61 items.

13. **24.** If the average of x, y, and z is 5, then $x + y + z = 15$. To find the average of the expressions $4x + y$, $2y - x$, and $3z + 27$, add them up and divide by 3. The equations $4x + y$, $2y - x$, and $3z + 27$ simplify to $3x + 3y + 3z + 27$. Because $x + y + z = 15$, $3x + 3y + 3z = 3(15)$, or 45. Add the 27 for a total of 72. And $72 \div 3$ is 24.

14. **D.** If the central angle is 45 degrees, then the resulting arc is also 45 degrees, which is $\frac{1}{8}$ of the circle. If the radius of the circle is 8, then the circumference is 16π. And $\frac{1}{8}$ of 16π is 2π.

15. **D.** On Test B, a score of 300 placed the examinee in the 94th percentile ranking. This means that the examinee scored higher than 94 percent of the other examinees. It also means that 5 percent of the examinees scored 300, which is 1 out of 20 examinees.

16. **E.** In the first graph, the line for Test A examinees crosses the 40,000 line at two points: 30 and 210. However, 30 isn't an answer choice, so if you chose Choices (A) or (B), you fell for the trap of not looking far enough on the chart. This examinee could also have a score of 210, which *is* an answer choice and the correct answer. Choice (C), 90, is the group of 40,000 like scorers on Test B, another trap. Choice (D), 180, is the score at which the two testing trend lines cross, but has nothing to do with a cohort of 40,000.

17. **C.** Using the line chart, approximately 75,000 examinees scored 100 and 80,000 scored 110. By jumping from 100 to 120, the examinee surpasses about 155,000 examinees.

18. **E.** The area of any circle is πr^2. Because the radius of the original circle increased by 50 percent, the new radius is $\frac{3r}{2}$. Plug the new radius into the area formula, or square it and multiply by π for $\frac{9\pi r^2}{4}$.

19. **C.** If the circle is inscribed within the square, then the diameter of the circle is equal to one side of the square, which is 6. This makes the radius of the circle 3 and the area 9π. The circle occupies $\frac{9\pi}{36}$ of the square, which reduces to $\frac{\pi}{4}$.

20. **5.** The volume of a cylinder can be found with $\pi r^2 h$. You're given the volume and height, so back solve to find the radius. Begin with $50\pi = \pi r^2 2$. Eliminate the π and 2 from both sides for $25 = r^2$, making the radius 5.

Section 3: Verbal Reasoning

1. **B.** A ***tome*** is a large, scholarly book or a volume of such a book, so the volumes that comprise the *Oxford English Dictionary* definitely meet the criteria. Because the size and weight of the tomes is specified, none of the other answer choices comes close. For future reference, a *novella* is a short novel — longer than a short story, shorter than the average novel.

2. **E.** ***Officious*** means intrusive or meddlesome. ***Banal*** (dull) may be a good second choice if the couple moved anywhere else, but because they moved to a remote location, presumably where neighbors would be more distant, officious makes more sense. If the neighbors had been ***accommodating*** or ***sincere***, the couple would have little reason to move. Nor would they likely move because the neighbors were ***ambivalent*** (wishy-washy).

3. **A, E.** People who are ***capricious*** tend to change their mind easily, so they have a ***penchant*** for or tendency to abandon their shopping carts before checking out. For the first blank, ***predictable*** doesn't work, because it's the opposite of capricious, and ***fatuous*** means silly or inane. For the second blank, neither ***inkling*** (hunch) nor ***passion*** (desire) make sense in this context.

4. **C, D.** Because the compensation was ***commensurate*** (proportional), Jerry wouldn't ***quibble*** (argue) over the deadlines. For the first blank, ***discordant*** (conflicting) means nearly the opposite of commensurate, and ***pursuant*** means in agreement with (as in the terms of a contract). ***Acquiesce*** and ***concede*** both mean to go along with, neither of which fit the connotation of this sentence.

5. **A, F.** Because the audience was impatient, it was more likely ***intractable*** (difficult to control) than ***imperturbable*** (calm and cool) or ***indolent*** (lazy). If everything the speaker said to silence the rabble didn't work, it must have ***exacerbated*** the situation (made it worse), not ***precipitated*** (triggered) or ***exonerated*** (forgave) it.

6. **C, D, G.** Reading the sentence from the end, you know that the teacher was concerned about student safety, so safety issues would have ***superseded*** (take precedence over) all other concerns, and not ***preceded*** (come earlier) or ***negated*** (canceled) them. If safety became a concern, the mixture must have become ***volatile*** (evaporating rapidly), definitely not ***piquant*** (spicy), but perhaps ***acidic***, although that wouldn't require an evacuation. Something changed the nature of the mixture, so that would be a ***catalyst*** (an agent of change), not just any old ***chemical***, and certainly not a ***neutralizer***, which would have made the mixture less volatile.

7. **A, F, H.** ***Pristine*** means perfect. ***Primordial*** is more along the lines of prehistoric, and ***rudimentary*** means basic. If the owner said that the vase *certainly was*, he ***averred*** (confirmed) that the vase was in pristine condition. ***Corroborated*** would have required someone else saying it before he did, and if he ***proved*** it, the vase really would have been in pristine condition. For the last blank, *however* is the key word; knowing that the owner claimed the vase was in pristine condition, *however* clues you in that it really wasn't, in which case the buyer was ***duped*** (fooled), not ***sidetracked*** (diverted) or ***ostracized*** (excluded).

8. **B, C.** The second sentence names three factors that contributed to Great Britain's ability to take an early lead in the Industrial Revolution: coal, waterways, and international trade. Choice (A), trade unions, is mentioned near the end but only as a reaction by the working class to the low pay and poor working conditions.

9. **D.** "Thus, employers had such a large labor pool to select from that they were able to dictate low wages and long hours, further suppressing the working poor." The sentence clearly states that the reason wages were so low is because "employers had such a large labor pool to select from."

10. **E.** "Great Britain's Industrial Revolution: Natural Resources, Migration, and Unions." The passage covers these three topics but isn't entirely based on any one. Choice (A) is wrong because the passage never says Great Britain went bust. Choice (B) is wrong because it describes only half the passage. Choice (C) is wrong because unions are mentioned only in the final sentence and the passage doesn't say that unions originated in Great Britain. Choice (D) is wrong because the perspective in the passage is one of historian, not one of the exploited poor.

11. **A.** If some teachers have a better track record than others in educating students at the same school, the difference in teacher expertise is probably the reason why. Choices (B), (C), and (E) would help point toward some other cause, while Choice (D) is off topic.

12. **C.** If population growth offsets any savings in resources from reducing consumption, then regardless of how much consumption is reduced, the population will eventually be too large for the planet to sustain it. Choice (A) is wrong because the fact that the population doubles every 40 years is not necessarily a problem in and of itself. Choice (B) is wrong because it doesn't counter the argument. Choices (D) is off topic, and Choice (E) is more in support of the argument.

13. **B.** Even if you don't know the meaning of ***rapprochement***, the parenthetical that follows it, *(rejection of)*, provides a clue that *rapprochement* means the opposite of rejection of, so it means something like acceptance of. ***Reconciliation*** is the closest in meaning to acceptance of.

14. **C.** The second sentence mentions the only answer choice that's correct: "It can be a triumphant parade of 'great men and women.'" Choice (A) is wrong because although the passage mentions psychoanalysis, it does so only as one of a sequence of paradigmatic shifts. Choice (B) is wrong because although the passage mentions film language, it does so only as an example of an orienting metaphor.

15. **B, E.** If Amanda was known as the life of the party and acted that way during a ceremony of any sort, her behavior would appear ***loutish*** or ***boorish***, both of which mean rude. At a ceremony, people are expected to be ***courteous*** or ***decorous***, both of which mean polite. ***Capricious*** means fickle, and ***contentious*** means quarrelsome, neither of which fits in this context.

16. **D, F.** ***Convoluted*** and ***tortuous*** both mean complex, full of twists and turns, which would make the manager's plans difficult to follow and execute. ***Desultory*** means aimless or unfocused, making it a good word to describe the manager's plans, but it doesn't have a match in the answer choices. If the plans were ***methodical*** (systematic), they'd be easy to follow, and if they were ***proscribed*** (prohibited), nobody on his staff would be allowed to carry them out.

17. **A, E.** If the candidates weren't strong and were pandering, they must have been ***pusillanimous*** or ***craven*** (cowardly). They certainly would not be ***impudent*** (bold, in a disrespectful way), ***audacious*** (daring), ***sanctimonious*** (self-righteous), or ***intransigent*** (stubborn).

18. **B, E.** When children misbehave, parents are expected to ***admonish*** (scold) or ***castigate*** (punish) them, but not ***vilify*** (slander) or ***disparage*** (ridicule) them. Of course, they should never ***sanction*** (approve of) such behavior or congratulate the child for it.

19. **A, C.** ***Obdurate*** and ***implacable*** both convey a sense of stubbornness; ***implacable*** is stubborn in a sense of not being satisfied with anything being offered. ***Recalcitrant*** and ***subversive*** are a little too strong, conveying a sense of rebellion. ***Assiduous*** means hardworking, which the couple may have been, but that wouldn't necessarily make them reluctant to move. ***Fundamentalist*** (die-hard, or one who is unyielding) isn't even in the ball park.

20. **B.** The answer is most clearly provided in the final sentence. Naturalism relied on accuracy of description, whereas symbolism requires vividness of expression. Choice (E) is tempting, but *authenticity* is used to describe both naturalism and symbolism. Choice (A) is also a little tempting, but the passage mentions two types of art — that which is rooted in the real world (such as nature) and that which originates in the artist's soul (symbolism) — so it's not exactly art versus nature. Neither of the remaining two choices comes close.

Section 4: Quantitative Reasoning

1. **B.** The percents profit and loss are based on the dealer's purchase price, not the dealer's selling price. If he sold a sofa for $400 at a 25 percent profit, then he sold it for 125 percent or $\frac{5}{4}$ what he paid for it, which is x, so

$$\frac{5}{4}x = \$400$$

$$x = \$\overset{80}{\cancel{400}} \times \frac{4}{\underset{1}{\cancel{5}}}$$

$$x = \$320$$

The dealer sold the other sofa for $400 at a 20 percent loss, or for 100% – 20% = 80%, or $\frac{8}{10} = \frac{4}{5}$ what he paid for it (call it y), so the dealer purchased it for

$$\frac{4}{5}y = \$400$$

$$y = \$^{100}\ \cancel{400} \times \frac{5}{{}_1\cancel{4}}$$

$$y = \$500$$

So just subtract 20% of $500 (or $100) from $500 to arrive at the price of $400. The net gain was $400 – $320 = $80 and the net loss was $500 – $400 = $100, so Quantity B is larger. If you chose Choice (A), then you calculated the profit and loss on the dealer's *sale* prices of $400, not the dealer's *purchase* prices.

2. **B.** The number of integers between 200 and 500 with a units digit of 5 is 30.
3. **B.** If $ab < 0$, then either a or b is negative, but not both. Making them both positive, as in Quantity B, and then adding them produces a higher number than adding them first (with one as a negative) and then making the result positive.
4. **D.** If you chose Choice (B), then you fell for the trap. Just because $\frac{a}{b} = \frac{2}{3}$, doesn't mean that $a = 2$ or $b = 3$. They could be 20 and 30, for example. Or a and b could also be negative, such as –2 and –3.
5. **A.** Draw the xy-coordinate plane and place the points A and C as directed. These are two points of the square, and you know they're the opposite corners because the question tells you the sides of the square are parallel to the axes. Measure the width and height and multiply for an area of 25.
6. **C.** Drawing a line from point A to point C splits the square into two 45-45-90 triangles. The side ratio of this triangle is $x : x : x\sqrt{2}$, so if two of the sides are 5, then the hypotenuse is $5\sqrt{2}$.
7. **D.** If n equals 2, then Quantity A is greater; if n equals $\frac{1}{2}$, then Quantity B is greater. All you know is that n is positive, but not whether it's an integer or a fraction that's less than 1.
8. **B.** Set up the conversions as fractions and do the math:

$$\left(\frac{2\cancel{0}\ \cancel{\text{meters}}}{1\ \cancel{\text{sec}}}\right)\left(\frac{1\text{ km}}{1{,}\cancel{000}\ \cancel{\text{meters}}}\right)\left(\frac{6\cancel{0}\ \cancel{\text{sec}}}{1\ \cancel{\text{min}}}\right)\left(\frac{1\cancel{0}\ \cancel{\text{min}}}{1}\right) = 12\text{ km}$$

Note that the three zeros in the numerators cancel the three zeros in the denominator of the second fraction.

9. **C, E.** If $(x - 5)^2 = 900$, then take the square root of both sides to get $x - 5 = 30$ or $x - 5 = -30$. Add 5s all around, and $x = 35, -25$.
10. **B.** If the radius of the pool is r, then the radius from the center of the pool to the outer circumference of the sidewalk is $r + \frac{r}{2}$. First, calculate the area of the pool and sidewalk by substituting $(r + \frac{r}{2})$ for r in the equation for the area of a circle:

$$A = \pi\left(r + \frac{r}{2}\right)^2$$

$$A = \pi\left(r + \frac{r}{2}\right)\left(r + \frac{r}{2}\right)$$

$$A = \pi\left(r^2 + \frac{r^2}{2} + \frac{r^2}{2} + \frac{r^2}{4}\right)$$

$$A = \left(\frac{4r^2}{4} + \frac{2r^2}{4} + \frac{2r^2}{4} + \frac{r^2}{4}\right)$$

$$A = \frac{9r^2}{4}$$

Next, calculate the area of the pool alone, which is easy: $A = \pi r^2$. Finally, subtract the area of the pool from the total area of the pool plus the sidewalk, remembering that you need a common denominator to subtract:

$$\frac{9\pi r^2}{4} - \pi r^2 = \frac{9\pi r^2}{4} - \frac{4\pi r^2}{4} = \frac{5\pi r^2}{4}$$

11. **120.** The sum of angles for any shape (other than a circle) can be found with the formula $(n - 2)(180°)$, making the sum of the hexagon's angles 720 degrees. Because the hexagon is a regular hexagon, meaning all sides and angles are the same, each angle is 120 degrees.
12. **3.** Pick a number that has a remainder of 3 when divided by 35, such as 38 or 73. Divide the number by 7, and it has the same remainder.
13. **E.** Pick simple numbers for the length and width of the rectangle, such as 5 and 5, for an area of 25. Increase one by 20 percent and decrease the other by 20 percent, for new sides of 6 and 4 and a new area of 24. Regardless of the numbers you pick for the original rectangle, the ratio of the area of that to the new rectangle is the same.
14. **D.** If you multiplied the Bachelor's-degree holder's median weekly earnings of $1,012 by 4 and chose Choice (C), you fell for the trap. An average month is $4\frac{1}{3}$ weeks long:

    $$\frac{52 \text{ wks}}{12 \text{ mnths}} = 4\frac{4}{12} = 4\frac{1}{3} \approx 4.3 \text{ wks/mnth}$$

    Now multiply the median weekly earnings of $1,012 by the number of weeks per month: $1,012 × 4.3 = $4,351.60, which is closest to Choice (D), $4,350.
15. **B.** To count the unemployed Doctoral-degree holders, take 2 percent of 10,000, which is 200. To count the unemployed Master's-degree holders, take 2.4 percent of 200,000, which is 4,800. Reduce the ratio of 200:4,800 to 1:24.
16. **D.** Good thing you can use a calculator. To find the annual earnings of the Associate-degree holder earning 20 percent less than the median, multiply the median amount of $757 by 0.8 and by 52, for an annual salary of $31,491. To find the annual earnings of the Bachelor's-degree holder earning 25 percent above the median, multiply the median amount of $1,012 by 1.25 and by 52, for an annual salary of $65,780. The difference is $34,290, making the closest answer choice $34,300.
17. **B.** You can find the area of an equilateral triangle by using the formula $\frac{s^2\sqrt{3}}{4}$, where s is any of the sides, including the base. You can also consider the equilateral triangle to be two 30-60-90 triangles, giving the triangle a height of $3\sqrt{3}$, and use the $A = \frac{1}{2} base \times height$ formula.
18. **B, C, D.** Of the 49 houses, the median value will be of house number 25, in order of value. This places the median house in the third group, valued in thousands from $150 to $199. The median value can be any value in that range.
19. **A.** With the two equations, solve for x by eliminating y. Because $y = x + 3$ and $y = 2x + 5$, replace the y in one equation with its value from the other equation: $x + 3 = 2x + 5$. Solve for x as -2 then substitute x in either original equation to get the value of y as 1.
20. **C.** The idea is to simplify this fraction as quickly and easily as possible. Factor the $\frac{5^{10} - 5^8}{5^9 - 5^7}$ into $\frac{5^8(5^2 - 1)}{5^7(5^2 - 1)}$. Cancel the $(5^2 - 1)$ from the top and bottom, and reduce the $\frac{5^8}{5^7}$ to 5.

Answer Key for Practice Exam 2

Section 1: Verbal Reasoning	*Section 2: Quantitative Reasoning*	*Section 3: Verbal Reasoning*	*Section 4: Quantitative Reasoning*
1. **B**	1. **C**	1. **B**	1. **B**
2. **E**	2. **B**	2. **E**	2. **B**
3. **A, E**	3. **D**	3. **A, E**	3. **B**
4. **A, F**	4. **A**	4. **C, D**	4. **D**
5. **C, D**	5. **C**	5. **A, F**	5. **A**
6. **C, D, G**	6. **C**	6. **C, D, G**	6. **C**
7. **B, F, H**	7. **A**	7. **A, F, H**	7. **D**
8. **C**	8. **B**	8. **B, C**	8. **B**
9. **A**	9. **A**	9. **D**	9. **C, E**
10. **A, C**	10. **E**	10. **E**	10. **B**
11. **E**	11. **A, B, C, D**	11. **A**	11. **120**
12. **D**	12. **61**	12. **C**	12. **3**
13. **B**	13. **24**	13. **B**	13. **E**
14. **C**	14. **D**	14. **C**	14. **D**
15. **B, D**	15. **D**	15. **B, E**	15. **B**
16. **E, F**	16. **E**	16. **D, F**	16. **D**
17. **C, D**	17. **C**	17. **A, E**	17. **B**
18. **A, D**	18. **E**	18. **B, E**	18. **B, C, D**
19. **B, C**	19. **C**	19. **A, C**	19. **A**
20. **E**	20. **5**	20. **B**	20. **C**

Chapter 20

Practice Exam 3

You're now ready to take another practice GRE. Like the actual, computer-based GRE, the following exam consists of two 30-minute essays, two 30-minute Verbal Reasoning sections (20 questions each), and two 35-minute Quantitative Reasoning sections (20 questions each). The actual GRE may also include an extra Verbal or Quantitative Reasoning section, which doesn't count toward your score, but this practice exam has nothing like that.

Take this practice test under normal exam conditions and approach it as you would the real GRE:

- **Work when you won't be interrupted.**
- **Use scratch paper that's free of any prepared notes.** On the actual GRE, you receive blank scratch paper before your test begins.
- **Answer as many questions as time allows.** Consider answering all the easier questions within each section first and then going back to answer the remaining, harder questions. Because you're not penalized for guessing, go ahead and guess on the remaining questions before time expires.
- **Set a timer for each section.** If you have time left at the end, you may go back and review answers (within the section), move on and finish your test early, or kick back and relax until time expires.
- **Don't leave your desk while the clock is running on any section.**
- **Take a one-minute break after each section and the optional ten-minute break after the first Verbal section.**
- **Type the essays.** Because you type the essays on the actual GRE, typing them now is good practice. Don't use software, such as Microsoft Word, with automatic spell-checker or other formatting features. Instead, use a simple text editor, such as Notepad, with copy and paste but no other features. The GRE essay-writing field features undo, redo, copy, and paste functionality but nothing else.

After completing this entire practice test, go to Chapter 21 to check your answers with the answer key and go through the answer explanations to *all* the questions, not just the ones you miss. The answer explanations provide a plethora of valuable insight — material that provides a good review of everything you went over in the previous chapters. Reviewing answer explanations to all the questions also ensures that you understand the reason why any answers you guessed correctly are correct.

Chances are good that you'll be taking the computerized GRE, which doesn't have answer choices marked with A, B, C, D, E, and F. Instead, you'll see clickable ovals and check boxes, fill-in-the-blank text boxes, and click-a-sentence options (in some Reading Comprehension questions). I formatted the questions and answer choices to make them appear as similar as possible to what you'll see on the computer-based test, but I had to retain the A, B, C, D, E, F choices for marking your answers.

Answer Sheet

Section 1:
Verbal Reasoning

1. Ⓐ Ⓑ Ⓒ Ⓓ Ⓔ
2. Ⓐ Ⓑ Ⓒ Ⓓ Ⓔ
3. Ⓐ Ⓑ Ⓒ Ⓓ Ⓔ Ⓕ
4. Ⓐ Ⓑ Ⓒ Ⓓ Ⓔ Ⓕ
5. Ⓐ Ⓑ Ⓒ Ⓓ Ⓔ Ⓕ
6. Ⓐ Ⓑ Ⓒ Ⓓ Ⓔ Ⓕ Ⓖ Ⓗ Ⓘ
7. Ⓐ Ⓑ Ⓒ Ⓓ Ⓔ Ⓕ Ⓖ Ⓗ Ⓘ
8. [A] [B] [C]
9. Ⓐ Ⓑ Ⓒ Ⓓ Ⓔ
10. Ⓐ Ⓑ Ⓒ Ⓓ Ⓔ
11. [A] [B] [C]
12. Ⓐ Ⓑ Ⓒ Ⓓ Ⓔ
13. Ⓐ Ⓑ Ⓒ Ⓓ Ⓔ
14. Ⓐ Ⓑ Ⓒ Ⓓ Ⓔ
15. [A] [B] [C] [D] [E] [F]
16. [A] [B] [C] [D] [E] [F]
17. [A] [B] [C] [D] [E] [F]
18. [A] [B] [C] [D] [E] [F]
19. [A] [B] [C] [D] [E] [F]
20. Ⓐ Ⓑ Ⓒ Ⓓ Ⓔ

Section 2:
Quantitative Reasoning

1. Ⓐ Ⓑ Ⓒ Ⓓ
2. Ⓐ Ⓑ Ⓒ Ⓓ
3. Ⓐ Ⓑ Ⓒ Ⓓ
4. Ⓐ Ⓑ Ⓒ Ⓓ
5. Ⓐ Ⓑ Ⓒ Ⓓ
6. Ⓐ Ⓑ Ⓒ Ⓓ
7. Ⓐ Ⓑ Ⓒ Ⓓ
8. Ⓐ Ⓑ Ⓒ Ⓓ
9. Ⓐ Ⓑ Ⓒ Ⓓ
10. Ⓐ Ⓑ Ⓒ Ⓓ
11. Ⓐ Ⓑ Ⓒ Ⓓ
12. Ⓐ Ⓑ Ⓒ Ⓓ
13. Ⓐ Ⓑ Ⓒ Ⓓ
14. [A] [B] [C]
15. [ ]
16. [ ]
17. [ ]
18. [A] [B] [C] [D] [E] [F]
19. [A] [B] [C] [D] [E] [F]
20. [A] [B] [C]

Section 3:
Verbal Reasoning

1. Ⓐ Ⓑ Ⓒ Ⓓ Ⓔ
2. Ⓐ Ⓑ Ⓒ Ⓓ Ⓔ
3. Ⓐ Ⓑ Ⓒ Ⓓ Ⓔ Ⓕ
4. Ⓐ Ⓑ Ⓒ Ⓓ Ⓔ Ⓕ
5. Ⓐ Ⓑ Ⓒ Ⓓ Ⓔ Ⓕ
6. Ⓐ Ⓑ Ⓒ Ⓓ Ⓔ Ⓕ Ⓖ Ⓗ Ⓘ
7. Ⓐ Ⓑ Ⓒ Ⓓ Ⓔ Ⓕ Ⓖ Ⓗ Ⓘ
8. Ⓐ Ⓑ Ⓒ Ⓓ Ⓔ
9. Ⓐ Ⓑ Ⓒ Ⓓ Ⓔ
10. [A] [B] [C]
11. [A] [B] [C]
12. Ⓐ Ⓑ Ⓒ Ⓓ Ⓔ
13. Ⓐ Ⓑ Ⓒ Ⓓ Ⓔ
14. Ⓐ Ⓑ Ⓒ Ⓓ Ⓔ
15. Ⓐ Ⓑ Ⓒ Ⓓ Ⓔ
16. [A] [B] [C] [D] [E] [F]
17. [A] [B] [C] [D] [E] [F]
18. [A] [B] [C] [D] [E] [F]
19. [A] [B] [C] [D] [E] [F]
20. [A] [B] [C] [D] [E] [F]

Section 4:
Quantitative Reasoning

1. Ⓐ Ⓑ Ⓒ Ⓓ
2. Ⓐ Ⓑ Ⓒ Ⓓ
3. Ⓐ Ⓑ Ⓒ Ⓓ
4. Ⓐ Ⓑ Ⓒ Ⓓ
5. Ⓐ Ⓑ Ⓒ Ⓓ
6. Ⓐ Ⓑ Ⓒ Ⓓ
7. Ⓐ Ⓑ Ⓒ Ⓓ
8. Ⓐ Ⓑ Ⓒ Ⓓ
9. Ⓐ Ⓑ Ⓒ Ⓓ Ⓔ
10. Ⓐ Ⓑ Ⓒ Ⓓ Ⓔ
11. Ⓐ Ⓑ Ⓒ Ⓓ Ⓔ
12. Ⓐ Ⓑ Ⓒ Ⓓ Ⓔ
13. Ⓐ Ⓑ Ⓒ Ⓓ Ⓔ
14. [A] [B] [C]
15. [ ]
16. [ ]
17. [ ]
18. [A] [B] [C] [D] [E] [F]
19. [A] [B] [C]
20. [A] [B] [C]

Analytical Writing 1: Analyze an Issue

Time: 30 minutes

Directions: Present and explain your view on the following issue. Although there is no one right or wrong response, be sure to consider various points of view as you explain the reasons behind your own perspective. Support your position with reasons and examples from your own reading, personal or professional experience, and observations.

"Consumerism has contributed significantly to alleviating human suffering."

Express the extent to which you agree or disagree with the preceding statement and explain the reasoning behind your position. In support of your position, think of ways in which the statement may or may not be true and how these considerations influence your position.

Analytical Writing 2: Analyze an Argument

Time: 30 minutes

Directions: Critique the following argument. Identify evidence that will strengthen or weaken the argument, point out assumptions underlying the argument, and offer counterexamples to the argument.

The following is a common argument used to support increased globalization — expansion of economics beyond national borders.

> "Microlending is the key to ending poverty. With microlending, investors make small loans to entrepreneurs in developing countries, so they can start a business and become self-sufficient. In return, the investor has the opportunity to profit from the interest. This helps the impoverished lift themselves out of poverty in a dignified way, instead of having to feel like beggars. To be successful, people need opportunities and the resources to pursue those opportunities. They want to work and are looking for a hand up, not a hand out. Microlending is the answer."

Write a response in which you examine the unstated assumptions of the previous argument. Be sure to explain how the argument depends on the assumptions and what the implications are if the assumptions prove unwarranted.

Section 1

Verbal Reasoning

Time: 30 minutes for 20 questions

Directions: Choose the best answer to each question. Blacken the corresponding oval(s) on the answer sheet.

Directions: For Questions 1–7, choose the one entry best suited for each blank from its corresponding column of choices.

1. In Shakespeare's *Julius Caesar,* Act II, scene I, lines 193 to 194, Brutus and Cassius make reference to a clock that struck three o'clock. Given the fact that at the time of Julius Caesar, the mechanical clock had not yet been invented, this reference is quite _____.

Ⓐ archaic
Ⓑ a relic
Ⓒ a tropism
Ⓓ an anachronism
Ⓔ a euphemism

2. Journalism students must study not only the craft of writing but also the ethics of accuracy. Journalists are responsible to the public and their profession for the _____ of their stories.

Ⓐ veracity
Ⓑ plausibility
Ⓒ tenacity
Ⓓ originality
Ⓔ righteousness

3. Galileo was not the first astronomer to question the (i)_____ view of the earth as being at the center of the universe, but he was certainly the most vocal. Ultimately, he was labeled a heretic for publicly supporting Copernicanism, and his ideas were (ii)_____ by the Catholic Church.

Blank (i)	*Blank (ii)*
Ⓐ heliocentric	Ⓓ authorized
Ⓑ Eurocentric	Ⓔ proscribed
Ⓒ geocentric	Ⓕ legitimized

4. The question of whether the common (i)_____ used in dental fillings poses a significant health risk plagues dental professionals. Although it contains mercury (along with several other metals), most dentists advocate its use, because it is inexpensive, easy to use, and durable. Experts question the (ii)_____ that because mercury is toxic, its use in fillings must be unhealthy. They believe that the level of mercury exposure is too minimal to pose a serious threat.

Blank (i)	*Blank (ii)*
Ⓐ element	Ⓓ supposition
Ⓑ metal	Ⓔ accusation
Ⓒ amalgam	Ⓕ allegation

Go on to next page

5. Law students often have (i)_____ to study the letter of the law at the expense of grasping the spirit of the law. As a result, many of these students become entangled in (ii)_____ legal language and technicalities to the extent of completely missing the point.

Blank (i)	*Blank (ii)*
Ⓐ an aptitude	Ⓓ sophisticated
Ⓑ the propensity	Ⓔ recondite
Ⓒ a desire	Ⓕ erudite

6. Teachers with a temperament that is more (i)_____, typically perform better and last longer than those who are choleric. In junior high especially, classroom management can become quite (ii)_____. Over time, an irritable temperament only deepens one's (iii)_____ to the students and the profession.

Blank (i)	*Blank (ii)*	*Blank (iii)*
Ⓐ phlegmatic	Ⓓ truculent	Ⓖ antipathy
Ⓑ sanguine	Ⓔ elementary	Ⓗ opposition
Ⓒ melancholic	Ⓕ onerous	Ⓘ hostility

7. Arguments for increasing domestic oil production instead of investing in renewable energy resources are (i)_____ at best. When you consider the fact that the entire world is at or about to reach peak oil (maximum world oil production) it is (ii)_____ obvious that regardless of how much oil we produce domestically, it will eventually be insufficient to meet the (iii)_____ demand.

Blank (i)	*Blank (ii)*	*Blank (iii)*
Ⓐ specious	Ⓓ deliberately	Ⓖ nascent
Ⓑ standard	Ⓔ consummately	Ⓗ escalating
Ⓒ surreptitious	Ⓕ menifestly	Ⓘ proliferating

Go on to next page

Directions: Each of the following passages is followed by questions pertaining to the passage. Read the passage and answer the questions based on information stated or implied in that passage. For each question, select one answer choice unless instructed otherwise.

This passage is an excerpt from Psychology *by Robin M. Kowalski, PhD, and Drew Westen (John Wiley & Sons, Inc.).*

Since its origins in the nineteenth century, one of the major issues in behavioral neuroscience has been **localization of function.** In 1836, a physician named Marc Dax presented a paper suggesting that lesions on the left side of the brain were associated with *aphasia,* or language disorders. The notion that language was localized to the left side of the brain (the left hemisphere) developed momentum with new discoveries linking specific language functions to specific regions of the left hemisphere. Paul Broca (1824–1880) discovered that brain-injured people with lesions in the front section of the left hemisphere were often unable to speak fluently but could comprehend language. Carl Wernicke (1848–1904) showed that damage to an area a few centimeters behind the section Broca had discovered could lead to another kind of aphasia: These individuals can speak fluently and follow rules of grammar, but they cannot understand language, and their words make little sense to others (e.g., "I saw the bates an cuticles as the dog lifted the hoof, the pauser").

For the following question, consider each of the choices separately and choose all that apply.

8. Which of the following, if true, supports the notion of localization of function?

   A A person suffers a lesion in part of the frontal lobe of the left hemisphere of the brain and can no longer recall certain words.

   B The area of the brain known as the fusiform gyrus is more active than other areas of the brain when engaged in facial recognition.

   C Unconsciousness occurs when almost the entire cortex has been destroyed or has been invaded by convulsive activity.

9. Which of the following statements, if true, would most effectively challenge the notion that complex thoughts or emotions happen exclusively in a single localized part of the brain?

   Ⓐ While nearly 95 percent of right-handed people are left-hemisphere dominated for language, only 18 percent of left-handed people are right-hemisphere dominated for language.

   Ⓑ While the back edge of the frontal lobes control voluntary motor movement, the occipital lobe controls one's ability to see.

   Ⓒ A woman with lesions in the top part of the temporal lobe suffers hearing loss, but her vision improves.

   Ⓓ Due to a lesion in one area of his brain, a man cannot consciously recognize his wife's face, but his heart rate increases upon seeing her face.

   Ⓔ Convulsions may be accompanied by a loss of consciousness.

10. The discoveries of Broca and Wernicke contribute to Dax's findings by showing that

    Ⓐ Language functions are not as localized as Dax had suspected.

    Ⓑ Language comprehension is not localized to the left hemisphere of the brain.

    Ⓒ Language functions are even more localized than Dax had suspected.

    Ⓓ Language acquisition and grammar are localized in different areas of the brain.

    Ⓔ Aphasia encompasses more than simply language disorders.

Go on to next page

This passage is taken from The Egyptians (Peoples of Africa) *by Barbara Watterson (Wiley-Blackwell).*

The Egyptian section of the Nile — the 1250 kilometers from the First Cataract to the Mediterranean — was, in its formative stage, much wider than it is today, and bordered by marshland and swamps. Gradually, the river bed cut deeper and the Nile narrowed, flowing through terrain that was rocky and barren. The land sloped very gently to the north, and large quantities of the gravel, sand and silt carried by the river were deposited at its mouth to form the delta, later to become one of the most fertile areas of Egypt. In addition, large amounts of detritus sank to the bottom of the river so that, over the millennia, it aggraded: the different levels of the river are still visible, in the form of cliffs and terraces on the east and west sides of the Nile Valley.

For the following question, consider each of the choices separately and choose all that apply.

11. According to the passage, compared to earlier times, the Nile river is now

- A Wider
- B Deeper
- C More fertile

12. Which of the following is the most accurate definition of the word *aggraded* as it is used in the passage?

- Ⓐ To build up
- Ⓑ To wash away
- Ⓒ To erode
- Ⓓ To level off
- Ⓔ To cut through

This passage is taken from The Idea of Culture (Blackwell Manifestos) *by Terry Eagleton (Wiley-Blackwell).*

'Culture' is said to be one of the two or three most complex words in the English language, and the term which is sometimes considered to be its opposite — nature — is commonly awarded the accolade of being the most complex of all. Yet though it is fashionable these days to see nature as a derivative of culture, culture, etymologically speaking, is a concept derived from nature. One of its original meanings is 'husbandry' or the tending of natural growth. The same is true of our words for law and justice, as well as of terms like 'capital', 'stock', 'pecuniary' and 'sterling'. The word 'coulter', which is a cognate of 'culture', means the blade of a ploughshare. We derive our word for the finest of human activities from labour and agriculture, crops and cultivation. Francis Bacon writes of 'the culture and manurance of mines', in a suggestive hesitancy between dung and mental distinction. 'Culture' here means an activity, and it was a long time before the word came to denote an entity. Even then, it was probably not until Matthew Arnold that the word dropped such adjectives as 'moral' and 'intellectual' and came to be just 'culture', an abstraction of itself.

13. Select the sentence in the passage that most accurately expresses the main idea of the passage.

- Ⓐ 'Culture' is said to be one of the two or three most complex words in the English language, and the term which is sometimes considered to be its opposite — nature — is commonly awarded the accolade of being the most complex of all.
- Ⓑ Yet though it is fashionable these days to see nature as a derivative of culture, culture, etymologically speaking, is a concept derived from nature.
- Ⓒ One of its original meanings is 'husbandry' or the tending of natural growth.
- Ⓓ The same is true of our words for law and justice, as well as of terms like 'capital', 'stock', 'pecuniary' and 'sterling'.
- Ⓔ We derive our word for the finest of human activities from labour and agriculture, crops and cultivation.

Go on to next page

14. Which of the following words does the author of the passage not cite as being a concept derived from nature?

Ⓐ Capital

Ⓑ Culture

Ⓒ Stock

Ⓓ Pecuniary

Ⓔ Manurance

Directions: Each of the following sentences has a blank indicating that a word or phrase is omitted. Choose the two answer choices that best complete the sentence and result in two sentences most alike in meaning.

15. In 1585, the missionary Luis Frois, in discussing Japanese music at the time, remarked, "Everybody howls together and the effect is simply awful." To most Western listeners, traditional Japanese music may sound _____, aimless, and even monotonous, but this is only because we lack the foundation for appreciating it.

[A] dissonant

[B] symphonic

[C] disparate

[D] raucous

[E] cacophonous

[F] mellifluous

16. Filmmakers have a tendency to stereotype scientists, choosing to depict them as either _____ humanitarians, like Paul Muni in *The Story of Louis Pasteur,* or passionately mad scientists, like Dr. Strangelove portrayed by Peter Sellers.

[A] dull

[B] stygian

[C] impassive

[D] zealous

[E] profound

[F] stolid

17. People with diabetes often struggle with _____ wounds that require long-term treatment.

[A] refractory

[B] recalcitrant

[C] acute

[D] severe

[E] perspicacious

[F] excruciating

18. Although communities often must deal with it locally, _____ is a global issue requiring global solutions. As long as the prosperous view it as the necessary result of laziness, however, the solution will always elude us.

[A] malnutrition

[B] illiteracy

[C] indigence

[D] famine

[E] penury

[F] squalor

19. By focusing almost exclusively on the contentious dialogue between the leaders of the United States and China, the media does a disservice to the people of both countries. With nothing to offset the highly polarized exchanges, misconceptions arise among the populace that often lead to irrational enmity between the people of the two countries. The media must do more to _____ this potential antagonism.

[A] mitigate

[B] augment

[C] assuage

[D] incite

[E] repress

[F] subjugate

Go on to next page

Directions: The following passage is followed by a question pertaining to that passage. Read the passage and answer the question based on information stated or implied in the passage. Select only one answer.

This passage is taken from Healing Gardens: Therapeutic Benefits and Design Recommendations *by Clare Cooper Marcus and Marni Barnes (John Wiley & Sons, Inc.).*

The idea of a healing garden is both ancient and modern. Long after humans had begun to erect dwellings, local healing places were nearly always found in nature — a healing spring, a sacred grove, a special rock or cave. The earliest hospitals in the Western world were infirmaries in monastic communities where herbs and prayer were the focus of healing and a cloistered garden was an essential part of the environment.

Over the centuries, the connection between healing and nature was gradually superseded by increasingly technical approaches — surgery, medicines, drugs, X-rays. A separation occurred between attention to body and spirit and increasingly, different parts of the body (eyes, heart, digestive tract, etc.) and different afflictions (cancer, arthritis, etc.) were treated by specialists. The idea that access to nature could assist in healing was all but lost. By the late twentieth century, in many health care settings, "landscaping" came to be seen as merely decoration used to offset the hospital building or perhaps to impress potential customers. Even when a courtyard or roof garden exists, it rarely appears on hospital way-finding maps or signage.

20. One could reasonably infer from this passage that the author believes which of the following?

Ⓐ Natural remedies are superior to modern medicine.

Ⓑ Hospitals should be located in natural settings.

Ⓒ Nature can improve the healing process.

Ⓓ The earliest hospitals are superior to their modern counterparts.

Ⓔ Every hospital should have a courtyard or roof garden.

STOP DO NOT TURN THE PAGE UNTIL TOLD TO DO SO. DO NOT RETURN TO A PREVIOUS TEST.

Section 2

Quantitative Reasoning

Time: 35 minutes for 20 questions

Notes:

- All numbers used in this exam are real numbers.
- All figures lie in a plane.
- Angle measures are positive; points and angles are in the position shown.

Directions: For Questions 1–8, choose from the following answer choices:

Ⓐ *Quantity A is greater.*

Ⓑ *Quantity B is greater.*

Ⓒ *The two quantities are equal.*

Ⓓ *The relationship cannot be determined from the information given.*

1.

Quantity A	Quantity B
$\frac{\sqrt{25}\times\sqrt{4}}{\sqrt{10}}$	3.5

2.

Quantity A	Quantity B
The sum of all integers from 99 to 198, inclusive	The sum of all integers from 101 to 199, inclusive

3. $9 < x < 10$

Quantity A	Quantity B
x^2	99

4. For all integers a and b, $a\Delta b = ab + 2(a+b)$.

Quantity A	Quantity B
$\frac{1}{1\Delta 2}$	$(0\Delta 1)^{-3}$

5. The perimeter of a certain right triangle with the two other angles measuring 30° and 60° is $3+\sqrt{3}$.

Quantity A	Quantity B
The hypotenuse of the right triangle	2

6. From a group of ten students, three are attending a meeting.

Quantity A	Quantity B
The number of different groups that could attend from the 10 students	720

7. A standard six-sided die is thrown.

Quantity A	Quantity B
The probability that the die will show either an odd number or a 2	$\frac{2}{3}$

8. Tom invested part of $8,000 at 3% and the rest at 5% annual interest for a total return of $340.

Quantity A	Quantity B
The amount invested at 3%	The amount invested at 5%

Go on to next page

9. If n is a positive even integer, which of the following represents the product of n and the consecutive even integer following n?

Ⓐ $n^2 + 2$

Ⓑ $(n + 2)^2$

Ⓒ $n^2 + 2n$

Ⓓ $2n^2$

Ⓔ It cannot be represented.

10. If a circular garden with a radius of three feet is surrounded by a circular sidewalk two feet wide, then the area of the sidewalk is

Ⓐ 4π

Ⓑ 9π

Ⓒ 12π

Ⓓ 15π

Ⓔ 16π

11. Billy has eight more cars than Joey. If Billy gives two of his cars to Joey, Billy will have twice as many cars as Joey has. How many cars does Billy currently have?

Ⓐ 2

Ⓑ 4

Ⓒ 6

Ⓓ 8

Ⓔ 10

Use the following graphs to answer Questions 12–14.

Percentage of Mothers in the Workforce in Country X by Age of Youngest Child (1985, 1995, and 2005)

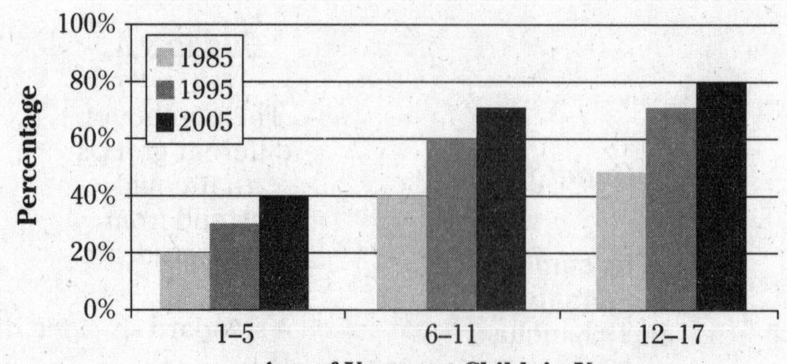

Approximate Number of Mothers with Children under the Age of 18 in Country X

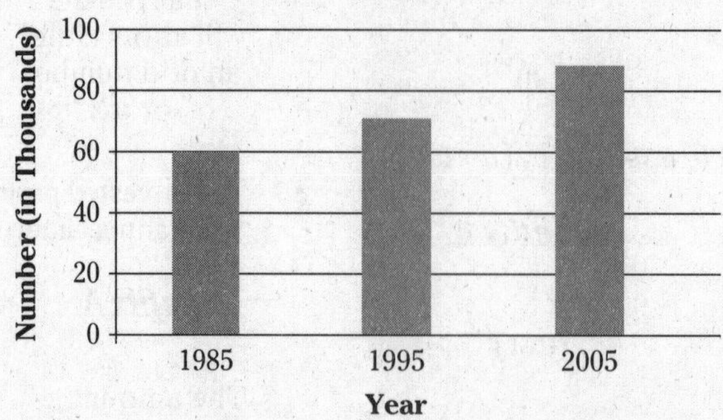

Note: Graphs drawn to scale.

Go on to next page

12. If the number of mothers with children under the age of 18 increased by 10% from 2005 to 2010, and the percentage of mothers in the workforce stayed about the same during that time, what was the approximate number of mothers with youngest children ages 12 to 17 in the workforce in 2010?

Ⓐ 75,000

Ⓑ 80,000

Ⓒ 85,000

Ⓓ 90,000

Ⓔ 95,000

13. What is the approximate ratio of the percent of mothers in the workforce in 1985 with youngest children ages 1 to 5 to the percent of mothers in the workforce in 1995 with youngest children ages 12 to 17?

Ⓐ 2 to 7

Ⓑ 4 to 7

Ⓒ 1 to 3

Ⓓ 5 to 9

Ⓔ 6 to 11

For the following question, choose all answer choices that apply.

14. Which of the following can be inferred from the data in the graphs?

[A] The population of Country *X* is steadily increasing.

[B] The percentage of single mothers is steadily increasing.

[C] The demand for daycare in Country *X* is steadily increasing.

15. In the given sequence $a_1, a_2, a_3, a_4, a_5 \ldots a_n$, where $n > 0$, $a_1 = 38$, and $a_{n+1} = \frac{a_n + 2}{2}$, what is the lowest value of n for which a_n is not an integer?

16. $\sqrt{(6)(7)(18)(21)} =$

17. What is the smallest prime factor of 120,248?

For Questions 18 and 19, choose all answer choices that apply.

18. A certain manufacturer produces an engine lift with three pulleys and seven levers. If each box contains eight pulleys, and the manufacturer is starting with unopened boxes and does not want to have a partial box of pulleys remaining, which of the following could *not* be the number of levers used in the manufacturing job?

[A] 56

[B] 84

[C] 112

[D] 168

[E] 196

[F] 224

Go on to next page

19. If n is an integer and $\frac{396}{n}$ is an integer, which of the following could be the value of n?

A 11

B 12

C 18

D 24

E 27

F 66

For the following question, choose exactly two answer choices.

20. If n is a positive integer, for which of the following would the units digit always be equal to the units digit of n?

A n^5

B n^{10}

C n^{25}

STOP

DO NOT TURN THE PAGE UNTIL TOLD TO DO SO.
DO NOT RETURN TO A PREVIOUS TEST.

Section 3

Verbal Reasoning

Time: 30 minutes for 20 questions

Directions: Choose the best answer to each question. Blacken the corresponding oval(s) on the answer sheet.

Directions: For Questions 1–7, choose the one entry best suited for each blank from its corresponding column of choices.

1. Many of Shakespeare's plays contain scenes or discussions that may appear, on their surface, to be _____. On closer inspection, however, most readers discover that these scenes and discussions are central to the theme.

Ⓐ essential
Ⓑ incisive
Ⓒ tangential
Ⓓ concurrent
Ⓔ predominant

2. After the speech, the issue was open for debate, but the floor remained silent. Apparently, the speaker had done such a fine job of presenting and supporting the case and anticipating questions, he had _____ the need for further discussion.

Ⓐ precluded
Ⓑ anticipated
Ⓒ adjourned
Ⓓ prohibited
Ⓔ obviated

3. A(n) (i)_____ existence typically leads to a loss of self-discipline followed by self-loathing. What once seemed a hedonistic paradise becomes a (ii)_____ asylum.

Blank (i)	*Blank (ii)*
Ⓐ ascetic	Ⓓ stygian
Ⓑ libertine	Ⓔ quixotic
Ⓒ Spartan	Ⓕ utopian

4. In Ayn Rand's *For the New Intellectual,* Galt questions the overriding belief at the time in the (i)_____ of body and soul. According to Galt, proponents of this belief have (ii)_____ the individual into two elements, both symbols of death — a corpse (a body without a soul) and a ghost (a soul without a body).

Blank (i)	*Blank (ii)*
Ⓐ paradox	Ⓓ dissected
Ⓑ irony	Ⓔ bifurcated
Ⓒ dichotomy	Ⓕ bisected

Go on to next page

5. In diplomacy, talks often fail or at least fail to move forward for some time. When this occurs, one party almost invariably accuses the other of (i)_____. In worst-case scenarios, negotiations break down completely, which may (ii)_____ conflict.

Blank (i)	*Blank (ii)*
Ⓐ tractability	Ⓓ expedite
Ⓑ indolence	Ⓔ precipitate
Ⓒ intransigence	Ⓕ motivate

6. Over the years, interrogators have learned a great deal about what works and what doesn't. They have discovered that overly aggressive interrogations often (i)_____ bad information. Rather than engage or give in, suspects often (ii)_____ to "give the interrogator what he or she wants." This calls into question not only the ethics of overly aggressive tactics but also their (iii)_____.

Blank (i)	*Blank (ii)*	*Blank (iii)*
Ⓐ dissemble	Ⓓ prevaricate	Ⓖ efficiency
Ⓑ elicit	Ⓔ prognosticate	Ⓗ alacrity
Ⓒ disseminate	Ⓕ adjudicate	Ⓘ efficacy

7. With no land masses to (i)_____ them, high winds and large waves are (i)_____ to the Southern Ocean. Plankton gather in relatively (iii)_____ pools, where they attract additional wildlife.

Blank (i)	*Blank (ii)*	*Blank (iii)*
Ⓐ debilitate	Ⓓ endemic	Ⓖ quiescent
Ⓑ impede	Ⓔ pandemic	Ⓗ dormant
Ⓒ disperce	Ⓕ intrinsic	Ⓘ truculent

Go on to next page

Directions: Each of the following passages is followed by questions pertaining to the passage. Read the passage and answer the questions based on information stated or implied in that passage. For each question, select one answer choice unless instructed otherwise.

This passage is taken from Better Living Through Reality TV: Television and Post-Welfare Citizenship *by Laurie Ouellette and James Hay (Wiley-Blackwell).*

To understand the political rationality of reality-based charity TV, a brief detour through the conceptual history of welfare will be helpful. We take our bearings partly from political theorist Nikolas Rose, who situates the changing "mentalities" of government leading up to welfare reform within the stages of liberalism. According to Rose's account, the liberal state was called upon to become more directly involved in the care of citizens in the late nineteenth and early twentieth centuries, a period of time that happens to correspond with the development and progression of industrial capitalism. As relations among elites and workers became increasingly antagonistic, rulers were "urged to accept the obligation to tame and govern the undesirable consequences of industrial life, wage labor and urban existence in the name of society." What Rose calls a "state of welfare" emerged to provide basic forms of social insurance, child welfare, health, mental hygiene, universal education, and similar services that both "civilized" the working class and joined citizens to the State and to each other through formalized "solidarities and dependencies." Through this new "social contract" between the State and the population, Rose contends, the autonomous political subject of liberal rule was reconstituted as a "citizen with rights to social protection and social education in return for duties of social obligation and social responsibility."

8. Which sentence explains the purpose of welfare in greatest detail, according to Nikolas Rose?

Ⓐ To understand the political rationality of reality-based charity TV, a brief detour through the conceptual history of welfare will be helpful.

Ⓑ We take our bearings partly from political theorist Nikolas Rose, who situates the changing "mentalities" of government leading up to welfare reform within the stages of liberalism.

Ⓒ According to Rose's account, the liberal state was called upon to become more directly involved in the care of citizens in the late nineteenth and early twentieth centuries, a period of time that happens to correspond with the development and progression of industrial capitalism.

Ⓓ As relations among elites and workers became increasingly antagonistic, rulers were "urged to accept the obligation to tame and govern the undesirable consequences of industrial life, wage labor and urban existence in the name of society."

Ⓔ What Rose calls a "state of welfare" emerged to provide basic forms of social insurance, child welfare, health, mental hygiene, universal education, and similar services that both "civilized" the working class and joined citizens to the State and to each other through formalized "solidarities and dependencies."

Go on to next page

This passage is taken from GMAT For Dummies, *5th Edition by Scott Hatch, JD, and Lisa Hatch, MA (John Wiley & Sons, Inc.).*

It is hard for us to imagine today how utterly different the world of night used to be from the daylight world. Of course, we can still re-create something of that lost mystique. When we sit around a campfire and tell ghost stories, our goose bumps (and our children's) remind us of the terrors that night used to hold. But it is all too easy for us to pile in the car at the end of our camping trip and return to the comfort of our incandescent, fluorescent, floodlit modern world. Two thousand, or even two hundred, years ago there was no such escape from the darkness. It was a physical presence that gripped the world from sunset until the cock's crow.

"As different as night and day," we say today. But in centuries past, night and day really were different. In a time when every scrap of light after sunset was desperately appreciated, when travelers would mark the road by piling up light stones or by stripping the bark off of trees to expose the lighter wood underneath, the Moon was the traveler's greatest friend. It was known in folklore as "the parish lantern." It was steady, portable, and—unlike a torch—entailed no risk of fire. It would never blow out, although it could, of course, hide behind a cloud.

Nowadays we don't need the moon to divide the light from the darkness because electric lights do it for us. Many of us never even see a truly dark sky. According to a recent survey on light pollution, 97 percent of the U.S. population lives under a night sky at least as bright as it was on a half-moon night in ancient times. Many city-dwellers live their entire lives under the equivalent of a full moon.

9. The primary purpose of this passage is to

Ⓐ Compare and contrast nighttime in the modern world with the dark nights of centuries past.

Ⓑ Explain why the invention of the electric light was essential to increasing worker productivity.

Ⓒ Lament the loss of the dark nights and the danger and excitement that moonless nights would bring.

Ⓓ Describe the diminishing brightness of the moon and the subsequent need for more electric lights.

Ⓔ Argue for an end to the excessive light pollution that plagues 97 percent of the U.S. population.

For the following question, consider each of the choices separately and choose all that apply.

10. The passage mentions which of the following as possible ways for travelers to find the path at night?

[A] Piles of light-colored stones or trees with the bark stripped off

[B] The moon or a torch

[C] Railings made of light wood

This passage is taken from Bad Medicine: Misconceptions and Misuses Revealed, from Distance Healing to Vitamin O *by Christopher Wanjek (John Wiley & Sons, Inc.).*

How can we be certain that we don't use only 10 percent of the brain? As Beyerstein succinctly says, "The armamentarium of modern neuroscience decisively repudiates this notion." CAT, PET and MRI scans, along with a battery of other tests, show that there are no inactive regions of the brain, even during sleep. Neuroscientists regularly hook up patients to these devices and ask them to do math problems, listen to music, paint, or do whatever they please. Certain regions of the brain fire up with activity depending on what task is performed. The scans catch all this activity; the entire brain has been mapped this way.

Go on to next page

Further debunking of the myth is the fact that the brain, like any other body part, must be used to remain healthy. If your leg remains in a cast for a month, it wilts. A 90-percent brain inactivity rate would result in 90 percent of the brain rapidly deteriorating. Unused neurons (brain cells) would shrivel and die. Clearly, this doesn't happen in healthy individuals. In Alzheimer's disease, there is a diffuse 10 percent to 20 percent loss of neurons. This has a devastating effect on memory and consciousness. A person would be comatose if 90 percent of the brain — any 90 percent — were inactive.

For the following question, consider each of the choices separately and choose all that apply.

11. Which of the following does the passage provide as scientific evidence to disprove the myth that humans use only 10 percent of their brains?

[A] Brain scans show activity in all regions of the brain, even during sleep.

[B] Brain cells shrivel and die when not in use.

[C] A loss of 10 to 20 percent of the brain results in Alzheimer's disease.

This passage is taken from The Daily Show and Philosophy: Moments of Zen in the Art of Fake News *by Jason Holt (Wiley-Blackwell).*

The fact that television provides entertainment isn't, in and of itself, a problem for Postman. He warns, however, that dire consequences can befall a culture in which the most important public discourse, conducted via television, becomes little more than irrational, irrelevant, and incoherent entertainment. Again, we shall see that this is a point often suggested by *The Daily Show's* biting satire. In a healthy democracy, the open discussion of important issues must be serious, rational, and coherent. But such discussion is often time-consuming and unpleasant, and thus incompatible with television's drive to entertain. So, it's hardly surprising to see television serving up important news analyses in sound bites surrounded by irrelevant graphics and video footage, or substituting half-minute ad spots for substantial political debates. On television, thoughtful conversations about serious issues are reserved for only the lowest-rated niche programs. Just as ventriloquism and mime don't play well on radio, "thinking does not play well on television." Instead, television serves as the sort of "gut"–based discourse celebrated by Stephen Colbert.

12. Which of the following most accurately expresses the main point of this passage?

Ⓐ Television can entertain, but it cannot inform.

Ⓑ Television inherently is a poor medium for discussion of important issues.

Ⓒ Conversations about serious issues play better on radio than on TV.

Ⓓ Television's drive to entertain is incompatible with serious discussion of complex issues.

Ⓔ Public discourse presented on TV is irrational, irrelevant, incoherent entertainment.

This passage is taken from GMAT For Dummies, *5th Edition, by Scott Hatch, JD, and Lisa Hatch, MA (John Wiley & Sons, Inc.).*

Snakes exist on every continent except for Antarctica, which is inhospitable to all cold-blooded animals. The continent of Australia is home to many of the deadliest snakes in the world. However, the nearby island nation of New Zealand has no snakes at all. Scientists estimate that snakes originated about 100 million years ago when the continents were joined and the snakes stayed on the main land masses of the continents when they split apart. Snakes are absent from New Zealand because they are unable to swim and therefore could not make the journey.

Go on to next page

13. Which of the following, if true, would most strengthen the conclusion of the preceding argument?

Ⓐ Snakes are found in South America at latitudes farther south than New Zealand.

Ⓑ Islands like Hawaii and New Zealand are very aggressive about preventing an accidental introduction of snakes.

Ⓒ Sea snakes can swim and are present in the warmer oceans of the world.

Ⓓ Snakes are also absent from other major islands, such as Hawaii, Ireland, and Greenland.

Ⓔ Snakes are found on many other islands of the Pacific Ocean.

Although many people in the United States complain about the tax burden, some of the countries with the highest taxes are ranked happiest in the world. One notable example is Denmark, where some of the happiest people in the world pay some of the highest taxes — between 50 and 70 percent of their total income.

How can that be? The reason is that Denmark does socialism and does it right. In exchange for handing over 50 to 70 percent of their income, Danes receive universal health-care coverage and free, quality education. While in school, students receive a stipend to cover living expenses and free daycare if they have children. The government also spends more per capita on caring for children and the elderly than any country in the world. Without having to worry so much about paying doctor bills and sending their kids to college, no wonder the Danes are so happy.

14. Which of the following, if true, most effectively challenges the connection between socialism and happiness?

Ⓐ The United States pays more per capita on healthcare.

Ⓑ Denmark is a relatively small country with a population of approximately 5.5 million people.

Ⓒ Between 2004 and 2008, Denmark's per capita GDP grew at an average annual rate of 1.5 percent — one of the 15 lowest in the world.

Ⓓ Several countries that provide universal healthcare and free college rank much lower in happiness than Denmark.

Ⓔ Denmark is ranked first in entrepreneurship and opportunity.

15. Which of the following does this passage most strongly imply?

Ⓐ Money can't buy happiness.

Ⓑ Higher taxes are essential to providing for the needs of citizens.

Ⓒ There's more to happiness than low taxes.

Ⓓ Universal healthcare coverage is essential for happiness.

Ⓔ We should all move to Denmark.

Go on to next page

Directions: Each of the following sentences has a blank indicating that a word or phrase is omitted. Choose the two answer choices that best complete the sentence and result in two sentences most alike in meaning.

16. In heated debate, anger often fuels emotions that result in one or both parties losing control. Communications experts recommend taking a time-out to remove the emotional component and return to discussions with a more _____ attitude.

A complaisant

B incendiary

C apprehensive

D conciliatory

E beguiling

F complacent

17. When the goal is to foster bipartisanship and encourage cooperation, one should consider delivering a prepared speech. Extemporaneous discourse can often lapse into an impassioned _____.

A supplication

B vernacular

C malapropism

D invective

E hyperbole

F diatribe

18. One of the unfortunate results of high unemployment is that it tends to transform even the most self-confident individuals into sycophants, which isn't good for the sycophant or his or her employer. Although most employers want team players, _____ individuals are more prone to cheer from the sidelines than get into the game.

A fawning

B assertive

C timorous

D obsequious

E indignant

F aggressive

19. The written request for funding appeared, at least on its surface, to convey a genuine desire to help the community. The presentation, however, seemed to exaggerate the needs of the community and thus came across as somewhat _____.

A erroneous

B duplicitous

C mendacious

D disingenuous

E sagacious

F pretentious

20. The age of consumer electronics is certainly a sign of technological progress; many are concerned about the potential negative effects of television and video games on the physical and psychological well-being of children and teenagers. Spending two hours outside is obviously more _____ than spending two hours in front of a TV.

A salacious

B specious

C salubrious

D pernicious

E wholesome

F propitious

STOP DO NOT TURN THE PAGE UNTIL TOLD TO DO SO. DO NOT RETURN TO A PREVIOUS TEST.

Section 4
Quantitative Reasoning

Time: 35 minutes for 20 questions

Notes:

- All numbers used in this exam are real numbers.
- All figures lie in a plane.
- Angle measures are positive; points and angles are in the position shown.

Directions: For Questions 1–8, choose from the following answer choices:

Ⓐ *Quantity A is greater.*
Ⓑ *Quantity B is greater.*
Ⓒ *The two quantities are equal.*
Ⓓ *The relationship cannot be determined from the information given.*

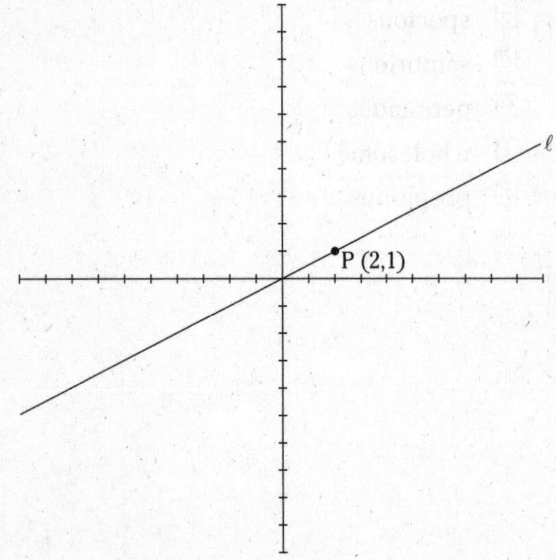

1. In the *xy*-coordinate plane, line ℓ passes through the origin, point P lies on line ℓ, and the x, y coordinates of point P are (2, 1).

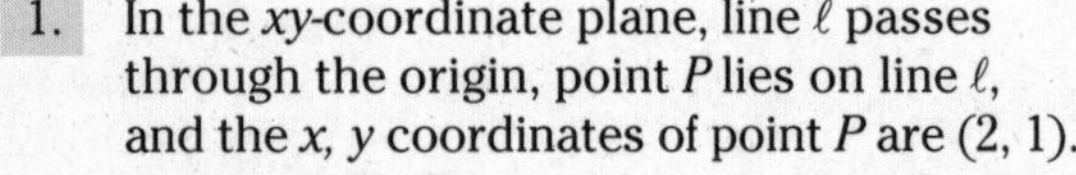

Quantity A	Quantity B
The slope of the line	1

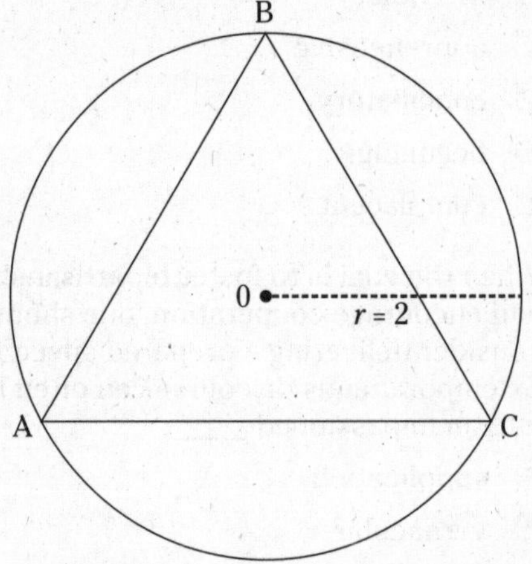

2. The equilateral triangle is inscribed within the circle of radius 2.

Quantity A	Quantity B
The length of minor arc AC	π

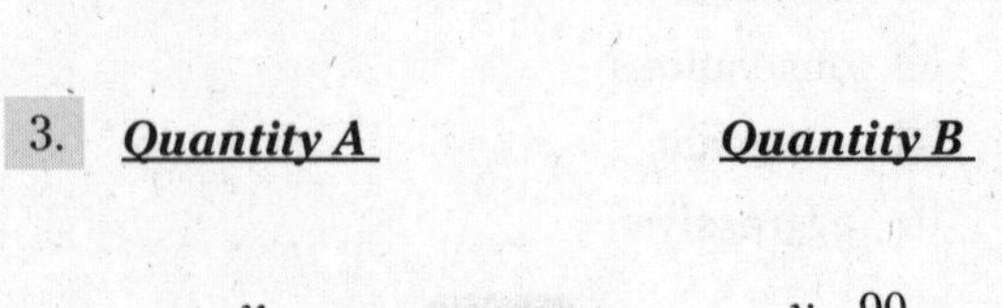

3.

Quantity A	Quantity B
x	$y - 90$

Go on to next page

4. **Quantity A** | **Quantity B**

$\frac{2^{20}}{3^{15}}$ | $\frac{16^5}{27^5}$

5. A car dealer purchased a used car, marked it up to make a 20% profit, and then sold it at a 20% discount from the sticker price.

Quantity A: The amount that the dealer paid for the car, before taxes and fees

Quantity B: The amount for which the dealer sold the car, before taxes and fees

6. **Quantity A** | **Quantity B**

$\frac{100!}{98!}$ | 99^2

7. **Quantity A**: The sum of all the integers from 1 to 20

Quantity B: 210

8. **Quantity A** | **Quantity B**

$\sqrt{4\times9\times25\times49\times121}$ | $\sqrt{2{,}310\times2{,}310}$

9. If a jogger runs 10 kilometers per hour, how many meters does he run in 30 seconds? (1 kilometer = 1,000 meters.)

Ⓐ $\frac{5}{54}$

Ⓑ $\frac{25}{18}$

Ⓒ $\frac{25}{9}$

Ⓓ $\frac{50}{9}$

Ⓔ $\frac{250}{3}$

10. If a chalkboard eraser measuring 1 inch by 2 inches by 6 inches is placed inside a tennis ball can with a radius of 1.5 inches and a height of 10 inches, what is the volume of the unoccupied space in the tennis ball can?

Ⓐ $3.0\pi - 12$

Ⓑ $22.5\pi - 12$

Ⓒ $30.0\pi - 12$

Ⓓ $225\pi - 12$

Ⓔ $300\pi - 12$

11. Given the equation $|x^2 - 2| > 1$, which of the following could *not* be a value of *x*?

Ⓐ –1

Ⓑ –2

Ⓒ –3

Ⓓ –4

Ⓔ –5

Go on to next page

Questions 12–14 refer to the following graphs.

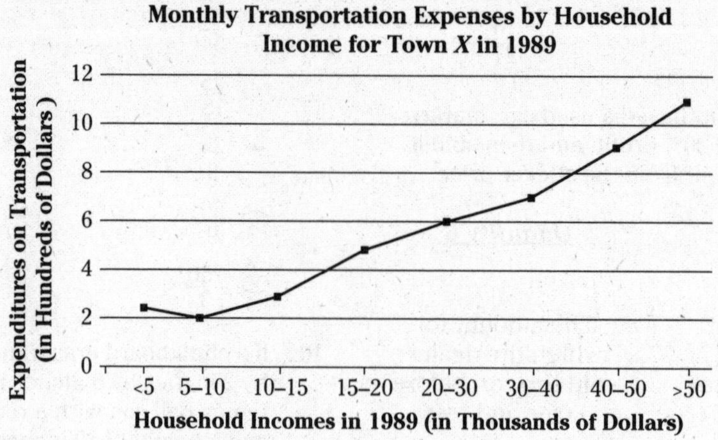

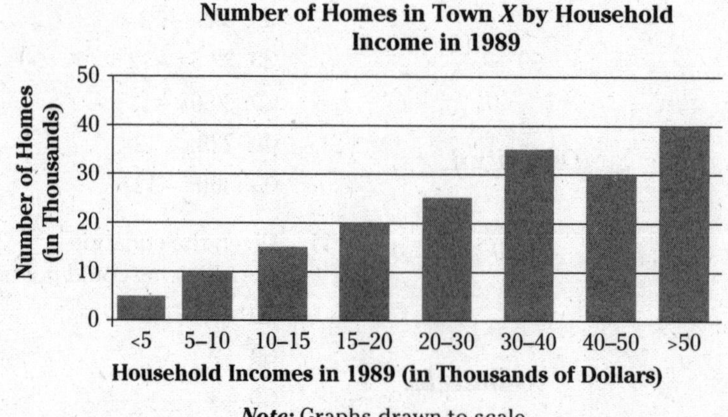

Note: Graphs drawn to scale.

12. For the homes with household incomes of $20,000 to $30,000, what was the approximate total expenditure on transportation in 1989?

Ⓐ $1,500,000

Ⓑ $15,000,000

Ⓒ $18,000,000

Ⓓ $150,000,000

Ⓔ $180,000,000

13. What is the approximate ratio of homes with household incomes between $5,000 and $10,000 to homes with household incomes between $30,000 and $40,000?

Ⓐ 2 to 7

Ⓑ 4 to 7

Ⓒ 1 to 3

Ⓓ 5 to 9

Ⓔ 6 to 11

Go on to next page

For the following question, choose all answer choices that apply.

14. Which of the following *cannot* be inferred from the data in the graphs?

A There are more homes with household incomes between $50,000 and $60,000 than homes with household incomes between $30,000 and $40,000.

B There are more homes being built for the $30,000 to $40,000 income demographic than for any other demographic.

C The median household income in Town X is between $30,000 to $40,000.

15. A decagon is a ten-sided polygon. What is the sum of its angles?

16. At a certain dinner party, there are three drinking glasses for every four utensils, and six utensils for every seven plates. If there are 27 drinking glasses total, how many plates are there?

17. If the average of x, y, and z is 1, what is the average of $8x + 2z$, $z - 2x + 3y$, $y - x + z$, and $4 - x$?

For the following question, choose all answer choices that apply.

18. If n is a positive integer, for which of the following would the units digit of n be equal to the units digit of n^3?

A 3

B 4

C 5

D 6

E 7

F 8

For the following question, choose exactly two answers.

19. If y is an integer and $\sqrt{60y}$ is an integer, which of the following could be the value of y?

A 15

B 30

C 60

For the following question, choose one or two answers.

20. If $x^2 - 4x = 0$, what could be the value of x?

A 0

B 2

C 4

STOP DO NOT TURN THE PAGE UNTIL TOLD TO DO SO. DO NOT RETURN TO A PREVIOUS TEST.

Chapter 21

Practice Exam 3: Answers and Explanations

After taking the Practice Exam 3 in Chapter 20, use this chapter to check your answers and see how you did. Carefully review the explanations because doing so can help you understand why you missed the questions you did and also give you a better understanding of the thought process that helped you select the correct answers. If you're in a hurry, flip to the end of the chapter for an abbreviated answer key.

Analytical Writing Sections

Give your essays to someone to read and evaluate for you. Refer that helpful person to Chapters 14 and 15 for scoring guidelines.

Section 1: Verbal Reasoning

1. **D.** An ***anachronism*** is a reference to something that couldn't have existed in the time it's referenced, like Brutus and Cassius discussing a mechanical clock (a clock that can strike a specific time) when no such clock existed. ***Archaic*** (out of date) also refers to time, but it doesn't quite work as well as anachronism in this context. *Relic* refers to something really old, which the reference itself may be, but in the context of referring to a mechanical clock, it doesn't fit either. ***Tropism*** refers to the orientation of an organism in response to a stimulus, such as a plant growing toward sunlight, so it obviously doesn't work here. And a ***euphemism*** is a mild form of an expression that may be offensive or not politically correct.

2. **A.** ***Veracity*** means truth, accuracy, which is an essential quality of any story a journalist may report. The only other choice that comes close is ***plausibility***, but that doesn't necessarily mean the story is true, only believable. None of the remaining choices (*tenacity,* meaning persistence, *originality,* and *righteousness*) work here.

3. **C, E.** ***Geocentric*** means, as the phrase after it explains, that the earth is at the center of the universe. If Galileo was labeled as a heretic for questioning a belief, his ideas would be ***proscribed*** (prohibited).

4. **C, D.** ***Amalgam*** is a metal alloy (mixture) commonly used in dental fillings. Although amalgam is *metal,* it contains several metals, as explained in the second sentence, so *amalgam* is the better choice. Experts would question the ***supposition*** (speculation), because people who believe amalgam fillings pose a health risk are not only making the *accusation* or *allegation* but are basing their hypothesis on the reasoning that because the fillings contain mercury, the mercury must leach out in levels high enough to pose a threat.

5. **B, E.** ***Propensity*** means the inclination. Law students may also have an ***aptitude*** (skill) and *desire,* but propensity conveys a sense that they're more likely than not to do it. As a result, law students would become entangled in ***recondite*** (obscure) language, not ***sophisticated*** (refined) or ***erudite*** (learned) language.

6. **A, F, G.** ***Phlegmatic*** (unflappable) teachers would be the opposite of ***choleric*** (irritable) and would perform better and last longer in junior high school, where classroom management can become ***onerous*** (burdensome), certainly not *elementary,* and not necessarily ***truculent*** (aggressive, hostile), although the students may be. ***Sanguine*** (confident, optimistic) could work for the first blank, but because the rest of the passage talks about oppositional students, *phlegmatic* is a better choice. ***Melancholic*** (sad) teachers would certainly not perform as well under such conditions. Over time, a choleric temperament would increase ***antipathy*** (aversion) not ***opposition*** (resistance) and usually not ***hostility*** (aggression), which is too strong a word.

7. **A, F, H.** ***Specious*** arguments are unsound, unsupported. In this case, arguments for increasing domestic oil production at the expense of developing renewable energy sources would be specious, because it's ***manifestly*** (clearly) obvious that oil production can't possibly keep pace with ***escalating*** (growing) demand. For the first blank, *standard* obviously doesn't work. ***Surreptitious*** (sneaky, underhanded) may make a good second choice, but *specious* is a better fit. For the second blank, *deliberately* obviously doesn't fit, and ***consummately*** means complete or perfect, which would also be a poor choice. For the third blank, ***nascent*** means emerging, as in being born, and doesn't work because the demand already exists. ***Proliferating*** is sort of like escalating, but refers more to growing in number than amount.

8. **A, B.** Choices **(A)** and **(B)** are correct because they demonstrate specific areas of the brain that control specific functions. The third choice is wrong, because it describes a case in which almost an entire area of the brain must be non-functional for unconsciousness to occur.

9. **D.** Choice **(D)** is correct because it shows that facial recognition is not linked solely to the damaged area of the man's brain.

10. **C.** The big clue here is the sentence that transitions from Dax's to Broca's research: "The notion that language was localized to the left side of the brain (the left hemisphere) developed momentum with new discoveries linking specific language functions to specific regions of the left hemisphere."

11. **B.** The passage specifically states that the river bed cut deeper and the Nile *narrowed* (the opposite of becoming wider), and although the delta may have become more fertile over time, nothing supports the idea that the river itself became more fertile.

12. **A.** ***Aggraded*** in this context means to build up. If large amounts of detritus sank to the bottom, it would aggrade, not wash away, erode, level off, or cut through.

13. **B.** The second sentence explains that the word *culture* is derived from nature. The rest of the passage provides details supporting that statement.

14. **E.** ***Manurance*** (cultivation) appears in the passage but only as part of one of the examples showing that the word *culture* was first used to describe an activity. All of the other words in the answer choices are specifically cited as being derived from nature.

15. **A, E.** ***Dissonant*** (harsh sounding) and ***cacophonous*** (grating) are the two correct answers. ***Symphonic*** and ***mellifluous*** both mean the opposite of what's needed here — harmonious. ***Disparate*** means dissimilar, and ***raucous*** means something more like loud and unruly, which is close but not quite the best match.

16. **C, F.** ***Impassive*** and ***stolid*** both mean unemotional, which would be the opposite of passionately mad. ***Dull*** means uninteresting and ***stygian*** means hellish, neither of which generally apply to scientists. ***Zealous*** (passionate, enthusiastic) doesn't work, because it doesn't contrast to the idea of a passionately mad scientist. Finally, although most scientists have *profound* thoughts, you wouldn't describe someone as profound.

17. **A, B.** ***Refractory*** and ***recalcitrant***, in this context, mean resistant to treatment. An *acute* wound would probably not require long-term treatment, and although the wounds may be *severe* or *excruciating,* neither of those qualities would necessarily make the wounds resistant to treatment. ***Perspicacious*** means wise, so it definitely doesn't work here.

18. **C, E.** ***Indigence*** and ***penury*** both mean poverty. They're the only two words in the list that match. *Malnutrition* and *famine* are close, but the second sentence, which describes how the prosperous view it, focuses the correct choices on poverty rather than starvation. *Illiteracy* has no match, and ***squalor*** means something more like filth or uncleanliness, which may accompany poverty but isn't poverty.

19. **A, C.** ***Mitigate*** and ***assuage*** both mean to lessen or alleviate. ***Augment*** (amplify) and ***incite*** (provoke) obviously don't work, and ***repress*** and ***subjugate***, both of which mean to put down by force, are too strong.

20. **C.** "Nature can improve the healing process" is the best answer. The answer is in the third sentence of the second paragraph: "The idea that access to nature could assist in healing was all but lost." All the other choices go too far and lack support in the passage.

Section 2: Quantitative Reasoning

1. **B.** Combine the $\sqrt{25} \times \sqrt{4}$ to equal $\sqrt{100}$, and reduce $\frac{\sqrt{100}}{\sqrt{10}}$ to $\sqrt{10}$. Because $\sqrt{10}$ is closer to $\sqrt{9}$ than to $\sqrt{16}$, its value is closer to 3 than to 4.

2. **C.** For each quantity, count only the numbers that aren't in the other quantity. Both quantities have the numbers 101 to 198, so those numbers won't affect which is greater. Only Quantity A has 99 and 100 (which total 199), and only Quantity B has 199.

3. **D.** Because x is between 9 and 10, it could be equal to 9.001 or 9.999. Don't square those — square the 9 and the 10 instead for 81 and 100.

4. **C.** To use the equation $a\Delta b = ab + 2(a+b)$, substitute the numbers before and after the triangle for a and b, respectively, in the equation. For Quantity A, $\frac{1}{1\Delta 2}$ becomes $\frac{1}{(1\times 2)+2(1+2)}$ then $\frac{1}{8}$. For Quantity B, $0\Delta 1$ becomes $(0 \times 1) + 2(0 + 1)$ then 2. To the power of –3, it becomes $\frac{1}{8}$, same as Quantity A.

5. **C.** The side ratio of the 30-60-90 triangle is $x : x\sqrt{3} : 2x$, with $2x$ being the hypotenuse. The only way that the perimeter could be $3+\sqrt{3}$ is if x were 1, making the hypotenuse 2.

6. **B.** The formula for combinations is $C_r^n = \frac{n!}{r!(n-r)!}$, with C being the number of possibilities, n being the group of students, and r being the students attending the meeting. And $\frac{10!}{3!7!}$ reduces to 120.

7. **C.** The formula for probability is $P = \frac{\text{Number of possible desired outcomes}}{\text{Number of total possible outcomes}}$. The number of desired possible outcomes is four (three odd numbers plus one even number), and the number of total possible outcomes is six. So $\frac{4}{6}$ reduces to $\frac{2}{3}$.

8. **B.** Let x represent the amount invested at 3% and set the equation up like this:

   $$(x)(0.03) + (8{,}000 - x)(0.05) = 340$$

   Solve for x, and Tom invested \$3,000 at 3% and \$5,000 at 5%.

9. **C.** Pick two consecutive even integers, such as 8 and 10, giving you a product of 80. Only one formula will return 80 if you plug in 8 for n.

10. **E.** This is basically a large circle around a small circle, and the task of finding the difference between the two. The large circle has a radius of 5 (the 3-foot-radius garden plus the 2-foot-wide sidewalk), giving it an area of 25π. Subtract from that the area of the small circle (the garden), 9π, for a difference of 16π.

11. **E.** Set this up as two different equations: $b - 8 = j$, and $b - 2 = 2(j + 2)$. Solve for b by substituting $b - 8$ for j in the second equation: $b - 2 = 2(b - 8 + 2)$. Solve for b as being equal to 10.

12. **B.** The number of mothers with children under the age of 18 in 2005 is about 90,000. A 10% increase in 2010 brings the number to about 100,000. The percentage of mothers in the workforce with youngest children ages 12 to 17 in 2005 is 80%. Because the percentage stays about the same in 2010, 80% of 100,000 is 80,000.

13. **A.** The first number is 20%, and the second number is 70%. This produces a ratio of 2 to 7.

14. **A, C.** Choice **(A)** is correct because more mothers are having children, so the population is increasing. Choice (B) is wrong because mothers in the workforce aren't necessarily single. Choice **(C)** is correct because with more mothers working, and more babies in Country *X,* the demand for daycare increases.

15. **4.** Use the equation to solve for a_2. Substitute a_1 for a_n and a_2 for a_{n+1}. Because $a_1 = 38$, solve for a_2, which equals 20. Now use the equation to solve for a_3 by substituting 20 for a_2 and a_3 for a_{n+1}. Thus, a_3 equals 11. Do this process again for a_4, which equals 6.5. This is the first non-integer value of a_n, so 4 is the lowest value for n that gives you an answer that isn't an integer.

16. **126.** Factor the numbers under the radical: $\sqrt{(6)(7)(18)(21)}$ becomes $\sqrt{(2\times3)(7)(2\times3\times3)(7\times3)}$. Find number pairs to remove from the radical: Two 7s mean a 7 comes out; two 2s mean a 2 comes out; four 3s mean two 3s come out. Nothing is left under the radical. Multiply all the numbers that came out: $7\times3\times3\times2 = 126$.

17. **2.** Because 120,248 is even, it can be divided by 2, which is the smallest prime factor.

18. **B, E.** Each engine lift uses three pulleys, and each box contains eight pulleys. To avoid having any pulleys left over, the number of pulleys used has to be a multiple of 24. The ratio of pulleys to levers is 3:7, so the ratio used in the manufacturing job has to be a multiple of 24:56. Any number of levers that isn't a multiple of 56 can't be the number used in the manufacturing job.

19. **A, B, C, F.** Because $396 = 2\times2\times3\times3\times11$, any answer choice that cancels completely with those primes produces an integer. The remaining answer choices don't work because 24 has too many 2s and 27 has too many 3s.

20. **A, C.** The units digit of any product depends on the units digit of the numbers multiplied, for any integer. For example, any number with the units digit of 7 times any number with the units digit of 3 produces a number ending with the units digit of 1 ($7\times3 = 21$, so just use the units digit of 1). The units digit of any number to the fifth power is the same as the units digit of the original number. For example, $2^5 = 32$, $3^5 = 243$, and $4^5 = 1{,}024$, making n^5 one of the answers. And $n^{10} = (n^5)^2$, so if n were 2, 32 squared has a units digit of 4. However, $n^{25} = (n^5)^5$, preserving the n^5 rule and making n^{25} the other answer.

Section 3: Verbal Reasoning

1. **C.** ***Tangential*** conveys a sense of not being essential or central to the play. ***Essential*** (necessary) is the opposite of what's needed here, and neither ***incisive*** (perceptive) nor ***predominant*** (main, principal) fit the context. Scenes could be ***concurrent*** (happening at the same time), but this wouldn't convey the sense that the scenes are of less importance.

2. **E.** ***Obviated*** means something along the lines of "made unnecessary." ***Precluded*** (prevented) and ***prohibited*** (banned) are too strong, and although the speaker had *anticipated* the questions, that would not anticipate the need for discussion. *Adjourned* doesn't work, because you adjourn a meeting, but you don't adjourn a need.

3. **B, D.** A ***libertine*** (morally unrestrained) existence could conceivably lead to a loss of self-discipline, but a ***Spartan*** (simple) or ***ascetic*** (puritan) lifestyle would tend to make someone more disciplined. For the second blank, you'd expect something opposite to "hedonistic paradise," making ***stygian*** (hellish) the only choice. ***Quixotic*** means idealistic, and ***utopian*** means perfect (in a good way).

4. **C, F.** This passage is all about two's — the body and soul, so filling the first blank is relatively easy: ***Dichotomy*** is a separation into two. A ***paradox*** is an apparent contradiction that may be true, and ***irony*** is the use of words to express the opposite of what the words mean. Finding the right match for the second blank is more challenging because all the words have *two* or *separation* in their meaning. ***Bisected*** (divided in two) is the best choice. ***Bifurcated*** is divided but more like a fork in a road, while ***dissected*** is more along the lines of dividing into several parts.

5. **C, E.** ***Intransigence*** is inflexibility, and ***precipitate*** means to bring about. ***Tractability*** (compliance) is the opposite of what's needed for the first blank, and ***indolence*** means laziness. For the second blank, ***expedite*** (hasten) would make a decent second choice, but *precipitate* is more fitting. ***Motivate*** (provide with a motive) doesn't work, because you may motivate individuals but not actions, such as conflict.

6. **B, D, I.** During an interrogation, you want to ***elicit*** (extract) information, not ***dissemble*** (mislead) or ***disseminate*** (spread) it. To stop interrogations without giving in, suspects may ***prevaricate*** (mislead, lie), not ***prognosticate*** (predict) or ***adjudicate*** (mediate), which would call into question the ***efficacy*** (effectiveness) of such methods, not their ***efficiency*** (ability to accomplish something with minimal effort) or ***alacrity*** (speed).

7. **B, D, G.** High winds and large waves would occur if nothing was in their way to ***impede*** (slow), not ***debilitate*** (incapacitate), them. ***Disperse*** (scatter) would make a good second choice. These high winds and large waves would be ***endemic*** (characteristic of) instead of ***pandemic*** (epidemic) or ***intrinsic*** (fundamental). Plankton would gather in pools, which tend to be more ***quiescent*** (calm) than a wavy ocean, not ***dormant*** (sleeping), and definitely not ***truculent*** (hostile).

8. **E.** "What Rose calls a 'state of welfare' emerged to provide basic forms of social insurance, child welfare, health, mental hygiene, universal education, and similar services that both 'civilized' the working class and joined citizens to the State and to each other through formalized 'solidarities and dependencies.'" Several other sentences explain the purpose of welfare, but this sentence does so in the greatest detail.

9. **A.** *Compare and contrast, explain,* and *describe* reflect the author's purpose, but *lament* and *argue* imply more emotion on the part of the author than is displayed in the passage, so eliminate Choices (C) and (E). Worker productivity has nothing to do with showing how our ancestors perceived night differently, so you can eliminate Choice (B). Choice (D) is simply wrong; the author doesn't maintain that the moon is actually getting darker, just that it's become overshadowed by electric lights.

10. **A, B.** This specific information exception question asks you to refer to the text to eliminate answers that *are* ways in the passage that travelers can find a path at night. The second paragraph specifically mentions Choice **(A),** light-colored stones or trees with bark stripped off; and Choice **(B),** the moon or a torch. Railings aren't mentioned anywhere in the passage.

11. **A.** Choice (B) is wrong because although the passage implies that brain cells shrivel and die when not in use, it provides no scientific evidence to support this claim. Choice (C) is wrong because the cause-effect is flipped; although a 10 to 20 percent loss of neurons may occur in Alzheimer's, the passage doesn't state that a 10 to 20 percent loss of neurons causes Alzheimer's.

12. **D.** "Television's drive to entertain is incompatible with serious discussion of complex issues." The other choices go too far, saying that TV *cannot* instead of that it *does not.* The passage doesn't criticize television itself but how it's used.

13. **D.** To strengthen the argument, find an answer that promotes the lack of swimming as the primary cause of a lack of snakes. If snakes are absent from the other large islands, the reason would seem to be that they can't swim.

14. **D.** "Several countries that provide universal healthcare and free college rank much lower in happiness than Denmark." This would mean that something other than socialism is boosting Denmark to the number one position.

15. **B.** "Higher taxes are essential to providing for the needs of citizens." The passage focuses on taxes and how Denmark uses them to provide for the needs of its citizens. Choice (C) is a reasonable candidate, but the phrase *more to happiness* extends its reach outside the scope of the passage.

16. **A, D.** ***Complaisant*** and ***conciliatory*** mean inclined to please. ***Incendiary*** (provocative) means the opposite, and ***beguiling*** means deceiving with trickery. ***Apprehensive*** means anxious, and ***complacent***, which is included to trip you up with its similarity to *complaisant,* means satisfied, content.

17. **D, F.** ***Invective*** and ***diatribe*** refer to bitter, abusive language, something you'd want to avoid if your goal was to foster bipartisanship and cooperation. None of the other choices are good matches: ***Supplication*** (plea), ***vernacular*** (dialect), ***malapropism*** (confusion of words with similar sounds), and ***hyperbole*** (exaggeration).

18. **A, D.** ***Fawning*** and ***obsequious*** refer to brownnosing, which would incline people to act as cheerleaders instead of players. ***Assertive*** and ***aggressive*** mean the opposite of what's required here. ***Timorous*** means shy, which would make a good second choice, but it has no match. ***Indignant*** is more along the lines of expressing anger over injustice.

19. **B, D.** ***Duplicitous*** and ***disingenuous*** mean deceitful. ***Erroneous*** means false. ***Mendacious*** is more along the lines of being a compulsive liar. ***Sagacious*** means wise, and ***pretentious*** describes someone who's phony.

20. **C, E.** ***Salubrious*** and ***wholesome*** are both good for you. ***Salacious*** (scandalous), ***specious*** (unsupported), and ***pernicious*** (malicious) aren't. ***Propitious*** (favorable) could be good for you, but doesn't express the meaning of being healthy, which is what's needed here.

Section 4: Quantitative Reasoning

1. **B.** Because the line passes through both the origin and point (2, 1), calculate the slope of the line as 0.5: Slope $= \frac{\text{rise}}{\text{run}} = \frac{(y_2 - y_1)}{(x_2 - x_1)} = \frac{(1-0)}{(2-0)} = \frac{1}{2} = 0.5$.

2. **A.** The degree measure of an arc is twice its inscribed angle. So minor arc *AC*, which originates from the angle of the equilateral triangle, is twice 60 degrees. Therefore, minor arc *AC* is 120 degrees, or one-third of the circle. Because the circle has a radius of 2, its circumference is 4π. One-third of 4π is $\frac{4\pi}{3}$, which is greater than π.

3. **C.** The angle supplementary to *y*, inside the triangle, can be represented as $(180 - y)$ degrees. Because the triangle's angles total 180 degrees, add up the angles and set them equal to 180:

   $x + 90 + 180 - y = 180.$

   Solve for *x*, which equals $y - 90$.

4. **C.** The two numerators are equal: $2^{20} = (2^4)^5 = 16^5$. The two denominators are also equal: $3^{15} = (3^3)^5 = 27^5$. Therefore, the two quantities are equal.

5. **A.** Because no price is given, pick \$100 as the starting point for the value of the car. So \$100 marked up 20 percent is \$120, and the 20 percent discount from \$120 brings the price to \$96.

6. **A.** From Quantity A, $\frac{100!}{98!}$ becomes $\frac{100 \times 99 \times 98!}{98!}$, which reduces to 100×99 and is greater than 99^2.

7. **C.** The sum of all integers from 1 to 20 can be found using the formula $\frac{n(n+1)}{2}$, where n represents the 20. And $\frac{20(21)}{2} = 210$.

8. **C.** Don't fall for the trap of multiplying all these numbers and looking for the square roots. Instead, solve for Quantity A by finding and multiplying the square roots of each of the numbers under the radical: $\sqrt{4\times 9\times 25\times 49\times 121} = 2\times 3\times 5\times 7\times 11 = 2{,}310$. To compare this to Quantity B, consider that $2{,}310 = \sqrt{2{,}310\times 2{,}310}$.

9. **E.** Set up the conversion steps as a series of fractions and cancel out as much as you can: $\left(\frac{\overset{5}{\cancel{10}}\text{ km}}{1\ \cancel{\text{hour}}}\right)\left(\frac{\overset{50}{\cancel{1000}}\text{ meters}}{1\ \cancel{\text{km}}}\right)\left(\frac{1\ \cancel{\text{hour}}}{\underset{3}{\cancel{60}}\ \cancel{\text{mins}}}\right)\left(\frac{1\ \cancel{\text{min}}}{\underset{1}{\cancel{2}}\text{ units}}\right) = \frac{250}{3}$ meters. The *unit* represents the 30-second interval that the question asks for. Avoid putting *30 sec* as the unit, which will lead to a math mistake.

10. **B.** To find the volume of the remaining space, subtract the volume of the eraser, which is $1\times 2\times 6 = 12$, from the volume of the tennis ball can, which is $\pi r^2 h = \pi(1.5)^2(10) = 22.5\pi$.

11. **A.** Plug in each answer choice for x and see what works. The only number that doesn't work is –1: $\left|(-1)^2 - 2\right| > 1$ becomes $|1-2| > 1$ then $1 > 1$, which isn't true.

12. **E.** Check both graphs at the 20–30 points. The first graph shows \$600 per month. The second graph shows 25,000 homes. Multiply these together for a monthly expenditure of \$15,000,000. Multiply this by 12 for an annual expenditure of \$180,000,000.

13. **A.** The graph shows approximately 10,000 homes with household incomes between \$5,000 and \$10,000 and approximately 35,000 homes with household incomes between \$30,000 and \$40,000. The ratio of 10,000 to 35,000 reduces to 2 to 7.

14. **A, B.** This question asks you to choose the answer choices that *cannot* be inferred. For Choice **(A)**, how many of those homes have incomes between \$50,000 and \$60,000 isn't known. For Choice **(B)**, how many homes are being built and for what demographic isn't known. Finally, Choice (C), 75,000 homes have incomes lower than \$30,000 to \$40,000, and 70,000 homes have higher incomes. Because 35,000 homes are within the \$30,000 to \$40,000 bracket, the median income is also in that bracket.

15. **1,440.** The formula for calculating the sum of angles of any polygon is $(n-2)180$, where n represents the number of angles. Therefore, $(10-2)180$, or 8×180, is 1,440.

16. **42.** Combine the ratios so that 3:4 glasses to utensils combined with 6:7 utensils to plates produces a combined ratio of glasses to utensils to plates of 9:12:14. To get 27 drinking glasses total, multiply the entire ratio by 3, for a proportion of 27:36:42.

17. **4.** Because the average of x, y, and z is 1, write out the equation as an averages formula: $\frac{x+y+z}{3} = 1$, which tells you that $x + y + z = 3$. From the question, simplify the $8x + 2z$, $z - 2x + 3y$, $y - x + z$, and $4 - x$ by adding them together, giving you $4x + 4y + 4x + 4$. Divide this sum by 4 for the average of $x + y + z + 1$. Because $x + y + z = 3$, the answer is 4.

18. **B, C, D.** Try each answer choice: $3^3 = 27$, $4^3 = 64$, $5^3 = 125$, $6^3 = 216$, $7^3 = 343$, and $8^3 = 512$.

19. **A, C.** For any square root to be an integer, each factor under the radical has to be in a pair. For example, $\sqrt{4}$ is an integer because it equals $\sqrt{2\times 2}$, and the 2s are in a pair. For $\sqrt{60y}$ to be an integer, all the factors of 60 have to be in pairs: $\sqrt{60y} = \sqrt{2\times 2\times 3\times 5\times y}$. The 2s are in a pair, but the y has to complete the 3-pair and the 5-pair to make an integer. So y has to contain 3 and 5, making 15 one possible value. However, y could also be 15 times any other perfect square, such as 4. So $15\times 4 = 60$, which is the other possible value of y in this list.

20. **A, C.** Factor $x^2 = 4x = 0$ into $x(x-4) = 0$, making both 0 and 4 possible answers for x.

Answer Key for Practice Exam 3

Section 1: Verbal Reasoning	*Section 2: Quantitative Reasoning*	*Section 3: Verbal Reasoning*	*Section 4: Quantitative Reasoning*
1. **D**	1. **B**	1. **C**	1. **B**
2. **A**	2. **C**	2. **E**	2. **A**
3. **C, E**	3. **D**	3. **B, D**	3. **C**
4. **C, D**	4. **C**	4. **C, F**	4. **C**
5. **B, E**	5. **C**	5. **C, E**	5. **A**
6. **A, F, G**	6. **B**	6. **B, D, I**	6. **A**
7. **A, F, H**	7. **C**	7. **B, D, G**	7. **C**
8. **A, B**	8. **B**	8. **E**	8. **C**
9. **D**	9. **C**	9. **A**	9. **E**
10. **C**	10. **E**	10. **A, B**	10. **B**
11. **B**	11. **E**	11. **A**	11. **A**
12. **A**	12. **B**	12. **D**	12. **E**
13. **B**	13. **A**	13. **D**	13. **A**
14. **E**	14. **A, C**	14. **D**	14. **A, B**
15. **A, E**	15. **4**	15. **B**	15. **1,440**
16. **C, F**	16. **126**	16. **A, D**	16. **42**
17. **A, B**	17. **2**	17. **D, F**	17. **4**
18. **C, E**	18. **B, E**	18. **A, D**	18. **B, C, D**
19. **A, C**	19. **A, B, C, F**	19. **B, D**	19. **A, C**
20. **C**	20. **A, C**	20. **C, E**	20. **A, C**

Part VI
The Part of Tens

In this part . . .

No *For Dummies* book is complete without a Part of Tens. After working the previous, challenging chapters, you can wind down and enjoy some easy reading that still helps you prepare for the GRE.

This Part of Tens includes ten key facts about the GRE, ten common mistakes to avoid, and ten ways to warm up, relax, and recharge before and during the test. Though fun, these chapters provide good, useful information based on years of preparing students for the GRE. Read on.

Chapter 22

Ten Key Facts about the GRE

In This Chapter

- Highlighting important points relevant to taking the GRE
- Setting yourself straight about what the GRE does and doesn't test

You've probably heard horror stories from your friends about the GRE. Rumors abound, growing wilder with each telling: "You have to know calculus!" (Absolutely not true.) "It's an open-book test this year!" (You wish!) "You get to use an on-screen calculator!" (Actually, this one is true.)

As a GRE-prep instructor, I field questions all the time from students trying to get a sense of what to expect on the test. This chapter reveals several key facts you need to know when prepping for the exam and heading into the testing center.

You May Return to Previous Questions in the Same Section

The GRE allows you to return to previous questions in any given section as long as you haven't moved on to the next section, which wasn't true with earlier versions of the GRE. One effective strategy is to plow through a section from beginning to end answering all the easy questions first and then go back through and tackle the difficult questions at the end.

You can flag questions for review by clicking the Mark for Review button at the top of the screen. You can also visit a review screen at any time during the section by clicking the Review button (also at the top of the screen). At a glance, the review screen shows you which questions are unanswered and which are marked for review. From there, you can jump directly to any question. Practice navigating through the questions and review screen with the Powerprep software provided by ETS at `www.ets.org` and with the practice tests included with the Premier edition of this book so that you're familiar with this feature on test day.

The GRE Doesn't Penalize for Guessing

To discourage examinees from making wild guesses, some standardized tests deduct points for wrong answers. The GRE doesn't do this. Questions answered incorrectly count exactly the same as questions left unanswered, so you're better off guessing than skipping.

By going through the chapters, practice questions, and practice tests included in this book, you dramatically reduce the chances of having to guess on the GRE. Make sure to spend extra time on the areas you need more help with — closing the gaps is the most important thing you can do to prepare for the GRE.

The GRE Uses a Percentile-Based Scoring System

The GRE is a competitive test. Immediately after you complete the test, you receive an estimated percentile ranking based on the test-takers' scores from the previous year.

The number of GRE test-takers worldwide increases each year. More test-takers mean more graduate-school applicants, which makes admissions more competitive. This means that scoring as well as you can on the GRE is more important than ever.

Find out what the acceptable GRE score range is for admissions and scholarships at the schools you're applying to and ask whether that range is expected to change.

Practice Makes All the Difference

Although you may not be able to dress-rehearse the entire test-taking experience, practicing the test makes the actual test-taking experience feel more familiar and reduces the element of surprise. Take advantage of the practice tests included in this book — and on the CD if you purchased the Premier edition. Also, the practice software ETS provides has the exact feel of the actual GRE, so make it something you know well. Write the practice essays, too, making the entire experience as familiar as a day at the office (flip to Part IV for more on essay writing).

Reviewing your practice tests also helps you discover a lot of silly mistakes that can lead to wrong answers. Making these mistakes *in practice* is okay. Knowing you're prone to these mistakes decreases your chances of making the same types of mistakes in the actual test.

A good sense of familiarity and knowing what to expect truly boosts your confidence on test day. I require a five-practice-test minimum from my students, and getting them to do each of the tests is like pulling teeth. But I also track their progress and always see a marked improvement from one practice test to the next. At what point on the improvement curve do you want to be when you take the actual GRE?

You Must Study for the GRE

Though stories of unprepared folks scoring dramatically high are out there, incidents of unprepared folks bombing and having to retake the GRE are far more common. I'd put my money on an average Joe or Josephine who's well prepared over a budding Einstein going in cold — every time. So be prepared. This book is your best resource and includes all the study materials you need.

The GRE Is Different from the SAT

You're not the same person you were in high school. You've matured, acquired better study habits, and suddenly come to the shocking realization that you're in charge of your own destiny. Maybe you didn't study much for the SAT, figuring that you could always get into *some* college, somewhere, regardless of your score. You were probably right. But getting into graduate school isn't as easy, and the GRE is much more difficult than the SAT.

As you mature, you tend to become more serious, so approach the GRE with a more mature, serious mindset. Doing so allows you to leverage the power of your improved study habits and concentration to better prepare yourself for the test.

The GRE Also Measures Your Stamina and Performance under Pressure

The GRE measures a number of things besides your math and verbal aptitude. It measures your ability to prepare, your stamina, and your performance under pressure. Many people are quite capable of solving math problems with all the time in the world, but only those who have honed their skills through practice can come up with the right answers when the timer is ticking.

The good news: You can build or strengthen all the skills that the GRE measures.

Other Than the Math, the General GRE Is Subject-Neutral

You're a high-school and college graduate. Everything on the GRE is stuff you've seen before. In other words, the material is *subject-neutral* (not requiring specialized knowledge).

The GRE is required for entrance into graduate programs ranging from Construction Management to Physician Assistant to Master of Social Work. Regardless of your background, current major, or area of study, you *can* ace the GRE.

You Can Practice the GRE on Your Own Computer

The only way to experience the real GRE is to take it. However, you can simulate the test-taking experience on your own computer and get as close to a real-life experience as possible. After you've studied and acquainted yourself with the different question types, practice on your own computer. If you purchased the *GRE For Dummies,* Premier 7th Edition, you have an accompanying CD that includes two practice tests. Take these sample tests to get comfortable with the format.

Set aside a good chunk of time, pop the CD into your computer, and take one of the tests to make the test-taking experience as familiar and comfortable as possible. If you live alone or have a room in your house or apartment insulated from the usual hustle and bustle, that's perfect. Otherwise, consider taking the test in a library or other quiet place.

If you didn't buy the Premier edition or you want additional practice, you can download the practice software provided by ETS. Go to `www.ets.org/gre`, click the link that takes you to the Revised General Test, scroll down to find and download the Powerprep software, install it on your computer, and then take one of the sample tests.

You Can't Bring Anything into the Testing Center

I once saw a photo of a confiscated plastic water bottle with math formulas printed on the inside of the label. Though you may not go to such lengths, the testing center staff wants to ensure zero opportunities of cheating on the GRE. Because of this, you can't take anything in with you — not even a wristwatch. You can store food and water in a locker, but be prepared to empty your pockets and be fingerprinted upon entering the actual testing area.

Don't store any GRE books in the locker. If the proctors suspect you of checking the books during your breaks, you may not be allowed to finish the test.

Chapter 23

Ten Mistakes You Won't Make (And Others Will)

In This Chapter

- Avoiding the temptation to cheat
- Building endurance and taking advantage of breaks to finish strong
- Taking charge of what you can control and letting the rest fall into place
- Testing with the clock (or your best bud)

Throughout this book, you discover techniques for doing your best on the GRE. I'm sorry to say, however, that you may encounter just as many pitfalls for messing up big time on the test. The good news is that this chapter can help you avoid those pitfalls. Take a few minutes to read through these mistakes now to see what crazy things people do to totally blow the exam. By becoming aware of these catastrophes, you may prevent them from happening to you.

Cheating

Cheating on the GRE is just plain stupid, so don't even consider it. Apart from the ethical issues, cheating simply doesn't work. When you get to the testing center, and before you begin your test, the proctors separate you from anything that you can possibly use to cheat, including your cellphone, wristwatch, water bottle, jacket, and hat. On top of that, you're monitored by a camera while taking the test. Any semblance of privacy goes right out the window.

How would you cheat anyway? You can't copy all those vocabulary words or write all the math formulas on anything accessible during the test. Besides, the GRE tests your critical-reasoning and problem-solving skills more than your memorization skills.

Those caught cheating can be banned from taking the test for up to ten years! In the world of education, that's nearly a life sentence.

Running Out of Steam

The GRE tests your stamina as much as anything else. Most people aren't able to maintain these levels of concentration for four straight hours, so they end up petering out. Through preparation and practice, you have a definite edge over the other test-takers.

Like practicing for a marathon, you must slowly build yourself up for the long GRE. Practice for a few hours at a time and stop when you get tired. Repeat this exercise, and eventually you'll be able to go the full distance without fail. Don't push yourself too hard, though, because you'll burn yourself out. As they say in the weight room, "Train, don't strain."

Planning for Your Breaks

Some people don't take advantage of the short breaks offered during the GRE. Be sure you don't miss the opportunity to take a breather. You're offered a short break (one- or ten-minute increments) between sections. If you don't take these breaks, you'll be sitting still for hours. Though your stamina may be good (because you practiced), you still want to stay hydrated, eat a power bar, and walk around every now and then to keep your mind clear. Don't plan on studying during your breaks, though — the review of any GRE-prep materials during breaks is strictly forbidden.

Pack some water bottles and power bars to keep in a locker for your breaks. You won't have time to go grab something. Don't drink too much water, though — you can't pause the test to run to the restroom.

Worrying about the Past Questions or Sections

When skipping a question or marking it for further review, let it go until the end of the section so you can focus on the other questions at hand. When you reach the end of the section (but before moving on to the next section or before the time expires), you may return to the questions you skipped or marked and check or change your answers.

When you move on to the next section, however, that's it: You can't go back to a previous section. You have no choice but to move forward, so don't waste mental energy and focus on past questions you can do nothing about.

Although you can go back and change answers within each section, it's not always a good idea unless you had serious doubts about your answer. Examinees tend to change more right answers to wrong answers than the other way around. Think twice and rule out all other choices before changing your answer.

Panicking over the Time Limit

Some test-takers fret over the clock. The key to success is to be aware of the clock while remaining calm. Practice working with a timer. As you become more accustomed to working with the clock during practice, you'll eventually settle into a comfortable pace and be used to the timer on test day.

The mistakes you make while under pressure from the timer are different from the mistakes you make while relaxed. Practice with a timer to become aware of the timer-pressure mistakes and fix them *before* the test.

Rushing through the Questions

Some test-takers are so worried about finishing the test that they rush through it, taking shortcuts and making careless errors. As a result, they finish early then don't have time to check all their work.

Because the easy questions are worth exactly as much as the hard questions, it makes sense to knock out the easy ones first. For the medium questions that you're not so sure of, take advantage of the Mark for Review button available for each question. At the end of each section, you have a review screen that shows which questions aren't answered and which are marked for review. You can jump straight to those questions to work them further.

Choking on the Essays

Choking, by definition (on the GRE), means getting stuck on something and becoming so flustered that you can't focus on anything after that. Choking can happen at any point on the test, but because you can flag the multiple-choice questions and go back to them at the end of the section, you're unlikely to choke on the questions.

Essays, however, are another story. On the GRE, you have to write two essays and you have only 30 minutes each to write them. What's worse, they're at the beginning of the test, so if you choke on one, you're toast for the entire test. Of course, this won't happen to you, because in Chapters 14 and 15, I guide you through writing two perfect essays, step by step, and making writer's block something of the past.

Practice writing the essays! Like any skill, essay-writing takes practice, and you don't want to be at the start of the learning curve on test day.

Fretting over the Hard Questions

The GRE contains some incredibly difficult questions. Most test-takers don't get perfect scores, and you're not expected to either. Do the best you can, score in the high percentiles, and get accepted to graduate school! No one expects a perfect score, so you shouldn't either.

The GRE is only one of many parts of the application process. Your GPA, work experience, essays, and any other relevant character-building experience (such as playing sports, military service, volunteer work, or leadership training) also count toward your chances of admission.

Taking the Test with Your Best Friend

You and your buddy may be able to schedule your tests for the same time. Big mistake. Two of my students from the same class took the exam at the same time, side by side, and both told me afterward that the distraction was almost unbearable. Fortunately, they both scored well, but I wonder how different their results would have been if they'd tested separately. If you want to rely on your friend for support, study with him or plan a celebration afterwards, but don't buddy up to take the test.

Changing Your Morning Routine

The GRE is stressful enough. The last thing you need to do is add more anxiety to the whole nerve-racking experience by changing your morning routine.

If you normally have one cup of coffee, should you have an extra cup for more energy or only half a cup to reduce anxiety? Should you have an omelet for more protein or just have toast to avoid the food crash later? Here's a suggestion: *Do what you normally do.* It works every other day, and it'll work just as well the day of the test. Don't break routine.

If you're tempted to try an energy drink or something unusual for an enhanced test-taking experience, try it first on a practice test! Make sure your new concoction doesn't upset your stomach, give you a headache, or zone you out.

Chapter 24

Ten Ways to Warm Up and Relax Before and During the GRE

In This Chapter

- Getting your head in the game
- Keeping the blood flowing
- Shaking out the test jitters
- Banishing any negative self-talk

The GRE is as much a physical workout as it is mental and more like a marathon than a sprint. If you come out of the blocks at a sprinter's pace, you're sure to quickly exhaust yourself.

The keys to reaching the end and finishing strong are warming up mentally and keeping in tune physically. This chapter describes ten mental and physical exercises that can keep you going before and during the test and carry you through to the very end.

Work Some Easy Math First

Make sure your first math warm-up problem on the day you take the GRE isn't finding the possible values of k in $f(x) = x^2 + 2xk - 13$. Instead, warm up before the test by getting some simple math flowing through your head. During your drive to the testing center, review the squares of numbers 1 through 10, find the circumference and area of a circle with a radius of 6, and review the side ratios of the common right triangles (see more on these math problems in Chapters 8 and 10).

Taking a test is like running a race. Before you run a race, you want to jog a little to warm up. Before you take the GRE, you want to get your brain going with some easy mental math exercises.

Do Some Light Reading

Just as you want to warm up with some easy math, you also want to warm up with some verbal exercises. Make sure the Verbal sections, including the monster GRE Reading Comp passages, aren't where you do the first verbal reasoning of the day.

While eating your breakfast, read a magazine or newspaper article and look for the introduction, supporting detail, main idea, and author's perspective. (Check out Chapter 5 for more on reading comprehension.) Also look at the vocabulary words in the article and separate the roots, prefixes, and suffixes. (Brush up on vocabulary in Chapter 7.)

Breathe Deeply

The value of breathing deeply is grossly underrated. Take a deep breath, hold it for a few counts, and then expel the air through your nose.

Avoid short, shallow breaths, which can cause you to become even more anxious by depriving your body of oxygen. Try breathing in and out deeply while reciting something in your mind, such as dialogue from a movie or lyrics to a good song.

Rotate Your Head

Work the kinks out of your neck by trying to see behind you without turning around. Slowly rotate your head as far as possible to the right until you feel a tug on the left side of your neck. Then rotate your head all the way to the left until you feel a tug on the right. Return your head back to center and then move it straight back, as if you're looking up at the sky, and then down, as if looking at your feet. You'll be surprised at how much tension drains out of you when doing these moves a few times.

During the test, be careful to perform this exercise with your eyes closed and make what you're doing obvious. You don't want a suspicious proctor to think you're craning your neck to look at someone else's computer screen.

Cup Your Eyes

Cup your hands, fingers together. Put them over your gently closed eyes, blocking out all the light. You're now in a world of velvety-smooth darkness, which is very soothing. (Try not to let your hands actually touch your eyes.) Do this for 10 to 15 seconds.

Hunch and Roll Your Shoulders

While breathing in, scrunch up your shoulders as if you're trying to touch them to your ears. Then roll them back and down, breathing out. Arch your back, sitting up super straight, as if a string is attached to the top of your head and is being pulled toward the ceiling. Then slump and round out your lower back, pushing it out toward the back of your chair. These exercises relax your upper and lower back and are especially useful if you develop a kink in your spine.

Shake Out Your Hands

You probably shake out your hands automatically when you need to get rid of writer's cramp. Go ahead and do it more consciously and more frequently. Put your hands down at your sides, hanging them below your chair seat, and shake them vigorously. Imagine all the tension and stress pouring out through your fingers onto the floor.

Extend and Push Out Your Legs

While you're sitting at your desk, straighten your legs out in front of you and think of pushing something away with your heels. Point your toes back toward your knees. You'll feel a stretch on the backs of your legs. Hold for a count of three and then relax.

Curtail Negative Thoughts

Suppose you catch yourself thinking, "Why didn't I study this math more? I saw that formula a hundred times, but I can't remember it now!" Change the script to, "I got most of the math right. I can get this one, too. I'm doing fine, and I'm almost done!"

Don't panic over something you may not have done your best on, because the panic will carry over into the next section. I've seen students doubt themselves and then do great, proving that doubt is a poor indicator of performance. Doubt can lead to panic, though, which negatively affects your performance, so banish doubt and focus on acing the next question or section.

Visualize Success

Before the exam, close your eyes gently and visualize yourself as the champion. Believe in yourself and envision kicking the GRE's butt:

- You're in the testing center, seeing questions you know the answers to and cheerfully punching the Next button.
- You're leaving the exam room, shouting, "YES!" because you got your unofficial score right off the computer. You eagerly rush home to begin your mailbox vigil for the official good news.
- You're opening the envelope containing the acceptance letter from the graduate school of your dreams.
- Years from now, you're working your dream job and telling the magazine reporter in the seat next to you that your success started with your excellent GRE scores, thanks (at least in part) to *GRE For Dummies.*

Index

• A •

• B •

• E •

• F •

• G •

• J •

• K •

• L •

• M •

• N •

• O •

• P •

• S •

• T •

• W •

• Y •

• Z •

Workspace

Workspace

Workspace

Workspace

Workspace

Apple & Macs

iPad For Dummies
978-0-470-58027-1

iPhone For Dummies, 4th Edition
978-0-470-87870-5

MacBook For Dummies, 3rd Edition
978-0-470-76918-8

Mac OS X Snow Leopard For Dummies
978-0-470-43543-4

Business

Bookkeeping For Dummies
978-0-7645-9848-7

Job Interviews For Dummies, 3rd Edition
978-0-470-17748-8

Resumes For Dummies, 5th Edition
978-0-470-08037-5

Starting an Online Business For Dummies, 6th Edition
978-0-470-60210-2

Stock Investing For Dummies, 3rd Edition
978-0-470-40114-9

Successful Time Management For Dummies
978-0-470-29034-7

Computer Hardware

BlackBerry For Dummies, 4th Edition
978-0-470-60700-8

Computers For Seniors For Dummies, 2nd Edition
978-0-470-53483-0

PCs For Dummies, Windows 7 Edition
978-0-470-46542-4

Laptops For Dummies, 4th Edition
978-0-470-57829-2

Cooking & Entertaining

Cooking Basics For Dummies, 3rd Edition
978-0-7645-7206-7

Wine For Dummies, 4th Edition
978-0-470-04579-4

Diet & Nutrition

Dieting For Dummies, 2nd Edition
978-0-7645-4149-0

Nutrition For Dummies, 4th Edition
978-0-471-79868-2

Weight Training For Dummies, 3rd Edition
978-0-471-76845-6

Digital Photography

Digital SLR Cameras & Photography For Dummies, 3rd Edition
978-0-470-46606-3

Photoshop Elements 8 For Dummies
978-0-470-52967-6

Gardening

Gardening Basics For Dummies
978-0-470-03749-2

Organic Gardening For Dummies, 2nd Edition
978-0-470-43067-5

Green/Sustainable

Raising Chickens For Dummies
978-0-470-46544-8

Green Cleaning For Dummies
978-0-470-39106-8

Health

Diabetes For Dummies, 3rd Edition
978-0-470-27086-8

Food Allergies For Dummies
978-0-470-09584-3

Living Gluten-Free For Dummies, 2nd Edition
978-0-470-58589-4

Hobbies/General

Chess For Dummies, 2nd Edition
978-0-7645-8404-6

Drawing Cartoons & Comics For Dummies
978-0-470-42683-8

Knitting For Dummies, 2nd Edition
978-0-470-28747-7

Organizing For Dummies
978-0-7645-5300-4

Su Doku For Dummies
978-0-470-01892-7

Home Improvement

Home Maintenance For Dummies, 2nd Edition
978-0-470-43063-7

Home Theater For Dummies, 3rd Edition
978-0-470-41189-6

Living the Country Lifestyle All-in-One For Dummies
978-0-470-43061-3

Solar Power Your Home For Dummies, 2nd Edition
978-0-470-59678-4

Available wherever books are sold. For more information or to order direct: U.S. customers visit www.dummies.com or call 1-877-762-2974. U.K. customers visit www.wileyeurope.com or call (0) 1243 843291. Canadian customers visit www.wiley.ca or call 1-800-567-4797.

Internet

Blogging For Dummies, 3rd Edition
978-0-470-61996-4

eBay For Dummies, 6th Edition
978-0-470-49741-8

Facebook For Dummies, 3rd Edition
978-0-470-87804-0

Web Marketing For Dummies, 2nd Edition
978-0-470-37181-7

WordPress For Dummies, 3rd Edition
978-0-470-59274-8

Language & Foreign Language

French For Dummies
978-0-7645-5193-2

Italian Phrases For Dummies
978-0-7645-7203-6

Spanish For Dummies, 2nd Edition
978-0-470-87855-2

Spanish For Dummies, Audio Set
978-0-470-09585-0

Math & Science

Algebra I For Dummies, 2nd Edition
978-0-470-55964-2

Biology For Dummies, 2nd Edition
978-0-470-59875-7

Calculus For Dummies
978-0-7645-2498-1

Chemistry For Dummies
978-0-7645-5430-8

Microsoft Office

Excel 2010 For Dummies
978-0-470-48953-6

Office 2010 All-in-One For Dummies
978-0-470-49748-7

Office 2010 For Dummies, Book + DVD Bundle
978-0-470-62698-6

Word 2010 For Dummies
978-0-470-48772-3

Music

Guitar For Dummies, 2nd Edition
978-0-7645-9904-0

iPod & iTunes For Dummies, 8th Edition
978-0-470-87871-2

Piano Exercises For Dummies
978-0-470-38765-8

Parenting & Education

Parenting For Dummies, 2nd Edition
978-0-7645-5418-6

Type 1 Diabetes For Dummies
978-0-470-17811-9

Pets

Cats For Dummies, 2nd Edition
978-0-7645-5275-5

Dog Training For Dummies, 3rd Edition
978-0-470-60029-0

Puppies For Dummies, 2nd Edition
978-0-470-03717-1

Religion & Inspiration

The Bible For Dummies
978-0-7645-5296-0

Catholicism For Dummies
978-0-7645-5391-2

Women in the Bible For Dummies
978-0-7645-8475-6

Self-Help & Relationship

Anger Management For Dummies
978-0-470-03715-7

Overcoming Anxiety For Dummies, 2nd Edition
978-0-470-57441-6

Sports

Baseball For Dummies, 3rd Edition
978-0-7645-7537-2

Basketball For Dummies, 2nd Edition
978-0-7645-5248-9

Golf For Dummies, 3rd Edition
978-0-471-76871-5

Web Development

Web Design All-in-One For Dummies
978-0-470-41796-6

Web Sites Do-It-Yourself For Dummies, 2nd Edition
978-0-470-56520-9

Windows 7

Windows 7 For Dummies
978-0-470-49743-2

Windows 7 For Dummies, Book + DVD Bundle
978-0-470-52398-8

Windows 7 All-in-One For Dummies
978-0-470-48763-1

Available wherever books are sold. For more information or to order direct: U.S. customers visit www.dummies.com or call 1-877-762-2974. U.K. customers visit www.wileyeurope.com or call (0) 1243 843291. Canadian customers visit www.wiley.ca or call 1-800-567-4797.